# Meeting the Challenge
## Corrective Reading Instruction in the Classroom

**Eunice N. Askov**
The Pennsylvania State University

**Wayne Otto**
University of Wisconsin—Madison

Charles E. Merrill Publishing Company
A Bell & Howell Company
Columbus   Toronto   London   Sydney

Published by Charles E. Merrill Publishing Company
A Bell & Howell Company
Columbus, Ohio 43216

This book was set in Garamond.
Production coordination: Rebecca Money Bobb
Text design: Cynthia Brunk
Cover design: Cathy Watterson
Cover photo: The Eyes, Inc./Bob Milnes

Photo credits: Photographs on pp. xviii, 16, 40, 64, 108, 134, 192, 218, 240, 264, 284, and 320 by Jean Greenwald; pp. 86 and 340 by Strix Pix; pp. 166 and 384 © C. Quinlan; p. 368 by Buster P.L. Prewitt Diaz.

International Standard Book Number: 0−675−20303−1
Library of Congress Catalog Card Number: 84−71917
1  2  3  4  5  6  7  8  9—90  89  88  87  86  85
Printed in the United States of America

*To our friends and colleagues*
*of the American Reading Forum*

# Preface

Classroom teachers today are faced with greater responsibilities for teaching children with reading problems within the regular classroom than ever before. Parents and the public are showing a more active interest in reading instruction and in children's reading performance, and recent legislation calls for greater efforts to mainstream into the regular classroom children with a wide range of handicaps, including but not necessarily limited to reading problems. Fortunately, many resources are available to classroom teachers to help them meet the challenge. But whatever the resources, the buck stops with the classroom teacher. It is the classroom teacher who is expected to select and coordinate resources and, often, to take initiative in implementing special programs designed to help children return to the mainstream of reading instruction. This book is for teachers who accept the challenge.

We assume that the readers of this book have had an introductory, developmental reading methods course. The book is suitable for a second undergraduate level course in reading, a beginning graduate level course, or an inservice project. While *Meeting the Challenge* is intended primarily for regular classroom teachers, it will also be useful to reading specialists and special education teachers who work closely with regular classroom teachers. The book focuses on the elementary grades, 1–8.

As we wrote and revised the chapters, we often wanted to introduce, elaborate, or explain our main points in an informal way. Rather than repress that urge to "talk" directly with our readers, we decided to include our comments; they appear in *italics*.

At the ends of the chapters, you'll find activities that will help you check your understanding and apply what you have learned. Many of the activities are appropriate for use either in a field experience linked to a reading course or directly in your classroom.

We provide examples of actual teaching materials, many of them contributed by classroom teachers, to help illustrate our suggestions. While some of these suggestions may be used directly, they are probably more useful as models. Readers adapt the models to create teaching materials that are most appropriate for their own classrooms.

We begin the book by "setting the stage." First we describe the corrective reading process and show how it rounds out a comprehensive approach to reading instruction. Then we address two essential aspects of successful corrective teaching: direct instruction and the firm foundation for it, adequate assessment.

Next we examine the foundations—word recognition, comprehension, and study skills—from a diagnostic-prescriptive viewpoint. We present strategies for helping readers who are unable to read grade-level textbooks; we suggest writing as a means for reinforcing and extending reading development; and we consider the role and impact of affective factors in teaching reading.

We give special attention to several types of learners with unique instructional needs—slow learners, special education students, and bilingual children. Finally we "bring it all together" with a discussion of effective schools and effective teaching.

We hope this book will help each of our readers meet the challenge of providing effective reading instruction for all students. We invite you to share your reactions and experiences with us.

# Acknowledgments

We owe much more to former students—now colleagues and friends—than we can adequately express in this short space. Some have taken major responsibility for certain chapters or sections of this book, and we have borrowed freely from the words and ideas of others. We have benefited from the experiences and insights that they have shared with us.

We owe a particular debt to these "Wisconsin people": Roger Eldridge, who prepared the draft version of Chapter 15; Don Richgels, who wrote parts of Chapter 9 and provided comments and examples throughout that chapter; Mary Bredeson, who supplied the two real-life examples of direct instruction in Chapter 3; Kaybeth Camperell; Carol Dana; Ruth Hansen; Beverly Morrison; Susan Toms-Bronowski; Sandy White; Pauline Witte; and Petey Young. We are indebted to the following Penn Staters for their contributions: Connie Maclay, for creating the end-of-chapter "Check Your Reading Comprehension" activities; Anna Gajar, for her guidance on Chapter 15; Joyce Lee, Joe Prewitt Diaz, Carol Fishel, Mary Dupuis, and Linda Merchant, who authored portions of the book. We have invited the contributions of all these educators because of their unique perspectives on reading. We also thank the teachers who have permitted us to include their materials in the book as examples.

We thank Susan C. Griffith and Ginny Moore Kruse for the Cooperative Children's Book Center (CCBC) list of children's literature in Appendix C. We recommend the CCBC and its publications as valuable resources for educators.

The senior author is grateful to Peter Cole and other Australian colleagues and friends who enriched her stay in Perth, Western Australia. She also thanks her family for their patience and her mother for being understanding about the letters she did *not* receive.

We owe much to our editor, Vicki Knight, who guided us through the process of creating this book. We gratefully acknowledge the helpful suggestions of our reviewers, particularly Bernard Hayes of Utah State University, Stinson E. Worley of Southwest Texas State University, Carol Hodges of Park School of Buffalo, Albert Shannon of Rider College, Janell P. Klesius of the University of South Florida, and Roger DeSanti of the University of New Orleans. We thank Penn State doctoral candidate Bernard Badiali for writing the *Instructor's Manual* that accompanies this book.

# Contents

# 6 Word Recognition Skills 109

# 7 Diagnosing and Teaching Word Recognition Skills 135

# 8 Words to Meaning: Easing the Transition 167

# 9 Helping Students Understand Their Textbooks   193

# 10 Guiding Students' Reading and Study Skills   219

# 11 Content Area Reading   241

# 12 Integrating Reading and Writing   265

# Meeting the Challenge

# 13 Affective Factors in Corrective Teaching   285

# 14 Adapted Teaching for Slow Learners   321

# Appendices

# 1

# The New Teacher

Congratulations! You are now a new fifth-grade teacher at Model Elementary School. You're pleased at getting the job and feel well prepared to teach. You confidently pack a box of teaching materials from student teaching—plus your methods textbooks—and set off for your first teaching job.

The first day goes all right, but let's check the scenario later in September. You discover that not all the children seem so eager to learn as you thought on the first day. Some children can't even read the textbooks they are supposed to be using for social studies, science, and math. Perplexed, you seek the guidance counselor's help in understanding these children's difficulties. You find that some of the children have extensive files, including reports of individual psychological testing and IEPs (Individual Educational Programs). The guidance counselor suggests that you compile a chart listing the reading achievement scores from the most recent achievement testing last spring in fourth grade as well as other scores. This chart is reproduced as Table 1.1.

The guidance counselor cautions you that these tests scores do not nicely translate into reading levels—that Tiffani cannot necessarily be given a book at the fifth grade level because she scored 5.2 on the test. The scores of most achievement tests represent a maximum level of performance, which would not be appropriate for daily work.

You see the necessity for administering individual informal reading inventories (IRIs), especially to those children having difficulty. An IRI will help you know at what reading level a child can actually function.

You compare the score on a group intelligence (IQ) test with performance on a standardized achievement test for each child. You are troubled that the teacher from the previous year placed no child, regardless of test scores, higher than fifth-grade basal reader level for instruction. You decide to consider these groupings only tentative until you become more familiar with the reading abilities of your children.

You want to spend some time studying the cumulative folders to learn what others have discovered about those children. The reading specialist offers to show you what he has been doing with some of the children. You meet with the special education teacher for the educable mentally handicapped (EMH), for two of the children are placed (or "mainstreamed") into your classroom for social studies and science only. You must obtain individual achievement test scores from the special education teacher since these children do not take group tests. The learning disabilities (LD) teacher offers information about LD children who come to your room only for social studies and science. You also consult the speech therapist, who has been working with one child for several years. Finally, you talk with the classroom teacher that the children had last year, fortunately a kindly veteran teacher willing to help you.

Let's now look at some of these children to see why they are having difficulties with the usual fifth-grade curriculum, particularly with reading.

# Children With Special Needs

## John (#29)

From the moment John was able to walk, he never stopped running. He was always adept at physical activities, being the first picked for every team on the playground. His kindergarten teacher noted that he came to school without knowledge of letters, numbers, or book concepts. He appeared to have not been read to, having no interest in the teacher's reading aloud to the children.

Even though John repeated kindergarten, his first grade teacher noted his extreme difficulty with reading. John still did not show much interest in reading but knew it was expected of him. John's reading consisted primarily of saying isolated sounds strung together with limited success. This process was complicated by his speech problem, a difficulty in pronouncing some sounds and blends.

John's primary teachers discovered that he could learn reading skills best if he could be physically involved while learning. He liked manipulative materials and games; he finally learned some sight words when he was given the opportunity to print the words in sand as he said them.

John had been sent to a special reading class since first grade and is still attending three times per week. The reading specialist reported that John appeared to learn best using sight words; phonics, or letter sounds, were taught only after he had learned

**Table 1.1** Classroom Screening Chart: Fifth Grade

| Student's Name | Sex | CA | 3rd Grade IQ on Otis-Lennon (Group) | Instructional Basal Level for Beginning 5th | California Achievement Test (Grade Placement 4.6) | | | | | Teacher's Comments |
|---|---|---|---|---|---|---|---|---|---|---|
| | | | | | Reading Vocabulary | Reading Comprehension | Reading Total | Language Total | Math Total | |
| 1. Robert | M | 10–3 | 116 | 4 | 7.4 | 6.2 | 6.5 | 6.9 | 6.6 | Moved to district middle of grade 4. B student in other school. |
| 2. Kelley | F | 10–4 | 114 | $3^2$ | 3.8 | 4.7 | 4.2 | 4.7 | 5.9 | Chapter I help reading in grades 2 & 3. |
| 3. Tony | M‡ | 11–2 | 97 | $2^1$ | 2.4 | 2.2 | 2.4 | 2.1 | 3.9 | Poor progress reports, referred for psychological testing middle of grade 2 and placed in LD in grade 3. Chapter I, grade 2. |
| 4. Allison | F* | 11–1 | 112 | $3^2$ | 4.2 | 2.5 | 3.7 | 4.1 | 4.5 | Chapter I, grade 3 & 4. |
| 5. Robin | F | 10–4 | 93 | $3^2$ | 3.9 | 4.7 | 4.3 | 3.9 | 5.3 | Capable, good speller. |
| 6. Tiffani | F | 10–3 | 117 | 4 | 5.2 | 6.5 | 5.8 | 5.6 | 4.3 | Poor homework. Does pay attention in class. |
| 7. Carl | M‡ | 11–0 | 95 | $1^2$ | 2.0 | 2.1 | 2.0 | 2.5 | 4.0 | Diabetic, hyperactive—difficulty organizing thoughts. Needs teacher or peer help on all work; trouble understanding directions |
| 8. Guy | M | 10–6 | 126 | 5 | 8.3 | 7.6 | 7.9 | 9.0 | 5.3 | |
| 9. Maria | F* | .11–3 | 93 | $3^2$ | 3.6 | 3.7 | 3.7 | 3.7 | 4.0 | Chapter I, grade 3. Poor comprehension in classroom work. Non-native speaker. |

(Table 1.1, *continued*)

| Student's Name | Sex | CA | 3rd Grade IQ on Otis-Lennon (Group) | Instructional Basal Level for Beginning 5th | California Achievement Test (Grade Placement 4.6) | | | | | Teacher's Comments |
|---|---|---|---|---|---|---|---|---|---|---|
| | | | | | Reading Vocabulary | Reading Comprehension | Reading Total | Language Total | Math Total | |
| 10. Jeff | M | 10–8 | 93 | 4 | | | | | | Attended this district grades 1–3. Moved during grade 4, returned for end of grade 4. |
| 11. Sherry | F | 11–1 | 109 | $3^2$ | 4.7<br>6.6 | 3.7<br>4.2 | 4.1<br>4.9 | 4.1<br>4.9 | 3.3<br>3.9 | + Repeated grade 4. Psychological testing grade 1, classified LD. Behavior problem grade 1. |
| 12. Scott | M | 11–5 | 87 | $3^2$ | 4.0 | 4.6 | 4.3 | 3.8 | 4.0 | + Repeated grade 1, psychological testing. University report indicated below average intelligence and recommends less dependence on mother. Testing done end of K year and middle of grade 1. |
| 13. Jeanette | F† | 11–2 | 75 | $3^1$ | | | | | | She and twin sister have sweet dispositions. Has progressed well in reading; in grade 5 will be mainstreamed for all subjects except language. |
| 14. Greg | M | 10–6 | 114 | 5 | 6.6 | 6.9 | 6.7 | 7.8 | 5.9 | |
| 15. Angela | F | 10–5 | 108 | 5 | 5.2 | 5.3 | 5.3 | 9.0 | 6.3 | |

| | | | | | | | | | | |
|---|---|---|---|---|---|---|---|---|---|---|
| 16. Raymond | M | 11–6 | 94 | 4 | 4.8 | 4.3 | 4.6 | 3.8 | 5.5 | Doesn't do assigned work, cheats on other student's papers. Moved to district beginning of grade 3. Reading grades for 1–3 were E's. |
| 17. Stacey | F | 10–8 | 117 | 5 | 5.4 | 8.6 | 6.7 | 8.5 | 6.3 | |
| 18. Joe | M† | 11–0 | kindergarten 66 | $2^2$ | | | | | | Assigned to special education after grade 1. |
| 19. Rosemary | F§ | 10–7 | 139 | 5 | 8.3 | 8.6 | 8.9 | 10.9 | 7.6 | Referred for gifted program end of grade 1 and placed in grade 2. |
| 20. Thomas | M | 10–3 | 101 | 5 | 5.4 | 5.5 | 5.5 | 8.5 | 4.8 | |
| 21. Dan | M* | 10–10 | 91 | $3^1$ | 4.3 | 3.8 | 4.0 | 3.5 | 3.4 | Moved into district in grade 2. Chapter I help at other district. Moved to different attendance area, dropped from Chapter I Feb. of grade 4. Excellent speaking vocabulary. |
| 22. Cathy | F | 10–7 | 109 | $3^2$ | 5.0 | 5.3 | 5.2 | 4.4 | 5.4 | Sloppy handwriting—Chapter I in grade 3. |
| 23. Jon | M | 10–11 | 90 | $3^2$ | 7.4 | 6.9 | 7.0 | 8.5 | 7.6 | + Repeated grade 2. |
| 24. Susan | F* | 11–3 | 88 | $2^1$ | 4.0 | 3.2 | 3.7 | 1.6 | 3.4 | + Repeated grade 1. Referred for psychological testing grades 3 & 4—not placed. Poor behavior in classroom. Father is blind. Chapter I help grades 3 & 4. Gates-MacGinitie scores 1.6 comprehension pre and post. |

(Table 1.1, *continued*)

| Student's Name | Sex | CA | 3rd Grade IQ on Otis-Lennon (Group) | Instructional Basal Level for Beginning 5th | California Achievement Test (Grade Placement 4.6) | | | | | Teacher's Comments |
|---|---|---|---|---|---|---|---|---|---|---|
| | | | | | Reading Vocabulary | Reading Comprehension | Reading Total | Language Total | Math Total | |
| 25. Michael | M | 10–6 | 105 | 5 | 7.4 | 11.0 | 10.0 | 6.4 | 5.5 | Moved to district beginning of grade 4. Doesn't do assignments, very careless. Math computation 4.5, math concepts 7.0. |
| 26. Brad | M[§] | 9–4 | 129 | 5 | 6.9 | 6.6 | 6.7 | 7.5 | 7.9 | Outstanding math student both on computation and concepts; gifted program began in grade 4. |
| 27. Mary Ann | F | 10–1 | 97 | $2^2$ | 3.5 | 3.7 | 3.6 | 3.8 | 4.2 | Chapter I grades 2–4. Doesn't pay attention. Hard worker. |

| 28. Jill | F | 10–4 | 117 | 4 | 8.3 | 7.6 | 7.9 | 7.8 | 5.6 | |
|---|---|---|---|---|---|---|---|---|---|---|
| 29. John | M* | 11–8 | 95 | 3¹ | 3.3 | 2.9 | 3.3 | 4.2 | 4.7 | + Repeated K. Chapter I grades 1–4. Speech problem—bisyllables and blends. Poor homework. |
| 30. Todd | M | 10–5 | 107 | 4 | 4.7 | 5.3 | 5.0 | 4.9 | 5.8 | |
| 31. Jennifer | F | 10–4 | 143 | 5 | 8.3 | 10.0 | 10.0 | 10.9 | 5.8 | Tested in grade 3 on Slosson test; scored 130. Psychologist doesn't feel she would score high enough on the WISC-R for gifted placement. |

Source: Prepared by H. Robert Mencer and Diane Farr, Bellefonte, PA, Public Schools, adapted from school records. Students' names and teacher's comments have been modified. *Chapter I— Reading ‡Educable mentally handicapped ‡Learning disabled/emotionally disturbed §Gifted program + Grades repeated

many words containing a given sound. Attempts to teach him isolated letter sounds that were to be blended together had not been productive. Through early training in phonics—probably inappropriate given his speech problem—John had learned to say new words by sounding letters individually, but he was rarely able to blend them together successfully. The words he did know had been acquired primarily through the language experience approach, in which the reading teacher used John's dictated stories written on charts as his reading material. John remembered these words, and he was able to read his own stories fluently without saying individual letter sounds. The reading teacher also reported that John enjoyed "high interest, low difficulty" books about sports—books appropriate to his interests and age but written at a readability level of two or more years below grade level. John's involvement in special reading activities had improved his language and reading test scores.

His math achievement scores showed normal grade-level progress. The group intelligence test administered in third grade indicated average ability. John's difficulty in learning to read apparently resulted from lack of early reading experiences—that is, being read to as a preschooler—and from being taught initially by the phonics method, which he could use with only very limited success.

John has not been a discipline problem in class except when required to remain in his seat for long periods of time. He then shows signs of frustration, wiggling in his seat, tapping his pencil, and moving his lips when silently reading from his social studies text. Since he is reading with understanding at approximately a third-grade level, his social studies textbook, intended for average fifth-grade readers, is too difficult for John. He is easily distracted from this task and, in fact, distracts others by his restlessness.

The counselor reports sporadic parental cooperation. While John's parents seem eager for John to learn to read, they readily admit that no one in the family reads regularly. Family activities usually involve sports and outdoor activities. The father, a factory worker, enjoys television after work. The mother has not worked in recent years, staying at home to care for John and his three brothers. They have attended PTA events occasionally, including the "Back to School" night at the beginning of the school year. They were friendly and eager to meet John's new teacher.

## Joe (#18)

Joe has only recently been mainstreamed into the regular classroom from the EMH (educable mentally handicapped) room. He returns to the special education program daily only for reading and math.

The cumulative records reveal that Joe had been categorized as mentally retarded at the end of his kindergarten year. His individual full-scale IQ score on the Weschler Intelligence Scale for Children–Revised (WISC–R) was in the mid-60s, indicating a lower than average capacity for school learning. His reading and math achievement scores are several years below grade-level expectations.

The counselor tells you that Joe comes from a large family living at subsistence level on welfare support. Joe's father deserted the family several years ago, leaving his mother with sole responsibility for eight children. Most of Joe's older and younger siblings have also been placed in special education classes. The mother was a high school drop-out because of premarital pregnancy. Her own unsuccessful experiences with school make her reluctant to communicate with school personnel, who have found it difficult to obtain her consent for placement of her children in special education classes.

Your classroom observations of Joe have led you to suspect some of this information. His lack of cleanliness and unkempt appearance often make him the target of teasing by other children. He sometimes retaliates by hitting other children; more often he keeps to himself. His responses to questions are usually monosyllabic. You determine from talking with his special education teacher that a bright spot in his life seems to be that his uncle has recently permitted Joe to help him at his service station. Joe seems very proud to be allowed to pump gas and do odd jobs at the station, though he is not paid for these tasks.

In response to your assignments in the social studies and science textbooks, Joe usually sighs and puts his head down on the desk. Even when prompted, he usually refuses to attempt the work. On tasks appropriate to his abilities, such as daily measuring and graphing the height of a bean plant, he works slowly and methodically. The special education teacher has suggested that he needs much drill and repetition in order to learn.

On the first day of school when you asked the children to write a paragraph about what they did last summer, Joe scrawled "nothing." Upon questioning him, you discovered that his summer was spent caring for his younger siblings—he never traveled beyond this local area. You were astonished to discover that he had never visited the state capital or ridden any form of public transportation. Joe's only enriching experiences seem to have been provided by the school.

## Tony (#3)

Tony is being mainstreamed from a learning disabilities (LD) classroom where he still returns for daily instruction in reading. His math abilities seem average except on word problems, which cause him great difficulty.

When asked to read aloud, Tony reads painfully slowly. He attacks each word individually, seeming to have no sense that words fit together meaningfully in sentences. He is unable to paraphrase what he has read. The phonics approach being used in his LD class appears to be working, but progress is slow. He astutely avoids reading tasks whenever possible.

During class discussion, however, Tony actively contributes, drawing on his background experiences to supplement what he is learning. He responds particularly well to films and other media presentations.

Tony's handwriting is almost illegible. He reverses many letters, especially *b, d, p,* and *q.* Because he crowds upper- and lower-case letters together, it is hard to tell where words begin and end. He spells the same words several ways.

The counselor informs you that Tony was placed in an LD class in third grade after exhibiting extensive reading problems. Even now he functions only on a second-grade level on his reading achievement tests. In math he scores slightly higher.

His individual full-scale IQ score on the WISC–R indicates at least average learning ability.

His family is portrayed by the guidance counselor as close-knit and of Italian descent. His parents are highly supportive of school efforts in his behalf. His mother volunteers as a library aide, and both his parents have been active in the local ACLD (Association of Children with Learning Disabilities).

*The guidance counselor has been a tremendous help. You have gained a more complete picture of these children through their cumulative files, anecdotal records, and the counselor's comments.*

*Now it is time to enlist the help of the reading specialist. He has offered to help you find more appropriate instructional materials and techniques for the children he serves in the Chapter I program, a compensatory reading program providing additional assistance for children who are educationally or economically disadvantaged. In particular, you are puzzled about Allison, one of several black children in your room, who goes to the reading specialist three times each week.*

## Allison (#4)

You are puzzled about Allison, who appears to be a very good reader. During the first week of school you noted that her oral reading was perfect. In fact, Allison was considered a good reader through second grade. She was referred for special reading help and placed in the Chapter I program beginning in third grade. Why?

The reading specialist explains to you that Allison is a "word caller." Early and intense phonics instruction taught her to decode, or sound out, words easily. But for Allison reading was only saying the words. She did not understand that reading is also a "meaning-getting" process. Thus Allison appears to be able to read her fifth-grade social studies and science textbooks because she can say the words; but she does not completely understand what she can decode. Now you understand why Allison has difficulty with reading assignments in her content subjects. She can, however, understand material when it is read aloud to her.

Allison's parents were understandably upset when she was referred for special reading assistance. They had also thought Allison to be a good reader and had diligently listened to her read at home. Her problem was not noticed at school until she had to read silently for meaning. Her parents now understand the problem and have discontinued oral reading at home. Instead they ask her to talk about the books she is reading silently so that they can be sure she understands what she is reading.

## Maria (#9)

Maria, whose native language is Spanish, has also been receiving assistance from the reading specialist. From your student teaching you know that a bilingual education program provides students instruction in both their native language and English. Extra assistance in English is provided by an ESL (English as a Second Language) teacher. This small school district, however, has few bilingual students, so a bilingual program is not feasible. One part-time ESL teacher must travel throughout the district. Because Maria receives only limited help from the ESL teacher, the reading specialist provides daily help to Maria. He emphasizes learning to read through the language experience approach, which also builds her oral language abilities.

Maria is from a Puerto Rican family who recently moved into the school district. Because her father is unemployed (her mother is employed as a house cleaner), the family may move back to Puerto Rico. Since the family has periodically moved back and forth between "the island and the mainland," Maria's schooling has lacked continuity. Although she is fairly adept at oral reading, having learned to read in Spanish, she, like Allison, does not understand what she is reading. Furthermore, she lacks the conceptual background and vocabulary to understand the fifth-grade content subjects. Her oral English language abilities are weak, making it difficult for her to follow along in class. She is learning English quickly, however, because of having made new friends in her class.

The reading specialist reports that her parents are very cooperative and have high academic aspirations for their children. Because their English language abilities are severely limited, they are unable to help Maria with her school work. Maria needs extra assistance from you in building background concepts and vocabulary. Reading

Some kids need special help. (Photo by Jean Greenwald)

assignments from the fifth-grade textbooks are unrealistic. You are grateful that the reading specialist has offered to help.

# Corrective Reading

Having portrayed the challenges to the new fifth-grade teacher, let us consider how to address them. For example, what is corrective reading? A brief definition from *A Dictionary of Reading* (1981), published by the International Reading Association, follows.

> **corrective reading:** supplemental, selective instruction for minor reading difficulties, often within a regular classroom by the regular teacher, an aide, or peer tutor. *Corrective reading instruction is more specific than developmental instruction, but less intensive than remedial reading instruction.* (p. 71)

Chapter 2 deals with how the developmental, corrective, and remedial programs relate to the total reading instructional program design. For now, remember that the responsibility for corrective reading instruction rests with the classroom teacher. Problems should be within the range of expertise of the classroom teacher, assisted by resource specialists. While the *Dictionary* definition of corrective reading states that it involves "minor reading difficulties," teachers frequently encounter more complicated problems that were perhaps at first only minor.

Mainstreamed special needs students may receive specialized services in resource rooms but spend much of their school day in the regular classroom. Public Law 94–142 entitles special needs students to education in "the least restrictive environment." Special needs children may thus spend none, or all, of their day in a regular classroom, depending upon their needs.

The IEP, Individual Educational Program, is the educational guide for each child for the school year. It is formulated cooperatively by the special education teacher, school psychologist, classroom teacher, parents, and appropriate specialists, such as a speech teacher, reading specialist, and social worker. The procedure varies in different school districts, but the IEP in any case must be signed by both a school district representative and the parents.

Classroom teachers must often implement the IEP, with the guidance of the special education teacher and various resource personnel. In effect, as special needs students spend more time in the regular classroom, teachers must coordinate the efforts of various specialists, many of whom are employed not by the local school district but by a special services unit that serves several counties. To assist the classroom teacher in assuming this new and often overwhelming role of coordinator, we will discuss in this book the various types of special education.

Some veteran teachers have "grown" into their new roles without difficulty while others have resisted. Someone must orchestrate the various efforts in behalf of the child. As federal, state, and local budgets for education are cut, the classroom teacher must assume more and more responsibility for the education of children with special learning needs and differences.

## Applying Corrective Reading

*Compiling the chart in Table 1.1 has taught you more about the special needs of children who have been mainstreamed into your classroom. Through talking with the specialists, you have reached some decisions about appropriate corrective reading programs for those children.*

John will continue to learn new words primarily by sight, looking for the root words in new vocabulary words and expanding his knowledge of affixes. While Joe and Tony receive reading instruction away from the regular classroom, you still must help them read content area materials. You decide to try to find alternative reading materials at lower levels of difficulty. If these cannot be located, you will try other strategies, discussed in Chapter 11. Joe will need to learn new material slowly and thoroughly, as described in Chapter 14.

Allison and Maria, both competent decoders, need help with comprehension. You will use strategies discussed in Chapters 8, 9, and 10 to assist them. Maria, who lacks concepts and vocabulary in English, needs many background experiences to which labels are attached. You will use the suggestions in Chapter 16 for teaching bilingual students.

While this chapter has focused on the particular needs of five learners, all children shown in Table 1.1 have needs of one kind or another. For example, Guy (#8) was recommended for a fifth-grade basal reader group by last year's teacher. Yet his achievement test scores in reading appear to be two to three grade levels higher. While achievement test scores do not translate directly into instructional reading levels, Guy's do indicate that he appears to be performing above grade level on test scores. A similar pattern is noted for Jennifer (#31) who appears to have reached the maximum score of the test (10.0) on both Reading Comprehension and the Reading Total.

It appears that last year's teacher believes in grade-level progress rather than continuous progress. In other words, she apparently accommodated those reading below grade level by using appropriate basal readers. But rather than allowing those who were competent readers to progress beyond the basal level intended for their grade, she probably spent the instructional time enriching and broadening what they already knew.

You wonder how appropriate a $2^1$ (beginning of second grade) basal reader is for Susan (#24). Surely her interests are not those of a beginning second grader even if her reading abilities are. You will try some of the other instructional approaches described in this book in an attempt to find one that will help her want to learn to read.

## Summary

We have portrayed various types of problem readers that a classroom teacher typically meets. Corrective reading has been defined as the classroom teacher's responsibility. Coordination of various resource personnel in dealing with mainstreamed special education students is also the classroom teacher's responsibility.

# Reference

Harris, T. L., & Hodges, R. E. (Eds.). (1981). *A dictionary of reading and related terms.* Newark, DE: International Reading Association.

# Check Your Reading Comprehension

1.  What is corrective reading instruction?

2.  Who is responsible for corrective reading instruction?

3.  Study the Classroom Screening Chart (Table 1–1). Which students might be candidates for corrective reading instruction?

4.  Study your own class. Which students might be candidates for corrective reading instruction?

# 2

# Corrective Teaching in a Comprehensive Reading Program

As the case studies in Chapter 1 suggest, there are many different reasons why children experience reading difficulties. Students may have physical and emotional disabilities or come from impoverished environments and lack the language development they need to respond to classroom reading instruction. Others just don't seem to care much about reading or school. Still others seem to care very much, but just don't seem able to "get it." Successful teachers soon recognize that they must deal with their students as they are. We talk about that in the chapters that follow.

A good reading program is everyone's responsibility. (Photo © Jack Hamilton)

In Chapter 2 we present program-related aspects of corrective reading. To work effectively with students who have reading difficulties, teachers need to have a comprehensive view of reading development. We suggest that schools must develop comprehensive reading programs that encourage and enable teachers to help students correct minor difficulties before they become major problems.

The main topics discussed in Chapter 2 are:

- the need for and features of a good comprehensive reading program,
- the place of corrective teaching in a school's overall reading program,
- a view of corrective teaching in the classroom.

# A Comprehensive Reading Program[1]

A few students seem to bog down at the initial stage of learning to read. They have trouble grasping the essential skills and strategies for decoding—sounding out—words. Until they can move beyond this basic stage, reading remains a mystifying and frustrating task. They are effectively shut out from participation in most of the learning

---

[1] The discussion is adapted from parts of a publication of the Wisconsin Department of Public Instruction, *The K–12 Reading Program, A Planning Resource for Wisconsin Schools.* One of your coauthors was on the committee of reading educators who prepared the resource book.

experiences schools provide. Many more students have no problems decoding words or acquiring the skills and strategies taught in typical developmental programs. Yet they experience difficulty when confronted by the complex reading tasks of the school curriculum and of the world outside school. They are unable to apply what they learn in reading classes. They "read," but often without meaning. They miss much of the enlightenment and joy reading can provide.

Schools have traditionally given more attention and resources to the non-decoders than to the underachievers—those students who seem to know how to read (i.e., to decode words) but not how to use that ability as teachers and society demand. Yet schools do have a responsibility far beyond providing remedial help for students with obvious decoding problems. Schools must develop comprehensive reading programs.

## The Need for a Comprehensive Reading Program

Reading is so closely intertwined with the process of schooling that it is difficult to imagine a school without some kind of reading program. But many programs tend to be dominated by available materials, usually a basal reader series; limited to the elementary level; and lacking in specificity, comprehensiveness, and contact with local realities. We suggest that a worthwhile reading program, must, first, systematically address the needs of all students at all levels *within the limits imposed by available resources.* Further, the program should provide teachers with guidelines for assessing students' progress and for providing appropriate instruction for individual students. Most important, the program must assure coordination and continuity from grade to grade and from teacher to teacher.

Some of the reasons why a school needs a comprehensive reading program follow.

*To anticipate and accommodate the changing demands of the developmental reading task.* As a student moves grade by grade through school, the nature of the reading task shifts from *learning to read* to *reading to learn.* A systematic reading program provides structure, transition, and guidance as students first learn how to read and then apply what they have learned to all areas of the curriculum. A comprehensive program can also enable students to deal with the increasing complexity of reading as subject matter becomes more difficult.

*To provide for application as well as acquisition of reading skills and strategies.* Many schools adequately teach the acquisition of reading skills and strategies. But few provide the systematic instruction that students need to apply those skills and strategies in their content areas and other day-to-day reading. Thus, for many students the program breaks down at the very point where they could begin to profit most from what they have learned. Certain reading skills are most appropriately applied in certain subject areas. A planned program promotes development of the skills that have the highest yield in given content areas.

*To permit coordination of "special and remedial" services and programs that have been instigated in response to federal and state funding, special interest groups, and other demands.* Many schools have a smorgasbord reading program—a collection of bits and pieces offered to satisfy a wide range of appetites. A comprehensive plan can assure that special offerings (such as remedial reading classes, programs for the learning disabled, programs for the developmentally disabled, and supplementary "developmental" classes) are in line with and contributing to a balanced program.

*To assure that students' reading needs and teachers' responsibility to teach reading are kept visibile at all levels and in all areas of the curriculum.* The ability to read is basic to success throughout the school experience. This fact is so obvious that it becomes commonplace. As a result, the implications are often neglected. A prominent, all-school, all-level program assures that reading instruction gets the attention it requires. Students are more likely to be assigned reading tasks that are in line with their abilities and to get special help when they need it.

*To give assurance to the community that reading is getting the attention it deserves.* Students' ability to read is probably the single most visible product of the schools. The public expects, first, that students will succeed in learning how to read and, then, that they will be able to cope with the reading tasks they encounter both in and out of school. A well-planned, comprehensive program is the only credible evidence of a school's efforts to meet those expectations.

The development of a comprehensive reading program is everybody's responsibility—school administrators', classroom teachers', reading teachers', reading specialists', and other specialized teaching and supervisory personnel's. Unfortunately, when something is everybody's responsibility it often turns out to be nobody's responsibility. If your school does not have a comprehensive reading program, do not sit quietly and wait for someone else to start one. Do whatever you can to get people interested. Share good ideas about teaching reading. Ask your fellow teachers about students who have reading problems; tell them about any insights you may have. Be an avid reader yourself.

You can help students with reading difficulties all by yourself. Never pass up a chance to do so! But the big payoff comes when students can benefit from the continuity and coherence of an all-school program.

## Obstacles to Program Development and Implementation

Are you convinced that schools need comprehensive reading programs? If so, you may be wondering why every school does not have one. The reason is not disinterest. Most schools direct many of their resources to teaching reading and to remedial instruction; but resources tend to be dissipated in dealing with bits and pieces rather than an overall program. Following are some of the most troublesome obstacles.

***Inertia.*** Total disinterest in a comprehensive program is seldom a problem. Partial inertia is much more troublesome. Planning may have been done and comprehensive goals adopted; but there have been no real changes in teaching practices, available materials, coordinated programs, or scheduling practices. There are lots of "paper" programs on file in curriculum libraries.

***Contradictory programs.***   "Special" programs often seem to fly in each other's faces. One reason is that "special" programs soon become vested and then tend to be continued whether the continuation makes sense or not. A school might base its developmental instruction on a series of basal readers, its remedial instruction on an assortment of kits and workbooks, and its "enrichment" instruction on still another set of materials. How can these materials-based programs share a coherent focus when there is no coordination among them?

***False security.***   Some upper-level teachers do not concern themselves with teaching reading because "they teach that in the lower grades." Some teachers are reluctant to teach reading in the content areas because they think that reading is (or should be) taught in reading classes.

***Lack of leadership.***   An effective reading program requires careful planning initially, but then it requires creative and aggressive leadership for implementation. Too often a fully qualified coordinator is not designated, or lines of responsibility and support are not made clear.

***Lack of effective teacher training.***   Teachers cannot do what they do not know how to do. They need a task-specific inservice program that deals with perceived and emerging problems.

***Budget problems.***   There is no point in spending all your money on a Jaguar if it means you cannot afford to buy gasoline. Nor is there any point in spending money on implementing a fancy reading program if funds for its continuation are not available. A reading program must be designed with a realistic view of resources as well as needs.

***Lack of planning.***   Some schools do not have a sensible reading program because the staff has not expended the effort to plan one. Good reading programs never just happen; they are purchased at the price of careful, long-term planning.

Don't think that these obstacles are insurmountable or that the efforts of any individual are likely to be insignificant. To the contrary! The first step toward dealing with obstacles is to recognize them.

## Features of a Good Comprehensive Program

Each school must develop its own unique reading program, but good programs have in common certain characteristics. They share three main purposes: (a) to provide *direct instruction* in how to read, (b) to provide guidance in *applying* reading skills and strategies to the full range of reading tasks encountered in and out of school, and (c) to provide experiences and activities that foster reading as a lifelong habit, for personal achievement and enjoyment.

Good programs include four components, in line with the preceding purposes: (a) word analysis, (b) comprehension, (c) reading-study skills and habits, and (d) independent reading. Each contributes to the development of students' competence and maturity as readers. A well-coordinated program helps to assure balance in both the instructional emphasis given to each component and the instruction offered to each student. We will return to the matter of balance a bit later. As we examine each component, notice that we identify a number of unresolved questions. We will deal with these later in the chapter.

***Word analysis.***     Decoding—making sense of the letter-sound correspondence code that enables pronunciation of written words—is basic to meaningful reading. Word analysis is a term commonly used to designate a full array of skills that enable readers to discover both the pronunciation and the meaning of written words. The components of word analysis, then, should be taught in a sequence that is in tune with the materials students are expected to read, or, in other words, that permits readers to cope with the written words they encounter.

Although reading educators do not agree completely on which specific word analysis skills should be taught, there is reasonable consensus regarding the following:

*Prereading competencies.*     In order to respond to formal reading instruction, children need to have developed some prereading, or readiness, competencies. Among these are (a) awareness of the importance of letter orientation (e.g., that *d* is significantly different from *b,* even though the basic letter shapes are the same); (b) awareness that in reading one moves from left to right; and (c) ability to discriminate among the sounds of the various letters. Educators disagree about when to teach the prereading competencies.

*Sight words.*     While quick recognition of sight words is not, in a pure sense, a word analysis technique, there are good reasons for teaching sight words. They let a new reader experience success in reading at a very early stage; they provide a basis for teaching letter sounds; and a very few of them account for a large percentage of all the words one will ever encounter in print. Although many sight word lists exist, there is almost total overlap among them. Questions that arise are whether to teach sight words before or after initial phonics instruction, and how many should be taught.

*Phonics.*     By phonics we mean skills that enable readers to pronounce words they have not seen before in written form by associating sounds with written symbols. The development of a "phonics sense" and an inclination to use it are essential prerequisites to independent reading. (Notice that we said "essential," not "sufficient." Successful readers must go beyond efficient decoding. Chapters 6 – 8 deal with the matter in much more detail.) Reading educators do not agree on the content of or the sequence for teaching phonics.

*Structural analysis.*     Structural analysis goes a step beyond phonics, enabling the reader to pick out already known, meaningful parts of words. By recognizing meaningful parts, readers may be able to figure out both the pronunciation and the meaning of unfamiliar words when they first encounter them in print. Structural analysis includes attention to root words, affixes, and inflected words; it may also include attention to plural forms, tenses, comparisons, contractions, and compound words. But what specifics ought to be taught directly, and when should they be taught?

*Contextual analysis.*  While phonics and structural analysis deal mainly with individual words, contextual analysis goes beyond the word to the surrounding context for clues to pronunciation and meaning. It involves attention to typographic, pictorial, stylistic, syntactic, and semantic clues. We think of contextual analysis as a general orientation on the part of the reader rather than a collection of specific skills. It is an inclination to figure out a word by the way it is used in a sentence or passage. Questions related to teaching contextual analysis are whether the "clues" should be taught explicitly, in reading class, or implicitly, in content area classes; and when certain specifics should be taught.

### Comprehension.

Some educators doubt that comprehension can be taught at all. They argue that comprehending is thinking, so the best that teachers can do is help students acquire the facts and concepts they need to think clearly. Most, though, find good evidence that readers' ability to comprehend can be enhanced by learning certain skills and strategies. But what specific skills and strategies ought to be taught? And how can teachers best make allowances for differences in students' backgrounds and in the materials they are expected to understand?

An individual's reading comprehension is influenced by many factors. Some are related to the written message itself, such as sentence complexity and organizational clarity. Others involve the individual's reading environment—the home and the school. Still others are within the reader, such as linguistic competence, interest, motivation, and decoding ability.

We have found it useful to organize reading comprehension skills into four major clusters: skills for getting meaning from (a) words, (b) sentences, (c) paragraphs, passages, and selections, and (d) the overall organization of a text, including sequence clues.

### Reading-Study skills and habits.

These are, for the most part, additional comprehension strategies. They have probably come to be set apart because they deal with rather specialized abilities: strategies for reading maps, graphs, and charts; techniques for recognizing implicit organizational schemes in different types of texts; and adjustment of reading rate in accordance with purpose for reading and difficulty of the material. Students also need to learn how to use basic reference materials such as dictionaries, encyclopedias, card catalogs, and other library resources.

Some activites that seem to go considerably beyond reading are considered study skills, for example, techniques for taking tests and for preparing term parpers and reports. Which of the wide range of possible study skills should be taught in a given program? To what extent should the teaching of specific strategies be integrated into instruction in given content areas? The latter question is particularly important because the unique demands of different subject areas may best be met by specific study strategies. We talk more about the issues related to teaching study skills and strategies in chapters that follow.

***Independent reading.***     Guidance in reading for recreation, pleasure, and personal growth deserves explicit attention in a comprehensive program. Teaching students *how* to read is not enough; schools must try to instill an *inclination* to read. Teachers at all levels can provide a model and show that they value reading by reading aloud and by sharing their personal reading experiences. Some schools even allocate time during the school day for personal reading by students and faculty. We should note, however, that this practice does not have unequivocal support. Proponents say that setting school time aside for reading demonstrates how much it is valued. Critics suggest that providing unstructured time for reading demonstrates only that reading can be a pointless activity. What are other ways to encourage students to acquire a reading habit?

*We have talked about the main purposes and components of a good reading program, pointing out questions that reading educators have not answered. In fact, there are no "right" answers. The answers will always depend on the beliefs and attitudes of whoever does the answering.*

*Yet one must attempt to answer questions such as these if one is to proceed with the teaching of reading. Furthermore, a school faculty must come to agreement about the answers when planning a coherent, comprehensive reading program.*

A good reading program provides balance. A school might have aggressive procedures for teaching word analysis skills but no systematic plan for developing comprehension skills or independent reading habits. Some teachers are confident when helping students understand reading assignments but very uncomfortable about helping students with decoding difficulties. Some students never reach a point where they are good enough at decoding to give most of their attention to understanding what they read. In each of these instances, a comprehensive plan could better achieve balance among the various components.

# Corrective Teaching in the Overall Program

The primary goal of a comprehensive reading program is to enable individuals to cope with the reading tasks they encounter in their lives, both in and out of school. Specific goals for students must take into account personal capacities, background experiences, and progress in achieving component skills.

Oddly enough, teachers often seem to be more inclined to accept and deal with major individual differences in ability and background than with relatively minor differences in achievement. There is, for example, a range of special and remedial options available for students experiencing serious reading problems. But students who encounter minor obstacles, who may be confused and "hung up" at a given point in their reading development, often get no special attention at all. In the best of circumstances, they "figure it out" and move ahead. But in far too many instances minor difficulties are permitted to develop into major problems. Sensibly focused corrective teaching can clear up small difficulties before they become big ones. The place for corrective teaching is in the classroom and it is the responsibility of the classroom teacher.

## Instructional Aspects of a Comprehensive Reading Program

One conception of the instructional aspects of a comprehensive reading program is summarized in Figure 2.1. Note that each of the instructional aspects is directed toward the goal of the overall program: *Reading achievement that approaches the limit of each student's capacity to learn.*

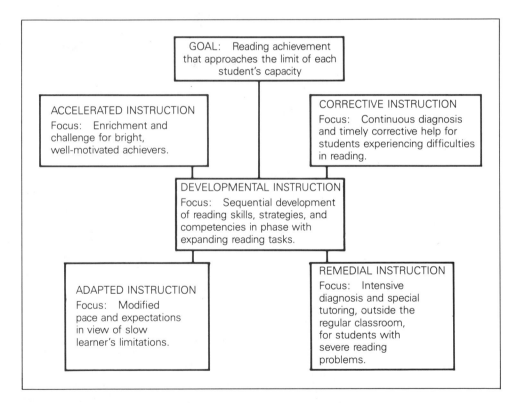

**Figure 2.1.** Instructional Aspects of a Comprehensive Reading Program. (Figure 2.1 and the discussion concerning it are adapted from *Corrective and remedial teaching* (3rd ed.), by W. Otto and R. J. Smith, 1980, Boston: Houghton Mifflin; *The school reading program: A handbook for teachers, supervisors, and specialists* by R. J. Smith, W. Otto, and L. Hansen, 1978, Boston: Houghton Mifflin; and *Reading problems: A multidisciplinary perspective* by W. Otto, N. A. Peters, and C. W. Peters (Eds.), 1977, Reading, Mass.: Addison-Wesley.)

***Developmental instruction.***    In the literature of reading education the term *developmental program* has a broad meaning similar to our description of a comprehensive, or overall, reading program. The *developmental program* subsumes all levels of the entire reading curriculum, including special programs for students with exceptional needs. *Developmental instruction,* on the other hand, is designed for the normal child who moves through the school experience without special problems of any kind. Basal reader programs, designed to move students step by step through the acquisition of reading ability, exemplify developmental instruction.

***Accelerated instruction.***    The focus here is on enrichment and challenge for bright, well-motivated achievers. Students who experience no difficulty with the developmental tasks of reading should—if they have the ability and desire—be permitted to move more rapidly or to take on a broader scope of work, or both, than their grade-level peers. To permit or force bright, eager students to loaf along with unchallenging work is a waste and a disservice.

***Adapted instruction.***    Adapted instruction modifies both pace and expectations in view of "slow learners' " limitations. "Slow learner" is a euphemism designating students whose limited ability makes it unlikely that they can ever achieve at grade level. Unfortunately, in age-graded schools such children are often pushed into remedial classes. There they remain, because they lack the ability to maintain the pace set by their age-level peers.

    Given a normal, bell-shaped distribution of cognitive ability, about one fourth of the children in a typical school have substantially limited ability. To treat these children like underachievers—i.e., children whose performance is below their capacity—is neither realistic nor humane. We return to a more detailed consideration of slow learners and adapted instruction in a later chapter.

***Remedial instruction.***    Remedial instruction differs from adapted instruction mainly in terms of expectations. Remedial instruction is typically offered to students with severe reading difficulties. This is done with the expectation that their deficits will be eliminated or substantially reduced. Students with limited cognitive abilities need adapted instruction; students who are not achieving at their capacity level may need remedial help. Remedial instruction is usually offered outside the student's regular classroom by a specially trained teacher.

    Textbook discussions of how to identify students eligible for remedial instruction are many and long. They tend to be quite legalistic and to bog down in comparison of test scores. A much simpler rule of thumb is: *Refer for remedial instruction when a student who is a substantial underachiever is no longer able to benefit from classroom instruction.* Regardless of whether the reason stems from the student's problems, the teacher's inability to handle individual diagnosis and instruction, or a combination of factors, referral should be made when there is no longer any real potential for learning in the classroom.

***Corrective instruction.***    Corrective instruction differs from remedial instruction in that it is offered (a) when the nature and degree of the difficulties do not appear to demand intensive diagnosis or prolonged, individual instruction, and (b) in the regular classroom by the regular classroom teacher. Corrective instruction differs from adapted instruction in terms of *expectations.* Corrective instruction should help students overcome their underachievement.

*A word of caution is in order. Do not treat the categories in Figure 2.1 as if they were inflexible. To label a given student or a given act of instruction as either developmental or corrective would be foolish. We use the term corrective teaching to underscore the need to tackle little problems before they become big ones. We refer to remedial and adapted instruction to show that expectations and practices must reflect practical realities.*

## Focus on Corrective Teaching

In the first edition of his popular text on reading instruction, Heilman (1961) elucidated the difference between developmental and remedial teaching when he wrote "in remedial reading we conscientiously adhere to the principles that we often only verbalize in regular classroom instruction" (p. 475). He meant that the difference is not so much in materials and techniques as in care and rigor. It is one of degree. In good remedial teaching, diagnosis is more intensive, instruction is more finely focused and carefully paced, reinforcement is more systematic, and the assessment of students' ability to apply what they have learned is more rigorous. Corrective teaching falls squarely between developmental and remedial teaching in terms of rigor, intensity, and focus.

But to say that good corrective teaching adheres more rigorously to sound principles is not to say that developmental teaching is sloppy and insensitive. Students with reading problems simply need more careful attention than students without problems. Unlike learners who succeed, learners who fail in reading are characterized by their general inability—or at least their greater difficulty—to put things together for themselves. A teacher we know put it like this: "It's as if they [poor readers] just don't know how to play the game. Good readers will have a dozen different ways to figure out words and what they mean. They play the game without thinking about the rules. But I have to teach the poor readers exactly what to do, and then I have to help them do it."

## The Classroom Teacher and Friends

One of the classroom teacher's most available resources for teaching reading is a reading specialist who might be called a reading resource teacher, reading consultant, reading supervisor, or just plain reading teacher. An effective working relationship between classroom teacher and reading teacher can be very productive, but there can be problems. Briggs and Coulter (1977) have pointed out some stumbling blocks to effective working relationships:

> The lack of articulation between remedial and regular classroom programs is a . . . problem. For the most part, special reading services operate in a vacuum, largely independent of the classroom and with no impact on the pattern of developmental instruction. Nothing makes less sense than for a child to be sent regularly to the

"reading room" for special help while receiving daily reading instruction in the classroom from materials in which she or he has been inappropriately placed by a well-intentioned but misguided teacher. Without doubt, neither teacher is cognizant of what the other is doing. The child is like a ping-pong ball, propelled from one teacher to the other, making it over the net in remedial sessions, but programmed to crash headlong into it when faced with classroom reading demands. A further irony may be the requirement that the disabled reader be responsible for completing classroom work missed while attending remedial reading classes. Such situations occur because specialists and/or classroom teachers fail to understand the need to support each other if disabilities are to be overcome. Instead, classroom teachers see responsibility for corrective instruction belonging to the specialists and want them to accept the burden. More often than not, specialists are happy to do so and devote the school day exclusively to work with disabled readers, leaving classroom teachers free to maintain their individual spheres of influence, including whatever reading instruction they deem appropriate. This pattern has been firmly established over the past two decades (pp. 224–225).

To change this pattern, the classroom teacher and the specialist must have an open, working relationship that focuses on the needs of the students—not on the personal convenience of the teachers. A comprehensive reading program would go a long way toward enhancing such a relationship. The balance and coherence of an overall program would make individual teachers much less likely to operate in their personal vacuums.

We do see a positive trend in many schools. Reading specialists are spending more time as "consultants" to classroom teachers. This means that more students with reading problems can remain in the classroom, receiving the help they need in the context where they most need it. Of course there will always be a need to diagnose and tutor a few severely disabled readers outside the classroom. Our point is that most reading specialists we know are well-informed, helpful, friendly people. If one is available, invite him or her to work with you.

## Corrective Teaching in the Classroom

If your efforts at corrective teaching fit into the overall plan of an all-school program, they are more likely to be effective and to have a lasting effect on students' reading performance. As an individual teacher you can participate and contribute, but you must also rely on the collaborative efforts of others.

In your classroom you are on your own. You may do as much corrective teaching as you can handle with any students you choose. *How much you can handle* depends largely on how much you know about teaching reading in general and corrective teaching in particular. We hope to help you with that in the following pages. *Which students you choose* will always depend on your view of the reading process and how you define reading "difficulties."

Every student learns to read in a very personal, idiosyncratic way. So students' performance will always be distributed over a rather broad continuum. A temporary set-back for one student may be a serious difficulty for another.

One way to gain perspective on corrective teaching in the classroom is to take a close look at a single classroom. In the remaining pages of this chapter we present a combined classroom of fourth- and fifth-grade students, borrowing heavily from a study by Eldridge (1981). Eldridge observed everything that went on in a classroom related to the teaching and learning of reading for four months. He tried to discover and understand the teacher's and students' (a) knowledge and beliefs about reading, and (b) teaching and learning behaviors in the classroom.

We have included our comments with Eldridge's observations. We do not suggest that observations, no matter how intense or insightful, are a basis for sweeping generalizations about the teaching and learning of reading; but they provide a perspective for dealing with corrective teaching in the classroom.

## Three Categories of Readers

Eldridge decided that there were three basic "types" of readers in the classroom he observed: appliers, tacit appliers, and nonappliers. The categories are worth a closer look because they describe a range of reading behaviors found in many classrooms. They also provide a basis for identifying students who would be likely to profit from corrective teaching.[2]

***The appliers.*** *Appliers* are defined as individuals who are able to identify reading skills, to describe the skills, to use their reading skills to complete assigned school-work, and to apply the skills independently when reading for pleasure. In Eldridge's study, "specific reading skill" was defined as any skill presented in the basal reader series, such as *determining sequence, drawing conclusions, identifying variant sounds of consonants, and pronouncing consonant blends.* A specific reading skill was also any skill the teacher taught during the reading group discussion, such as *getting the main idea, drawing inferences, or evaluating characters.* The appliers shared certain characteristics.

They could list reading skills when asked to. For example, Monica identified one reading skill as "getting the meaning of the story." She also referred to "finding similes and comparing things" as reading skills. Leslie, on the other hand, talked about following the sequence of a passage and "saying things in your own words." The list of skills identified by the appliers includes skills incorporated in the basal reader series as well as skills their teacher taught. It is interesting to note that although at no time during the course of the study did the teacher identify any of the appliers' group activities or assignments as skill-development activities, the appliers did identify their reading activities as skills.

Once a student named a particular skill, he or she was asked to explain or describe it. Without exception the appliers were able to do so; most could provide an example of the use of the skill to illustrate the intended meaning. Paul, for example, defined getting the main idea of a story as telling "mainly what happens in a chapter

---

[2] The discussion of the three categories is, for the most part, in Eldridge's own words. We have made minor modifications.

. . . or story." He used an example, "Your eyes are like pearls" to exemplify a simile. To define what he meant by sequence, Karl listed the steps Jodi (a character in *The Yearling* ) took to get help after a rattlesnake bit Penny.

Each applier was able to use reading skills by completing assigned work in both reading and social studies.

Finally, the appliers said they read lots of materials on their own, outside of school, "to get information and for the fun of it." They also said that their parents encourage them to read at home "before bedtime and during free time."

To sum up, appliers are able to identify reading skills, define or describe the skills, use the skills in completing their assignments, and apply the skills independently when they read for pleasure or personal profit. Six of the children in the classroom observed were designated appliers.

The appliers are successful readers. They know how to tackle a reading task and why they succeed. There may be a variety of reasons for each individual's success; but in the terms introduced in Figure 2.1, all of the appliers seem to be responding well to developmental instruction.

**The tacit appliers.**    *Tacit appliers* were not able to name any reading skills on their own. When the name of a reading skill was provided, however, they remembered having heard of it. Still, the students were unable to describe the skill or to ascribe meaning to it beyond recognizing its name. A puzzling characteristic was that these students were able to engage in productive reading—they could apply the requisite skills—so as to complete required assignments in both reading and content area classes.

Tacit appliers were apparently using good reading skills. All of them passed the skill pre-assessments in their workbooks and continued to work successfully in the basal reader materials at or above their grade placements. Further, the tacit appliers progressed at an even pace through the basal reader levels—they completed three or more text levels in the basal reader series during the school year. They could answer questions during their reading group instruction that probed beyond literal comprehension. That is, they were able to make inferences from the content of stories, to evaluate aspects of the stories, and to show appreciation and understanding of the characters in stories and of the author's efforts and motives. Finally, the tacit appliers consistently completed the reading assignments for their social studies class and participated in subsequent discussion.

To sum up, the tacit appliers could not name a reading skill, but when skills were named they indicated having heard of them. They could not define or describe the content of reading skills named for them. They could, however, use reading skills, consistently completing reading assignments and participating in group discussions. Seventeen of the children in the classroom observed were designated tacit appliers.

The tacit appliers present a dilemma. They appear to know how to read in a global sense; but they do not seem to know how to go about reading. Some reading educators suggest that it is unnecessary to belabor the teaching of specific skills if the end result is satisfactory. Others argue that merely getting the right results is not enough; one should know both how to achieve them and when they have been achieved.

*We find ourselves somewhere between the two positions. While it would be foolish to teach certain specific skills to students who are able to cope with their day-to-day reading tasks, we are convinced that competent, fully mature readers are able to attain their independence and versatility as readers because they have a reasonably clear understanding of the process of reading. Not to help students reach some level of understanding of the reading process would be irresponsible.*

*We suggest that tacit appliers are prime candidates for corrective teaching. While they do not manifest typical difficulties in their day-to-day reading, they appear to lack understanding of the process of reading. Through well-planned, direct teaching they can develop insights that will assure their continued growth and development as readers.*

Allison, one of the children introduced in Chapter 1, is a good example of a tacit applier. She can decode, or sound out, words and perform quite well at oral reading. Yet she has no real sense of the importance of getting meaning from what she reads. She needs very much to develop a better understanding of her own involvement in the reading process. This can be accomplished through well-directed corrective teaching.

**The nonappliers.**    The *nonapplier* was unable to name or identify any specific reading skill. Nor could the nonapplier describe or define a reading skill. (Remember that the appliers consistently defined reading skills by giving examples, by reciting definitions previously learned, or by defining in their own words.) The nonapplier was unable to apply specific skills either in doing reading assignments or in doing assignments for content area classes such as social studies.

Patty, for example, was designated a nonapplier because she showed the following attributes. First, she was unable to name specific reading skills when asked to do so. Even though the question was asked directly after she had received teacher-directed instruction in the use of skills with basal reader materials, she could not name a skill. Second, Patty was unable to define a single specific skill, even after certain, presumably familiar skills were identified for her. Third, Patty was not able to use the reading skills she was exposed to in her reading group. She continued to have trouble with word analysis, and her comprehension was limited to understanding the literal meaning of printed words. Consequently, Patty's ability to participate in certain group activities, such as the discussion of stories, was very limited. In her reading group she had difficulty answering questions the teacher asked. She did not participate in discussions with her social studies group.

To sum up, nonappliers were characterized by being unable to name specific reading skills, incapable of describing or defining the content of reading skills, and inept at applying reading skills to complete assignments. Three of the children in the classroom observed were designated nonappliers.

It is clear that the nonappliers need special attention. They give little evidence of having profited from previous reading instruction and they seem unable to participate fully in reading-related activities. Without additional information, however, one cannot prescribe the appropriate type of instruction—corrective, remedial, or adapted (see Figure 2.1 and the related discussion). Adapted instruction would be indicated for a nonapplier who is also a slow learner, unable to participate in or to benefit from regular developmental instruction. Remedial instruction might be in order for a student who, though unable to profit from instruction in the classroom, shows potential for improvement. Corrective instruction would be on target for a nonapplier who seems to be generally confused about the reading process.

John, from Chapter 1, is a good example of a nonapplier. Although he appears to have potential for doing better, his reading performance is bogged down by difficulties with decoding. He is unable to apply phonics principles except in isolation. John is "glued to print"; he needs corrective teaching to develop greater reading fluency and the ability to go beyond word attack to seeking meaning from the words. (See particularly Chapters 6, 7, and 8.)

The three categories just discussed describe a range of reading behaviors found in most classrooms. The categories are most useful for planning instruction appropriate for different groups. Sensible decisions about how to help individuals learn to read better can only be made with some understanding of how those individuals view the reading process and their place in relation to it. Again, Eldridge's observations provide us with some insights.

## Readers' Views

Three individuals' comments on reading as they perceive it in the classroom are given in this section.[3] The comments describe the reading-related behaviors and beliefs of one student from each of the categories just discussed. Do keep in mind that although the individuals in each category share certain characteristics they differ in many important ways. The point is that you must consider personal knowledge and beliefs when planning instruction.

*An applier's views: Heather.*    Heather participated in a reading group of six members, five fifth graders and one fourth grader. The teacher did not assign selections or workbook exercises from the basal reader series. Instead, the group read widely from a variety of library books (*The Yearling, Caddie Woodlawn, The Bully of Barkham Street* ).

Heather maintained that one reason the teacher had her group read a variety of books "was for reading skills." (Josh, another member of the group, stated more bluntly that the group used library books "because he [the teacher] thought that those reader books [the basal readers] are too easy for us." He added, "The stories might be good for us but the workbook stuff would be too easy for us.") Heather pointed out that reading skills "help you read better" and "practice makes perfect." According to Heather, you are a good reader "if you read out loud and if you understand what you're reading . . . and if you are better with the meanings of words."

---

[3] Again, the description of each individual is largely in Eldridge's own words, but we have made some modifications.

Heather: An applier.  Gini: A tacit applier.  Patty: A nonapplier

When asked what reading skills she had learned, Heather mentioned "the mood of the story, . . . vocabulary, how the author feels." She also said that reading a story helps to develop one's feelings. For example, the teacher had encouraged the members of her reading group to tell how they felt when Jodi killed a friendly deer, Flag, in *The Yearling*. Heather claimed that knowing the mood of a story is important "to help you understand the story better." She went on to say, "but some books if you read 'em you can't understand what they're trying to make you feel." She concluded, "Well, in certain books like *The Yearling* just the words help you feel what's going to happen next." She felt that the author of *The Yearling* was trying to make the reader feel "mostly sad and angry."

Heather mentioned that the teacher often required her group members to make comparisons of different incidents in the book. For instance, they were asked to tell how Jodi felt after he killed Flag, the friendly deer, and then what his feelings were when the rattler bit Penny.

Heather stated regarding social studies that "the questions are mainly looking for facts . . . but you have to read carefully and think about what you're reading so that you can find the answers." She maintained that the tasks during the reading discussion sessions were similar.

Heather was not an active participant in the social-studies discussion sessions, but she worked hard to compile answers to the questions the teacher provided in study packets. When the teacher directed questions to Heather, she responded with appropriate answers. Although she expressed disappointment that the teacher did not collect the completed social studies questions "to see how good I did," she understood that if she had not finished the questions she could not have participated in the discussion sessions. She knew that the teacher did not check the written answers but she was aware that he checked to see which students participated in the discussions.

Heather is obviously both bright and perceptive. She is not hung up with decoding the words and is ready to go beyond the literal meaning of a passage or story to seek deeper meanings. She is aware of certain parallels between what she learns in reading class and what she is expected to know in social studies class. (If she needs any special help at all, it would be to help her take a more aggressive stance in social studies discussion group.)

**A tacit applier's views: Gini.**     Gini, a fourth grader, was in a group of four students working with the materials at a high fifth-grade level in the basal reader series.

According to Gini, the teacher assigned stories in the basal reader so that the children would "get the important parts or the high point of the story." She said the teacher could tell when a child understood the high point of a story by the way the child answered questions during the discussion session. Gini said the teacher usually asked the children to "think of another name for the story" they had read and to write that name in their workbooks. Then she added that the teacher asked each child to explain (orally) a reason for his or her selection. Gini thought the teacher could tell from this information whether or not each child had understood the story. Gini also maintained that the teacher assigned extra reading "to see if you understand what the high point is. What the story was talking about." Gini seemed to think that the main purpose for reading was to identify the climax or high point of a story.

Gini described the vocabulary pretests her teacher assigned from the workbooks as "pages given to help you understand the vocabulary. If you don't understand [the words] in the story go back here [workbooks] and read it." Gini said, too, that she used the pictures in the stories "to help understand the story." She explained that she often "forms images" while she reads to help her with the content of a story, even though "the author's pictures and my pictures would be different."

Unlike the other children in her reading group, Gini did not complete her workbook assignments before she read the assigned story. She read the story first "because the workbook is dependent on the story sometimes." Gini was the only tacit applier interviewed who acknowledged any connection between reading a story in the basal reader and completing the workbook exercise. In fact, Gini claimed that she read each story two times—"the second time to look for important parts"—before beginning her workbook assignments. She said she needed to read the story twice to be able to answer the teacher's questions during group discussions and to complete the workbook exercises.

Gini actively participated in social-studies discussion sessions. She was well-prepared, sought to answer the teacher's questions, and worked hard to prepare appropriate written answers. She said that "things in reading were similar to social studies." What she seemed to mean was that the types of questions and the discussion format were similar.

While Gini, a tacit applier, did not seem to have a good grasp of the nature or function of specific reading skills, she was aware of certain opportunities to apply what she learned in reading group. She said that what she had learned about suffixes she was able to use when writing her stories in language arts. Likewise, she made comparisons of various story characters in reading, and she employed a similar technique in making comparisons of the people she learned about in social studies.

Gini explained that report card grades were based on each child's success in submitting completed assignments on time. She believed that children who consistently failed to submit papers on time received lower grades, and she said that she tried to submit all of her work on time. For Gini, promptness seems to be the main criterion of good grades. This is in contrast to a view expressed by Paul, an applier, who said that grades depended on "getting stuff in on time *and* how well you express your feelings."

On one hand, Gini is a serious and sincere student. She looks for the good motives behind her assignments, she seeks parallels between what she learns in her reading group and what she must do in her other classes, and she takes her workbook exercises seriously. She also seems to have an inclination to "image" while she reads. On the other hand, Gini has no good idea of why she does her workbook exercises, she has only a distorted notion of the main purpose for reading, and she thinks that promptness is the sole basis for report card grades. While her imaging could become a positive factor in understanding what she reads, the existing evidence suggests that her efforts might not be very effective.

Gini would probably benefit from help in developing a better understanding of reading at two levels. First, she should have a clearer notion of multiple purposes for reading (e.g., for facts, for concepts, for the gist of a story or article). Second, she ought to see the relationship between the skills she studies in her exercise book and the tasks she must deal with when she reads to complete assigned work.

*As we mentioned earlier, we believe tacit appliers like Gini to be prime candidates for corrective teaching. Direct teaching in the classroom could help Gini to see different purposes for reading, point out opportunities to apply previously learned skills, and help her monitor her own efforts, including imaging, to understand content area materials.*

*A nonapplier's view: Patty.* Patty was working, with individual attention, in the third-grade level materials in the basal reader series.

Patty described reading as "the time I spend with Mr. Bell [the teacher] reading out loud." Then she added that the time she spent answering the questions in her workbook was also reading time. She thought that reading time was provided by the teacher so "we can think about what [a] story is about and what it's trying to explain." The content of Patty's oral reading was usually a story from her basal reader text. She had usually read the material prior to meeting with the teacher.

Patty gave several reasons for reading aloud for Mr. Bell. First, a story is read aloud "if we like the story." Next, a story is read aloud "because it is short." And finally, "So Mr. Bell would hear me read and know I understand what I read." Patty apparently equated reading aloud with understanding. She was, however, frequently unable to respond to the teacher's questions about stories she had read aloud. When asked why she had difficulty answering her teacher's questions, Patty admitted that often she didn't "know what [the] words mean."

Patty's pattern of working with reading materials was often erratic. When she did her workbook assignments, she completed the easiest parts of the pages first, then moved on to finish what she knew on subsequent pages. When Patty did not understand how to complete a specific exercise she was not hesitant to ask her teacher to re-explain the page to her. Yet she stated that she completed her workbook pages before she began to read the assigned story.

When the observer asked Patty to explain the directions and content of some of her workbook exercises, Patty was usually able to tell what was expected of her on each page. She could not, however, give any reasons why specific pages were assigned. When the observer asked Patty to explain the workbook assignments a day after the teacher had explained them to her, she was confused. She could not explain what she was to do or why she was expected to complete the pages.

Patty mentioned on several occasions that she did not read at home very much. She sometimes read "easy books" to her younger brothers and sisters, but "never read to self." She said that there were a few books at home for her to read, but that she didn't like to read. She added that neither her mother nor her father read to her but that her father read "a lot of books on his own." During recreational reading periods in the classroom, Patty would sometimes page through books looking at the pictures; but she spent most of the allotted time completing math assignments.

Patty thought that the words she encountered during reading time helped her in social studies and science work. Yet she could not apply the questions her teacher asked in the reading discussions to her social studies assignments. Patty did not actively participate in the fourth-grade social studies group discussions. In fact, during the four months of observation, Patty responded only once to a question from the teacher. The teacher noted that Patty seemed to have only a "minimal" understanding of what she read and what was expected of her in social studies.

*About the only thing we can say about Patty with any confidence is that she is having serious difficulties with her reading. This is so even though her teacher has provided her with materials closer to her achievement level and has attempted to individualize her instruction. Patty does not have even a fuzzy notion of what reading is all about or why one would voluntarily engage in reading activities.*

*Before we can make any suggestions about appropriate instruction for Patty we need more information. If we find that her reading performance is in line with her general ability, adapted instruction would best suit her needs. If her reading performance is below her general ability, she probably would benefit from corrective or remedial instruction. With the information we have, it appears that both Patty and her teacher are willing to give it their best shot. So intensive corrective teaching may be in order. A referral for remedial help outside the classroom should be made only if it appears that effective instruction cannot be offered in the classroom.*

# Summary

A well-planned, comprehensive reading program can bring coherence and balance to the reading instruction offered in a school or a school system. Such all-school programs can be developed only with the understanding and support of all responsible personnel. Components of a comprehensive reading program include teaching word analysis skills, comprehension skills, and reading-study skills as well as providing opportunities for independent reading.

When such a program is implemented, teaching responsibilities can sensibly be shared. Most important, teachers may proceed with confidence that individual's needs can be met and that reading difficulties can be detected and dealt with before they become debilitating and demoralizing problems. Classroom-based corrective teaching must play an important role in the overall instructional effort.

# References

Briggs, D. A., and Coulter, F. G. (1977). The reading specialist. In W. Otto, N. A. Peters, and C. W. Peters (Eds.), *Reading problems: A multidiciplinary perspective* (pp. 215 – 236). Reading, MA: Addison-Wesley.

Eldridge, R. G., Jr. (1981). *An ethnographic study of the acquisition and application of reading skills in one elementary school classroom* (Technical Report No. 579). Madison, WI: Wisconsin Research and Development Center for Individualized Schooling.

Heilman, A. W. (1961). *Principles and practices of teaching reading.* Columbus, OH: Charles E. Merrill.

Otto, W., Peters, N. A., & Peters, C. W. (Eds.). (1977). *Reading problems: A multidisciplinary perspective.* Reading, MA: Addison-Wesley.

Otto, W., & Smith, R. J. (1980). *Corrective and remedial teaching* (3rd ed.). Boston: Houghton Mifflin.

Smith, R. J., Otto, W., & Hansen, L. (1978). *The school reading program: A handbook for teachers, supervisors, and specialists.* Boston: Houghton Mifflin.

# Check Your Reading Comprehension

1. What should be the goal of a comprehensive reading program?

2. What are some of the reasons schools need a comprehensive reading program?

3. What are some of the obstacles to the development and implementation of a comprehensive reading program.

**4.** Matching exercise:

_____ **1.** Word analysis

_____ **2.** Comprehension

_____ **3.** Reading-study skills and habits

_____ **4.** Independent reading

_____ **5.** Accelerated instruction

_____ **6.** Corrective instruction

_____ **7.** Developmental instruction

_____ **8.** Adapted instruction

_____ **9.** Remedial instruction

_____ **10.** Appliers

_____ **11.** Tacit appliers

_____ **12.** Nonappliers

**a.** Instruction that emphasizes modified pace and expectations in view of slow learner's limitations.

**b.** Involves guidance in reading for recreation, pleasure, and personal growth.

**c.** Includes an array of skills that enable a reader to discover both the pronunciation and the meaning of written words.

**d.** Students who appear to know how to read but do not seem to grasp the meaning of reading.

**e.** Instruction emphasizing intensive diagnosis and special tutoring, outside the regular classroom, for students with severe reading problems.

**f.** Continuous diagnosis and timely corrective help for students experiencing difficulties in reading.

**g.** Students who give little evidence of having profited from previous reading instruction and who seem unable to participate fully in reading related activities.

**h.** Students who are able to read for whatever purposes they have and who also know how to tackle a reading task and know why they succeed.

**i.** Skills dealing with rather specialized activities and abilities, such as: strategies for reading maps, graphs and charts; adjusting reading rate based on the purpose for reading and the difficulty of material; techniques for test-taking.

**j.** Includes skills and strategies enabling a reader to get meaning from words, sentences, paragraphs, passages, selections, and complete texts.

**k.** Sequential development of reading skills, strategies, and competencies in phase with expanding reading tasks.

**l.** Instruction that emphasizes enrichment and challenge for bright, well-motivated achievers.

Answers:

| | | | |
|---|---|---|---|
| 6. f. | | 12. g | |
| 5. l. | | 11. d | |
| 4. b. | | 10. h. | |
| 3. i. | | 9. e. | |
| 2. j. | | 8. a. | |
| 1. c. | | 7. k. | |

**5.** Study the Classroom Screening Chart (Table 1 – 1) in Chapter 1. Which students might you consider appliers? tacit appliers? nonappliers? Which students might profit from developmental instruction? accelerated instruction? corrective instruction? remedial instruction? adapted instruction?

**6.** Study your own class. Which students might you consider appliers? tacit appliers? nonappliers? Which students might profit from developmental instruction? accelerated instruction? corrective instruction? remedial instruction? adapted instruction?

# 3

# Effective Corrective Teaching

In Chapter 1 we gave you some examples of children who, for a variety of reasons, need special attention—corrective teaching—when they are in the regular classroom. In chapter 2 we told you that corrective teaching is most effective when it is part of a comprehensive, all-school reading program. In both chapters we reminded you that the main responsibility for corrective reading instruction is yours, the classroom teacher's. Additional resources may be available in the form of special programs and specialized personnel, but it is only corrective help in the classroom that will enable certain pupils to participate in the mainstream of reading instruction.

The first two chapters provided an overview of the "clientele," the context, and the challenge of corrective teaching. The rest of the book tells you how to get on with it.

Think of Chapter 3 as an orientation to corrective teaching. You may be concerned that the definitions of corrective teaching given so far have not been precise. The dictionary definition in Chapter 1 (Harris & Hodges, 1981, p. 71) says, "Corrective reading instruction is more specific than developmental instruction, but less intensive than remedial reading instruction." In Chapter 2 we told you that sensibly focused corrective teaching can help students deal with minor difficulties and keep little problems from becoming big ones. Corrective teaching falls squarely between developmental and remedial teaching in terms of rigor, intensity and focus. These definitions, which explain how corrective teaching differs from both developmental (in-the-classroom) and remedial (outside-the-classroom) teaching, may tell you more about what corrective teaching isn't than what it is. That is because the term "corrective teaching" defies neat definition.

The basic premise of this chapter is that effective corrective teaching is no more—and certainly no less—than effective teaching at its very best. It is largely seeking out and applying sound teaching practices. We address certain aspects of teaching that seem to have particular promise for corrective teaching. The chapter is composed of three main topics: (a) long-term goals and short-term objectives, (b) effective teaching practices, and (c) direct teaching, where the teacher takes an assertive role in creating favorable conditions for learning.

# Long-term Goals and Short-term Objectives

Good teachers set *long-term goals* and *short-term objectives*. In other words, they have a good sense of where they are going and how they will try to get there. Take away the short-term objectives and many well-intentioned but poorly focused activities are apt to occur: page-by-page reading from the basal series, phonics lessons that follow the workbook, and oral reading without critique. Take away the long-term goals and you are likely to see lots of random activity in a classroom: tests given without reason, basal readers pursued without direction, and workbook pages assigned without purpose. The first instance is like a ship without a rudder; the second is like a rudder without a ship!

Long-term goals of corrective teaching might include the following:

- Morgan will read at second-grade level.
- Heidi will apply phonics principles to figure out the pronunciation of new words.
- Marvin will state the main idea of passages written at his reading performance level.

Related short-term objectives could be these:

- Morgan will recognize at sight (one-second exposure) ten high-frequency words chosen from a book he is currently reading.
- Heidi will apply the "silent *e* rule" when attempting to pronounce unfamiliar words in oral reading sessions.
- Marvin will find the topic sentence in paragraphs from the Every Pupil Skilltexts, Book H.

Long-term goals describe a desirable outcome, but are not specific enough for planning a lesson or even a week-long series of two to four lessons. Short-term objectives describe behaviors specifically enough for planning a lesson or a short

Set short-term and long-term goals!

series of lessons. Each short-term objective is related to a long-term goal: each focuses on a specific behavior that contributes to the long-term goal. Notice, too, that our examples of short-term objectives contain no specific criteria or performance levels. A formal behavioral objective would specify a performance criterion, for instance "... in eight out of ten tries" or "... with total accuracy." Use your own good judgment to set criteria for each student's performance. You might decide that Morgan, who tends to be a careless reader, needs to reach a criterion of total accuracy in recognizing sight words. Heidi, who tends to be overly cautious anyway, can perform satisfactorily with 80 percent accuracy in sight word recognition. You want to ensure that the student is able to perform a specific skill at a level that permits successful application in actual reading.

## Characteristics of Useful Goals and Objectives

Set long-term instructional goals for corrective teaching according to (a) your school's curriculum guide, if there is one, or, perhaps more realistically, the instructor's manual for your basal reader, (b) the needs and characteristics of the learner(s), and (c) your own common sense. Consider a long-term goal that says: "The pupil will read at the second-grade level." Reading at given grade levels is commonly called for by curriculum guides or by the overall goals of a school's reading program, so the outcome seems to be a sensible and desirable one to pursue in a given setting. If Morgan is reading at the first-grade level at the middle of second grade, the outcome certainly is a desirable one for him. If Morgan is an underachiever, capable of reading at a higher level, the outcome is a realistic one to pursue. By describing a realistic and desirable outcome, a long-term goal sets a direction and makes it possible to plan a sensible sequence of instruction.

Short-term objectives are sometimes called *behavioral* or *instructional* objectives. There is no need in this chapter to go into technical specifications for behavioral objectives or the shades of difference between formal behavioral objectives and less formal instructional objectives. Very briefly, a well-stated objective describes, first, the desired student performance in terms of specific, observable behaviors, and, second, a performance level that establishes a criterion for judging whether a student has mastered the objective. (See Otto, Rude, and Spiegel, 1979, Chapter 3, for a more detailed discussion.)

For present purposes, the function of the objective matters more than the form. Short-term objectives break long-term goals into teachable bits. The objectives help the teacher to (a) set a purpose for a lesson or a short series of lessons, (b) make the student(s) aware of that purpose, (c) plan instructional activities in line with that purpose, (d) organize time, space, and materials for carrying out the activities, and (e) establish a criterion for assessing the outcome of the instruction. (See Chapter 4 for a discussion of criterion-referenced assessment.) We stress that the technical elegance of an objective is less important than its potential utility. We have seen too many discussions bog down in trivial details because more importance was placed on form than on function.

The following are some characteristics of useful, workable objectives. Notice, though, that some of the examples may be too broad for day-to-day planning.

*The objective describes an observable behavior.* The objective "Flossie will develop more interest in reading" is not very useful because "more interest" cannot be observed, so it would be impossible to assess progress. A better objective would be "Flossie will voluntarily select and read a book of her own choice each week."

*The objective is clear and specific.* The words used in the objective should convey a precise and unambiguous meaning. "Gordon will understand material from his basal reader" is unclear because "understand" could mean anything from answering a simple multiple-choice question to giving a synopsis of the main points of an entire chapter. A better objective would state exactly how Gordon is to demonstrate comprehension: perhaps by answering three out of four factual questions, by paraphrasing passages, or by summarizing main points. A decision about how understanding is to be demonstrated has implications for how instruction should proceed.

*The objective focuses on a single behavior.* If an objective covers more than one behavior, you may find it difficult to focus instruction and assess the outcome. "Kim will *decode* and *define* words at her reading level" would be better stated as two objectives. Both decoding and defining words are important processes and in many instances should be taught concurrently; but pushing both into a single objective is likely to clutter planning and assessment.

*The objective should be attainable.* Again, you must combine common sense with a realistic appraisal of the learner's characteristics. Consider the time and resources available for corrective teaching as well as the learner's present skill development and potential. The objective "Henry will read at grade level by the end of the school year" would probably be unattainable if Henry is a slow learner reading two years below grade placement.

A good short-term objective has still another characteristic: it describes a behavior in terms specific enough to be a basis for planning a lesson or a short series of lessons (work that would take a week or so). The preceding examples might be too broad to serve such a purpose. When this is so, the objective needs to be broken down to focus on more specific behavior.

Remember, short-term objectives should be specific enough to give direction to day-to-day teaching, which is in turn directed by long-term goals. A case study, where the teacher actually sets long-term goals and short-term objectives, will help to clarify.

# A Case Report

This is the case of Alfred E. Nessman. (The case study is real; the name is fictitous.) His mother requested that he be given extra help in reading because his performance was poor and he was becoming increasingly frustrated by his unsuccessful attempts to improve. The teacher who prepared the case report was enrolled in a practicum course offered by the local university. Note, then, that she was acting as a tutor, not as Al's regular classroom teacher. Tutoring was scheduled twice a week for 30-minute sessions during the summer and into the first semester of third grade.

Do not be disturbed that the case study focuses on just one student. While it is true that in the classroom you are more likely to be teaching children in groups than as individuals, you must always consider the needs of individuals *before* you form groups for instruction. Once you know individuals' needs, you can bring those with common needs together for instruction. In the classroom Alfred would probably be taught in a group of students with similar needs. We present the case study more to demonstrate some points about corrective teaching than to provide a model for grouping students. Suggestions for organizing and managing corrective instruction in the classroom are given in subsequent chapters, particularly Chapter 15.

Alfred was an exemplary candidate for corrective help. That is, he was experiencing reading problems, but they were not so severe as to require the intensive individual attention of remedial teaching. Because the tutor set long-term goals and short-term objectives for her work with Al, we have a basis for commenting on the appropriateness and the function of her goals and objectives as well as other aspects of the work. The case report is only moderately edited from the tutor's original, and our comments are interspersed throughout. The pronouns "I" and "me" refer to the tutor.

## Background Information

I have been tutoring Al Nessman since June, at which time he was completing second grade. Al's mother contacted me to discuss Al's frustration with reading and his low self-concept.

First I met with Al's teacher, who stated that Al was, indeed, one of the poorest readers in second grade. He had displayed an intense dislike of reading and had often failed to meet school standards. He was in a special reading group and would very likely be retained at the end of third grade. The teacher added that Al was disruptive and had few, if any, friends. Children would often say, "We don't want Al in our group." His teacher suspected that Al had been trying to compete with two academically successful older brothers and had encountered a great deal of pressure at home from his father. She thought Al was signed up for the summer reading program and wondered whether tutoring might induce further pressure.

I next met with Al's mother. She expressed deep concern for his low self-concept, stating that he often would say, "I'm dumb. I can't read." She, too, indicated that Al's father was impatient with him, and she mentioned that Al had developed several tics.

We determined that Al should participate in either the summer school program or tutoring. We decided that I would tutor Al using a language experience approach and that no one else would work with him unless Al requested it. This was to be a fun, pressure-free experience—but first, lunch at McDonald's to get acquainted!

*Lunch at McDonald's? Not everyone would agree that such an activity is appropriate. Some teachers would say that poor readers need teachers, not pals; that lunch is an extrinsic reward, and therefore questionable; or even that their principal would never approve of a field trip. Others would argue that anything that would reduce anxieties and establish rapport would be worthwhile. What YOU should do will always depend very much on your own personal style. But you must also consider the learner and the context. So, what about lunch at McDonald's? Well . . . Al is feeling a lot of pressure and, after all, summer vacation is about to begin. One of your authors says "Two quarter pounders to go!" and the other says "Let's get down to business."*

## Diagnostic Procedures

After my contacts with Al's teacher and mother, I decided to limit my initial efforts to informal procedures. I did not see a need for additional formal testing, and it appeared that more work with Al's reading text would serve no useful purpose because of his negative association with "school work." I would, however, try to incorporate words from his basal reader into the language experiences. I was determined, at this point, to help Al break out of the failure-frustration-failure pattern and to pay attention to his emotional needs.

My second meeting with Al (after McDonald's) consisted of discussing his interests and the kind of experiences he would like to have. He expressed varied interests: art, cooking, fishing, animals, and a new puppy. He appeared to enjoy talking about and deciding which of these we would share. He was verbal, expressive, opinionated, and seemed to be a typical eight-year-old—not what had been previously described to me.

After several meetings I determined that Al had a very good grasp of phonics. I later viewed this to be an overdependence instead of a strength. Although I found Al to be a slow, choppy reader with a limited reading vocabulary, his verbal abilities were quite good. Another of Al's strengths was that he did use contextual clues when he failed to remember or recognize a word.

After several more meetings with Al, my "hunch" was that he was an underachiever with average capacity and a reluctant reader. He exhibited frustration and anxiety when reading by fidgeting, repeatedly clearing his throat, blinking, and jerking his head. His apparent discomfort and lack of motivation confirmed my early decision to try to stimulate and develop his interest through language experience. I would defer work on specific word attack skills and, particularly, work with his reading text until he was more comfortable with the reading task.

*The tutor's informal, easygoing style is evident. But what does it mean to say that ". . . Al had a very good grasp of phonics" and that this was ". . . an overdependence and not a strength." If there is, indeed, good evidence that Al knows how to "sound out" words he does not recognize at sight, but that he tends to overdo the sounding at the expense of fluent reading, then the diagnosis may be adequate. But if the "good grasp of phonics" is only a general impression, then some further, formal testing would be in order. The report does not make the bases for this important diagnostic conclusion clear, as it should. However, we will assume that the diagnostic conclusion is sound.*

## Summary Diagnosis

I concluded that Al's summary needs were an improved self-image, a better attitude toward reading, and more sight vocabulary development. Al also needed to become less dependent on his version of phonics and more attentive to fluent oral reading. Later we would work on his using those phonics skills to become an independent reader.

## Goals and Objectives

My intentions were to set two or three short-term objectives each week (and to repeat them as necessary) in order to pursue the long-term goals implied by the summary diagnosis.

Long-term goals:

1. That Al's self-concept will improve, as shown by fewer references to an inability to read.
2. That Al's attitude toward reading will improve, as shown by the development of a desire to read for purpose or enjoyment.
3. That Al's reading (sight) vocabulary will expand, as evidenced by (a) his ability to quickly recognize selected words, (b) greater independence,

(automaticity) in his word attack, and (c) more fluent oral reading; for example, increased speed and appropriate use of inflected speech at punctuation marks.

*Notice that the long-term goals are generally interrelated and that each speci-fies how the desired outcome is to be demonstrated. This specificity is appro-priate to these goals because they involve performance otherwise difficult to observe. "More fluent oral reading," for example, could be interpreted many different ways without the further mention of "increased speed and appropri-ate use of inflected speech at punctuation marks." ("Automaticity" is a concept we will explain fully in Chapter 8.) In general, though, look to your short-term objectives to specify behaviors.*
Short-term objectives (examples from subsequent weeks):

1. Allowed one-second exposure per word, Al will recognize 90 percent of the words in his word box.
2. Al will be able to pronounce with 80 percent accuracy new words he encounters in an unfamiliar paragraph at his instructional reading level.
3. Al will be taped reading a selection before and after practicing reading it. He will be able to observe his improved fluency and expression on the postpractice tape.

*The preceding short-term objectives are only a sampling from the objec-tives that were set for planning and assessment on a daily or weekly basis. Notice that each objective is in line with one or more of the long-term goals and is specific enough to serve as a basis for planning day-to-day instruction and for assessing progress.*
*Notice, too, that both the long-term goals and the short-term objectives describe relatively easy but important tasks that build upon Al's strength in "sounding out" words. A cardinal principle of both corrective and remedial teaching is: Success begets success! With "easy" tasks you can assure suc-cess and build a sound foundation for subsequent development. (In Chapter 8 we talk more about the need to develop fluent oral reading—automaticity—as a prerequisite to effective silent reading.)*

## Summary of Instruction

I followed a two-stage instructional plan. During the summer months we worked on the first three of the long-term goals. This was done entirely through language experience activities and a great deal of positive reinforcement. When school began in the fall, I met with Al's new teacher. Instruction from this point on was primarily in conjunction with his school reading program.
Al responded very well to the language experience approach. We made

baker's clay, bathed his puppy, baked a pizza, and painted each other with face paint. He kept a large scrapbook containing all of his stories along with riddle pages, classification work, and art work. The more I told Al that he was smart and a good reader, the more he was determined to keep me saying so!

Al's third-grade reading program included language experience activities and creative writing. Two days a week were devoted to a basal reader. The teacher and I decided that each week I would go over with Al the story from his reader that he was to read the following day in class.

To prepare for each classroom reading lesson we would practice, sometimes memorize, each page of the assigned story. We began by my reading a page first and Al reading it after me (echoic reading). This, I feel, gave Al a sense of how fluent oral reading should sound. In order to vary lessons, some days Al and I read in unison and some days I read alone, periodically leaving out words for him to fill in. Al thus returned to his reading class familiar with the story to be read. Many days he volunteered to read in class. Both his teacher and I soon noticed that most of his "tics" had disappeared!

The following are some typical instructional strategies I used:

1.  Recognizing words in word box. Al chose the words he wanted in his word box. Some were words from his language experience stories; others were words he liked or was interested in learning. At the beginning of each session we would go over his word cards. I would flash them at approximately one-second intervals. I would temporarily remove those that Al missed two consecutive times and add them at a later date.

2.  Pronouncing new words. I would use many of the words from Al's word box to create new stories. The stories would be unfamiliar to him but would contain many familiar words along with some new words. I tried to maintain a balance by challenging him but not frustrating him. We talked about the different phonics skills Al applied to figure out new words.

3.  Oral expression and fluency. We would tape Al reading a page from his reading book after he had practiced it once. Then we would talk about what fluent oral reading should sound like and do some echoic reading or reading together. When Al felt confident reading the page, after having practiced it several times, we would retape him reading it and see if he could hear an improvement in fluency and expression. Having his parents listen to the tape was a real source of pride for Al.

*This tutor's fairly relaxed, easygoing style would not work for every teacher, nor for every learner. But for this tutor and for Al it seems to have produced positive results. In later sections of this chapter we will discuss more structured approaches to teaching. Meanwhile, notice that the instruction— relaxed and easygoing as it is—is in line with the goals and objectives.*

## Evaluation and Prognosis

I feel a great sense of personal accomplishment from my work with Al. However, other people were also involved in his success: a very supportive mother, an understanding and flexible third-grade teacher, and Al himself. I strongly feel that if Al had not been able to respond so beautifully to positive reinforcement, we would have had much less success. I'm surprised at how relatively little help was required to get Al back on the right track. Apparently Al is one of those children who, at some point in learning to read, need some one-to-one attention.

I see no reason why Al can't continue to progress at a rate in line with his abilities. Fortunately, he has acquired a "friend" (neighbor woman) who loves to hear him read. Her interest, along with continued support from family and school, should provide much of the encouragement he needs, at least for the present, to maintain his interest in reading.

*"Prognosis" means "a forecast of what is likely to come next." It is the tutor's attempt to say how Al is likely to do in reading, now that the tutoring is done. She does a better job with prognosis than with evaluation. Evaluation should say whether, or to what degree, the long-term goals were attained. One could infer from the case report that, in general, the goals were attained. But the tutor did not return to the goals for evaluation, which is one of their most important functions. The goals did direct the short-term objectives and the instruction.*

# Effective Teaching Practices

In recent years a number of researchers have been trying to identify classroom management behaviors associated with effective instruction—how good teachers get good results. To date, there seems to be a good deal of agreement regarding certain practices (Otto, Wolf, & Eldridge, 1984). The following points can serve as a basis for developing a personal style of corrective teaching. (We return to a comprehensive discussion of organizing and managing the classroom in Chapter 15.)

When students spend more time working on tasks that are relatively easy for them, achievement scores tend to be higher and attitudes tend to be more positive (Marliave, 1978).

*The implications for corrective teaching are clear and important. Children who cannot read well probably get few chances in school to read materials that are easy for them. They probably do not enjoy reading enough to read much outside of school. As a corrective teacher you must find materials that are appropriate— relatively easy—for your students. One reason is simply that success breeds success. Another may be that reading with relative ease is a prerequisite to "automaticity," wherein the act of reading is habituated enough that the reader can direct most of his or her attention to understanding the material rather than to decoding the words. (This idea is discussed more fully in Chapter 8.)*

When teachers do more ongoing diagnosis and use the information to plan appropriate instruction, achievement scores tend to be higher (Rupley, 1977; Tinkunoff, Berliner, & Rist, 1978).

*Effective teachers do not teach solely on the basis of initial diagnosis. They diagnose constantly while they teach, and they modify their teaching procedures accordingly.*

When teachers spend more time on academic instruction, achievement scores tend to be higher (Medley, 1977; Rosenshine, 1979; Duffy, 1983).

*Don't interpret this to mean that you should never consider a trip to Mc-Donald's or that nonacademic activities are necessarily a waste of time. It means, rather, that much time spent giving general directions and asking questions would be better spent telling students exactly what they need to know to move ahead. Directly teaching students what they need to learn gets the best results.*

When teachers or other adults spend more time supervising students as they are working, achievement scores tend to be higher (Medley, 1977; Tinkunoff et al., 1978).

*Studies show that many students spend much, or even most, of their time guessing the answers to questions, trying to figure out how to proceed with tasks they do not fully understand, or simply remaining withdrawn from assigned tasks. Good supervision helps to keep students actively and productively engaged in learning activities.*

When teachers, other adults, or peer-tutors spend more time pacing the rate at which students work, engagement rates tend to be higher. (Filby, 1978.) Similarly, student engagement is higher when instruction is teacher-centered (Dunkin & Biddle, 1974).

*The first part says, in effect, that learners pay closer attention and move along at a more even rate when they have a reasonable idea of how long to spend on a task and when to move forward. Tutors can help by sharing the perspective they have gained from their own learning experience—but they must remember that it takes longer the first few times.*
*The second part says that students do better when the teacher stays with them while they complete an assignment than when they are left to complete an assignment on their own. The teacher should be there to help with pacing and to clarify, redirect, and explain as needed.*

When there is less deviant or disruptive behavior, achievement scores tend to be higher (Medley, 1977).

*This point may seem obvious. But remember that what is normal, or at least not disruptive, for one student could be totally distracting for another. Some people can read with concentration in a crowded bowling alley; others need quiet, calm surroundings. Good teachers are sensitive to the latter's needs as well as to controlling obvious deviant and disruptive behavior.*

When students are allowed more freedom to choose the activities they will work on, achievement scores tend to be lower (Medley, 1977; Rosenshine, 1979; Soar & Soar, 1979).

*This point may seem to fly in the face of certain ideas about students' self-selection and self-direction of learning activities. On closer examination, however, the conflict may be more apparent than real. The suggestion is certainly not that teachers should be authoritarian and rigid or that their classrooms should be joyless and uninteresting. It is simply that when teachers take an active role in directing their students' learning the results are better than when students are left to their own devices.*

When students work independently without direct supervision, achievement scores tend to be lower (Medley, 1977; Rosenshine, 1979).

*The same comments apply here as to the previous point. Both are particularly important for corrective teaching. Students experiencing problems in reading need direction and guidance more than they need freedom and independence.*

The distillation of all of these points is that students learn more when the teacher takes a more active role (Brophy, in press; Duffy, 1981). The effective teacher (a) allocates most classroom time to instruction and enhances student use of this time through efficient classroom management; (b) sets positive expectations for pupils and engages them in academic activities at which they can succeed; and (c) teaches actively, avoiding simply managing instruction (distributing, monitoring, and correcting assignments). Rosenshine (1979) called such an active, assertive approach to teaching "direct instruction," and the term has come to be widely accepted. Direct instruction is likely to be particularly productive with students who need additional help in the form of corrective instruction.

Review Chapter 2, if necessary, for a discussion of the characteristics and needs of students most likely to benefit from corrective teaching.

# Direct Teaching Strategies

Researchers agree that teachers invest a lot more time and effort making assignments and asking questions than following a sequence that goes from direct instruction—the clarification and demonstration of skills—to application and practice (Brophy, in press; Duffy & McIntyre, in press; Duffy, 1983; Durkin, 1978–1979). Typical classroom activities follow an "individualized diagnostic" teaching model:

- *Pretesting.* The teacher diagnoses student needs using instructional objectives and the results of criterion-referenced tests.
- *Teaching.* The instructor assigns groups or individuals to work in basal readers, workbooks, or labs on the basis of their weak skills.

- *Practice.* Students engage in these worksheet, game, or learning center activities.
- *Posttesting.* The teacher evaluates the progress of specific skills. (Merlin & Rogers, 1981)

This popular teaching model works with bright, highly motivated students who are good problem solvers. These students seem to need only a minimum of instruction—"mentioning (that is, naming specific skills or strategies) and assignment giving and checking," as Durkin (1978–1979, p. 523) puts it. They are able to figure out how to proceed with assigned activities from the minimal directions given for workbook exercises. They quickly learn to give answers likely to please the teacher during turn-taking sessions.

Other students—particularly those who are candidates for corrective/remedial instruction—profit little from the individualized diagnostic approach. Why? Probably because the teacher seldom teaches. When learners are unable to proceed on their own they bog down.

Look again at the model. There is no provision for direct instruction. Teachers assign students to workbooks, games, and learning centers, assuming that the brief, written directions for these activities will be sufficient. When students have completed the activities, they are tested to see what they learned, even though they may not have understood the directions. Teachers tend to assume that instruction is taking place when they ask questions or assign turns, the child responds, and the teacher reinforces or corrects, as in oral round robin reading. But turn taking, Duffy (1983) says, gives too little attention to sense making. Teachers interrogate rather than teach and assess rather than assist.

Some critics of public education claim that children must either come to school as successful problem solvers or be abandoned by the system. This is an extreme view; yet many students do fail to progress simply because instruction is inadequate. They need instruction that is explicit, painstaking, and direct.

## A Model for Direct Instruction

A better approach to teaching than traditional turn taking is direct instruction, where the teacher creates positive conditions for learning and actually helps students change their behavior and attitudes. An outline for direct teaching of reading skills follows. (See Duffy and Sherman, 1977, for a detailed description and Merlin and Rogers, 1981, for additional examples.) The outline assumes that long-term goals have already been set.

**I.** Set *short-term objectives* in line with long-term goals. The objectives may come directly from the basal reader series or skills management system used in the classroom.

**II.** *Direct the students' attention* to the task at hand. Make the directions explicit: "Today you will learn . . . ." Highlight specific characteristics and important features of the task: "Notice that the word begins with . . . ," or "so you see how the facts in this paragraph. . . ." Be certain that the material is at the students' instructional level and make it clear that you will be there to help as needed.

**III.** Proceed with *direct teaching,* taking either a deductive (modeling) or an inductive (discovery) approach.

    **A.** *Modeling*

        **1.** Tell the student how the skill works.

        **2.** Demonstrate how the skill is performed.

        **3.** Have the students imitate what you do.

        **4.** Provide many opportunities for responses and reinforcement.

        **5.** Reduce the cues as the students respond correctly.

    **B.** *Discovery*

        **1.** Ask questions and give information that leads the students to perform the skill.

        **2.** Have the students explain what they are doing while performing the skill.

        **3.** Ask clarifying questions and make frequent, reinforcing comments.

        **4.** Reduce your comments and questions as the students begin to make correct responses.

        **5.** If responses are incorrect, continue to shape correct responding with questions and comments.

        **6.** Praise correct responses and provide tangible demonstration of progress (for example, keep a progress log, draw a progress chart, or compare tapes or early performance with improved performance).

**IV.** Provide for *practice and application* of the skill.

    **A.** *Practice.* Remember that students who are experiencing difficulties with their reading will need to have more practice and to proceed at a slower pace than more efficient learners. Provide enough time for each student to learn *and remember* the skill by using a variety of practice activities.

    **B.** *Application.* Help the students identify instances where the skill should be applied in regular daily reading activities. Contrive instances requiring application if necessary.

## Direct Instruction of a Phonics Skill

In the following example the teacher applies the direct instruction model to teach a phonics skill to a small group (of course, the model applies also to individual instruction). Assume the long-term goal to be "The students associate appropriate long and short sounds with the vowels *a, e, i, o,* and *u.*"

***Short-term objective.***    The students will be able to decide whether the short (ŏ) or long (ō) *o* sound should be applied in unfamiliar CVC (consonant-vowel-consonant) and CVCE (consonant-vowel-consonant-plus *e* ) words.

### *Directing Attention.*

**Teacher**   You have learned that the letter *o* can stand for different vowel sounds in different words. Read these words to yourself and listen for the vowel sound in each word (pot, fox, not). Did you hear the same vowel sound in each word?

**Students**   Yes. It was the short sound of *o*, ŏ.

**Teacher**   Very good. Now look at these words (note, bone, rope). They all have the long sound of *o*, ō. Say them softly to yourself and listen to the sound of the vowel *o*. . . . What sound does the *o* have?

**Students**   It has the sound of its letter name, ō.

**Teacher**   Great! Now, sometimes the problem when we're reading is whether the *o* should be given the long sound or the short sound in a word. Have any of you ever been confused about which sound to give the *o* when you're reading?

**Students**   Yes. The letter *o* is in a lot of words and it takes so long to decide which *o* sound lets the word make sense.

**Teacher**   Today I'm going to teach you one way to decide if an *o* will get the short or long sound. Then your reading will go easier for you.

### *Direct Teaching—Modeling and Discovery.*

**Teacher**   Look at these two lists of words (robe, hope, and note; rob, hop, and not). The words in the first list all have long *o* sounds (teacher says words) and those in the second list all have the short *o* sound (teacher says words). Now, look again at the words in the first list that all have the long *o* sound. What else is the same about all those words?

**Students**   They all have the letter *e* at the end.

**Teacher**   Right. And what sound does the *e* make in each one of those words?

**Students**   It doesn't make any sound at all.

**Teacher**   Good. Those are the first two clues that help you decide if an *o* will have a short or long sound. So, a word ending in an *e* that is silent is a clue that the *o* will say its name. Read these words.

**Students**   Bone, stove, hole, rose.

**Teacher**   What kind of a letter is between the *o* and the *e*. A vowel letter or a consonant letter?

**Students**   A consonant letter.

**Teacher**   That's the last clue to help you see if the letter *o* has a short or long sound. If the three letters in the word are a vowel, then a consonant, and then an *e* at the end, the vowel will be long and the *e* will be silent. Let's look back at the first two lists of words. By just looking at the letters in each list, which list of words with *o*'s in the middle will have the long *o* sound? And why?

**Students**   The first list will have the long sound because the last three letters in each one have the vowel *o*, a consonant letter, and a final *e*.

### *Practice and Application Activities.*

*Practice.*

**Teacher**   Now let's practice what you've learned. Look at these sentences. Underline all the words you see with the vowel *o*, then a consonant letter, and finally an *e* at the end. (Students do so.) Now read them out loud. (Students read.) Excellent. Tell me why you didn't give this *o* the long sound?

**Students**   It has a short *o* sound because it doesn't have an *e* at the end.

*Application.*

**Teacher**   Right. Choose one of these books that you would like to read. Each one has a lot of words with short and long *o*'s in them. You will have to look at the last three letters in them to decide what sound to give the *o*.

**Student**   I choose this one, *A Note in the Hole.* (Others choose different stories.)

**Teacher**   *A Note in the Hole* is like a detective story. The boy is trying to find out who wrote the note he found. I liked it when I read it. Yours is about . . . (teacher tells a little about each story that is chosen). First I want you to record this tape of me reading this story and follow along in your book as I read. Then I will read the story a second time on tape and I want you to read along with me. Then turn off the tape recorder and read the story out loud to yourself several times, trying to read all the words correctly. When you think you're doing a pretty good job, choose a partner from the class but not from your reading group and read the story to your partner. In group tomorrow each one of you will get a chance to read aloud for all of us. What are you going to do first?

**Students**   Listen to you read the story on tape.

**Teacher**   What's next?

**Students**   Keep the tape on because you're going to read it again, only this time we read with you.

**Students**   Then we practice reading it out loud until we think we've got it pretty good. Then we can read it to a friend, but not someone from this group. We'll hear each other's stories tomorrow.

**Teacher**   Great. Let's get started. I'll help. And tomorrow let's see if everyone gets the long and short *o* words right.

Now that you have read the example, go back to the model for direct instruction and note how the teacher has tried to implement the suggestions at each step in the lesson. The teacher (a) sets up the lesson by directing attention to the specific skill; (b) uses a combination of modeling and discovery to teach the skill; and (c) provides opportunities for practice and application of the skill. In contrast, a teacher using the fairly typical individual diagnostic sequence would (a) identify students who are having trouble with long and short *o,* (b) briefly introduce, or mention, the skill to be learned, (c) assign a workbook page or sequence, and (d) check to see which items were correct. There would be little teacher-student interaction. The teacher's active, assertive role in direct teaching better assures that the students will understand the skill, be able to apply it in real-word reading activities, and remember and apply it in future instances.

## Direct Teaching of a Comprehension Strategy

In the next example, the teacher uses the direct instruction model to teach a comprehension strategy. Note that, even though the lesson deals with a fairly complex comprehension strategy, the teacher starts with a clearly stated, teachable short-term objective. Notice also that the teacher introduces repeated readings as a way for the students to get the words under control so they can pay more attention to meaning.

Using repeated readings requires that the group include no more than three or four students. (We will discuss the method of repeated readings more fully in Chapter 8.)

***Short-term objective.*** The students will actively seek to understand an expository passage, as demonstrated by an ability to (a) tentatively identify a main problem or purpose of the passage, (b) identify additional purposes or problems as reading unfolds, and (c) verify or modify the original hypothesis.

### *Directing Attention.*

**Teacher**   Sometimes when I'm reading, I can get to the end of a passage and not remember anything about what I read. Has that ever happened to you?

**Students**   Yes! And then sometimes we have a test we can't do.

**Teacher**   Today I'm going to help you solve that problem by teaching you some questions to ask yourself while you're reading. If you take the time to ask these questions and answer them to yourself, you will stand a better chance of answering those test questions after you've read. Do you think that would be helpful?

**Students**   Yes.

**Teacher**   I have four National Geographic Society books. Which one would you like to read from, *Wild Cats, Amazing Animal Groups, Strange Animals of Australia,* or *Life in Ponds and Streams?* Choose one that you don't know much about, but would like to learn more about.

**Students**   Animals are amazing. Let's read *Amazing Animal Groups.*

### *Direct Teaching—Modeling and Discovery.*

**Teacher**   Before I even start to read, the first thing I do is read the title and ask myself, "What do you think you'll be reading about?" Sometimes I find out I'm right, but sometimes I'm wrong. I thought this whole book, *Strange Animals of Australia,* would be about kangaroos. The *s* on the word in the title, Animals, should have been a clue that it was about lots of animals but I missed noticing it. Anyway, I was right about the kangaroos, but I was surprised to learn about all the other animals in Australia. I tried to guess the things the book would tell about kangaroos too. Again, I was right about some and forgot others, but throughout the whole book I thought about how the content actually compared with my guesses. Read the title of the book you chose. From the title, what do you think you'll be reading about?

**Students**   *Amazing Animal Groups.* For one thing, they'll tell about penguins. Their picture is on the cover. They'll tell about other animal groups, too, because of the *s* on groups.

**Teacher**   Good detective work using the clues on the cover. What do you think they'll tell about the different animal groups?

**Students**   Maybe they'll tell about where they live and what they eat.

**Teacher**   Good, that's certainly possible. The first question to ask yourself then, when you are reading and remembering what you read, is what?

**Student**   I have to ask myself, after reading the title, what I think the book or article will be about.

**Teacher**   Right. Now comes the part when you begin to read and check out your guesses, but first look over the pages in the book. As I looked at the Australia book I noticed all

|  |  |
|---|---|
| | the animals they were going to tell about. There were the kangaroos, but possums, koalas, numbats, wombats, and many more too. Look your book over. |
| **Students** | Wow. There are elephants, gorillas, zebras, ants, plus penguins and others in this book. |
| **Teacher** | The reason I quickly discover what's in the book is so that I can decide how logically to divide the book into sections. Then, after reading each "section," I stop and make sure I understood what I read by asking myself questions. In my book, every animal had two pages written about it, so I divided it that way. How about yours? |
| **Students** | Ours is organized the same way, so that idea would work with this book too. Should we read the first two pages now? |
| **Teacher** | Not at first. When I began helping myself in this way, I only read a paragraph or a few sentences before stopping. When you have done this lots of times it will become easier to read more at a time, quickly check yourself, and go on. For now, I'll help you. Read the five sentences on page 2 to yourself. (Students and teacher read.) Why did the elephants crowd together in a circle? |
| **Students** | To keep their young safe. |
| **Teacher** | What saved them? |
| **Students** | A female elephant. |
| **Teacher** | Good. Did you recognize the word huge before female? |
| **Students** | No. |
| **Teacher** | Notice the *e* at the end of the word, which is preceded by a vowel and then a consonant. |
| **Students** | Oh, yeah. The "magic *e* " rule we talked about yesterday. Huge. That's right, huge. |
| **Teacher** | These are the kinds of questions you need to ask yourself—at first even after each sentence. Read the last sentence on this page aloud. |
| **Students** | "Living in groups helps animals in different ways." |
| **Teacher** | It's easy to see why humans live in groups. We aren't all plumbers, or electricians, or teachers, or factory workers. But why do you think living in groups helps animals? |
| **Students** | They can protect each other. I wonder if that's the only reason, though. |
| **Teacher** | I wonder too. Let's each read the next page and find out. (Students and teacher read.) Why do elephants live together in groups? |
| **Students** | Besides for the protection talked about on the last page, the book said elephants help each other take mud baths to protect themselves against the sun and insects. |
| **Teacher** | Good. Can you see, now, what I do to help myself remember what I read? First, I read the title and guess what my reading is going to be all about, then I divide the book into parts. While I'm checking out my guesses and reading each part, I stop sometimes to ask questions of myself about what the words told me. I try to keep guessing what they are going to tell about in the next sentence or paragraph too. Go ahead now to the section on gorillas and try it out. What will you do first? |

### *Practice and Application Activities.*

*Practice.*

|  |  |
|---|---|
| **Students** | I'm going to ask myself, "What do you think this page is going to tell me about gorillas?" I think it's going to tell me about why gorillas live in groups. This page looks long. I'm going to just read the first three sentences before I check myself. |
| **Teacher** | Good planning; let's do that together. (Students and teacher read.) |

**Students** The book said one reason why gorillas live in groups is that the old ones watch over the young ones. That's just like humans. What else did the sentences tell me? Oh yes, they said gorillas aren't really fierce at all, but gentle and shy.

**Teacher** Remember when we read about goats last week? The same thing was said about them. Are you ready to finish reading the page?

**Students** Yes.

**Student** I wonder how the authors know they're gentle and shy? (Students and teacher read.) It says all gorillas do during the day is rest and find food.

**Teacher** Turn the page and use the pictures to ask yourselves what you're going to learn next.

**Student** This part must be about their babies. (Students and teacher read.) I'm done reading. (Remaining students soon indicate that they, too, have finished reading.)

**Teacher** Remember, always ask yourselves what you read about when you finish each section. Now tell yourselves what the authors told you about gorilla babies.

**Students** They told how the baby watches his mother carefully to learn what to do and that they run to their moms if they get hurt or scared.

**Teacher** Great. You remembered everything! Now read the next section about zebras and do all the questioning yourself. I'll ask you some questions when you're finished.

*Application*

**Students** (Students read with occasional, pondering pauses.)

**Teacher** Virgil, was your first guess about what you'd be reading correct?

**Student** Yes, I think all of these sections are going to tell some reasons that the animals live in groups.

**Teacher** Very good. You've found the author's plan for organizing the book. What was the reason for zebras to live in a group, Marcella?

**Student** Zebras always have some of the group stand guard to watch for enemies while the others are drinking or eating.

**Teacher** Good work, and all on your own. Sometimes the article or the paragraphs I'm trying to understand have words in them that are new. I have to concentrate so much on how to say the new words that I can't possibly remember what they mean. Has that ever happened to any of you?

**Students** Yes, and the next section on ants in this book looks like that's what's going to happen there.

**Teacher** What I do then is read it aloud, over and over as many times as it takes, until the words and sentences fall together so well that I can pay attention to what they mean. Usually I only need to read it three times until it begins to make sense. I think you're right about this section on ants—there are lots of words I'm sure you've heard but haven't seen before. Want to try this method of repeated readings?

**Students** Sure.

**Teacher** First, ask yourself what you think you'll learn from reading this . . . now quietly read it aloud.

**Students** (Students read aloud while teacher times them.)

**Teacher** Virgil, that took four minutes and twenty seconds. What was your guess about what you'd read? (Teacher notes the time for each student and carries on a brief discussion with each student in the group. An example of one discussion follows.)

**Student** I thought it would tell about what ants do together as a group, but I only remember that they make an ant bridge for some reason.

| | |
|---|---|
| **Teacher** | Read it aloud again and try to remember about that bridge of ants. |
| **Student** | (Virgil reads aloud and teacher times him.) |
| **Teacher** | Your time was much better—three minutes and ten seconds. Your reading was much smoother too. What did you remember about the bridge of ants this time? |
| **Student** | It is one of the jobs of an army ant. Making the bridge helps them to get to their food. |
| **Teacher** | This time as you are reading aloud, what do you think you'd like to remember? |
| **Student** | I'm going to remember as many of the jobs that ants have as I can. (He reads aloud as teacher times him.) |
| **Teacher** | Your reading sounded beautiful—just the way you sound when you talk. Your time was a little shorter too. But what do you remember about the jobs of the ant? |
| **Student** | (Student is able to point to nine out of twelve ants in the diagram of an ant colony and correctly identify what they are doing.) |
| **Teacher** | (Back with the entire group) Now you have learned two ways to help yourself remember what you read. What were they? |
| **Students** | One way was to keep asking myself questions about what I am going to read and what I have just read. I need to stop every few sentences and check myself to see if I'm remembering. If I'm having trouble reading the words, I should read it out loud over and over until the reading becomes easy. Then I'll be able to understand the sentences. Even when I'm reading out loud, though, I should ask myself questions. |

Of course, not every comprehension problem can be solved by repeated readings of a passage. But it is one technique that can help students who have difficulty understanding what they read shift their main attention from decoding the words to getting meaning from passages. The teacher used direct teaching to introduce, clarify, and apply a fairly complex technique.

# Summary

Chapter 3 is an orientation to corrective teaching. On the assumption that corrective teaching and effective teaching are essentially the same, we discuss practices used by successful teachers. Three topics are addressed: (a) long-term goals and short-term objectives, (b) research-based guidelines for effective teaching/learning, and (c) strategies for direct teaching. We stress that students' learning is improved when teachers take a more active role.

# References

Brophy, J. (in press). How teachers influence what is taught and learned in classrooms. *Elementary School Journal.*

Duffy, G. G. (1983). From turn-taking to sense-making: Broadening the concept of reading teacher effectiveness. *Journal of Educational Research, 76,* 134–139.

Duffy, G. G. (1981). Teacher effectiveness: Implications for reading instruction. In M. Kamil (Ed.), *Directions in reading: Research and instruction* (Thirtieth Yearbook of the National Reading Conference). Washington, DC: National Reading Conference.

Duffy, G. G., & McIntyre, L. (in press). A naturalistic study of instructional assistance in primary grade reading. *Elementary School Journal.*

Duffy, G. G., & Sherman, G. B. (1977). *Systematic reading instruction* (2nd ed.). New York: Harper & Row.

Dunkin, M. J., & Biddle, B. J. (1974). *The study of teaching.* New York: Holt, Rinehart and Winston.

Durkin, D. (1978–1979). What classroom observations reveal about reading comprehension and instruction. *Reading Research Quarterly, 14,* 481–533.

Filby, N. N. (1978). How teachers produce "academic learning time": Instructional variables related to student engagement. In. C. W. Fisher, L. S. Cahen, N. N. Filby, R. S. Marliave, & D. C. Berliner, *Selected findings from Phase III-B.* San Francisco: Far West Laboratory for Educational Research and Development.

Harris, T. L., & Hodges, R. E. (Eds.). (1981). *A dictionary of reading and related terms.* Newark, DE: International Reading Association.

Marliave, R. S. (1978). Academic learning time and engagement: The validation of a measure of ongoing student engagement and task difficulty. In. C. W. Fisher, L. S. Cahen, N. N. Filby, R. S. Marliave, & D. C. Berliner, *Selected findings from Phase III-B.* San Francisco: Far West Laboratory for Educational Research and Development.

Medley, D. M. (1979). The effectiveness of teachers. In P. L. Peterson & H. J. Walberg (Eds.), *Research on teaching: Concepts, findings and implications.* Berkeley, CA: McCutchan Publishing, 1979.

Medley, D. M. (1977). *Teacher competence and teacher effectiveness: A review of process-product research.* Washington, DC: American Association of Colleges for Teacher Education.

Merlin, S. B., & Rogers, S. F. (1981). Direct teaching strategies. *Reading Teacher, 35,* 292–297.

Otto, W., Rude, R., & Spiegel, D. L. (1979) *How to teach reading.* Reading, MA: Addison Wesley.

Otto, W., Wolf, A., & Eldridge, R. G. (1984). Managing instruction. In P. D. Pearson, R. Barr, M. Kamil, & P. Mosenthal (Eds.), *Handbook of research in reading.* New York: Longmans.

Rosenshine, B. V. (1979). Content, time and direct instruction. In P. L. Peterson & H. J. Walberg (Eds.), *Research on teaching: Concepts, findings and implications.* Berkeley, CA: McCutchan Publishing.

Rupley, W. H. (1977). Stability of teacher effectiveness on pupils' reading achievement over a two year period and its relation to instructional emphasis. In P. D. Pearson (Ed.), *Reading: Theory, research and practice* (Twenty-sixth Yearbook of the National Reading Conference). Washington, DC: National Reading Conference.

Soar, R. S., & Soar, R. M. (1979) Emotional climate and management. In P. L. Peterson & H. J. Walberg (Eds.), *Research on teaching: Concepts, findings and implications.* Berkeley, CA: McCutchan Publishing.

Tinkunoff, W. J., Berliner, D. C., & Rist, R. C. (1978). *Special study A: An ethnographic study of forty classrooms of the beginning teacher evaluation study known sample* (Technical Report 75-10-5). San Francisco: Far West Laboratory for Educational Research and Development.

# Check Your Reading Comprehension

1. Explain how effective corrective teaching is largely a matter of seeking out and applying sound teaching practices.

2. Your authors spend several pages of this chapter describing long-term goals and short-term objectives.
   a. What is the difference between the two?
   b. What are the characteristics of good long-term goals? Of good short-term objectives?
   c. What is the function of the long-term goal? Of a short-term objective?
   d. How should the two relate to one another?

3. Each of the following short-term objectives violates one or more of the guidelines outlined in this chapter. Describe what is wrong with each; then correct or rewrite each so that it would be more useful to the teacher planning a lesson or short series of lessons.
   a. The student will outline and summarize the main points of a selected reading passage.
   b. Within the next school year, all of the students in Class X will increase their reading level by at least one grade level.
   c. Following the completion of the social studies unit, the students will demonstrate a more patriotic appreciation of the Revolutionary War era.
   d. The student will read aloud, with fluency, a reading selection.

4. According to current research, teachers are more effective if they take a more active role in instruction. What does this mean? Briefly describe two classrooms: one in which the teacher does take an active role in instruction and one in which the teacher does not take an active role in instruction.

5. How does direct instruction differ from the individualized diagnostic teaching model described under "Direct Teaching Strategies?"

6. Imagine that you are a fourth-grade teacher. You are teaching a lesson on identifying the main idea of a selection from a basal reader.
   a. Describe the lesson if you followed a deductive approach (modeling).
   b. Describe the lesson if you followed an inductive approach (discovery).

7. Choose a skill that is appropriate for some or all of the students in your class. Plan a direct teaching lesson based on that skill.
   a. State your short-term objective.
   b. Give samples of statements you might use to direct the students' attention.
   c. Which approach will you use? Why? Briefly describe the sequence you will follow. Give samples of probable teacher and student statements.
   d. How will you provide practice of the skill? How will you emphasize the application of the skill?

# 4

# Interpreting and Selecting Standardized Tests

The first section of this chapter introduces you to basic measurement terms and concepts that should help you understand test manuals and reviews and discussions of tests. In the second section we discuss considerations for choosing and administering tests.

Most of you probably do not like to think about tests and testing. As a student, you may have experienced anxiety or frustration because of tests. As a teacher, you may feel that tests offer much more than they ever seem to give. You may have the impression that tests and testing have very little value for planning or directing your teaching. We cannot promise to change all that—particularly students' test anxieties. But we do believe that tests and testing could play a much more constructive role in the classroom than they do.

In Chapter 5, we talk about ways to use assessment techniques in planning and directing your teaching. Of course, there is more to worthwhile assessment than formal, paper-and-pencil tests. Yet formal, standardized tests are likely to continue to be an important aspect of most evaluation plans. Chapter 4 gives you a background for intelligently selecting and applying standardized tests so that they may begin to fulfill their promise.

# Basic Measurement

## Descriptive Statistics

Descriptive statistics are used to describe or summarize information about individuals or particular groups of people. Some of the more common terms and concepts follow.

***Scales of measurement.***    The scales you are likely to encounter most frequently are *nominal* scales, *ordinal* scales, and *equal-interval* scales. Ordinal and equal-interval scales are used most frequently in education and psychology.

    *Nominal scales* use numbers merely to designate people or objects when the numbers have no inherent relationship to one another. The arbitrary assignment of numbers to marathon runners or to racing cars are examples of the use of nominal scales.

    *Ordinal scales* order or rank information or scores on some continuum. A common example is a listing of students' test scores, as in Table 4.1. Students' raw scores on a 50-item reading test appear in the second column. The students are ranked from "best" to "worst" performance in the third column. Notice (last column) that there is a greater difference between the raw scores of Mark and Jennifer, who rank first and second, than between those of David and Jason, who rank fourth and eighth. Differences in adjacent ranks do not reflect the size of differences in raw scores. You may sometimes find it practical to rank students according to their relative performance, but remember that there may be greater differences in the performance of students who are closely ranked than students who are not so closely ranked.

    *Equal-interval* scales have an additional characteristic. The magnitude of difference between any two adjacent points on the scale is the same. A simple yardstick employs an equal-interval scale; the difference between 4 and 5 inches is the same as

**Table 4.1**    Ranking of Students in the Afternoon Reading Group

| Student | Raw-Score Total | Rank | Difference Between Score and Next Higher Score |
|---------|-----------------|------|-----------------------------------------------|
| Jennifer | 4 | 1 | 0 |
| Mark | 42 | 2 | 6 |
| Megin | 41 | | |
| Christopher | 41 | 4 | 1 |
| David | 41 | | |
| Sarah | 40 | 6 | 1 |
| Linda | 38 | 7 | 2 |
| Jason | 37 | 8 | 1 |
| Tim | 34 | 9 | 3 |
| Heidi | 31 | 10 | 3 |

between 21 and 22 inches. Ordinarily we assume that the raw score points on a test are distributed on an equal-interval scale, for example, that the difference between 42 and 41 items correct is the same as between 38 and 37 items correct.

***Basic notations.***   You will frequently find these symbols in discussions related to tests:

| Symbol | Meaning |
|--------|---------|
| X | Any score |
| Σ | A summation sign that means "add the following" |
| N | The number of scores in a distribution of scores |
| f | The frequency of occurrence of a particular score |
| $\overline{X}$ | The mean, or arithmetic average, of a distribution |
| $S^2$ | The variance of a distribution |
| S | The standard deviation |

***Measures of central tendency.***   You can expect to see three measures of central tendency: mean, median, and mode.

The *mean* is the arithmetic average of the scores in a distribution. Compute the mean of a set of scores by using this formula: $\overline{X} = \frac{\Sigma X}{N}$. The sum of scores ($\Sigma X$) from Table 4.1 is 393. Divide 393 by 10, the number of scores (N), to get a mean score ($\overline{X}$) of 39.3.

The *median* is the score that divides the top 50 percent from the bottom 50 percent of scores. In Table 4.1, three students earned the median score of 41.

The *mode* is the score most frequently obtained. The mode for the distribution in Table 4.1 is the same as the median, 41. A distribution might have no mode at all; or it might have two modes (be bimodal) or more.

***Measures of dispersion.***   There are three common measures of dispersion: range, variance, and standard deviation. The *range* is simply the distance between and including the extreme scores of a distribution. In Table 4.1, the scores range from 31 to 48; the *range* consists of 18 points.

The *variance* is a numerical index that describes the dispersion of scores around the mean of a distribution. It is a kind of average of the distance of all the scores in a distribution from the mean. Knowing the variance of a distribution has little value in itself. You must calculate variance, however, to compute the standard deviation.

The *standard deviation* is the most commonly reported measure of the variability of a distribution. It is a unit of measurement, as *inches* or *tons* are units of measurement. When scores are normally distributed—that is, when the distribution is not distorted by unusual numbers of scores at either end of the range—any score can be described in terms of standard deviation units from the mean. This is so because we know how many cases occur between the mean and any standard deviation, as in Figure 4.1, which shows a normal distribution, or *normal curve*. Approx-

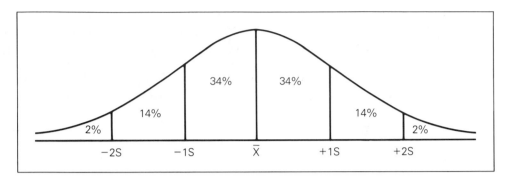

**Figure 4.1.** The Normal Distribution

imately 34 percent of the scores fall between the mean ($\overline{X}$) and one standard deviation (S) either above or below the mean. So about 68 percent of all scores will fall in the two standard deviations closest to the mean. Another 14 percent of the scores will fall between one and two standard deviations above the mean and still another 14 percent of the scores will fall between one and two standard deviations below the mean. Thus 96 percent of all scores will fall between two standard deviations above and two standard deviations below the mean. (See Salvia and Ysseldyke, 1981, or McLoughlin and Lewis, 1981, for a remarkably lucid discussion of all this.)

You do not need to learn how to calculate variance and standard deviations to interpret and use test scores sensibly. But you must pay attention to the means and standard deviations of test scores. Only when you know the mean of a test—or some measure of central tendency—can you begin to evaluate an individual's scores on that test. A third grader's raw score of 68 means nothing until you know that the mean score of a norm group of third graders who took the test was 50. Then you know, at least, that 68 is above the average score. Further, if you learn that the standard deviation for the test is 15, you know that a score of 68 is more than one standard deviation above the mean. So the individual who earned a score of 68 was among the top 16 percent of third graders who took the test.

***Correlation.***     Correlations measure relationships between variables (for example, sets of test scores). Suppose that we had a second set of reading test scores for the ten students whose scores on a first test are given in Table 4.1. We could find out how closely related the two sets of scores are by determining the *correlation* coefficient, a numerical index of the relationship. If there were a perfect relationship between the two sets of scores—if we could predict exactly how the students would do on the second test from how they did on the first—the correlation would be one (1.0). If there were no relationship at all, the correlation would be zero (0). Because perfect relationships between variables are unusual, most correlations fall somewhere between 0 and 1.0. Students' scores on reading achievement tests and group intelligence tests, for example, are fairly closely related; correlation coefficients for two such sets of scores commonly fall somewhere between .6 and .8. For two forms of a well-constructed reading test we would expect a high correlation, on the order of .9.

Correlations may be either positive (+) or negative (−). A positive correlation indicates that high scores on one variable are associated with high scores on the other variable. A negative correlation indicates that high scores on one variable are associated with low scores on the other. We would expect a negative correlation between students' scores on a reading achievement test and the number of errors they make on an oral reading test.

Finally, a word of caution about correlations. You cannot infer a cause-effect relationship simply because two variables are related. A third variable or set of variables could be responsible for the relationship between the two variables. For example, beginning readers who can name many letters of the alphabet tend to score high on early reading tests. Typically, the correlation between the two variables is positive and moderate, on the order of +.6. But it would be inappropriate to assume that by teaching letter names one would enhance students' reading performance. Chances are that other variables—for example, cognitive and perceptual abilities, pre-school experiences, or desire to read—account for both superior letter-naming ability and superior early reading performance.

## Description of Test Performance

Simply knowing how many correct or incorrect responses a student made on a test is not always helpful. An exception is if the test is *a criterion-referenced* test, because usually the goal is to get *all* of the items correct. (We talk more about criterion-referenced tests in Chapter 5). But a more general achievement test has no absolute criterion with which to compare the scores. You need a basis for interpreting the score by comparing it to the scores of a group with similar characteristics (age, grade, sex, and so on), a *norm group.* Such comparisons are typically made by changing raw scores into *derived* scores, which are either developmental scores or scores of relative standing.

*Developmental scores.* Developmental scores are *transformations* of raw scores. The most common types are *age-equivalent* scores and *grade-equivalent* scores. In the simplest terms, the scores are based upon the age (or grade) in the test standardization population at which the average person earns a given score. Age equivalents are expressed in years and months (for example, 7-11 means seven years and eleven months). Grade equivalents are expressed in grades and tenths of grades (for example, 4.5 indicates mid–fourth grade).

Interpret both age- and grade-equivalent scores with extreme caution, because a comparison group may have characteristics very different from those of any single individual. (Other reasons for exercising caution are given later in this chapter, under "norms.")

While grade equivalents are the most commonly reported scores in schools, they are, nevertheless, the most grossly inadequate scores. They are often so carelessly constructed by test makers that errors of several months are not uncommon. Then the scores do not reflect the average level of performance of children at any given grade level, so there is no way to use the scores sensibly. A second problem is that, in their apparent simplicity, grade-equivalent scores are subject to misinterpretation. An example is the common impression that a student who scores two years above or below a grade level is doing the same work as students in those grades. Similarly, the notion—perhaps it's merely wishful thinking, usually expressed by politicians and bureaucrats—that more than 50 percent of the population can score *at or above* grade level is incorrect. Further, it is wrong to assume that scoring at grade level is "good"; it is simply "average." Finally, there is a misconception that scoring a year or so below grade level has the same meaning for all grades. Actually, a second grader who scores a year below grade level would be in the lowest 10 percent of a national distribution; a sixth grader who scores a year below grade level would be only slightly below average.

***Scores of relative standing.***    The two main types of scores of relative standing are percentile ranks and standard scores.

*Percentile ranks* are derived scores that indicate the percentage of students or scores that occur at or below a given raw score. Do not confuse the percentile rank with the percentage of items correct. To say that a student's percentile rank for a given test is 57 is to say that the student scored equal to or better than 57 percent of the students in the comparison, or norm, group. Percentile ranks have the advantage of being the least complicated and least likely to be misinterpreted of the derived scores. One drawback, however, is that percentiles do not form an equal-interval scale. For instance, a gain of five percentile points is much larger if it occurs at either end of the distribution than if it occurs in the middle.

*Standard scores* are derived scores that transform raw scores so that the set of scores always has the same mean and standard deviation. There are several types of standard scores:

- *Z-scores.* The mean is set at 0 and a standard deviation is 1. Thus, a z-score of +1.5 means that the score is 1.5 standard deviations above the mean of the group. A z-score of −.8 means the score is .8 standard deviation below the mean.
- *T-scores.* The mean is set at 50 and the standard deviation is 10.
- *Deviation IQs.* The mean is set at 100 and the standard deviation is 15 or 16, depending on the test.
- *Stanines.* These are standard score bands that divide a distribution into nine parts. The second through eighth stanines are each .5 standard deviation in width; the first and the ninth stanines include all scores that are 1.75 standard deviations or more *below* or *above* the mean, respectively.

Standard scores are a convenience because they permit direct comparisons among test components or subtests. When the components of a test or test battery are set equal, the teacher can do a straightforward profile analysis (that is, identify relatively high or low performance areas).

***Normal curve equivalents.***    Normal curve equivalents, or NCEs, are another form of normalized standard scores. They deserve special mention because they have come to be widely used in standardized test reports, and federal projects (such as Chapter I and basic skills projects) often require students' scores to be reported in NCE format.

Like T-scores, NCEs have a mean of 50; and a score of 50 matches the 50th percentile on a national distribution. NCEs are constructed to have a standard deviation of 21.06, which produces an exact match between NCEs of 1 and 99 and percentiles of 1 and 99. Thus, NCEs have the same range (1 to 99) and midpoint (50) as percentiles. On the average one NCE equals one percentile; but in specific instances that equality almost never holds because NCEs form an equal-interval scale. You will remember that on an equal-interval scale the magnitude of difference between any two adjacent points is the same. A gain of five NCEs represents exactly the same amount of improvement in performance for pupils at the extreme low end of the achievement distribution as it does for average achievers. NCEs, therefore, represent an important improvement over percentiles for reporting achievement gains. A comparison of the two scales is shown in Figure 4.2. Notice that NCEs are the same size from one end of the scale to the other; percentiles are spread out at the ends and small in the middle.

## Reliability

Reliability refers to the stability of a test, as measured by repeated administration of the test or its equivalent to the same individuals. Specifically, the reliability of a test is expressed as a correlation coefficient that describes the extent to which two applications of the same measuring procedure would rank persons in the same way. A

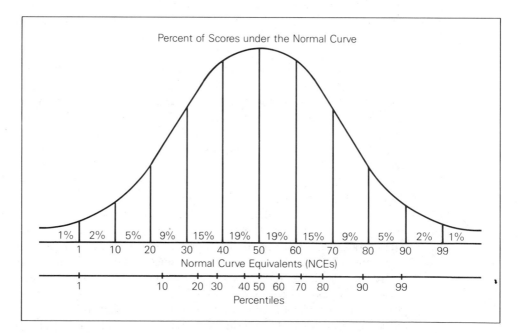

**Figure 4.2.** Comparison of Scales: Normal Curve Equivalents and Percentiles

highly reliable test (one with a reliability coefficient of .8 or better) would yield a relatively small range of scores when administered repeatedly to the same individual (assuming no learning effects). An unreliable or less reliable test would yield a wider range of scores under the same conditions.

***Factors influencing reliability.***    Several factors may inflate or deflate reliability estimates (coefficients):

*Test length.*    Long tests tend to be more reliable than short tests. Remember, though, that the effective length of any test is determined by the number of items appropriate for a given test taker. A test with many items that are too hard for a given individual is not likely to be very reliable for that person.

*Time between initial testing and retesting.*    In general, the shorter the interval, the higher the reliability estimate. The obvious reason is that the test taker's abilities change over time.

*Limited range.*    The greater the variance (or, the greater the range of scores obtained) of a test, the higher the reliability estimate.

*Guessing.*    A guess is a random response to a test item, so it introduces error into a test score.

*Variation within the testing situation.*    Anything that introduces variation and error into a testing situation will lower reliability estimates. Some sources of variation are inability to understand the directions, thinking about recess, and wondering what to do when a pencil point breaks.

***True scores.***    The score a test taker actually gets is called the *obtained score.* It is a raw score that generally reflects both random and systematic errors. A *true score* is the value the test taker would have obtained if the test score were entirely free of error. Unfortunately, we never know a student's true score on any test. The best we can get is an estimated true score. We do know, though, that when an obtained score is below the test mean and the reliability coefficient is less than 1.00, the estimated true score is always higher than the obtained score. When an obtained score is above the test mean and the reliability coefficient is less than 1.00, the estimated true score is always lower than the obtained score.

Test makers use what they call a *standard error of measurement* as a basis for estimating true scores. The standard error of measurement is an estimate of the standard deviation of obtained scores for a given value of the true score. The larger the standard error of measurement, the smaller the confidence in the estimated true score. It is desirable, then, to construct a range within which the exact probability of including a person's true score is known. This range is called a *confidence interval.* Thus, when a test manual includes 95-percent confidence intervals, it shows the range of scores within which an individual's true score will fall 95 percent of the time.

***Reliability standards.*** A test score is not interpretable unless it is reliable. As a consumer, or user, of test scores you must be concerned about the reliability of the tests you use and the scores you attempt to interpret. Test authors and publishers are responsible for providing adequate reliability data in their test manuals. They should include reliability indexes for each type of score reported (for example, raw scores, grade equivalents, and standard scores) and for each appropriate age or grade level.

Salvia and Ysseldyke (1981) recommend that when a test score is reported the estimated true score and a 68-percent confidence interval for the true score also be reported. Such a practice would help remind us that test scores are not absolute values. They are, at best, approximations and they should always be viewed with some skepticism.

Salvia and Ysseldyke also recommend that two standards of reliability be used in "applied settings" (schools, classrooms). First, if test scores are reported for groups and are to be used for general, administrative purposes, a reliability coefficient of .60 should be considered minimum. Second, if a test score is to be used in making a decision about an individual, the standard should be much higher. For important educational decisions, such as placing the student in a special class, .90 should be considered minimum. For more general purposes, the minimum should still be .80.

## Validity

The most important—some would say the *only* important—characteristic of a test is its *validity,* the characteristic that determines how well the test measures what it is supposed to measure. A test must be reliable before it can be valid. But even a very high reliability coefficient does not assure a test's validity. Validity must be judged after careful examination of an array of information.

***Judging validity.*** Validity is usually examined in terms of *content* validity, *construct* validity, and *criterion* validity.

*Content validity* describes how well the test covers the domain, or the content area, being measured. If, for example, the claim is to test word analysis skills, then the test must include sufficient and appropriate items to measure the word analysis domain. Content validity is generally determined by inspection of test items, by administration of test forms before and after instruction, and by inspection of the errors commonly made on the test.

*Construct validity* is an index of the relationship between a theoretical construct, such as *intelligence* or *anxiety,* and a test which proposes to measure the construct. In practice, construct validity is generally determined by correlations between the test and similar, established tests.

*Criterion validity* may be concerned with how well a test predicts future behavior (*predictive* validity); or how accurately a test can estimate current performance on another test or measure (*concurrent* validity); or both. Criterion validity is generally determined by correlating test scores with other measures of individuals' performance in the domain of the test. One might, for example, correlate students' scores on a reading achievement test with certain measures of their performance on real-life reading tasks, such as their ability to fill out an application form, to pass a written driver's test, or to read and pass the test on a chapter from a college history test.

Even though we discuss content, criterion, and construct validity individually, these three aspects of validity cannot be kept separate in the overall consideration of a test's validity. They are highly interrelated and interdependent.

***Factors affecting validity.***     Even when a test has been judged valid for general use, its validity can be threatened by any of the following factors during actual use.

*Reliability.*     A test must be reliable to be valid. Anything that reduces a test's reliability reduces its validity.

*Method of measurement.*     The method used to measure performance may determine the test taker's score. In a test of phonics skills, for example, a series of items may ask the student to identify the letters associated with sounds enunciated by the teacher. Such a measurement would have no validity for a child with a hearing loss. The example may be obvious, but the point is important. Question the validity of any score that includes variance due to the method of measurement.

*Enabling behaviors.*     An obvious enabling behavior is fluency in the language of the test—the ability of the test taker to understand the language of the test and the test administrator. Yet it is not at all uncommon to have tests in the English language administered to children and adults whose primary language—perhaps even whose second language—is not English. Such tests are not valid for these individuals.

*Item selection.*     The assumptions behind the items on many tests, particularly achievement tests, is that the test takers have been exposed to the skills, facts, and concepts measured by the test. In other words, a test should be in line with the curriculum of a given school or classroom. If it is not, you should question the test's validity for students in that school or classroom.

*Administration errors.*     If a test is not administered according to the standardized procedures, the results are not valid. Deviations from time limits or from standard directions are likely to affect students' scores—and to undermine the validity of the scores.

You, the consumer, must ultimately judge a test's validity. To evaluate properly you must first have a clear understanding of what is to be measured. With a purpose in mind you can then determine how the measuring is to be done. If the content of a test doesn't make sense to you and you can't see how you would use the results, don't give it.

## Norms

We give certain tests (norm-referenced tests) to find out how specific individuals or groups of individuals are performing in comparison to their age or grade peers. Such comparisons permit us to judge whether individuals or groups are making "normal" progress or performing in "normal" ways. Ordinarily, though, we cannot find the norm by testing everyone in an entire population. Not only is the population likely to be unmanageably large, it is constantly changing. So we rely on test makers to test subsets of individuals, or *samples,* from the population and from the scores infer characteristics of the entire population, or "norms."

Norms permit you, as a teacher, to evaluate a student's performance in terms of other students' performance. Most test manuals provide norms, but some are inadequate. Obviously, test scores may be misleading if compared to inadequate or inappropriate norms. You can evaluate a test's norms by judging the representativeness of the norm sample, number of scores in the sample, and relevance of the norms to a given situation or purpose for testing.

**Representativeness.**   Adequate norms faithfully reflect the characteristics of an entire population—the norms *represent* the entire population. You must ask whether the norm sample includes the full range of people the norms are supposed to represent. Further, are the people in the sample present in the same *proportions* as in the population? Consider the following factors when judging the adequacy of the range of people sampled.

*Age.*   Simple chronological age is a critical factor in children's physical, psychological, and cognitive development. Inappropriate age comparisons can be very misleading.

*Grade.*   In most instances, an individual's grade placement reflects the amount of exposure to academic instruction. It is inappropriate, then, to compare third graders to any other grade-level group.

*Sex.*   Sex role expectations are changing, but boys and girls continue to differ in some important aspects of development. Both boys and girls should be appropriately represented in normative groups.

*Social class.*   A norm group should include children of all social classes.

*Geographic areas.*   There are demonstrated differences in children's academic and intellectual performance relative to geographic area of residence and community size and type. "National" norms, then, must in fact cover the entire range.

*Race.*   This continues to be a highly sensitive issue. But so long as there is an issue, children of all racial and ethnic groups should be included in both standardized and normative samples.

*Date of norms.*   People change. Norms developed in 1930 probably do not adequately reflect the characteristics of any population in 1985. Norms for reading tests, in particular, should be current because reading expectations, reading instruction, and reading performance tend to change quite rapidly in our rapidly changing world. Norms that are over five years old need to be taken with more than the usual, single grain of salt.

***Sample size.***    The number of subjects in a normative sample must be large enough to give the norms stability, representativeness, and range. How many are enough? Salvia and Ysseldyke (1981) suggest that 100 should be the minimum number of people in any norm sample. They also say that if the test covers several age or grade levels, the norm sample should include 100 subjects per age or grade.

***Relevance.***    Most commercially published tests provide "national" norms in their test manuals. National norms are appropriate for considering an individual's general, or global, development—physical, intellectual, perceptual, and linguistic. "Local" norms may be more useful for examining a student's performance in a particular school or classroom. "Specialized" norms may be needed to deal appropriately with special cases, for example, certain handicapping conditions. But use specialized norms with caution. You may find it helpful to know how a deaf child is responding to reading instruction in comparison to other deaf children; but such a comparison says nothing about how that child's performance compares to the performance of a full range of age and grade peers.

# Choosing and Using Tests

The process of choosing an appropriate test is somewhat like preparing an instructional objective (see Chapter 3). You must begin with a clear idea of what is to be tested and then consider *how* it is to be tested and under what *conditions* the testing will be done. In this section we offer some specific guidelines for choosing and using tests by responding to six questions.

But first we want to say a bit more about why tests should be chosen in the first place. Venezky (1974) puts it this way:

> There is an instructional goal—and only one goal—which *may* be realized or aided through assessment,[1] and this is instructional decision making. Knowing a child's reading level or his competence in pronouncing initial consonant clusters or his ability to select the main point of a story from four options is of little value unless these data are collected as an aid to a particular decision. Collecting periodic data on reading ability, as many school districts do today, merely for "knowing" what is happening is a monstrous waste of time and money and serves no purpose other than to create suspicion among politicians and parents. (pp. 6–7. Reprinted with the permission of the National Council of Teachers of English.)

---

[1] Venezky (1974) applies the term *assessment* "to any procedures—including testing—for gathering performance data" (p. 4). He uses the term *testing* "in the narrow sense of a formal, critical examination" (p. 4). We use the terms more or less interchangeably; but we generally use "testing" in a broader, more informal sense.

Group testing for efficiency. (Photo © Anne Schull-strom)

Individual testing for precision. (Photo © Richard Khanlian)

In other words, giving tests simply as a matter of policy or curiosity is pointless. The only sensible reason you can ever have for giving a test is to find out something you need to know to make sound instructional decisions. Before you select an appropriate test, decide exactly what information you want and how you will use it.

With your purpose for testing clearly in mind you can proceed to answer the questions that follow.

***Who is to be tested?***    The essential concerns are (a) Will I be testing a single student or a group of students? and (b) Does the student, or any student in the group, have special limitations that must be considered while testing?

A group test offers an obvious advantage—it saves time. Any group test can also be given to an individual—in that sense, it is versatile. Individual tests are not as efficient, but most permit the tester and the test taker to interact much more freely. The tester can adapt the pace of testing and respond in other ways to the student's behavior—confusion, fatigue, frustration. In general, individual testing offers the possibility of a deeper, more intimate—therefore, more realistic—glimpse of a student's performance than group testing. The tester is in a position to gather *qualitative* as well as *quantitative* information.

Base your choice of a group test or an individual test on purpose and efficiency. Group tests are appropriate making decisions about a group—planning and evaluating all-school programs, designing classroom instruction, or screening students for general placement or further testing. Although individual tests could be used for such purposes, it would be difficult to justify the time and expense. Individual tests are more appropriate for making decisions about an individual—such as planning corrective or remedial instruction for a student.

Certain group tests, or parts of them, may be inappropriate for students with special limitations. For example, most group tests require that the test taker be able to read and understand the written directions and to respond by writing or marking. Some students will be unable or unwilling to cope with such seemingly straight-forward demands. Others may be unable even to turn pages or to respond to oral directions. Anticipate such problems whenever possible. When they arise in spite of your best efforts, let common sense be your guide, keeping in mind that helping the student—not giving the test—is your main purpose.

***What do I expect to learn from the test?***     You must determine exactly what more you need to know about a student's performance. Do you really even need additional information? Venezky (1974) offers some good advice:

> Before testing should be undertaken, one should ask whether or not the information already available is sufficient for making the required decision. Consider as an example the typical diagnosis-prescription unit. A pretest indicates who needs instruction in a particular skill. Those so identified are sequenced through instruc-tional materials . . . and then typically, a posttest is given to determine if mastery has been reached. But sometimes the information available from daily assignments allows as accurate an assessment of mastery as does the posttest. In such circum-stances, the posttest makes no unique contribution to the decision-making process and therefore is without value. (p. 8. Reprinted with the permission of the National Council of Teachers of English.)

Unless a student has just transferred from Katmandu, there is probably a fair amount of information already available. Or you may be able to learn what is needed through everyday instruction. If the test will not add anything to what is known, don't test!

Decide whether you want to learn about the student's actual level of skill devel-opment or to compare the student's performance to peer performance. You will then choose either a *criterion-referenced* test or a *norm-referenced* test. A norm-referenced test assesses the performance of an individual in relation to that of a norm group. A criterion-referenced test measures an individual's performance in terms of the kind of behavior that is expected (the criterion). (We talk more about norm-referenced and criterion-referenced tests in Chapter 5.) Choose the test that will give the information you are seeking.

To what extent will you be able to individualize instruction? There is no need to seek specific information about a student's performance unless you will use that data to plan and offer appropriate instruction. The exactness of the information sought should be in line with the adaptability of the instruction to be offered. There's no need to get all dressed up if all you can afford is a hamburger at Dotty's Good Eats Cafe!

Choose between giving a power test or a speed test. Tests with time limits—many standardized, norm-referenced tests—are speed tests. The time limits are often so short that many students cannot get to all the items. A power test usually includes items ranging from easy to very difficult. Its time limits are generous enough to permit all items to be attempted. A power test will let you see what a person can do when there is no time pressure; a speed test gives you some notion of a student's ability to perform in a competitive situation.

***What behaviors will I be testing?*** All tests sample behavior. Specific considerations are (a) whether the content of a particular test is compatible with the instruction the student has received and (b) if the stimulus and response demands of the test are within the student's capabilities.

Tests with the same general name very often differ greatly in the types of items they use and in the skills they assess. Be careful to choose a test in line with the instruction you have been giving. If, for example, you have been stressing word analysis skills and oral reading performance, a silent reading test would probably be inappropriate. You could find out which students were able to transfer what they had been taught to their silent reading; but you would have no way to know whether students who tested poorly had not learned the basic material or simply were unable to transfer what they had learned.

It would, likewise, be inappropriate to test vocabulary with unaided recall (asking the student to say what a word means) if instruction has been limited to matching words with their definitions. The two tasks are quite different, particularly within the constraints of a testing situation.

Children, particularly at the primary level, are easily distracted from the main task by variables associated with the test itself. So, remember: Don't be misled by the name of a test; look at the test itself to be sure that its content and format are in line with the test takers' previous instruction.

Additionally, be sensitive to a student's limitations in dealing with the stimulus and response demands of a test. An oral stimulus, for example, would probably be inappropriate for a deaf student. Requiring a written response would almost certainly be inappropriate for a student with no arms. But limitations are not always so obvious. More subtle examples of inappropriate stimulus-response demands include (a) a phonics test requiring the fine discrimination of sounds from a hearing impaired student; (b) a "readiness" test requiring fine visual discrimination from a visually handicapped student; and (c) separate answer sheets requiring coordinated motor behaviors from students who lack motor control.

***Should I use a commercially prepared test?*** All the test selection concerns we have raised apply equally to teacher-made and commercially prepared tests. Teacher-made tests are often called "informal" tests; published tests are called "formal" tests. (Of course, teacher-made tests may be quite "formal" in terms of directions to the student, format, and even use of local norms.)

Commercially prepared tests offer some fairly obvious advantages over teacher-made tests. First, they require no time to develop—extremely important to a busy teacher. Second, because many of them are widely used, they facilitate communication among educators. If everybody is familiar with Test X, they know what you're talking about when you say Melissa scored at the 53rd percentile on Test X. Third, commercial tests often include useful technical information—a good indication that the test has been carefully constructed. Such information describes standard procedures for administering and scoring the test and provides data on the validity, reliability, and norms of the test.

Informal tests may lack technical information. But because they are teacher-made, their content can be in closer touch with the content of instruction, making them superior for assessing the teaching-learning experiences of a given classroom.

Decide what kind of behavior sample you want. Informal tests give better information about the effects of day-to-day teaching and provide guidance on how to proceed. Commercial tests are likely to give a better picture of students' overall achievement or general development in comparison to a norm.

**Where can I look for help in selecting a test?** After you answer the four preceding questions, you will usually still have several tests to consider. The most comprehensive single source for help is *The Eighth Mental Measurements Yearbook* (Buros, 1978) or its companion volume *Reading Tests and Reviews II* (Buros, 1975). The Buros references contain descriptions and reviews of almost all commercially published tests. Both are revised periodically, on a six-to-ten-year cycle, so be certain to consult the most recent edition. Between revisions you can find the latest reviews in current professional journals. Test reviews can help you answer four basic questions (Kavale, 1979): (a) Which tests might serve my present purpose? (b) What are the new tests in the field? (c) What is text X like? (d) What do specialists in the field have to say about test Y?

You can also look to publications of the American Psychological Association, the old but venerable *Technical Recommendations for Psychological Tests and Diagnostic Techniques* (1954) and *Standards for Educational and Psychological Tests* (1974). The 1974 publication identifies essential standards for tests, manuals, and norms. A very brief summary of these standards follows:

- A test should be accompanied by a manual that provides the information required to substantiate any claims made for the test's use. The manual should fully describe the development of the test: the rationale, specifications followed in writing items or selecting observations, and procedures and results of item analyses or other research.
- The test, the manual, and record forms should help users make correct interpretations of the test results and warn against common misuses. There should be a clear statement of what, if any, interpretations are intended for each subscore as well as for the total test.
- The manual should state explicitly the applications for which the test is intended.
- The manual should specify any qualifications required to properly administer the test and interpret its results.
- The manual should present evidence of validity and reliability.
- Directions for administering the test should be clear, allowing the test giver to duplicate the conditions under which normative and reliability data were obtained.

- Scoring procedures should be specific and clear to reduce the chances of scoring error.
- Norms should be available when the test is released for general use.
- Norms should refer to defined and clearly described populations. (The test giver should seek assurance that the norm group is appropriate for the test takers.)
- Care should be taken to preclude misleading impressions about the generality of the normative data.

You must also consider a test's utility. Is it easy to administer, convenient to score, and economical? Are scores easily interpreted or will you need special training? Utility can be critical to your final choice of a test. Consider, for example, Reading Test X and Reading Test Z. Test X has exemplary validity and reliability characteristics; Test Z is not so great, but it is adequate. Test X requires an hour and 25 minutes to administer, per individual; the test giver will spend an additional thirty minutes scoring and plotting a profile of scores for each individual. Test Z requires 48 minutes to administer to a group; it can be scored quickly with an answer grid; and individual profiles can be plotted in a few minutes. The cost of test booklets, answer sheets, etc. per individual administration is almost identical. Chances are that you would choose Test Z on the basis of cost effectiveness. You get adequate data for the same money and substantially less time.

The best way to judge a test's utility is to give it (preferably to a tried and true friend!), score it, and think about its specifics.

### What must I consider in administering a standardized test?

Remember that a standardized test is made up of specified tasks and procedures so that comparable results may be obtained by testers working in different geographic areas. You must administer the test according to the specified procedures or there will be no basis for comparing the results with national or regional norms.

Keep the following factors in mind when you administer a standardized test:

*Group size.* In general, the smaller the group tested, the better. Lots of things can go wrong when children, particularly very young children, take tests—they misunderstand directions, turn pages out of order, break their pencils, lose their places, and let their attention wander. Obviously, the smaller the group, the easier it will be for you to offset distractions by careful monitoring.

*Adherence to standardized procedures.* Standardized testing must adhere exactly to the standardized procedures called for in the directions. Any departures may invalidate the test scores and render the norms useless. No coaching! No alterations in time limits!

*Length of sitting.* Consider the age of the test takers and the extent of any student's handicaps. Common sense is the best guide: If children become restless, unruly, or uninterested, give them a break. In general, a testing session should not exceed twenty to thirty minutes for children in primary grades, forty to sixty minutes for students in intermediate grades, or ninety minutes for any human beings.

*Elimination of distractions.*    Again, use common sense. Tests should not be scheduled during recess or other "fun" times, when other children are eating lunch, or just before or after a vacation. Nor should testing be scheduled in the room next to the one where the band rehearses, the cheerleaders practice, or the teachers are expounding on why Dewey's theories have not worked. The person who administers the test should keep a low profile—no discussions with other monitors, no small talk with the test takers, no setting up the chemistry demonstration for next hour.

*Encouragement.*    You can subtly encourage students without intruding on the standardized procedures. If the building next door catches fire, pull the shades. On second thought, postpone the test! But if Maynard starts watching a robin build its nest, remind him that he should be paying attention to the test . . . or quietly draw the shades. And a reassuring pat on the shoulder can't hurt.

*Knowledge of the test.*    Some tests call for oral presentation of directions, careful timing, or other specific actions on the part of the test giver. Know the test and the directions well to keep the testing situation smooth, stable, and standardized. Practice giving the test and practice taking it before you give it to real students. You can thus anticipate any problems that might arise.

## A Final Word About Tests

In this chapter we say a lot about the characteristics of standardized tests and how you should go about choosing and using them. We would be remiss if we did not also mention the controversy that surrounds the use of standardized tests. Critics raise important questions about the very assumptions that underlie standardized testing; the moral, social and political implications that may be involved; and the motives and competence of the people who construct and publish the tests. Are the tests an unjustified intrusion on personal privacy? Are the results likely to be misinterpreted—or worse, interpreted to advance certain beliefs or to support certain assumptions? Can test-wise students take undue advantage? Are school curriculums and students' attitudes toward schooling shaped by the very tests that are ostensibly designed to assess the outcomes of schooling? These important questions deserve serious consideration from everyone who uses tests and test results.

We readily acknowledge the legitimacy of many of the questions that the critics of tests raise, but we will not attempt to answer them—or to raise still more—in this chapter. Standardized tests will continue to be available and to be used in the schools for the foreseeable future. You, as a teacher, must strive to choose tests wisely and to make the best possible use of them once chosen. We recommend an excellent book by Ysseldyke and Algozzine (1982), *Critical Issues in Special and Remedial Education,* for those interested in pursuing the controversy.

## Summary

The purpose of this chapter is to help you choose and use tests effectively. Knowledge of basic measurement terms and concepts can help you understand and deal confidently with tests and test manuals. Remember, though, that the only good reason for testing is to get information that can and will be used. Before deciding *what* test to use, always decide *why* you want to test. The six guide questions in the chapter can help you select and apply tests intelligently.

## References

Buros, O. K. (Ed.). (1975). *Reading tests and reviews II.* Highland Park, NJ: Gryphon Press.

Buros, O. K. (Ed.). (1978). *The eighth mental measurements yearbook.* Highland Park, NJ: Gryphon Press.

Kavale, K. (1979). Selecting and evaluating tests. In R. Schreiner (Ed.), *Reading tests and teachers: A practical guide.* Newark, DE: International Reading Association, 9–34.

McLoughlin, J. A., & Lewis, R. B. (1981). *Assessing Special Students: Strategies and Procedures.* Columbus, OH: Charles E. Merrill.

Salvia, J., and Ysseldyke, J. E. (1981). *Assessment in special and remedial education* (2nd ed.). Boston: Houghton Mifflin.

Venezky, R. L. (1974). *Testing in reading: Assessment and instructional decision making.* Urbana, IL: ERIC Clearinghouse on Reading and Communication Skills and National Council of Teachers of English.

Ysseldyke, J. E., and Algozzine, B. (1982). *Critical issues in special and remedial education.* Boston: Houghton Mifflin.

## Check Your Reading Comprehension

1. What is the purpose for standardized testing in education?

2. How should one decide which test to use? What questions should one consider?

3. Matching Exercise:

_____ 1. Validity

_____ 2. Scores of relative standing

_____ 3. Reliability

_____ 4. Developmental scores

a. Age equivalents and grade equivalents

b. The score most frequently obtained by a particular group of students

c. Representative characteristics that allow you to evaluate an individual's performance in terms of other people's performance

_____ **5.** Norms

_____ **6.** True score

_____ **7.** Obtained score

_____ **8.** Correlation

_____ **9.** Median

_____**10.** Standard deviation

_____**11.** Variance

_____**12.** Mode

**d.** The extent to which a test measures what it claims to measure

**e.** The score that divides the top 50 percent from the bottom 50 percent of scores

**f.** A numerical index that describes the dispersion of scores around the mean of a distribution

**g.** A measure of the relationship between variables

**h.** The value the test taker would have obtained if the test scores were entirely free of error

**i.** A raw score that generally reflects both random and systematic errors; the score a test taker actually gets.

**j.** A measure of the stability of a test

**k.** The most commonly reported measure of the variability of a distribution

**l.** Percentiles and standard scores

Answers:

| | |
|---|---|
| 1. d | 7. i |
| 2. l | 8. g |
| 3. j | 9. e |
| 4. a | 10. k |
| 5. c | 11. f |
| 6. h | 12. b |

**4.** The following information was taken from the student information chart (Table 1.1) in Chapter 1.

|  | Reading Total (CAT) |
|---|---|
| Robert | 6.5 |
| Kelley | 4.2 |
| Tony | 2.4 |
| Allison | 3.7 |
| Robin | 4.3 |
| Tiffani | 5.8 |
| Carl | 2.0 |
| Guy | 7.9 |

  a. Rank the students from highest to lowest.
  b. Compute the range of the scores.
  c. Compute the mean of the scores.

  Answers:  a.  Guy, Robert, Tiffani, Robin, Kelley, Allison, Tony, Carl
  b.  $7.6 - 2.0 = 5.6$ (Highest Score − Lowest Score = Range)
  c.  $36.5 \div 8 = 4.56$ (Sum of Scores ÷ Number of Scores = Mean)

**5.** As a classroom teacher, how might you use the information from question 4?

**6.** In question 4 you are told a reading score for each student from a standardized test. What other information concerning the student might be helpful in deciding on reading group placement for each child? Would you want any additional information about the test? If so, what information?

# 5

# Assessing and Teaching: Striking a Balance

Certain terms related to tests and testing have come to connote different, sometimes very highly specialized, things to different people. We had a hard time deciding whether to use "diagnosis," "assessment," or "evaluation" to describe Chapter 5. We finally decided that "assessing" was best suited to our purpose. Now let us tell you why.

Our trusted reference, *A Dictionary of Reading and Other Terms* (Harris & Hodges, 1981) suggested that the process of diagnosis should have a specific focus—the identification and/or classification of disorders from their symptoms. Evaluation, on the other hand, involves making rather broad judgments on the basis of data from various sources, including tests. Assessment is the act of gathering data. We do intend to talk about using diagnostic tests to identify students' strengths and weaknesses in reading skill development in this chapter and in subsequent chapters. And we will continue to remind you that you must evaluate all the information you have to make judgments about your instructional program. But our deliberate emphasis in Chapter 5 is on gathering data and on getting the information needed to teach reading effectively—on assessment.

Making informed decisions about what to teach and what to stress with whom requires careful and constant assessment. Unfortunately, teachers sometimes gather information without any clear notion of how they will use it. Then they begin to think that time spent on assessment only diminishes time available for teaching. They need to strike a balance between assessment and teaching. They must begin to apply the knowledge gained from assessment to improve their teaching. A balance is struck when assessment becomes a part of, not a prelude to or an excursion from, an overall teaching effort.

To choose the most effective tools or techniques for assessment you must decide upon your reasons for assessing. What is it you want to find out? Various assessment procedures generally fall into five categories, or reference bases. Use them to organize existing information and to decide how to go about seeking new information.

The five categories, and the basic question each is designed to answer, follow.[1]

1. *Norm-referenced assessment:* How well is this student (or group) doing compared to others?
2. *Materials-referenced assessment:* What materials can this student read with confidence and understanding?
3. *Criterion-referenced assessment:* What objectives has this student (or group) mastered?
4. *Strategy-referenced assessment:* Which reading strategies is this student able (or unable) to use appropriately?
5. *Person-referenced assessment:* What are this student's positive and negative personal characteristics in relation to the acquisition of reading abilities?

The five categories overlap somewhat. Certain norm-referenced tests would be appropriate for strategy-referenced assessment. Some tests are both norm- and criterion-referenced. We discuss informal reading inventories under materials-referenced assessment, but an informal inventory can reveal a good deal about a student's preference for and competence with certain strategies (person-referenced assessment). So don't think of the categories as being closed or exclusive. Think of them as a way to help you seek and organize the information you need.

# Norm-referenced Assessment

Norm-referenced tests are those used to compare individual performance to that of a norm group, which presumably represents an appropriate larger population. The norm-referenced tests you are probably familiar with are the standardized achievement tests you took during your elementary and high-school years, such as the *California Achievement Tests* the *Iowa Tests of Basic Skills,* the *Metropolitan Achievement Tests,* or the *Stanford Achievement Tests.*[2] As discussed in Chapter 4,

---

[1] The categories and questions are suggested by a discussion in *How to Teach Reading Successfully* by J. D. McNeil, L. Donant, and M. C. Alkin, 1980, Boston: Little, Brown.

[2] See Appendix A for publication information and a brief description of the tests named in Chapter 5.

Choose the best test for your purpose. (Photo by Jean Greenwald)

standardized tests are used to compare a student's performance to that of a norm group, which presumably represents an appropriate larger population. The tests let you know how well a student (or group) is doing compared to others.

These tests are multiple-skill batteries; they assess skill development in several subjects, including reading, spelling, math, science, and social studies. *The Gates-MacGinitie Reading Tests* have a single-skill focus—reading. Norm-referenced tests used to assess reading achievement can be further categorized as either *survey* or *diagnostic* devices; they are administered either to groups or to individuals. Figure 5.1 categorizes some of the most commonly used of these tests.

Survey tests are essentially for screening purposes, to estimate a student's current level of performance in comparison to that of age or grade peers. Diagnostic tests allow a closer look at an individual's strengths and weaknesses in skill development. The group tests in Figure 5.1 may be given one-on-one if there is reason to believe the test taker would benefit from such an arrangement.

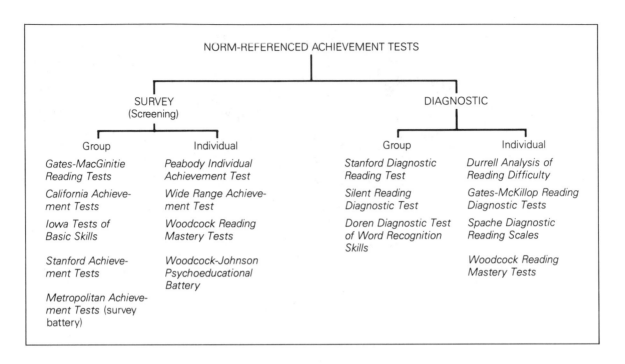

**Figure 5.1** Categories of Tests for Norm-Referenced Assessment of Reading (See Appendix A for the test publishers and addresses)

## Tests for Screening

Survey achievement tests may be given for purposes of *accountability,* to obtain evidence of how local students are doing in comparison to nationwide norms. But for our present purposes the tests' *screening* function is the most important one: the survey tests permit us to identify individuals who seem to be falling behind, who may need corrective teaching.

***Group survey tests.***      Keep in mind that survey tests were never intended to yield specific information about individuals' strengths and weaknesses in reading skill development. Rather, they measure the extent to which students have profited from previous instruction or other learning experiences compared to others of the same age or grade.

*We suggest that you approach survey tests as you would approach an 800-pound gorilla: very carefully! Although we have seen some rather explicit directions for using survey test scores to group students and even to plan instruction (see, for example, Canney, 1979), our own experience suggests that survey test scores are best reserved for general screening and very tentative grouping of students.*

Otto and Smith (1980) offer some perspective by suggesting three levels of diagnosis:

> Readers do not need equally prolonged, intensive, or sophisticated diagnosis to permit successful instruction. Nor is it necessary or even desirable that all diagnostic work be done by highly trained specialists. The purpose of diagnosis is to gather information for planning good instruction. In some cases an examination of complex, underlying causal factors by experts in fields such as education, medicine, and psychology may be needed; but in other cases a very straightforward assessment of the student's reading strategies by the classroom teacher will be adequate for planning effective lessons. We have systematized the diagnostic process by organizing it into three steps or levels: the survey level, the specific level, and the intensive level. Generally, each succeeding level requires more expertise in collecting and interpreting information about the student's strengths and weaknesses as a reader. (p. 99)

Group survey tests gather relatively small amounts of information about large numbers of students. Diagnosis at the survey level serves one or more of three main purposes: (a) to examine the overall impact of an instructional program by noting achievement trends from year to year, (b) to discover relative strengths and weaknesses in the reading performance of groups of students, and (c) to identify students who appear to be having reading problems requiring more detailed diagnosis.

The last purpose is most applicable to corrective teaching. Group survey tests help you limit further—more specific diagnostic—testing to students who need it most. You can identify those students who, on the basis of their survey test scores, seem to be falling behind. You can then take a closer look at their reading performance with more specific diagnostic tests.

***Individual survey tests.*** At least in theory, individual survey tests provide an alternative that could permit you to avoid some of the limitations of group testing. You might choose to give an individual survey test to get better rapport with the test taker, to have more options for presenting stimuli and getting responses, or simply to deal with a single student who, for some reason, has no other scores available. Two widely used individual survey tests are the *Peabody Individual Achievement Test* (PIAT) and the *Wide Range Achievement Test* (WRAT). Both are multiple skills tests; they are not limited to the assessment of reading performance.

The PIAT samples behaviors in (a) Mathematics; (b) Reading Recognition, which includes matching letters, naming capital and lower-case letters, and recognizing words in isolation; (c) Reading Comprehension, in which the student reads a sentence and then indicates comprehension by choosing the right picture out of a group of four; (d) Spelling; and (e) General Information. The test can be used with students from kindergarten through 12th grade.

The WRAT samples behavior in (a) *Reading,* including letter recognition, letter naming, and pronunciation of words in isolation; (b) *Spelling;* and (c) *Arithmetic.* The test is available at two levels: level 1 for students younger than 12, and level 2 for those over 12.

While both tests are used rather extensively for screening purposes, neither provides very satisfactory assessment of reading performance. The sampling of reading behavior is very superficial. If you see scores from these tests, remember where they came from. If you use either test, let it serve only as a tentative screening device, not as a basis for long-term decisions.

The *Woodcock Reading Mastery Tests* are also often used for screening purposes. They differ from the PIAT and the WRAT in that all of the subtests relate to reading behaviors: letter identification, word comprehension, and paragraph comprehension. Because the tests are often used for more specific diagnostic purposes we also mention them in the discussion of individual diagnostic tests.

The Woodcock-Johnson Psychoeducational Battery, an individually administered multiple-skill battery, purports to assess cognitive ability, scholastic aptitude, academic achievement, and interests in individuals from 3 to 80 years old. In addition to the reading interest subtest, a number of subtests related to reading behaviors are included in the cognitive ability and achievement sections. These include visual auditory learning, blending, visual matching, letter identification, word attack, and passage comprehension. These tests, too, could be used either for screening or for more specific diagnostic purposes. If you can manage not to be overwhelmed by the range of subtests and the variety of scoring and interpretation options offered, you may be able to use effectively some of these subtests.

## Tests for Diagnosis

Whereas survey tests provide relatively global information about students' reading performances, diagnostic tests help teachers assess skill development and plan instruction. Norm-group comparisons are less important because the emphasis shifts from determining individuals' relative standing in reading performance to examining the pattern of each individual's specific skill development. (This is fortunate because the norms provided for the diagnostic tests—particularly the individual tests—tend to be less than adequate. Use them with care and a bit of skepticism.)

Time limitations will probably always restrict you to using formal diagnostic tests only with students who you believe need further testing. It is particularly important that you choose your tests with care so as to get the precise information you are seeking. No diagnostic reading test can sample all aspects of reading. Each test samples specific behaviors that the test authors believe are important to successful reading. Be sure to consider an individual's performance on a diagnostic test in light of the behaviors sampled by the test and to put more emphasis on actual performance than on norm-referenced interpretations.

*Group tests.*     Group diagnostic tests resemble survey achievement tests in format and appearance, but they include subtests for a greater number of reading skills. Scores from the subtests can be used to create a profile of a student's specific reading skills. The obvious advantage of all group tests applies—they are relatively easy to administer and score. But because group diagnostic tests attempt to sample from many areas in limited time they tend to have too few items on their subtests to attain adequate reliability or validity.

The *Stanford Diagnostic Reading Test* is a widely used group diagnostic test. It is published at four levels, each with two alternate test forms. The skills tested at each level are

- *Red Level* (grades 1.6 – 3.5): Auditory Vocabulary, Auditory Discrimination, Phonetic Analysis, Word Reading, Reading Comprehension (sentence reading and paragraph comprehension).
- *Green Level* (grades 2.6 – 5.5): Auditory Vocabulary, Auditory Discrimination, Phonetic Analysis, Structural Analysis (syllabication and blending), Reading Comprehension (literal and inferential).
- *Brown Level* (grades 4.6 – 9.5): Auditory Vocabulary, Reading Comprehension (literal and inferential), Phonetic Analysis, Structural Analysis (syllabication and blending), Reading Rate.
- *Blue Level* (grades 9 – 13): Reading Comprehension (literal and inferential), Word Meaning, Word Parts, Phonetic Analysis, Structural Analysis, Fast Reading, Skimming and Scanning.

The Stanford is both norm-referenced and criterion-referenced. Norms are provided for comparison purposes; but the test can also be used to assess individuals' strengths and weaknesses in specific reading skills. You must be careful to test only what you've taught.

The *Silent Reading Diagnostic Test,* like the *Stanford,* covers a wide range of reading skills. Its eight subtests assess (a) recognition of words in isolation, (b) recognition of words in context, (c) identification of root words, (d) skill in separating words into syllables, (e) application of the common rules of syllabication, (f) synthesizing of beginning sounds, (g) skill in distinguishing ending sounds, (h) skill in distinguishing vowel and consonant sounds. Notice that the test is actually limited to assessing word-recognition and word-analysis skills—despite the general scope implied by the name of the test. As we have mentioned, test titles can be misleading. Look at the test, not the title, before you decide to use it. The *Silent Reading Diagnostic Test* does appear to have adequate norms and reliability.

A group diagnostic test with a more aptly chosen name is the *Doren Diagnostic Test of Word Recognition Skills.* The problem with the *Doren* is its norms. There are no grade-level standards for the various subtests, so it is difficult to see how the author intends the norms to be used for diagnostic purposes. Common sense suggests that one look at the specific items and the test taker's performance on each subtest in view of previous instruction.

***Individual tests.***   Group tests are relatively efficient to administer and score, but they cannot be relied on for planning specific instruction for individuals, particularly individuals with severe or complex reading difficulties. Individual diagnostic tests can be useful for gathering more specific information, if they are chosen with care.

Four individually administered diagnostic reading tests are widely used: the *Durrell Analysis of Reading Difficulty,* the *Gates-McKillop Reading Diagnostic Tests,* the *Spache Diagnostic Reading Scales,* and the *Woodcock Reading Mastery Tests.* The *Durrell,* the *Gates-McKillop,* and the *Spache* all have subtests that assess a variety of specific word recognition and word analysis skills. All three tests contain graded passages for assessing students' oral reading, and the *Durrell* and the *Spache* also have these for silent reading and listening comprehension. The tests are similar, too, in that they cover a range of skills from prereading to about sixth-grade level. We agree with the test authors that the tests can also be used to diagnose severe reading problems of older students.

We prefer the *Spache* overall. Directions for administering the various subtests are relatively clear, and the manual offers particularly helpful suggestions for interpreting scores and planning instruction. Two equivalent sets of 11 passages ranging in difficulty from first to eighth grade are used to assess oral reading, silent reading, and listening comprehension (passages are read to the students). The passages can help a teacher to assess the nature and extent of a student's reading errors, to identify a student's instructional and independent reading levels,[3] and to estimate a student's reading potential. Eight subtests assess recognition and use of letter sounds, use of consonant blends, use of syllabication, ability to translate (blend) letter sounds into words, skill in initial consonant substitution, and skill in auditory discrimination. The battery takes about 45 minutes to administer.

The *Woodcock Reading Mastery Tests,* for students in kindergarten through grade 12, include five subtests: Letter Identification, Word Identification, Word Attack, Word Comprehension, and Passage Comprehension. The battery is widely used in some circles; but in view of the low reliability of the subtests and the complex procedure for developing a performance profile we really don't know why.

Two advantages of a diagnostic battery are exemplified by the *Spache, Durrell,* and *Gates-McKillop.* First, the subtest scores may be reasonably compared because the tests were standardized with the same population. Second, there is a single test and a single manual, so learning to administer and interpret is not the overwhelming task it could be with a combination of different tests.

These tests do have serious limitations. Many subtests are too brief to be reliable, so the cornerstone of validity is missing. The bases for the norms tend to be inadequately described, so the norms may be misleading. Scoring and interpretation of the scores is demanding, requiring either advanced training in teaching reading or extensive practice. Most importantly, though, the subtests may not assess the types of skills that have in fact been taught. If so, then no amount of interpretive skill or sophistication as a test giver will make a student's scores meaningful.

***How to use diagnostic tests.***    Reading specialists, not classroom teachers, ordinarily administer individual diagnostic tests—particularly those just described—and to a lesser extent group diagnostic tests. This is not because the tests require extraordinary training or skill to be used properly. Most teachers can handle them very well after studying the manual and making a few trial runs. But most teachers have trouble finding the time to give the test; finding the opportunity for one-on-one testing in a busy classroom; or, most importantly, scheduling time to plan and offer the instruction that is indicated.

How, then, should you as a classroom teacher use diagnostic tests? First, make tentative decisions on the basis of survey test scores and limit further testing to students who need it most. Second, do not bother to test what you have not taught. Third, use formal diagnostic tests sparingly. Use them only to gather information that

---

[3] See Chapter 7 for a thorough discussion of *independent* and *instructional* reading levels.

you need to plan appropriate instruction and expect to be able to use in modifying your instructional program.

Better still, use formal diagnostic tests mainly as models for developing your own informal tests and testing procedures. Only occasionally will you be seeking a complete diagnostic profile of a student's skill development. In your day-to-day teaching you will more often be seeking insights into students' ability to handle a specific skill or a few related skills. If you become familiar with the various diagnostic subtests, you can choose the ones that are appropriate for your purpose. You may decide to use a subtest just as it is or as a model for making a test of your own.

Finally, remember to use the norms provided for diagnostic tests with care. The reference groups for the norms are not adequately described, particularly for the individual tests, so comparisons of individual scores to the norms may be misleading. More importantly, you usually give a diagnostic test not to find out how an individual is doing in comparison to others but to learn about specific skill development. You can learn more by looking at qualitative information from the subtests than by comparing scores to norms. Think of the test items as samples of students' reading behaviors.

Why bother with norm-referenced tests? First, there is value in knowing when and how much an individual or group is performing differently from a peer group. When there are differences, there is cause to look for the reasons. Second, certain norm-referenced tests have been and continue to be widely used. Knowing the tests can help to keep communication lines open among teachers and specialists. Third, many norm-referenced tests—particularly the diagnostic tests—are also criterion-referenced. You can learn about specific strengths and needs by attending to a student's response to specific items and subtests.

## Materials-referenced Assessment

The question addressed by materials-referenced assessment is: What reading materials can this student read with confidence and understanding? The question is particularly important for students who are experiencing some difficulty with reading. Too often their reading tasks are a little too difficult and their understanding is not quite clear. Such students seldom have a chance to read with confidence and understanding, so they do not perceive reading as a comfortable and fulfilling activity. They need many more opportunities to read materials appropriate to their abilities and interests.

Norm-referenced test scores are not very useful for matching up students and appropriate reading materials. Knowing that Juan scored at the 38th percentile for fifth graders or that he scored at the 4.3 grade level does not help you select appropriate reading material for him. Julian's grade-equivalency score of 4.3 gives no assurance that he can read a fourth-grade basal reader, much less a fourth-grade science text or trade book, with confidence and understanding. Grade-equivalent scores and the readability ratings of materials are much too imprecise to be relied on for matching a reader and a text.

Informal reading inventories and cloze tests are much more appropriate instruments for materials-referenced assessment. Both can be created from materials available in the classroom.

## Informal Reading Inventories

Informal reading inventories (IRIs) assess students' word analysis, comprehension, and listening abilities, and, to an extent, their reading potential. We discuss IRIs in detail and describe how to construct them in Chapter 7. Here we discuss them only as they apply to finding appropriate reading materials for students.

Bader (1980) calls IRIs Graded Paragraph Tests. IRIs do usually consist of series of paragraphs taken from basal readers or other carefully graded materials. Giving the test then, amounts to having the test taker read increasingly difficult passages until word analysis or comprehension problems become frustrating. The test taker attempts to respond to questions about each passage or to restate the content; the test giver may keep a running tally of word analysis errors as oral reading progresses.

The essential purpose for administering an IRI is to discover three reading levels: (a) the *independent level,* where the student has no difficulty with word analysis or comprehension and is able to read without supervision or support; (b) the *instructional level,* where the student needs some help with word analysis and comprehension is approaching minimum standards; and (c) the *frustration level,* where word analysis errors are so frequent as to frustrate understanding and further performance. The criteria for establishing each level are

| Level | Word Analysis | Comprehension |
|---|---|---|
| Independent | 99% correct | 90% correct |
| Instructional | 95% correct | 75% correct |
| Frustration | 90% correct | 50% correct[4] |

An IRI usually is most effective when constructed from the actual reading materials under consideration. So if you want to find out what book in Basal Reader Series X is appropriate for Martha, use passages from the books in Basal Reader Series X. On the other hand, Phillips and Colwell (1981) suggest that it may be acceptable to administer a "neutral" informal inventory—a published, commercially available IRI-type test, or one constructed from "neutral" materials—if students are to be instructed from a wide array of reading materials. In other words, if what you want is a fairly rough estimate of a student's reading level, it is okay to use an IRI constructed from materials other than the ones to be read directly. Using a "neutral" IRI saves preparing an IRI for each specific application.

We consider the best feature of informal inventories to be their informality. When they are formalized, neutralized, or generalized they begin to take on all the limitations of standardized tests. If the question is: *Can this student read this material*

---

[4] Betts (1946) described these levels years ago and offered criteria for determining each level. Betts' standards are still at least as good as any of the alternatives that have been suggested.

Independent level. (Photo by Jerry Bushey/Trinity Photos)

Instructional level. (Photo by Strix Pix)          Frustration level. (Photo © C. Quinlan)

*with confidence and understanding?,* the most straightforward way to find out is to have the student read a passage of the material while you observe any difficulties with word analysis and comprehension. Then apply Betts' criteria.

## Cloze Tests

You can use cloze tests, like IRIs, to assess students' ability to cope with specific reading materials (Taylor, 1953). One of their main appeals is their simplicity; they are easy to construct, administer, and interpret (Dieterich, Freeman, & Griffin, 1978).

You can develop a standard cloze test by the following procedure: First, select a passage of about 100 words (fewer for young children, more for older) from material at hand that the students have not yet read. For a book, select three passages, from near the front, the middle, and near the end. Second, delete every fifth word from each passage, beginning with the second sentence. Don't delete proper nouns and dates. Third, insert equal length lines for the deleted words (Rush & Klare, 1978). That's it! You have made a cloze test. To administer the test, simply have the test taker read the passage and attempt to fill in the missing words. Try to make the testing atmosphere gamelike to sustain the student's interest in what amounts to a rather difficult task.

Measurement specialists and reading educators have argued endlessly about whether the student must fill the blanks with the author's exact words or if reasonable synonyms are okay. Accepting synonyms assures more "correct" responses but makes scoring much more difficult because the person who scores the test must decide which words are acceptable. We favor accepting only the author's exact words as correct responses. Research has shown that accepting synonyms does not improve the functional value of the test; but it does destroy the ease of scoring, one of the most appealing attributes of cloze tests. (See also Harris and Sipay, 1980.)

Scoring a cloze test is easy if you accept only the author's exact words. A student's score is the percentage of words correct (Bormuth, 1968). You should not penalize incorrect spelling. Interpret the percentage scores as follows:

| | |
|---|---|
| 60–100% | Independent level |
| 40–60% | Instructional level |
| below 40% | Frustration level |

People who use cloze tests disagree on whether to delete every fifth, or every seventh, or every tenth word. Some suggest deleting selectively, letting function words remain and deleting only nouns or verbs or some combination. Again, the research suggests that not much is gained by deviating from the every-fifth-word pattern; and much is lost when a simple test construction routine is made more complex.

To give you the flavor of a cloze test, here is a passage from Chapter 2 with every fifth word deleted. See how you do with materials that should be both familiar to you and at your independent reading level.

But to say that good corrective teaching adheres more rigorously to sound principles is not to say that developmental teaching is sloppy and insensitive. Students
with reading problems _____ need more careful _____ than
students without problems. _____ learners who succeed, learners
_____ fail in reading are _____ by their general inability—
_____ at least their greater _____—to put things together
_____ themselves. A teacher we _____ put it like this:
"_____ as if they [poor _____] just don't know how
_____ play the game. Good _____ will have a dozen
_____ ways to figure out _____ and what they mean.
_____ play the game without _____ about the rules.
But _____ have to teach poor _____ exactly what to do,
_____ then I have to _____ them do it."

The deleted words are *simply, attention, Unlike, who, characterized, or, difficulty, for, know, It's, readers, to, readers, different, words, They, thinking, I, readers, and, help.* How did you do? Fourteen or more correct responses would put you at the independent level, with more than 60 percent of the items correct.

Some reading educators would argue that our 60 percent criterion for the independent reading level is too high if we are insisting on the author's exact words. They would say that 40 percent or so is adequate. This is probably true, if the author's style is unfamiliar or if the passage contains many technical terms or jargon words. It is fair to say, too, that the cloze procedure tests a students' associational fluency. Some students may be penalized by their inability to deal effectively with the associational task. As you gain experience with the cloze technique you will be able to make adjustments to serve your purposes.

By establishing students' independent, instructional, and frustration levels with given materials you can better help them select books and other materials for independent study; know when certain students need extra help, particularly with assigned reading from a content-area text; and decide when to provide a more readable alternative. Keep in mind, though, the other factors influencing a student's ability to deal with reading materials, including such nebulous ones as personal attitudes, interests, and experiences.

Remember, too, that attempting to select reading materials in line with students' abilities is different from attempting to help students deal with reading tasks as they are presented. There are no simple rules for deciding when to seek alternate materials and when to teach the requisite skills for coping with a given task. You must consider both options. The tacit appliers and the nonappliers we talked about in Chapter 2 need to be able to read materials they can understand and enjoy. But they also need to learn to apply specific skills and strategies as they tackle difficult reading tasks. (We offer suggestions for how to provide that help in Chapter 9.)

## Criterion-referenced Assessment

The objective of criterion-referenced testing is to find out which reading skills, as determined by the instructional objectives of the reading program, a student does and does not have. Venezky (1974) summed up the difference between norm-referenced and criterion-referenced tests:

> Norm-referenced and criterion-referenced tests differ in both content and utility. Writers of test items for norm-referenced tests generally do not begin with a well-defined set of performances which they intend to measure, and further, because of the need to obtain variability among individuals, they avoid items that are either too easy or too difficult, regardless of their importance for the subject matter of the test. Writers of test items for criterion-referenced tests, on the other hand, begin with a definition of desired behaviors (instructional objectives), from which test items are derived. Since variability across the total range of students is not an issue for criterion-referenced tests, the percentage of students who pass or fail an item does not by itself serve for selection or rejection of the item. Finally, norm-referenced tests have their main application in assessing individuals when selec-

tivity is a factor, for example, in determining which students should be placed in a special program which can accommodate only a small number of them. Criterion-referenced tests are applicable when individuals are to be matched to instructional alternatives. (pp. 12 – 13. Reprinted with the permission of the National Council of Teachers of English.)

Venezky's discussion underscores two important facts. First, criterion-referenced diagnostic tests are designed to analyze individuals' strengths and weaknesses with regard for criterion behaviors (described by instructional objectives), not for the performance of a comparison group. Second, norm-referenced tests are appropriate for general grouping; criterion-referenced tests are more useful for making specific instructional assignments. For example, you might refer a student for remedial reading partly on the basis of relatively poor norm-referenced test scores. You could, on the other hand, use criterion-referenced test scores to establish specific instructional groups (for example, to practice quick recognition of common sight words, to seek the main idea in passages with a topic sentence, to scan passages for specific facts) or to assign individuals for specific skill instruction.

In theory, criterion-referenced tests assess students' performance in relation to specific, predetermined instructional objectives. The sequence is first to state instructional objectives, then to use them to plan instruction, and finally to use criterion-referenced tests to see if the objectives have been attained. (A comprehensive reading program, as described in Chapter 2, helps to assure such an orderly sequence.) In practice, however, criterion-referenced tests are often used in the absence of clearly stated instructional objectives, without which there is little assurance that the tests are in line with students' instruction. The sequence then starts with testing.

Does it ever make sense to start with a criterion-referenced test instead of well-conceived instructional objectives? Yes, if two conditions are met. First, the criterion-referenced tests must be reasonably in line with the instruction that has been offered. Second, testing must be followed by using the test results to plan instruction in view of students' strengths and needs; reteaching as needed; and retesting on the same tasks. By carefully selecting criterion-referenced tests, teachers can not only clarify their instructional objectives but also get direction for their instructional efforts.

You, the teacher, might approach criterion-referenced assessment with carefully selected criterion-referenced tests or with thoughtfully developed instructional objectives, which you could then use to construct your own criterion-referenced tests. In the two sections that follow, we offer suggestions for doing both.

## How to Select a Criterion-referenced Test

Some norm-referenced tests are also criterion-referenced. They assess how well students have attained specific instructional objectives as well as provide a basis for comparing the performance of individuals and groups. These tests include the *Stanford Achievement Tests,* the *Stanford Diagnostic Reading Test,* and the *Metropolitan Achievement Tests.*

Strictly criterion-referenced tests are usually part of an entire reading system.[5] Some examples of commercially published reading systems are: *Diagnosis: An Instructional Aid* (Science Research Associations), *Criterion Reading* (Random House), *Fountain Valley Teacher Support System in Reading* (Zweig Associates), *Prescriptive Reading Inventory* (California Test Bureau/McGraw Hill), and *The Wisconsin Design for Reading Skill Development* (Learning Multisystems). While each of these systems presents a unique list of instructional objectives, their common feature is a series of criterion-referenced tests sequenced by the instructional objectives from least to most difficult.

Blanton (1981) nicely points out considerations for selecting a test in line with the skills you teach. Although his comments refer to a particular test, the *Prescriptive Reading Inventory* (PRI), they apply to any criterion-referenced test.

> The most important consideration in selecting a criterion-referenced reading test is the correspondence between the skills covered by the test and those of the reading program. In order to best determine the extent of this match, the skills of the test must be stated in terms which specify not only the reading behaviors, but also the criteria for meeting them. . . .
>
> In deciding whether the match between the PRI objectives and the objectives of the reading program is close enough to justify the use of the PRI, it is necessary to consider a variety of factors.
>
> 1. Many of the word recognition objectives in the PRI are tested by items that assess the skill in an activity that involves the total reading act. . . . Testing of skills in such a context often complicates the analysis of reading performance. A specific skill may be completed with a variety of strategies—it is not always possible to infer, for example, that a student who selects a word from a set of words, only one of which has the correct initial consonant to complete a sentence with a word omitted, can recognize initial consonant sounds. Performance might be attributable to sight word recognition or the use of context rather than the ability to recognize initial consonant sounds.
>
> 2. . . . If the instructional program teaches a skill in a particular way, it is important that performance of the skill be measured in a similar manner.
>
> 3. The distribution of PRI skills across the various reading areas should approximately match the distribution of skills in the school's reading program. The scope and sequence of reading programs vary. Some programs place heavy emphasis on phonics or other decoding skills from the beginning, while others emphasize comprehension. . . . The PRI appears most appropriate for those reading programs that lay equal emphasis on the various skills of reading. . . .
>
> 4. The placement of skills in the various levels of the PRI should correspond reasonably well with that in the school's reading program. A criterion-referenced test is generally administered to make an instructional decision. . . . Consequently, the measurement of skills should be placed immediately before or after instruction. This does not mean, however, that it is inappropriate to measure performance at

---

[5] That is, the tests are part of a comprehensive set of materials that includes instructional objectives, guidelines and/or materials for teaching, and criterion-referenced tests. Many basal reader series now provide criterion-referenced tests for each book or for each level in the series.

some time after instruction, particularly if the purpose is to determine whether mastery has been retained. (pp. 71–72. Reprinted with the permission of the author and the International Reading Association.)

Choosing appropriate criterion-referenced tests involves seeking not only a match between your instructional program and the skills tested but also assurance that the format, placement, and procedures of the tests are in line with classroom practices. Well-chosen tests present no surprises to the students who take them.

## How to Construct a Criterion-Referenced Test

Start with a clearly stated instructional objective. Salvia and Ysseldyke (1981) put it like this: "Criterion-referenced assessment is tied to instructional objectives, the individual items are designed to assess mastery of specific objectives" (p. 217).

Refer to Chapter 3 for some advice on how to state worthwhile instructional objectives. Kamil (1979) sums up the process as follows:

> Objectives should be constructed by first determining the desired student behavior. . . . Performance should then be specified, preferably using active verbs like *to answer, to define, to say,* or *to locate.* Verbs such as *to feel, to think,* or *to grow* should be avoided. Finally, an outcome should be stated. The outcome should be an observable or measurable performance and should include a statement of the task and a level of mastery or a criterion to be achieved. For example: "The students will be able to categorize known words with the long or short sound of *oo* into two groups with 90 percent accuracy." . . .
>
> Notice that [the] objective specifies, in itself, a test. If a student satisfies the objective, instruction should move to new objectives. If a student does not meet the criterion, revisions in instruction, in the objective itself, or in the needs assessment may be necessary. (p. 48)

In effect, you engage in criterion-referenced assessment any time you look for evidence that a student has or has not attained a given instructional objective. Consider, for example, the objective stated in the preceding passage. You could proceed very informally, simply noting students' correct or incorrect pronunciations of words with the long or short *oo* sound as they read out loud. Or you could construct a formal test, listing words with the long or the short *oo* sound and then asking students to categorize them as having either the long or short sound. In either case you must decide what you will accept as adequate demonstration of mastery of the objective. Our example arbitrarily sets 90 percent accuracy; ideally, though, you would expect a reader to pronounce all *oo* words correctly.

# Strategy-referenced Assessment

Criterion-referenced assessment enables you to find out what specific skills a student has and has not mastered. Strategy-referenced assessment goes beyond that to whether a student needs help with certain more general strategies for word analysis and comprehension. Decoding words and understanding what one reads involve not just the application of specific skills, but also (a) having a sense of balance in the use of skills and (b) choosing the best alternative for a given task. Phonics skills might help you decode words in some instances; but other times sight recognition, context clues, or structural analysis would be more appropriate. Likewise, efficiency in finding specific facts calls for a different strategy than reading for the gist of a passage.

In the chapters that follow, we discuss two techniques that particularly apply to both strategy-referenced assessment and teaching. The techniques are miscue analysis and glossing.

Very briefly, *miscue analysis* (Chapter 7) focuses on students' oral reading responses that differ from expected responses to written material. Analysis of miscues can reveal strengths and weaknesses in the students' reading strategies and provide information for planning corrective instruction. *Glossing* (Chapter 9) involves making instructional notations to accompany a specific text. The notations—based on careful analysis of the reader, the text, and the teacher's expectations—are designed to enhance the reader's comprehension strategies.

# Person-referenced Assessment

Person-referenced assessment addresses this question: What are this student's positive and negative personal characteristics in relation to the acquisition of reading abilities? The question deserves your careful attention and consideration. The success of all your assessing and teaching will be determined by the responses of your students. Even the most carefully planned and skillfully delivered instruction will fail if it falls upon unhearing ears, unseeing eyes, or unreceptive minds.

Unfortunately, we cannot outline techniques and strategies for person-referenced assessment as we have done with the preceding assessment areas. We do not think tests of personality, social-emotional behavior, or social maturity are particularly useful or even relevant to the purpose. We have found the available checklists, inventories, and behavior-rating scales to be of limited use for assessing individual students' interests, motives, and "adaptive behaviors" insofar as teaching reading is concerned. Person-referenced assessment amounts more to watching for the full range of personal attributes, aspirations, and needs that relate to each student's reading performance.

This is not the place for us to launch into a discussion of all the personal characteristics that relate to reading performance. Even an exhaustive discussion, however, might not be very useful because the very instruction that seems to contribute to one person's success in reading may contribute to another's failure. Some students, for example, respond very well to intensive phonics instruction. They learn the "rules," apply the rules when it serves their purpose, and quickly become self-sufficient readers who understand what they read. Other students seem to be hopelessly befuddled by phonics instruction. Even when they learn the rules successfully, they tend to overapply them; they become seemingly mindless word-callers with no concept of reading to understand. The difference seems to be influenced less by the phonics instruction, than by students' diverse, highly personal—and often unpredictable—reactions to instruction.

Person-referenced assessment goes beyond an awareness of and a sensitivity to personal attributes, aspirations, and needs. You must focus on each reader's reaction to instruction and to the instructional situation. Does Maynard, for example, appear to be totally uninterested in that new book on dinosaurs—which is, of course, at his instructional reading level—that you think is so beautifully illustrated and so interesting? It could be time for you to find out more about Maynard's interests. Is Jennifer, who tests at the 4.6 grade level in reading ability, reading a "high school level" paperback with obvious appreciation and enjoyment—and apparent ease? Maybe you ought to take another look at Jennifer's reading ability and interests as well as your own ideas about what makes a book readable.

Does Roger stay interested when he works with the microcomputer, but drop out when he joins his reading group? Does Linda seem to have a hard time getting the book the right distance from her eyes? Does Harold always seem to be "out to lunch" when you give oral directions? Does Tim spend hours daydreaming when you know he understands the assignment? There are reasons for all of these behaviors. The reasons may be quite obvious, but you won't see them unless you look. And unless you see them, you'll never do anything about them.

## Summary

The effective teaching of reading involves making informed decisions about what to teach, when to teach it, and what to stress with whom. You will base your decisions on assessment that is well-focused and in balance with instructional activities. The information gathered through assessment should have a clear and direct impact on instruction. Assessment activities come into focus when you consider the reference base of the desired information.

We identify and discuss five reference bases for reading assessment: (a) norm-referenced, determining how well a student (or group) is doing compared to others; (b) materials-referenced, determining what reading material a student can read with confidence and understanding; (c) criterion-referenced, considering what objectives (or skills) the student (or group) has mastered; (d) strategy-referenced, finding out which reading strategies a student is able (or unable) to use appropriately; and (e) person-referenced, determining an individual's positive and negative personal characteristics in relation to the acquisition of reading abilities.

## References

Bader, L. A. (1980). *Reading diagnosis in classroom and clinic.* New York: Macmillan.
Betts, E. A. (1946). *Foundations of reading instruction.* New York: American Book Company.

Blanton, W. E. (1981). *Prescriptive Reading Inventory,* levels A and B. In Leo M. Schell (Ed.), *Diagnostic and criterion-referenced tests: Review and evaluation.* Newark, DE: International Reading Association, pp. 70–76.

Bormuth, J. R. (1968). The cloze readability procedure. In J. R. Bormuth (Ed.), *Readability in 1968.* Champaign, IL: National Council of Teachers of English, pp. 40–47.

Canney, G. (1979). Organizing and applying test results. In Robert Schreiner (Ed.), *Reading tests and teachers: A practical guide.* Newark, DE: International Reading Association, pp. 53–71.

Dieterich, T., Freeman, C., & Griffin, P. (1978). Assessing comprehension in a school setting. Arlington, VA: Center for Applied Linguistics.

Harris, A. J., & Sipay, E. R. (1980). *How to increase reading ability* (7th ed.). New York: Longman.

Harris, T. L., & Hodges, R. E. (Eds.). (1981). *A dictionary of reading and related terms.* Newark, DE: International Reading Association.

Kamil, M. L. (1979). Construction and analysis of reading tests. In Robert Schreiner (Ed.), *Reading tests and teachers: A practical guide.* Newark, DE: International Reading Association, pp. 35–52.

Otto, W., & Smith, R. J. (1980). *Corrective and remedial teaching* (3rd ed.). Boston: Houghton Mifflin.

Phillips, K., & Colwell, C. G. (1981). Classroom reading inventory. In Leo M. Schell (Ed.), *Diagnostic and criterion-referenced tests: Review and evaluation.* Newark, DE: International Reading Association, pp. 17–22.

Rush, R. J., & Klare, G. R. (1978, Summer). Re-opening the cloze blank issue. *Journal of Reading Behavior, 10,* 208–210.

Salvia, J., & Ysseldyke, J. E. (1981). *Assessment in special and remedial education* (2nd ed.). Boston: Houghton Mifflin.

Taylor, W. L. (1953). Cloze procedure: A new tool for measuring readability. *Journalism Quarterly, 30,* 415–433.

Venezky, R. L. (1974). *Testing in reading: Testing and instructional decision making.* Urbana, IL: ERIC Clearinghouse on Reading and Communication Skills and National Council of Teachers of English, pp. 12–13.

# Check Your Reading Comprehension

1. What kinds of informed decisions are necessary for effective teaching of reading? Upon what should these decisions be based?

2. What is meant by a balance between teaching and assessment? How does one know when such a balance has been achieved?

3. Matching Exercise:

_____ **1.** Assessment

_____ **2.** Norm-referenced assessment

**a.** Attempts to identify reading materials that the student can read with confidence and understanding.

_____ **3.** Materials-referenced assessment

_____ **4.** Criterion-referenced assessment

_____ **5.** Strategy-referenced assessment

_____ **6.** Person-referenced assessment

_____ **7.** Tests for screening

_____ **8.** Tests for diagnosis

_____ **9.** IRI

_____**10.** Cloze test

**b.** Attempts to identify what strategies the student can or cannot use appropriately.

**c.** Attempts to identify objectives that the student has or has not mastered.

**d.** Attempts to identify a student's personal characteristics that are related to the acquisition of reading abilities.

**e.** Attempts to identify how well a student is performing compared to others.

**f.** A test involving a sample passage of reading material from which words have been systematically deleted.

**g.** Tests intended to provide relatively global information about students' reading performance.

**h.** The act of gathering data.

**i.** Tests intended to provide information that will help teachers assess skill development and serve as a basis for planning instruction.

**j.** Graded paragraph tests used to evaluate a student's word analysis and comprehension skills.

Answers:

| | |
|---|---|
| 10. f | 5. b |
| 9. j | 4. c |
| 8. i | 3. a |
| 7. g | 2. e |
| 6. d | 1. h |

4. Often the most appropriate type of assessment is determined by the reference base, or reason for testing. Read each situation and decide what type of assessment that you as a classroom teacher feel would be most helpful. Explain why.

   **a.** You are trying to determine which students have mastered the syllabication skill you have been teaching.

   **b.** You want to choose a science text that will be appropriate for your class.

   **c.** You want to identify which students may need more help with word analysis.

   **d.** You want to compare your group's performance with the rest of the second-grade classes in your district.

   **e.** You want to understand the interests and motivation of one of your students.

5. Study the "Classroom Screening Chart" (Table 1.1) from Chapter 1. Using the data from the group-administered, standardized test, establish a tentative grouping plan. Using the basal level from the previous year, establish another tentative grouping plan. How are the plans similar? How are they different? What other information might you use to establish your "just-to-get-started" grouping scheme? Which students would you plan to test individually as soon as possible?

6. Study your own class. Using data from previously administered tests, establish a tentative grouping plan. Indicate which students will probably require individual testing.

# 6

# Word Recognition Skills

Teachers sometimes become so concerned with word recognition that they lose sight of the ultimate goal of reading—to extract meaning. If Oscar reads fluently and understands what he reads, does it matter whether or not he has mastered all the phonics skills? Some children, especially brighter ones, devise their own decoding strategies without formal instruction. As long as Oscar's own strategies work for him, he shouldn't have to be put through one skill lesson after another.

A few children, on the other hand, decode very poorly, yet seem to grasp the meaning of the passage. These children, also usually fairly bright, are using their background experiences and knowledge to fill in the unknown portions of the passage. While their using context clues as an aid to word recognition is good, these readers will ultimately run into trouble as they reach more difficult reading material. They need a thorough word attack instructional program to supplement their already excellent use of context clues and background knowledge.

Like any good thing, word recognition instruction when taken to excess can do more harm than good. Some children, taught to analyze each word using all the available word attack rules, become overly dependent on the rules. Reading may become to them a matter of just "saying the words," not getting meaning from a passage. Such children need to learn to use context as a clue to word recognition, to draw upon their background experiences and knowledge.

We mention these various types of students because no single approach to word recognition instruction works with all children. Too often, phonics is the *only* strategy taught. When children have difficulty, the only solution seems to be *more* phonics instruction. Instead, a teacher should use a well-balanced reading program—one that is eclectic, drawing the best from a variety of approaches. If children do not progress at the expected rate of learning, the teacher must be able to draw upon other approaches to word recognition instruction.

We make a rather arbitrary distinction between word recognition and word meaning, dealing in this chapter only with word recognition. (Word meanings are treated in Chapter 8.) This distinction is made only for purposes of presentation. In the classroom, word recognition and meaning would be developed together, for they are two sides of the same coin.

## Hierarchy of Word Recognition Skills

The mature reader does not analyze each word. Indeed, many researchers (for example, Goodman, 1976) suggest that the mature reader does not even see every word. Reading instead has been called a "psycho-linguistic guessing game" (Goodman, 1976) in which we, as mature readers, use the familiar to derive the unfamiliar. In practice, then, our eyes fixate, or stop, only upon the substantive information in a passage. We fill in the familiar "little" words through our knowledge of the English language and the context of what we are reading.

Take a moment now to observe a friend's eye movements while she or he reads silently. (Have your friend hold a book up to almost eye level so that you can easily observe the eye movements.) Draw a graph showing the eye movements, using X's for fixations or stops and a straight line for eye movements. You may see regressions, during which the eyes retrace the path they have already taken. Regressions occur when the reader is uncertain of the meaning and rereading is necessary for clarification.

Did you see something similar to what Figure 6.1 indicates? The mature reader's eyes might fixate (shown by X's) about three or four times on a line of print. If the material is difficult or unfamiliar, more fixations (and possibly regressions) may occur.

If you have a chance to observe a child's eyes during silent reading, you may notice several more fixations per line. Again, the number of fixations will be determined in large part by the material's difficulty and the reader's familiarity with its content. But fluency in applying word recognition strategies is also a factor. Children

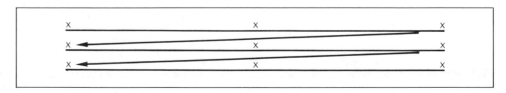

**Figure 6.1**  Eye Movements during Reading

who exhibit many fixations and regressions may lack mastery of the basic word recognition strategies or lack fluency in applying them.

Word recognition strategies fall into a natural hierarchy. The mature reader tends to use the top two while the novice reader relies primarily on structural/phonic analyses.

- Automatic recognition
- Contextual analysis
- Structural/phonic analyses

Specific word recognition skills fall under each category of the hierarchy. Objectives may be written to define each skill and assessments derived to test mastery. The essential word recognition skills with objectives included in the Wisconsin Design for Reading Skill Development (Otto & Askov, 1972) are shown in Appendix D. The levels of the skills progress in difficulty, with Level A corresponding to the end of kindergarten and Level D corresponding to the end of third grade for the average student. (The levels are lettered to avoid grade level designations; children of any age may progress through the levels as quickly as possible.) The list of skills and objectives may give you a sense of what the average child should be mastering at each level. It also indicates what skills come first—you would teach diphthongs, for example, only after students had mastered short and long vowels.

The long-range goals of word recognition programs are (a) to move as many words as possible into automatic recognition and (b) to teach children the skills necessary to analyze words that are not recognized automatically.

While a student may need to analyze a word the first few times, with repeated exposures the word should eventually become part of the student's automatic recognition vocabulary. If the student persists in analyzing a word that should be known immediately, then that student is "overanalyzing," or lacking fluency in reading.

Now let's take a closer look at the development of automatic recognition, which is at the top of the hierarchy, being the mature reader's main strategy for word recognition.

## Automatic Recognition

The mature reader recognizes most words instantly, stopping the flow of reading only to analyze unfamiliar words. In fact, reading appears to be automatic. La Berge & Samuels, 1976, call this process "automaticity." We might also use "fluency" to describe the easy flow of word recognition in which virtually no thought is given to the recognition processes.

The most obvious way to expand a child's automatic recognition is to increase the child's exposures to words. Children who have learned the basic word attack strategies often make rapid progress in reading if encouraged to do much silent reading. Teachers sometimes wonder how children can be making gains if they are not being directly taught either by the teacher or through skill development exercises. Simply reading seems too easy to be instructional.

But let's look at what prerequisites make sustained silent reading improve word recognition (Hunt, 1971). (We talk more about this as the individualized reading instructional approach in Chapter 7.) The first prerequisite to effective sustained silent reading is that the student has learned some basic word attack strategies, such as structural and phonic analysis skills. The student as yet, however, does not apply the skills easily but has to stop frequently and study a word to decode it. Through repeated exposures to that word the student will come to recognize it instantly. The word eventually becomes part of the student's automatic recognition vocabulary. Sustained silent reading provides the repeated exposures necessary for word recognition to become automatic.

The second prerequisite is that the material used for sustained silent reading is of appropriate difficulty. Teachers or parents may think that material must always be "challenging" to the child. In fact, reading material at the independent reading level, when the student recognizes most of the words and comprehends easily, best enables the student to arrive at fluency, or automaticity, in word recognition. The reading level may gradually be increased as the student's automatic recognition vocabulary expands. We discuss this process in greater detail in Chapter 8.

Samuels (1979) has found that reading the same material over and over builds automaticity or fluency. As discussed in Chapter 8, repeated readings helps students memorize new words; it moves them from the level of analyzing new words to the level of instant recognition.

LEA (language experience approach) stories or other short interesting selections are excellent for repeated readings. Both oral reading and silent reading are helpful. The student might use a tape recorder to ensure good voice inflection. The emphasis, however, should be upon reading the story for meaning rather than for just saying the words.

As a teacher, you can use the technique of repeated readings to help older students who are poor readers by having them read to kindergarten and first-grade children. Select a storybook that the older children can read with practice. Then instruct them on techniques for effective oral reading to young children. The students should repeatedly read the story until they feel that they are reading it fluently. They can record their reading on a tape and then critique it. They might also work with partners (other poor readers who are also engaging in the experience with younger children) in critiquing their oral reading. After much practice they will finally make the trek to the kindergarten or first-grade classroom, where each student will read the story to one child. (Reading to a group might be overwhelming.) Even if the reading performance is not perfect the younger child will enjoy the contact with an older student and benefit from hearing a story read aloud. The older student will gain expanded automatic recognition and practice in oral reading.

Similarly, encourage students to read aloud at home to younger siblings. Stress the importance of repeated readings to parents, for if the child reads without adequate practice, the resulting embarrassment may only aggravate the reading difficulty. If a parent cannot assist the student in preparation, then perhaps the teacher can help the student prepare to read aloud.

Reading to a younger child improves a student's automatic recognition. (Photo courtesy of Northshore Publishing Company, Bothell, Washington)

Sustained silent reading and repeated practice may not be enough for some readers. Students who need corrective reading instruction because of limited automatic recognition may require more direct instructional approaches. These are described in the next sections.

***High-frequency word lists.*** The Dolch list (Dolch, 1942) resulted from an early attempt to identify a list of core words that appear most frequently in children's reading materials. Dolch identified 220 words that appeared with the highest frequency in children's basic readers, literature, and oral vocabulary. His theory was that mastery of these words would enable the child to read easily. In other words, if initial reading material contained words that the child already knew by sight, then reading could become an enjoyable task. The child could concentrate primarily on the new words being introduced. The high-frequency words tended to be the "little" words that are often phonically irregular (for example, *to, done, mother*). Students had to learn these words by sight anyway, because word analysis strategies would not work in decoding them.

The idea behind sight word lists makes sense. Since Dolch's list proved to be so useful, other educators have formulated more up-to-date lists, using modern reading materials as the basis for arriving at the basic words. We do not think the particular word list is as important as the notion of consciously expanding the sight vocabulary. Otto and Chester's (1972) Great Atlantic and Pacific Word List is provided in Table 6.1.

You can put the words from the list onto index cards. Test students individually to determine the words that are already part of their automatic recognition vocabulary—those words recognized instantly. A student should be able to say the word following no more than a one-second exposure. (If the word is shown for a greater time period, the student may then analyze the word rather than recognize it instantly.)

Place the words that the student knows in a small file box, which the student may decorate and label with his or her name. The idea, of course, is to add as many words as possible to the box each week.

Students can make their own word cards. On one side of the card the word is printed (legibly); on the other side the word appears in a simple sentence, preferably a sentence written by the student. The new word should be underlined or highlighted in some way.

The student may keep together words not yet mastered and study them during free time. Allow the students to take their cards home so parents can help their children learn to recognize the words. The teacher or parent must expose the side with the word only for one second. If the student does not recognize it instantly, he or she looks at the sentence. If the student still does not recognize the word, he or she must either use one of the other word analysis strategies or be told the word.

Weekly quizzes on the new words are useful, especially if they contain words already mastered for review. A word should not be considered mastered until the student recognizes it for three consecutive weeks. Then it may be added to the box.

**Sight vocabulary.**     Sight vocabulary consists of words that the student frequently encounters when reading any set of instructional materials, whether specifically for reading or for one of the content area studies. Basal readers usually provide a list of vocabulary words included in each level, sometimes with a frequency count of the number of times a particular word is used. Phonically irregular words, which cannot be unlocked using word attack skills, are also taught as sight vocabulary.

Select for sight vocabulary instruction those words, especially phonically irregular words, that are important throughout the reading materials. Focus on these words, moving them into the students' sight vocabulary, so that the students can easily recognize them in context. Underachieving readers thus experience success when they meet these known words in new contexts.

You can base development of sight vocabulary on the sample lesson that follows on page 118. The italicized words, selected for sight vocabulary instruction, will occur in subsequent reading materials pertaining to a science unit on animals. Because the students are unfamiliar with these words, both in recognition and meaning, introduce only a few words at a time. Present these first in context.

**Table 6.1** The Great Atlantic and Pacific Word List

| Rank | Word | Rank | Word | Rank | Word | Rank | Word |
|------|------|------|------|------|------|------|------|
| 1 | the | 45 | we | 89 | just | 133 | help |
| 2 | a | 46 | then | 90 | big | 134 | looked |
| 3 | to | 47 | her | 91 | very | 135 | why |
| 4 | and | 48 | or | 92 | back | 136 | work |
| 5 | of | 49 | out | 93 | first | 137 | through |
| 6 | in | 50 | some | 94 | way | 138 | here |
| 7 | you | 51 | them | 95 | over | 139 | animals |
| 8 | is | 52 | write | 96 | too | 140 | place |
| 9 | he | 53 | their | 97 | than | 141 | before |
| 10 | it | 54 | words | 98 | good | 142 | three |
| 11 | that | 55 | about | 99 | use | 143 | home |
| 12 | was | 56 | by | 100 | day | 144 | house |
| 13 | on | 57 | like | 101 | where | 145 | again |
| 14 | for | 58 | see | 102 | called | 146 | another |
| 15 | are | 59 | so | 103 | me | 147 | number |
| 16 | they | 60 | if | 104 | went | 148 | our |
| 17 | I | 61 | these | 105 | put | 149 | must |
| 18 | with | 62 | make | 106 | around | 150 | off |
| 19 | his | 63 | into | 107 | new | 151 | name |
| 20 | said | 64 | him | 108 | know | 152 | mother |
| 21 | at | 65 | other | 109 | come | 153 | asked |
| 22 | as | 66 | word | 110 | who | 154 | picture |
| 23 | have | 67 | would | 111 | things | 155 | most |
| 24 | she | 68 | water | 112 | its | 156 | part |
| 25 | what | 69 | little | 113 | came | 157 | used |
| 26 | one | 70 | two | 114 | right | 158 | food |
| 27 | this | 71 | has | 115 | air | 159 | saw |
| 28 | all | 72 | did | 116 | sound | 160 | different |
| 29 | had | 73 | people | 117 | think | 161 | live |
| 30 | from | 74 | an | 118 | tell | 162 | well |
| 31 | be | 75 | which | 119 | after | 163 | any |
| 32 | can | 76 | could | 120 | Mr. | 164 | school |
| 33 | but | 77 | time | 121 | man | 165 | even |
| 34 | there | 78 | more | 122 | may | 166 | under |
| 35 | not | 79 | down | 123 | much | 167 | line |
| 36 | when | 80 | my | 124 | does | 168 | because |
| 37 | how | 81 | no | 125 | say | 169 | thought |
| 38 | were | 82 | go | 126 | same | 170 | next |
| 39 | your | 83 | get | 127 | been | 171 | small |
| 40 | do | 84 | now | 128 | take | 172 | every |
| 41 | each | 85 | long | 129 | only | 173 | going |
| 42 | will | 86 | find | 130 | old | 174 | want |
| 43 | up | 87 | look | 131 | away | 175 | something |
| 44 | many | 88 | made | 132 | children | 176 | earth |

| Rank | Word | Rank | Word | Rank | Word | Rank | Work |
|------|------|------|------|------|------|------|------|
| 177 | last | 221 | I'll | 265 | ever | 309 | green |
| 178 | men | 222 | while | 266 | kinds | 310 | gave |
| 179 | plants | 223 | soon | 267 | might | 311 | across |
| 180 | read | 224 | let | 268 | four | 312 | yes |
| 181 | left | 225 | hard | 269 | few | 313 | says |
| 182 | hear | 226 | hearts | 270 | move | 314 | learn |
| 183 | show | 227 | side | 271 | sure | 315 | can't |
| 184 | end | 228 | until | 272 | (1) | 316 | change |
| 185 | don't | 229 | should | 273 | miss | 317 | both |
| 186 | found | 230 | sometimes | 274 | feet | 318 | Indians |
| 187 | eat | 231 | own | 275 | tree | 319 | sounds |
| 188 | boy | 232 | dog | 276 | knew | 320 | turn |
| 189 | need | 233 | door | 277 | often | 321 | places |
| 190 | still | 234 | once | 278 | add | 322 | warm |
| 191 | keep | 235 | birds | 279 | better | 323 | Sam |
| 192 | together | 236 | days | 280 | room | 324 | without |
| 193 | sun | 237 | enough | 281 | such | 325 | between |
| 194 | us | 238 | near | 282 | vowel | 326 | short |
| 195 | got | 239 | trees | 283 | almost | 327 | lived |
| 196 | Mrs. | 240 | kind | 284 | ground | 328 | times |
| 197 | great | 241 | oh | 285 | sea | 329 | turned |
| 198 | father | 242 | top | 286 | heard | 330 | stop |
| 199 | along | 243 | didn't | 287 | try | 331 | family |
| 200 | night | 244 | draw | 288 | ways | 332 | form |
| 201 | took | 245 | letters | 289 | pictures | 333 | black |
| 202 | sentence | 246 | told | 290 | money | 334 | others |
| 203 | story | 247 | country | 291 | box | 335 | those |
| 204 | land | 248 | white | 292 | cut | 336 | am |
| 205 | never | 249 | large | 293 | thing | 337 | living |
| 206 | always | 250 | I'm | 294 | far | 338 | horse |
| 207 | sentences | 251 | year | 295 | Mother | 339 | front |
| 208 | play | 252 | letter | 296 | today | 340 | seen |
| 209 | began | 253 | wanted | 297 | cold | 341 | started |
| 210 | give | 254 | fish | 298 | inside | 342 | makes |
| 211 | years | 255 | (2) | 299 | run | 343 | ready |
| 212 | below | 256 | car | 300 | cried | 344 | eggs |
| 213 | boys | 257 | city | 301 | fast | 345 | body |
| 214 | also | 258 | ran | 302 | (4) | 346 | whole |
| 215 | head | 259 | page | 303 | answer | 347 | blue |
| 216 | grow | 260 | spelling | 304 | best | 348 | stood |
| 217 | set | 261 | (3) | 305 | light | 349 | table |
| 218 | paper | 262 | world | 306 | red | 350 | Jim |
| 219 | it's | 263 | eyes | 307 | means | 351 | moon |
| 220 | morning | 264 | high | 308 | hand | 352 | song |

| Rank | Word | Rank | Word | Rank | Word | Rank | Word |
|------|------|------|------|------|------|------|------|
| 353 | miles | 394 | hold | 435 | catch | 476 | carry |
| 354 | baby | 395 | comes | 436 | everyone | 477 | slowly |
| 355 | beautiful | 396 | face | 437 | Tom | 478 | woman |
| 356 | girls | 397 | stopped | 438 | legs | 479 | hole |
| 357 | second | 398 | wind | 439 | A | 480 | remember |
| 358 | above | 399 | window | 440 | grass | 481 | ship |
| 359 | leaves | 400 | done | 441 | Jack | 482 | King |
| 360 | girl | 401 | half | 442 | tried | 483 | stand |
| 361 | sat | 402 | true | 443 | listen | 484 | tiny |
| 362 | bird | 403 | walk | 444 | someone | 485 | friend |
| 363 | town | 404 | dark | 445 | happy | 486 | kept |
| 364 | cannot | 405 | sing | 446 | being | 487 | ride |
| 365 | friends | 406 | summer | 447 | happened | 488 | Sally |
| 366 | walked | 407 | missing | 448 | everything | 489 | tail |
| 367 | fire | 408 | outside | 449 | gone | 490 | seeds |
| 368 | call | 409 | behind | 450 | numbers | 491 | against |
| 369 | plant | 410 | learned | 451 | order | 492 | covered |
| 370 | talk | 411 | open | 452 | sleep | 493 | wood |
| 371 | that's | 412 | book | 453 | strong | 494 | bright |
| 372 | animal | 413 | six | 454 | anything | 495 | cars |
| 373 | important | 414 | glass | 455 | try | 496 | Father |
| 374 | really | 415 | ice | 456 | let's | 497 | game |
| 375 | soil | 416 | coming | 457 | snow | 498 | rest |
| 376 | ball | 417 | start | 458 | tall | 499 | Eddie |
| 377 | hot | 418 | ten | 459 | round | 500 | sets |
| 378 | sky | 419 | five | 460 | Bucky | | |
| 379 | study | 420 | watch | 461 | care | | |
| 380 | ago | 421 | road | 462 | hands | | |
| 381 | spell | 422 | winter | 463 | names | | |
| 382 | looking | 423 | milk | 464 | store | | |
| 383 | stay | 424 | goes | 465 | Ann | | |
| 384 | toward | 425 | gold | 466 | built | | |
| 385 | feel | 426 | rain | 467 | ones | | |
| 386 | young | 427 | river | 468 | hit | | |
| 387 | Bill | 428 | garden | 469 | maybe | | |
| 388 | himself | 429 | Indian | 470 | class | | |
| 389 | tells | 430 | John | 471 | fun | | |
| 390 | fly | 431 | piece | 472 | street | | |
| 391 | (6) | 432 | buy | 473 | space | | |
| 392 | cat | 433 | fine | 474 | bed | | |
| 393 | (5) | 434 | nothing | 475 | complete | | |

Source: "Sight Words for Beginning Readers" by W. Otto and R. Chester, 1972, *Journal of Educational Research, 65,* 436–443. Reprinted by permission.

- Many animals in Australia are *marsupials,* carrying their young in a pouch.
- Marsupials are *mammals* because they *nurse* their young.
- Many of them are also *nocturnal,* sleeping during the day and feeding at night.
- Many of them are *herbivorous,* preferring to eat grasses rather than meat.

Have the students read the sentences as best they can while you supply unknown words. Then discuss with the students definitions that they can derive from the words' use in context. (See Chapter 8 for these procedures.) Compare these definitions to those provided in the glossary of the textbook. Next instruct the students to make up new sentences using the new words. Collect these and place some of them on the chalkboard for the students to read. The new words may be included in a word bank, similar to the personal file box described in the preceding section. Or the students, either individually or as a group, may record the new words in a personal or class dictionary. As the students study new words, they enter them in alphabetical order, writing the words' pronunciation, definition, and context (use in a sentence).

Underachieving readers may need additional practice to learn sight vocabulary. They may need to visualize the word. Ask them to close their eyes and "see" each word in their minds. They may also need more repeated exposures than an average student. Games can be good reinforcement for teacher-directed instruction.

Many commercial games exist for teaching sight vocabulary. It is not difficult, however, to devise simple word recognition games. You can use almost any kind of "universal" game board. "Kangaroo Hop," shown in Figure 6.2, is an example. Two teams or two individuals compete by drawing cards alternately from each of two stacks. Cards from one stack display words in isolation; cards from the other show words in sentences. A die is also rolled. For each word read correctly the team or student advances the number of spaces on the die except when landing on a hazard of some type. (Correctness can be judged by the other students playing the game.) The winner is the first to reach the grasslands.

Young children may enjoy "fishing" for words with a magnet on a string tied to a pole. Magnets are also glued to the back of the word cards, which are in the shape of fish. The child must read any word that he or she "catches." A variation is that the child must create a sentence for the word caught. Again, correctness is evaluated by others playing the game.

Card games, such as Concentration and Old Maid, offer opportunities for students to practice sight words. Instead of matching numbers or pictures, the student matches words. The player must also say the word and use it in a sentence (or read the sentence provided).

*You will note that we have stressed that the games require students to use the words in context. We feel it is a mistake to present words only in isolation. Students constantly need to practice the transfer of recognizing the isolated word to recognizing it in a sentence. If they become accustomed to seeing the word in a sentence, they will be more likely to recognize it when they see it in contextual reading.*

You can also apply the language experience approach (LEA) to teach sight vocabulary. Ashton-Warner (1963) describes an approach used with Maori children in New Zealand that is effective in corrective reading instruction. (It is not appropriate,

**Figure 6.2** Kangaroo Hop Sight Vocabulary Game

however, if you have specific words to teach.) Ask the student to name a word that he or she wants to learn, thereby guaranteeing interest and motivation. Write the word on one side of a card and the student's sentence using the word on the other. The student studies several word cards, all created in the same manner. Assess the student's mastery of these words daily.

You can have your students combine word cards to build sentences and stories. Record the sentences they create onto a language experience chart, which can be read and used for additional practice in sight word recognition.

Instead of starting with the student's word cards, you might employ the more usual LEA procedures described in the next chapter. Briefly, discussion of an event elicits the key vocabulary and concepts related to the experience. (You might show a film, for example, to present vocabulary related to the study of marsupial animals.) The student or group dictates the main ideas, which you record, using students' exact words. Then the student or group reads and rereads the story until word recognition becomes automatic. Usually the student or group recognizes unknown words through the flow of the story, which is highly meaningful because it is a student creation.

Save the stories thus created to be reread frequently. You may also want to make another copy to cut apart into sentence strips or isolated word cards. If a student has difficulty reading the isolated word or sentence, refer that student to the story as an aid to word recognition.

## Contextual Analysis

*What do you do if you do not know a word as you are reading? Be honest! Do you really stop to analyze the word, breaking it into syllables and sounding it out? Most readers don't need to go that far. It is inefficient to analyze a word if you don't need to. Most of us just skip the word and read to the end of the sentence. We usually have that "ah ha" reaction as we realize what the word means. (We may have heard the word spoken but not recognized its written form.)*

Occasionally skipping a word is not necessarily a bad practice. In fact, we are using contextual analysis as an aid to word recognition. This technique of skipping words need not be a deep, dark secret. Children, especially poor readers, often feel that they are somehow cheating if they skip an unknown word. In fact, they are doing exactly what their teachers do in their own reading.

Instruct students to skip an unknown word and read on to the end of the sentence. Then they should backtrack to see if they recognize the word, based on their knowledge of the rest of the sentence. If they think they recognize the word, they should try rereading the sentence with the new word in it to see if it makes sense. If so, they have just successfully applied contextual analysis to recognize a new word. If the sentence does not make sense, they need to move to the next level in the hierarchy of word recognition skills (structural and phonic analyses).

Askov and Kamm (1976) found that teaching a system of context clues (those presented in the Wisconsin Design for Reading Skill Development) produced significant gains in students' abilities to do cloze-type activities. Students were better able to supply words that had been deleted from context. We present further discussion of context clues in Chapters 8 and 9, but we offer a simple system for using contextual analysis for word recognition as follows.

When we read, we use three main cueing systems—semantic, syntactic, and graphic—which help us recognize words and their meanings. We will limit this discussion to word recognition. Developing awareness of these systems helps students use contextual analysis.

***Semantic cueing system.***    The content of a passage provides clues to word recognition; a reading selection about Australian animals would be more likely to contain the word *marsupial* than would a passage about the United States government. Awareness of content, or meaning, is the semantic cueing system. You can adapt the cloze technique, described in Chapter 5, for instruction. Instead of deleting every fifth word delete those words that can be inferred from the context. For example, in the sentence "Flowers bloom in the _____ ," *spring* would be a logical choice because of the context of the sentence. Cloze exercises encourage the student to draw upon background knowledge and experience in supplying deleted words. You must be prepared, however, to accept other plausible answers (such as *garden* or *summer* for the preceding example) that fit the content of the passage or sentence. If using a multiple-choice format for the answers, be sure that only one choice is semantically correct (for instance, *spring, winter, snow, pavement*).

***Syntactic cueing system.*** The function of a word in a sentence (its part of speech) is also a cue to word recognition. For example, in the sentence "Tom ran to the _____ ," we know that the deleted word must be a noun (such as *store*) for two reasons: (a) A noun always follows a determiner (*the, a, an*); (b) The deleted word is the object of the preposition *to,* forming a prepositional phrase. Students who seem to be unaware of the syntactic cueing system—perhaps supplying a verb where a noun belongs—could benefit from work with systematic deletions of a particular part of speech, followed by instruction in the function that it serves in the sentence. Multiple-choice exercises should include choices among different parts of speech (such as *store, jump, on,* and *pretty* for the example above). Students should be able to choose a correct answer by knowing the part of speech. Avoid words, such as *race,* that may serve more than one function in a sentence.

***Graphic cueing system.*** An initial graphic cue may be provided by supplying the first letter or letters of a deleted word, as in "The wombat w _____ across the road." The graphic cueing system cannot be used apart from the other two cueing systems, however, for in this sentence we need to use semantic cueing to know that a wombat is a four-legged animal, not a flying creature. We also need to use the syntactic cueing system to realize that a verb is required. If we supplied *woolly,* we would be ignoring the syntactic cueing system while attending only to the initial graphic cue. We might correctly suggest the verb *waddled,* considering the wombat's physique. (We would also have to accept other answers, such as *wandered* and *went,* as correct.)

Knowledge of the three cueing systems can help you, the teacher, analyze a student's errors in oral reading—we'll see how to do that in the next chapter. The preceding cloze-type exercises can help students become aware of using the three cueing systems consciously. Many poor readers, especially those still needing help with word recognition, tend to rely too heavily on the graphic cueing system while ignoring semantic and syntactic cues. Exercises in contextual analysis can help overcome this problem.

## Structural and Phonic Analyses

When Mandy comes to an unknown word—one that is not part of her automatic recognition vocabulary—she should first attempt to recognize the word through contextual analysis. Initially she should skip the word and read to the end of the sentence; then she should return to the word, considering the semantic, syntactic, and graphic cues. If she still does not recognize the word, she must resort to the next level of the word recognition hierarchy: structural and phonic analyses.

Structural analysis refers to breaking a word apart. Phonic analysis involves sounding out the parts following structural analysis. The two processes thus work together. For the sake of discussion, we will consider each separately. (Practice exercises to help you learn structural and phonic analysis skills may be found in Durkin, 1981, and Wilson and Hall, 1984.)

***Structural analysis.***   Structural analysis may be applied to any word that is more than one syllable in length. Multisyllabic words may be broken into components by two methods:

1. *Morphemic Analysis,* or Using the Meaningful Structure. This involves breaking the word into *meaningful* components. If the separate components are recognized, the student can combine them to arrive at the pronunciation and possibly the meaning of the word. For example, the word *undone* is best attacked by separating it into the root *done* and the prefix *un.*
2. *Syllabic Analysis,* or Using Spelling Patterns. This entails dividing the word into syllables. If the word is multisyllabic but contains no root word, then the student should apply generalizations about spelling patterns to break the word apart into syllables. These patterns assist in pronunciation but do not help the student figure out word meaning. *Skirmish,* for instance, contains no meaningful root; therefore, the word is syllabicated following the syllabic generalization between the *r* and *m.*

*Morphemic analysis.*   A student using the *meaningful structure* in a word recognizes a word's root plus affixes. Some poor readers have no idea how words are made. For them each word is different. They need to understand how words can be built to know how to take them apart in decoding.

At the elementary level you can build the concept of root words by adding inflectional endings to base words. For example, students can try to create as many forms of *walk* as they can by adding *s, ed,* and *ing.* They should also write sentences for each form of the word. Present sentences in which the various forms are used.

- He will walk to school tomorrow.
- He walks to school every day.
- He walked to school yesterday.
- He is walking to school now.

Ask the students to determine what is different in the sentences. Highlight or underline the common element *walk.* You should also point out that the inflectional endings indicate time.

Once students have grasped the concept of a base word with inflectional endings, you might ask them to identify familiar roots in longer words containing affixes (for example, *return, preview,* and *unhappy* ). Carefully select the words to be sure that a meaningful root is present—that the meaning of the word is indeed based on the root. Consider the word *mother.* If children identify *moth* as the root (after all, *er* is a common suffix), not only is the meaning distorted but also the pronunciation. While it used to be common practice for teachers to tell students to look for the "little words inside the big words," teachers today generally avoid this practice because the "little words" may not be meaningful roots. (Fathers, particularly, may object to being called *fat hers!* )

When students are having difficulty in reading text materials in science, social studies, or other content areas, it is particularly important that you identify the most commonly encountered roots in the subject field. Teach these roots thoroughly so that the students will recognize them in various forms (for instance, *astro* as in *astronomy, astronaut,* and *astronomical* ).

A learning center—as described in Dupuis and Askov, 1982, and shown in Chapter 11 of this book (Figure 11.3)—may be set up in the corner of the room for any content area, such as social studies. The students manipulate small cubes, on each side of which is printed a different root related to social studies. On other cubes of a different color are prefixes and on others of still a different color are suffixes. The students can create real and made-up words using the cubes from each of the three categories (prefix, root, and suffix). They must use their real or made-up word in a sentence to show its meaning.

Another type of activity for teaching root words is to have students cut apart word cards into components and sort the parts into piles according to prefix, root, and suffix. The students can then form new words by combining parts for each pile and write sentences for the new words.

Similar procedures may be followed for teaching compound words, which are two roots combined. Sometimes these are easier for children to understand because so many common words can be combined into compound words (*football, bookworm, doghouse* ).

Students enjoy working in small groups (two to four children) on these types of tasks. They see how words can be constructed and, thus, how they may be taken apart for decoding. Students having trouble using phonics especially profit from this approach, because structural analysis is more visual in modality of learning (see Chapter 7).

Using the meaningful structure of words can also help students to decode contractions. Manipulative games, as just described, can provide meaningful practice. Students can match word cards on which the contracted and uncontracted forms are printed (such as *could not* and *couldn't* ). Or the two forms can be printed in random order in two lists, contracted and uncontracted, on a bulletin board. Students can connect the two forms of the same word with pieces of yarn.

Decoding possessives is another type of structural analysis skill based on the meaningful structure in a word. Students easily confuse possessives with contractions and plurals. They need to be taught each separately until they achieve mastery. Then they need to be able to distinguish instances of each. They will experience less confusion if they encounter the forms in sentences.

*Syllabic analysis.*    If a new multisyllabic word does not contain a meaningful root, the student can then only look for *spelling patterns* to decode the word. Divisions based on meaningful structure, however, should take priority over those based on spelling patterns. The patterns are useful only when no meaningful root can be found.

Students must first understand what a syllable is. (As obvious as this seems, even preservice teachers sometimes have difficulty identifying the number of syllables in a word!) Have the students place their hands on their jaws. Every time their jaws drop they are uttering a syllable. Try this now on a mutisyllabic word—even on the word *multisyllabic*—since every syllable contains a vowel sound that causes the mouth to drop open. You should feel your jaw drop, even if you do feel a bit foolish!

Students should also learn that every syllable contains one vowel *sound,* but not necessarily one vowel. For example, the word *reach* contains only one vowel *sound* (long *e*) although it is spelled with two vowels. This can be confusing to students.

The most useful spelling patterns that help students divide words into syllables are the VC/CV, V/CV, and /Cle. *V* stands for vowel and *C* represents a consonant.

In the VC/CV pattern the syllables are divided between the two consonants (as in *vac/cine, scar/let*). Sometimes the double consonants may actually appear to be three consonants because of a consonant digraph (see *Phonic Analysis* following). The consonant digraph is considered a single consonant because the two consonants together make a single sound. Never split a consonant digraph when dividing a word. For example, *hat/chet* follows the VC/CV generalization with *ch* functioning as a consonant digraph.

The V/CV pattern is not as reliable as the VC/CV in producing the correct syllabication, but it is still helpful. Using the V/CV pattern, one would divide *ago* and *decent* before the single consonant between two vowels.

The other generalization frequently taught is /Cle. When a word ends in *le,* the immediately preceding consonant belongs with the final syllable, as in *ta/ble* and *fum/ble.* A frequently occurring exception exists, however, affectionately dubbed by some as the "pickle exception." In the word *pickle, ck* forms a consonant digraph that belongs with the preceding syllable (*pick/le*). When a consonant digraph occurs instead of a single consonant in the *Cle* pattern, divide after the consonant digraph.

**Phonic analysis.**    Remember that structural analysis works together with phonic analysis. The student first uses structural analysis skills to divide a multisyllabic word into meaningful parts or syllables. If syllabication is based upon the meaningful structure in a word, the student may recognize the word once the root and affixes are detected. If so, phonic analysis is not needed. If, however, the student still does not recognize the word, then he or she must apply phonic analysis to sound out each syllable. The student then blends the syllables together to make a complete word, which is tested in context to see if it makes sense.

Usually the short and long vowels are taught early in a phonics program, following instruction in some initial consonants. Vowels combined with single consonants can form simple words. In spite of the fact that vowels are taught early, they seem to cause the most problems for poor readers. Even the poorest readers can usually pronounce single consonants in words, but vowels may completely befuddle them.

Why are vowel sounds so difficult for poor readers? One obvious reason is that each vowel letter has a variety of sounds, not just one, as do many consonants. The rules for knowing which sound to use are complex, and exceptions to the rules further complicate matters.

*We are writing this section in an attempt to simplify phonics instruction. Using research on the utility of various phonic generalizations (Bailey, 1967; Burmeister, 1968; Clymer, 1963; Emans, 1967), we attempt to present only those generalizations with the highest utility—those that work most often when applied to real words. We hold that some phonics practice materials present too many generalizations, almost as if a generalization must be contrived to cover every instance. We believe instead that many words must be attacked by structural analysis or learned as sight words—that phonics simply won't work every time a student needs to decode a word.*

*Short vowels.* A little verse of unknown origin has helped the authors remember the short vowel sounds: "F*a*t *E*d *i*s n*o*t *u*p." Say these words to yourself listening for the short vowel sounds. Children may learn the sounds more easily when they occur in the initial position, as in *a*pple. The short vowel appears most often in the VC or CVC pattern (as in *an* and *can*). This is known as a "closed" syllable, presumably because the final consonant "closes" the syllable.

*Long vowels.* Long vowel sounds are simply the vowel letter names. If you say *a, e, i, o, u,* you approximate the sounds of the long vowels. Three generalizations apply to long vowels:

1. When a syllable ends in a single vowel (CV), the syllable is "open" and the vowel is usually long, as in h*i*, m*e*, fl*y,* and p*i*/lot.
2. When the pattern VCe occurs, the vowel is usually long and the final *e* is silent. In fact, the pattern is usually written as VC¢ to show that the final *e* is silent, as in *dine, late,* and *mute.* Many common monosyllabic words are exceptions (*have, give, done*) that must be taught as sight words.
3. When two vowels appear together in one syllable, called a vowel digraph, the first vowel is long and the second is silent (shown as V̄ʬ). The most common vowel digraphs are: *ai* (b*ai*t), *ay* (r*ay*), *ea* (*ea*ch), *ee* (b*ee*t), *oa* (b*oa*t), and *ow* (gl*ow*). (Be careful, because *ow* can also be a diphthong.) The vowel digraph *ea* is frequently pronounced with the short *e* sound, as in h*ea*d. Students should learn to try the long *e* sound first when encountering *ea* in a word; if that doesn't make sense, they should try the short *e* sound.

*Diphthongs.* Two vowels appear together, as in vowel digraphs, but they blend together instead of one being heard and the other silent. The most common diphthongs are *oi* (bo*i*l), *oy* (bo*y*), *ou* (mo*u*se), and *ow* (c*ow*). Note that *oi/oy* have the same sound and *ou/ow* have the same sound. Students should learn to try *ow* both as a digraph and diphthong to see which fits the context better, because no rule determines which sounding is appropriate.

*Other vowel sounds.*     When an *r* follows a single vowel, it modifies the vowel sound so that it is neither long nor short: *ar* (c*ar*), *or* (f*or*), *er* (h*er*), *ir* (d*ir*t), and *ur* (f*ur*). (Note that *er, ir,* and *ur* all have the same sound.) These are known as the r-controlled vowel sounds.

Other modified vowel sounds occur in the following: *a + l* (ba*l*l), *a + u* (*Au*gust), and *a + w* (s*aw*). These combinations produce a similar modified sound for the vowel *a.* (Sometimes these combinations are classified as diphthongs.)

The *oo* combination may be either short (as in f*oo*t) or long (as in b*oo*t). A ditty to help you remember the two sounds is: "The *foot* is shorter than the *boot.*" The student should try the long sound first to see if a meaningful word is created. If not, the short *oo* sound should apply.

The schwa, a favorite of the authors, is indicated in dictionary pronunciation guides by *ə*. While some reading systems do not teach the schwa, it is perhaps worth knowing that it exists. The schwa sound, the short *u* sound, may be produced by any vowel in an *unaccented* syllable. (It's not a schwa if it's in a single or accented syllable.) Some examples are the *a* in *a*go, *e* in writt*e*n, *i* in beaut*i*ful, and *o* in beck*o*n. The *le* combination frequently has the schwa sound, as in humb*le*.

*Consonants.*     As we have said, poor readers have the most difficulty with vowels. Consonant sounds seem to be less tricky. Again, we believe in simplicity—here are a few generalizations that students need to know.

Two consonants have variant sounds that could cause difficulty for poor readers. The letters *c* and *g* may have either a hard or soft sound depending on the letter following them in the syllable. If an *e, i,* or *y* follows either *c* or *g* in the same syllable, the *c* or *g* has a soft sound. The *c* sounds like an *s* and the *g* like a *j* (as in *c*ertain, *c*ity, and *c*ycle; angel, *g*inger, and *g*ym).

*Consonant blends* occur when two or three consonants blend together in a word. Some consonant blends are *bl* (*bl*ack), *br* (*br*own), *gr* (*gr*ow), *gl* (*gl*ow), *sl* (*sl*ime), *spl* (*spl*ash), *str* (*str*ing). Note that each consonant retains its own sound; the sounds are simply blended together.

When two consonants combine to produce one sound, they are called a *consonant digraph.* While the name suggests similarity to vowel digraphs, the sound produced is usually different from either consonant separately (as opposed to a vowel digraph, in which the first vowel is long and the second one silent). Some common consonant digraphs are *ch* (*ch*urch), *sh* (*sh*ip), *th* (*th*at or *th*in), *ph* (*ph*armacy), *gh* (rou*gh*), *wh* (*wh*isk), and *ck* (che*ck*). (Sometimes *ck* is considered a silent letter combination instead of a consonant digraph.)

Note that *th* has two sounds. This is academically interesting but probably not necessary to teach to students. You can determine whether the *th* is voiced (*th*at) or unvoiced (*th*in) by placing your hand on your throat as you say the words. The voiced *th* causes vocal chord vibration that you can feel with your hand. (Since this is also the

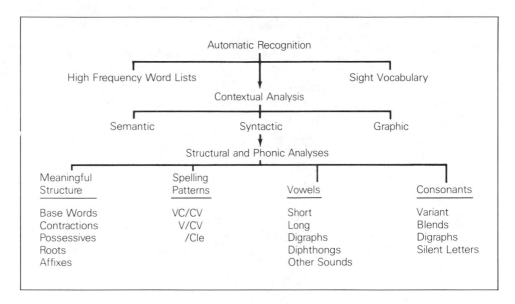

**Figure 6.3** Hierarchy of Word Recognition Skills

international sign to indicate you are choking, don't be too surprised if someone starts pounding you on the back!)

Some double consonants commonly form patterns that contain *silent letters:* *kn* (*kn*ife), *gn* (*gn*aw), *wr* (*wr*ench), *mb* (la*mb*), *tch* (i*tch*). Alert students to the distortion that can occur from trying to pronounce all the letters in silent letter combinations.

*As we said earlier, we have chosen to present only what we consider to be the major phonics generalizations. We have tried to identify from the research literature those with the greatest utility—those that work most often in real words. We believe that poor readers often suffer from the attempts of well-meaning teachers and commercially developed materials to teach generalizations that cover every word. We prefer that students develop larger sight vocabularies of irregular words than to learn phonics generalizations that may apply to only a few words.*

Some phonic elements may be categorized in other ways. Study the generalizations taught in your instructional materials and adapt to the categorizations and terminology used in them. Students need not be burdened with the terminology unless it would help them distinguish among the various phonic elements.

Now that you have studied the hierarchy of word recognition skills, review the hierarchy by examining the schema in Figure 6.3.

## Word Attack Strategies

Students cannot attack irregular words by phonics but should learn them by sight. While they need not memorize words with meaningful roots (as they do sight words) they should incorporate such words into their automatic recognition vocabulary. The nature of the word determines, in large part, which set of skills from the word-recognition hierarchy to apply.

When using the directed reading-thinking activity (described in Chapter 9) you, as teacher, should identify words likely to cause difficulty before assigning a selection to students. Present these words in context—perhaps using sentences from the selection—to the students before they read the selection. They will then be able to read the selection without difficulty, having already become familiar with the new words. But how should you teach students to recognize the new words?

Context, of course, is very important in teaching new words. By presenting new words in sentences, you provide semantic and syntactic cues that would not be available if you presented the words in a list. Perhaps students would recognize the new word *remodeled* by seeing it in this sentence: "Last year the Thomases *remodeled* their house." They would consider the meaning (semantic cues)—what could the Thomases have done to their house that begins with *r?* They would also consider the word's part of speech, or function in the sentence—what action word, or verb, begins with *r?* But contextual analysis may not be enough to help a student recognize an unfamiliar word.

When selecting new words for presentation, categorize each word as (a) a word that contains a meaningful root plus affixes; (b) a word that contains no meaningful root but that would be considered "regular" according to the generalizations of structural and phonic analyses; or (c) a word that contains no meaningful root and is "irregular"—cannot be correctly decoded by structural and phonic analyses. Figure 6.4 shows this categorization graphically.

The strategy you should choose for introducing a given word depends on the word. Consider again the word *remodeled.* Is there a meaningful root with affixes? Yes, *model* is the root word with the prefix *re* and the suffix *ed.* Therefore, you would select Strategy A for that word. The thrust of the instruction would be showing students how to remove affixes to recognize the meaningful root.

Another example is the word *mother.* Since no meaningful root exists in the word, you must then decide whether or not the word is regular. If your students divided the word following spelling patterns (the V/CV pattern yields *mo/ther*), they might not pronounce it correctly since the first syllable is open (ending in a long *o*). Therefore, you have no choice but to follow Strategy C, teaching the word as a sight word. If, on the other hand, the word were *thimble* (also containing no meaningful root), the word could be divided into syllables following spelling patterns (/Cle) and sounded out following phonics generalizations (Strategy B).

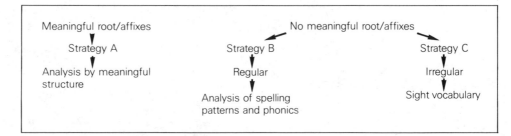

**Figure 6.4**  Word Attack Strategies

You must thus consider each new word, deciding which strategy, beyond contextual analysis, would be most appropriate. This procedure is particularly important for teaching poor readers who are less able to apply word recognition strategies independently. They need direct instruction and guided practice (as described in Chapter 3) to learn how to analyze words.

# Guidelines for Word Recognition Instruction

We have already presented most of these guidelines in earlier sections. We highlight them here to stress their importance in teaching word recognition skills.

*Present new words in context,* not in list form. Poor readers need the benefit of context to help them recognize new words. They often need assistance in using context to their advantage; they need reminders of semantic and syntactic cues.

*Establish visual and auditory readiness* for phonics instruction. In presenting the short vowel sounds, for example, be sure that students can hear the differences in the sounds (auditory discrimination) and can distinguish among their visual shapes (visual discrimination). After presenting the new words in sentences, ask students to listen to the words, with their eyes closed, to identify whether or not they hear a particular vowel sound. They can indicate recognition by raising their hands. If they cannot hear the differences among the sounds, then further skill instruction is pointless. Auditory discrimination is an essential prerequisite to learning phonics generalizations. (See Chapter 7.)

*Provide direct instruction* (as described in Chapter 3) on word-recognition generalizations. As obvious as it sounds, instruction should *precede* practice. Unfortunately, many teachers assume that they have taught a skill because they have "mentioned" it and assigned a practice exercise. They assume that somehow the students will "catch on." The better readers generally do, but they may not have needed the practice in the first place! The poor readers are left to flounder with a workbook exercise they may not understand.

*Follow instruction with guided practice,* both group and individual exercises. Guided practice—practice closely monitored by a teacher—is necessary in learning any skill. Group practice opportunities, such as playing a game or working at a learning center, allow children to help each other in a nonthreatening way. After students have tried a new skill with group support, they need to practice the skill individually to ensure that they have correctly understood instruction. You must monitor individual practice especially closely; that is the time to rectify misconceptions or bad habits. If you allow a student to practice mistakes, then the misconception becomes more firmly rooted. While the students engage in independent practice, quickly circulate around the room, checking progress. A few students may even need to be retaught; if so, interrupt their exercise until you can offer further instruction.

*Vary the methods of presentation.* The inductive method, in which students form a generalization based on seeing specific instances, is appropriate in first presenting a concept. For example, when teaching students to identify the VC¢ pattern, you might present numerous examples of words following that pattern. You would lead students to note that the first vowel is long and the final *e* silent, in contrast to words following the VC pattern (as when comparing *rate* to *rat*). The generalization becomes more meaningful and memorable if the students derive it themselves.

The inductive approach is more time consuming than the deductive approach, in which the generalization is stated for students to apply to specific instances. Often the deductive approach is used with practice exercises, after students have already induced the generalization being taught.

Some slow learners benefit more from the deductive method. They are able to apply a stated generalization, but they may be unable to arrive at the generalization on their own. They benefit from multiple exposures to the same generalization. (See Chapter 14 for guidance on teaching slow learners.)

*Teach for transfer of skills to connected reading.* Once you have taught word recognition generalizations, you are understandably eager for students to apply them in daily reading. In fact, transfer of word recognition instruction to daily reading tasks is most difficult for poor readers. Often they appear to have mastered a skill, but they fail to apply it unless specifically reminded to do so. They need contextual reading that provides many opportunities for specific skill applications. If students have recently learned the short vowel sounds, they should read passages containing many short vowel words. Application of the skill in context during instruction helps this transfer process.

*Teach for skill mastery;* often this involves overteaching. We recommend that teachers use criterion-referenced tests that assess skill mastery both in isolated words and in context. Proper application of a skill in context indicates that students have successfully made the transfer from skill exercises to everyday reading. Only through this type of criterion-referenced tests can you know whether or not the students have really learned what you taught.

*Know when and when not to teach word recognition skills.* If a student encounters an unknown word in an exciting book—perhaps the first book this student has ever read—that is not the right time for a lesson on diphthongs! Supply the word to the student so that he or she can keep the flow of the story, and make a note to teach diphthongs at a later date. Some teachers prefer to offer word recognition instruction at a separate time from directed reading activities so that any drudgery connected with skill learning would not interfere with enthusiasm for reading. The danger of this is teaching skills in isolation, thereby making transfer of skills to the reading process difficult, especially for poor readers. Nonetheless, the point is well taken that sustained reading should not be interrupted when enjoyment and comprehension are the major goals.

*We conclude this discussion of word recognition with the reminder that our distinction between word recognition and comprehension is an artificial one. In reality, the two processes complement each other. They are, indeed, two sides of the same coin. Not only do we need to understand this, but we also need to help our students see that the two processes are closely related.*

# Summary

We have used a natural hierarchy—the sequence that a mature reader follows—in presenting word recognition skills. (Review the hierarchy by studying Figure 6.3.) The mature reader recognizes words as part of his or her automatic recognition vocabulary. If the word is unknown, the reader applies contextual analysis (including semantic, syntactic, and graphic cues). If that does not help in figuring out a new word, the mature reader applies structural and phonic analyses, processes for breaking a word into parts and sounding out the parts.

Strategies for teaching words are determined by whether or not the words contain meaningful structure (such as roots and affixes) or only spelling patterns (forming syllables). The use of phonic analysis is appropriate only if the word is regular, that is, following structural and phonic generalizations. (See Figure 6.4.)

Guidelines for word recognition instruction include: presenting new words in context; establishing visual and auditory readiness for phonics instruction; providing direct instruction on word-recognition generalizations; following instruction with guided practice (group and individual); varying the methods of presentation; teaching for transfer of the skills to connected reading; testing for skill mastery with criterion-referenced tests; and knowing when and when not to teach word recognition skills.

# References

Ashton-Warner, S. (1963). *Teacher.* New York: Simon and Schuster.

Askov, E. N., & Kamm, K. (1976). Context clues: Should we teach children to use a classification system in reading? *Journal of Educational Research, 69* (9), 341–344.

Bailey, M. H. (1967). The utility of phonic generalizations in grades one through six. *Reading Teacher, 20,* 413–418.

Burmeister, L. E. (1968). Usefulness of phonic generalizations. *Reading Teacher, 21,* 349–356, 360.

Clymer, T. (1963). The utility of phonic generalizations in the primary grades. *Reading Teacher, 16,* 252–258.

Dolch, E. W. (1942). *Dolch Basic Sight Word Test.* Champaign, IL: Garrard.

Dupuis, M. M., & Askov, E. N. (1982). *Content area reading: an individualized approach.* New York: Prentice-Hall.

Durkin, D. (1981). *Strategies for identifying words* (2nd ed.). Boston: Allyn and Bacon.

Emans, R. (1967). The usefulness of phonic generalizations above the primary grades. *Reading Teacher, 20,* 419–425.

Goodman, K. S. (1976). Behind the eye: What happens in reading. In H. Singer & R. B. Ruddell (Eds.), *Theoretical Models and Processes of Reading.* Newark, DE: International Reading Association.

Hunt, L. C. (1971). Six steps to the Individualized Reading Program (IRP). *Elementary English, 48* (1), 27–32.

La Berge, D., & Samuels, S. J. (1976). Toward a theory of automatic information processing in reading. In H. Singer & R. B. Ruddell (Eds.), *Theoretical Models and Processes of Reading*. Newark, DE: International Reading Association.

Otto, W., & Askov, E. N. (1972). *The Wisconsin Design for Reading Skill Development, Rationale and Guidelines*. Minneapolis: National Computer Systems.

Otto, W., & Chester, R. (1972). Sight words for beginning readers. *Journal of Educational Research, 65,* 436–443.

Samuels, S. J. (1979). The method of repeated reading. *The Reading Teacher, 39,* 403–404.

Wilson, R. M., & Hall, M. A. (1984). *Programmed word attack for teachers* (4th ed.). Columbus, OH: Charles E. Merrill.

# Check Your Reading Comprehension

1. Obtain a copy of a scope and sequence statement of a basal reader series. Compare the list of skills and objectives to those of the Wisconsin Design for Reading Skill Development.

2. Which word-recognition skills are used most often by fluent readers? Which skills are used most often by less fluent readers?

3. Which word-recognition skills should the classroom teacher emphasize? How does a teacher make such choices?

4. What guidelines should the teacher follow in planning word-recognition instruction?

5. Matching exercise:

_____ 1. Fluency

_____ 2. Sight vocabulary

_____ 3. High-frequency word lists

_____ 4. Repeated readings

_____ 5. LEA (Language Experience Approach)

_____ 6. Contextual analysis

_____ 7. Semantic cues

_____ 8. Syntactic cues

_____ 9. Graphic cues

_____ 10. Phonic analysis

a. A strategy for building fluency in reading; the student reads the same material repeatedly.

b. A method of decoding words based on clues in the environment of the word.

c. Words that are recognized instantly.

d. Lists of core words that are used throughout children's reading materials (e.g., Dolch list).

e. Usually the first letter or letters of an unknown word, as an aid to word recognition.

f. A method of decoding words based on meaningful structures (morphemic analysis) and/or spelling patterns (syllabic analysis).

_____**11.** Structural analysis

Answers:

| | |
|---|---|
| 1. h | 6. b |
| 2. c | 5. j |
| 3. d | 4. a |
| 9. e | 10. k |
| 8. g | 11. f |
| 7. i | |

**g.** The function of an unknown word in a sentence (its part of speech) as an aid to word recognition.

**h.** The easy flow of word recognition in which virtually no thought is given to the recognition processes.

**i.** Content or meaning of a passage as an aid to word recognition.

**j.** A strategy for increasing fluency, in which words (and passages) are suggested by the child.

**k.** A method of decoding words based on letter-sound generalizations.

**6.** Imagine yourself a third-grade teacher. You will be planning a reading lesson including the following words: _cowboy, horse, herd, corral, mustang, lariat, stallion, bucked, galloped, mare, roan, canyon, ridge._ What would be the most appropriate word attack strategy for each word?

**7.** Plan a word recognition lesson for a group of your children needing help with one of the following skill areas: automatic recognition, contextual analysis, structural analysis, or phonic analysis.

# 7

# Diagnosing and Teaching Word Recognition Skills

Now that we have provided a framework for word recognition skills and some suggestions for teaching them, we will next look at how you can determine where a student's strengths and problems lie. In Chapter 5 you learned about the informal reading inventory (IRI), which you can use to determine a student's reading level and thereby select reading materials at the appropriate level of difficulty. (You should probably review the IRI reading levels and scoring in Chapter 5 before reading the rest of this chapter.) Now we will show you how to derive further information about a student's reading strengths and weaknesses by using miscue analysis, which may be based on an IRI.

# Miscue Analysis

Miscue analysis arose from the realization that not all oral reading errors are of equal importance. Consider the following example:

| | |
|---|---|
| Print: | The canary is in its cage. |
| Tom reads: | The bird is in its cage. |
| Dick reads: | The cannery is in its cage. |
| Harry reads: | The can run is in its cat. |

While all students read the print incorrectly, are all errors of equal magnitude? Tom, though not reading the correct word or even using a word beginning with the correct letter sound, did have the correct meaning in mind. In other words, while he did not use the graphic cues by reading the correct word, *canary,* he derived the correct meaning of the sentence—semantically, Tom made no error. He also chose a word that was syntactically correct. *Bird* and *canary* belong to the same part of speech—they have the same function in the sentence.

On the other hand, Dick chose a word that began with the correct letter sound and that was the correct part of speech, but whose meaning did not fit the rest of the sentence. Dick was responding to the graphic and syntactic cues but ignoring the semantic cue. Harry appeared to have distorted even the graphic cue—although his substitution did begin with the correct letter sound. He also substituted a verb phrase for a noun (subject of the sentence) and lost the meaning altogether.

So which student's error is the most serious? Most teachers would agree that Harry's was the most serious. He responded only partially to the graphic cue—the initial consonant in the word—while ignoring the syntactic and semantic cues. Dick's error was also serious because he too ignored the semantic cue, although he did use the syntactic and graphic cues correctly. Tom committed the least serious error in that he ignored only the graphic cue while using the semantic and syntactic cues. These cueing systems, discussed in Chapter 6 under Contextual Analysis, can help teachers analyze a student's reading.

*In Chapter 8 we will discuss the stages of learning to read (Chall, 1983). In the first stage the child acquires accurate decoding skills—becomes "glued to print." Tom's error, therefore, is highly improbable since as a competent reader he would not ignore the printed word so blatantly. Our point is, however, that Tom reads the way we, as mature readers, do. We sometimes do not read each word accurately, but we do keep the meaning intact.*

Because all errors are not equal, Goodman & Burke (1972) have substituted the term *miscue* for *error.* Some miscues are acceptable, especially those that are semantically correct—those that retain the meaning of the sentence. A student's reading a sentence in dialect is also considered an acceptable miscue. (For example, "We are going" might become "We be goin'," in black dialect. See Shannon, 1983, for further information.) An unacceptable miscue is one in which the meaning is distorted, as in the cases of Dick and Harry.

Goodman & Burke (1972) have devised the *Reading Miscue Inventory,* which helps teachers analyze patterns of miscues to determine a student's strengths and weaknesses in reading. While a useful instrument, it is too time consuming for the classroom teacher to administer (Pikulski & Shanahan, 1982). Various simplifications have been devised; we have chosen to present procedures adapted from those used in the Madison, Wisconsin, Metropolitan School District.

## Procedures

Be sure that material used for the miscue analysis is at an instructional reading level or slightly above—that is, generally appropriate for classroom use. Research (discussed by Pikulski & Shanahan, 1982) indicates that the types as well as the amount of oral reading errors change when the student reaches frustration level, the level at which the reading material is too difficult. The student tends not to use the context clues employed with easier materials. Therefore if you use frustration level material in performing a miscue analysis, the miscues may not be typical of those made with instructional level materials.

Because the sample of miscues from an IRI is limited to those passages at the instructional level or slightly above, many teachers prefer to make the miscue analysis a separate endeavor from the IRI. In fact, Pikulski and Shanahan (1982) recommend keeping the two analyses separate. The IRI provides quantitative information; miscue analysis provides quantitative information about students' strengths and weaknesses. While both types of information are valuable, their separate functions should not be confused.

The student reads a complete story (at instructional level) aloud. Approximately 25 miscues are necessary for meaningful analysis. It may, therefore, be necessary to have the student read more than one story, perhaps on different days. The student then retells all that he or she can remember from the reading(s).

Tape record the oral reading so you can analyze the miscues later. Keep a running tally of the miscues, as discussed in Chapter 5 regarding IRIs. Analyze the miscues by entering them in a chart like that shown in Figure 7.1.

Dick's response to reading "The canary is in its cage" is shown in Figure 7.1. A minus (−) indicates that he did not attend to the semantic cueing system—he ignored the meaning of the sentence. A plus (+) indicates that the miscue was syntactically correct (the correct part of speech). Because the miscue was similar graphically (it began and ended with the same letters), a plus (+) was also placed under "Graphically Correct." Dick did not correct himself; therefore, a minus (−) was recorded in the column labeled "Self-Corrections." A check (√) under "Repeated Miscues" indicates

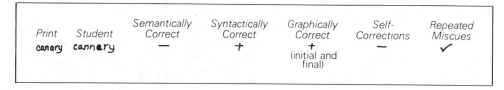

**Figure 7.1** Miscue Chart

that he made the same miscue again later in the selection. If that column had not been checked, he either did not encounter the word again or read it correctly the next time.

If your students speak a nonstandard dialect, you might add another column—"Correct in Dialect." In our example "We be goin'," instead of "We are going," *be goin'* would be the miscue. Pluses (+) would appear in all columns to indicate that the miscue is semantically, syntactically, and graphically correct as well as correct in the student's dialect.

When you have analyzed at least 25 miscues, you may begin to see a pattern by adding the number of pluses (+) in the semantic, syntactic, and graphic columns. If we assume that Dick's 25 miscues consisted of 11 that were semantically correct, 15 syntactically correct, and 24 graphically correct, we conclude that he is overly dependent upon graphic cues at the expense of the other two cueing systems. He ignores the meaning of the sentence while relying too heavily upon phonics in recognizing words. He correctly used syntactic cues only about half the time.

The self-correction score indicates how closely Dick is monitoring his own comprehension. Even though his rendition of the material did not make sense, he corrected his miscues only twice. He seemed unaware that reading ought to make sense. Dick's score, then, may be taken as an indication of his level of metacognitive awareness of the reading task. (See Chapter 8 and Yussen, Matthew, and Hiebert, 1982, for further information on metacognition and reading.)

You can also analyze the student's retelling of the story. Rather than questioning the student, ask him or her to retell the story from memory. The number of details provided as well as the correct sequence of events and main ideas indicate how well the student comprehended the story. Of particular importance is whether the miscues have affected the student's comprehension. Dick, for example, was totally unaware that the passage was about a bird as he retold the story.

## Interpretation

From filling in miscues in a chart, as shown in Figure 7.1, and calculating the total number of miscues in each category, you can judge the relative utilization of each cueing system. Good readers use all three cueing systems. Poor readers tend to rely too much on one to the exclusion of the others. We will discuss the implications of each commonly found pattern as follows. These generalizations are probably not exactly accurate for individual students, but they may provide some guidance for you as a teacher.

***High semantic/syntactic, low graphic.*** Tom's oral reading miscues followed this pattern. He has strengths that can be used to advantage in planning corrective reading. He attends closely to the meaning of what he is reading. He makes good use of context clues. In fact, he is so intent upon the meaning that he tends to be careless about reading the printed words. His reading is usually characterized by many omissions and additions, most of which, however, do not change the meaning. His substitutions, likewise, are meaningful ones. Mispronunciations or nonsense words do not occur at the instructional level. He recognizes most words by sight. If he does not know a word instantly, he either omits it or substitutes another word that fits the meaning of the sentence.

Students like Tom tend to be at least of average learning ability or better; sometimes their imaginative renditions of the reading material may be more interesting than the printed material itself. Meaning, however, remains paramount. Usually the syntax of the sentence remains intact.

Tom's retelling of the story is detailed and accurate. He uses the words he has substituted rather than the printed words, but the meaning is intact.

Tom's carelessness about the words he actually reads may not be apparent except when he reads orally. It may go undetected if he is required to do only silent reading.

***High graphic, low semantic.*** Dick's oral reading is heavily reliant on the graphic cues. He substitutes words that are similar in their beginning and ending sounds and of similar configuration. Because he attends closely to what is printed, he does not often make omissions or additions. His substitutions do not make sense; his reading is also characterized by mispronunciations or nonsense words. His reading tends to be conducted laboriously in a word-by-word fashion, as if he is reading words in a list rather than connected discourse. His notion of reading is "saying the words" rather than grasping meaning. He tends to analyze all words, even those that he should know by sight.

His syntactic score is better than Harry's but lower than Tom's. Dick is not especially aware of syntax because he is not thinking of the meaning of what he is reading. Some of the time, however, his substitutions are the correct part of speech, probably because he follows the graphic cues closely. For example, if a word ends in *ly*, he might substitute another word with the *ly* ending and thereby correctly use an adverb (*quickly* for *quietly*).

His retelling of the story is vague and inaccurate. His version focuses primarily on a few words he remembers. From these he tries to piece together, largely unsuccessfully, a scanty story.

***Low semantic/syntactic/graphic.*** Harry appears to use none of the cueing systems successfully. His reading is generally filled with mispronunciations, probably even more so than Dick's, which indicates that he does not perceive reading as a meaning-getting process. He has even more problems than Dick because his attempts to use the graphic cueing system are largely unsuccessful. The few words he does recognize are those he knows by sight. Remediation will be a long-term process for Harry.

His retelling of the story is also vague and unsuccessful. He does not even use complete sentences in his version, but hesitantly suggests a few words as an outline for the story.

## Corrective Instruction

It is probably obvious that the corrective instruction to be offered in each instance ought to be different. Once you have determined on which cueing system the student is relying you can plan appropriate corrective instruction.

***High semantic/syntactic, low graphic.***     Tom's major strengths lie in his strong comprehension and use of context clues. He is good at monitoring his own comprehension of what he is reading—his metacognitive knowledge of his own reading can assist in the corrective process.

First, Tom needs to become aware that he is not reading words correctly. You could raise his level of awareness by having him critique his own oral reading. He should record on tape a passage he has already read silently. Then he should listen to the tape, following along in the passage. He should mark any miscues with a pencil. Further experiences in critiquing his own oral reading should make him aware of the importance of reading what is printed.

You could teach Tom to pick up graphic cues using a modified cloze technique with an initial graphic cue. Delete key words, except their initial letters (for example, "The c_____ is in its cage"). Tom should have no difficulty using surrounding context to supply an appropriate word beginning with the given letter. Since the cloze is used here for instruction rather than as a test, you need not delete every fifth word but rather the more meaningful words.

As Tom's teacher you must determine whether Tom's lack of use of the graphic cueing system is due to an ignorance of letter-sound relationships or carelessness. If the latter, the awareness activities already described are probably sufficient.

On the other hand, if Tom's failure to use the graphic cueing system is from a lack of knowledge, he needs thorough instruction in word attack skills. You should encourage Tom to continue his use of contextual analysis, but explain to him that structural and phonic analyses are also important in attacking unknown words. Because Tom does attend to the meaning, instruction in the meanings of roots and affixes may help him with not only word recognition but also word meanings.

Expanded automatic recognition is always a goal, but Tom also needs to acquire the skills that will help him unlock words not in his sight vocabulary.

***High graphic, low semantic.***     Because Dick is heavily dependent upon the graphic cueing system, and because he is somewhat successful in using letter-sound relationships, Dick's instruction does not need to focus primarily on structural and phonic analyses. As Dick's teacher, however, you would face the challenge of convincing Dick that reading is a meaning-getting process. A mind-set for reading as merely a decoding process is very hard to overcome.

A variation of the cloze technique can help the student to identify the significant words in a sentence by using context cues. Ask Dick to cross out with a marking pen those words in a passage that are important and essential to meaning. Have another student with similar needs perform the same task on another selection. They then exchange papers and try to fill in the deleted words. They can check the cloze exercises together, discussing the importance of each deleted word.

You can also construct cloze exercises from Dick's own written material or language experience stories that he has dictated to you. Because he has written the reading material, it is highly meaningful to him. Again, the cloze technique requires him to focus on the meaning of what he is reading.

Another technique is to have him stop his reading after each sentence or paragraph and paraphrase what he has read. If he is unable to restate the passage in his own words, ask him literal comprehension questions focusing on *who, what, where,* and so forth. Study guides (see Chapter 10) may also help Dick pick out the important information from a passage and understand that reading is a meaning-getting process.

Because Dick reads in a word-by-word manner, he also needs help with fluency. He can benefit from repeated readings of material at his independent reading level. The emphasis should be on inflection appropriate to the meaning of what he is reading. He can critique his own oral reading using a tape recorder, read aloud to younger children as described in Chapter 6, or perhaps practice reading a script for a puppet show. The focus should be on conveying the meaning through proper expression.

To overcome his word-by-word reading, encourage Dick to do lots of silent reading at his independent reading level. For him to build fluency in word recognition—to expand his automatic recognition of words and break the habit of analyzing every word—the material must be easy for him. Encourage him to read as quickly as possible, possibly by some type of reward chart for the number of books read. But either you or a parent should talk with him daily about the books to ensure that he is comprehending.

Dick, like Tom, may also benefit from instruction in roots and affixes. He needs to be encouraged to search for the meaningful components in words rather than to rely exclusively upon letter-sound relationships.

A puppet show helps these readers develop fluency. (Photo by Joseph B. Bodkin)

***Low semantic/syntactic/graphic.***    Harry does not have the benefit of Tom's able use of context and meaning in word recognition. Nor does he have Dick's command of letter-sound relationships in using the graphic cueing system. Harry thus needs a complete and thorough instructional program that covers what he appears to have missed during initial instruction. He may have received the instruction before he had acquired the basic readiness skills. Or it may be that Harry is a slow learner. (See the guidelines provided in Chapter 14.)

His reading instruction needs to incorporate a complete word recognition program, focusing on all word recognition skills in the hierarchy described in Chapter 6. Awareness of meaning should also be fostered through directed reading-thinking activities and comprehension checks, as described in Chapter 9.

A study of the patterns of reliance on the various cueing systems, as shown in this section, will help you plan appropriate corrective instruction. Through miscue analysis you can also identify strengths and weaknesses in word recognition skills. Just as you like activities that you do well—whether they include roller skating or reading—so students have more positive feelings about instruction that is matched to their strengths. You need to be aware of these strengths and use them while you are bolstering the weak skills.

# Word Recognition Skills

We will now look at the skill areas presented in Chapter 6 to note how you might identify strengths or weaknesses in each area, using a modified miscue analysis, and how you can conduct corrective instruction. Review the hierarchy of word recognition skills presented in Figure 6.3 of Chapter 6 before proceeding.

## Automatic Recognition

Fluent reading is a good indicator of strength in the automatic recognition of words. The student does not laboriously sound out words but recognizes most words instantly, including the high-frequency, irregular words.

A student who is weak in automatic recognition may guess words at random, guess words based on an initial graphic cue, or use phonics to decode familiar words that should be instantly familiar. Such a reader does not even recognize by sight high-frequency words, such as those shown in Table 6.1, nor words that have been repeated throughout the instructional materials. We'll now consider how to deal with both a limited sight vocabulary and a tendency to analyze all words.

***Limited sight vocabulary.***    Most preschool children learn a few words by sight, usually in association with a favorite cereal, advertisement, or television show. This recognition is primarily a paired associates learning task (Gough & Hillinger, 1980), in which the word is learned in association with some object. The child recognizes the word because of its shape or some unusual feature within the word or because of its consistent presentation in a certain color or typeface, as in an advertisement.

Most young children do not have difficulties recognizing highly memorable words of such distinctive shapes as *elephant* with several ascenders and descenders. Nor is *look* a problem if they are taught that "two eyes are looking at them." But many children have difficulty with the short, functional words, with which no object may be associated, and which lack distinctive features. Words such as *our, are,* and *in* have neither vivid associations nor distinctive features to make them memorable.

When children enter school they must learn by sight many more words, especially those short, functional words. They can no longer recognize words just by association with a picture or advertisement. As the children are expected to learn more and more new words it becomes more difficult for them to identify distinctive features for all the words (Gough & Hillinger, 1980). It becomes necessary to use other strategies, such as phonic cues, in learning new words.

Since phonics is often taught using words that children have learned to recognize by sight, we are back to the original problem of how to develop sight vocabulary. Frequently memorable words are paired with pictures, such as *cat* with a picture of Morris. But this approach is limited to words that stand for objects.

Another technique commonly used to teach sight words focuses on the configurations or shapes of the words. Children draw boxes around the letters to give a word a distinctive shape, such as elephant . They try to match words with their configurations in practice exercises. This technique builds visual discrimination of words while expanding sight vocabulary.

The difficulty with configuration exercises is that some words have the same configurations. While bed is sometimes taught as being in the shape of a four-poster bed, bad , unfortunately, is the same shape. Therefore, use configuration cues sparingly as a visual discrimination exercise and a means of encouraging students to observe distinctive features of words. Many students, for example, confuse *then* and *when.* Configuration cues for those words should make the difference apparent ( then and when ).

***Overanalysis of sight vocabulary.***   Some students inappropriately try to analyze words that should be part of their sight vocabulary. They overemphasize phonics as a word attack skill and have a mind set that reading is primarily a decoding process. Their reading lacks fluency as they try to sound out every word.

Corrective instruction can include the games and activities for sight-vocabulary development described in Chapter 6. Flash cards may be sent home to enable parents to assist in drill. It is important for the student to say the words as fast as possible to ensure that words are recognized by sight rather than analysis. A good technique is to record each student's time and accuracy in identifying a given set of flash cards each week. The student can keep these records on an individual progress chart and receive stickers or rewards when he or she attains mastery level (perhaps 90 percent correct in 50 seconds).

The words on flash cards should also appear in sentences, the reading of which is also timed. Transfer of the isolated words to use in context is extremely important.

## Context Clues

A student who substitutes words in oral reading that are semantically acceptable is using context clues effectively. A student weak in using context clues usually relies too much on the graphic cueing system, losing the meaning of the sentence.

Context clues are of two types: global and local (Gough, Alford, & Holley-Wilcox, 1978). The global context refers to the book, chapter, or passage in which an unknown word is embedded. The local context refers to the sentence in which the word appears.

An example will clarify this distinction. The word *run* appearing in an article about baseball has a different meaning than it has in a Heloise column on the care of stockings. The global context thus provides semantic cues for words with multiple meanings as well as other words. The local context provides syntactic cues in addition to semantic cues, because the unknown word is used as a particular part of speech; it has a particular function in the sentence. Within the baseball article *run* could logically be either a noun or a verb.

A student who uses context clues effectively responds to both the global and local contexts—to both the semantic and syntactic cueing systems. A student who does not use context clues effectively probably attends to neither type of context. Instructional activities should focus on both semantic and syntactic cues.

You can effectively adapt the cloze technique for corrective instruction by deleting some of the important, meaning-bearing words, especially those used repeatedly. Focus discussion on the reasons that certain choices are appropriate or inappropriate considering the global context or semantic cueing system.

Likewise, you can employ the cloze technique to develop awareness of the local context using the syntactic and semantic cues. Again, instead of making random deletions, delete words of a particular part of speech, such as verbs. This makes students sensitive to the function of the word in a sentence, which helps limit the number of possible words that could apply.

If students experience difficulty with deletions of a particular part of speech in sentences, try to build awareness of the function of the part of speech in a game format. On an index card, print an adjective, for example, followed by a space for a deleted word (the red _____ ). On small strips of paper print other words, some of which have the functions of the deleted words and some which do not (*hat, dress, blue, run, fast, pretty*). The student must sort through the strips of paper to identify those that could follow the word on the index card. Focus discussion on whether the various combinations "sound right."

You should also provide direct instruction in the types of context clues, which we discuss in Chapters 8 and 9.

## Structural Analysis

A student demonstrates strength in the use of structural analysis by being able to break an unknown, multisyllabic word into meaningful components (roots and affixes) or syllables. A weakness in this area is evident when a student refuses to attempt to pronounce a multisyllabic word or makes a wild guess, perhaps based only on the initial graphic cue. This student does not understand the structure of words and is unable to recognize familiar roots.

Corrective instruction should focus first on using the meaningful structures— roots and affixes. Systematically teach the meanings of common morphemes (the smallest meaningful parts of words). Focus activities on building words by putting together prefixes, roots, and suffixes.

Teach readers to break apart words that do not contain roots by using spelling patterns to divide the words into syllables (syllabic analysis). Poor readers, however, may have difficulty applying syllabic generalizations because of their abstractness. It may be more effective to teach them to look for common syllables in words, such as *ake, at, al, an, ain, ope, er, ite, ast,* and *est.* These may be taught in single syllables by consonant substitution of the initial grapheme (p*al,* g*al,* S*al,* H*al* ). Later these may help the student to recognize multisyllabic words, such as mod*al*ity.

## Phonic Analysis

Many students have trouble applying phonics generalizations to recognizing words in context. Therefore, we suggest instruction in only a limited number of generalizations (Chapter 6). Nevertheless, it has been well-established that children who receive phonics training are better readers (Chall, 1967). (See Chapter 8 for a more complete discussion.)

Some students have difficulty with phonics because they lack the essential auditory discrimination readiness skills. A student who cannot hear the differences in letter sounds (or who has not yet learned to discriminate among them) will have difficulty learning phonics generalizations. Phonemic awareness tasks should precede phonics instruction, especially for young children, as the phonemic awareness tasks do not require reading or writing. Lewkowicz (1980, pp. 687 – 688), using the International Phonetic Alphabet, lists ten tasks that have been identified in the research literature for developing phonemic awareness.

1. *Sound-to-word matching.* "Does *fish* start with /f/? Does *dog* end with /g/?"
2. *Word-to-word matching.* "Does *fish* start with the same sound as *feather?* Does *dog* end like *pig?*"
3. *Recognition of rhyme.* "Does *fish* rhyme with *dish?*"
4. *Isolation of a beginning, medial, or final sound.* "What is the first sound of *fish?* What is the last sound of *dog?*"
5. *Phonemic segmentation.* "What are the (three) sounds in *fish?*"
6. *Counting the phonemes in a word.* "How many sounds to you hear in the word *fish?*"
7. *Blending.* "What word is this—/f/, /ɪ/, /š/?"
8. *Deletion of a phoneme.* "Say *fish.* Now say it without the /f/."
9. *Specifying which phoneme has been deleted.* "Say *meat.* Now say *eat.* What sound was left out of the second word?"
10. *Phoneme substitution.* "Say meat. Now say it with /f/ instead of /m/."

Lewkowicz (1980) identifies blending and segmentation as the basic phonemic-awareness tasks. The isolation of the initial phoneme is especially useful preparation for learning segmentation. She also identifies two basic principles of teaching segmentation (p. 693): (a) that pronunciation of the word to be segmented should be very slow so that the student can hear the separate sounds; (b) that the student must also do the slow pronouncing in order to receive articulatory as well as auditory clues.

Lewkowicz (1980, p. 696) also suggests "having some kind of visible, manipulatable representation of the sounds of the word to clarify and guide the task for the beginner." This manipulative representation, such as squares to count the number of phonemes, enables the student to keep track of the sounds as they are heard or spoken.

Lewkowicz (1980) further suggests that encoding, or writing, not just decoding, is a natural follow-up to the phonemic-awareness tasks. Some schools, in fact, are now using this technique in the early grades. Children are encouraged to write, attempting to spell words independently as they sound. Letter-sound correspondences are reinforced as the child systematically attempts to write a word. The teacher supplies the correct spelling of words above the child's version only for those words that have been explicitly taught. The child is thus freed from the burden of having to spell all words correctly, able to learn to write independently, and given practice with letter-sound relationships through writing. (Phonetic spelling is described in greater detail in Chapter 12.)

Students who have trouble hearing the differences among sounds and learning phonics generalizations may profit from phonemic awareness training. While they are receiving this training, they can be taught to read through another modality (see later in this chapter).

Now that we have considered corrective instruction in word-recognition skills, we need to know how to implement this instruction. Once you have identified a problem area, how do you monitor progress so that both you and the student know that improvements are being made?

# Diagnostic-Prescriptive Instruction in Word Recognition Skills

Students with reading difficulties usually have been taught word recognition skills, but for some reason they have not learned them. This may be because many teachers do not teach to the point of mastery. They teach a particular skill as long as the instructional materials direct or until most of the students appear to have grasped it and then move on to a more difficult skill for which the first skill may be a prerequisite. Students who never mastered the first skill fall further and further behind those of average reading ability. Feelings of failure and despair may complicate what might have been at one time a minor reading problem.

A diagnostic-prescriptive approach to instruction can prevent this snowballing effect. According to a diagnostic-prescriptive model, skills are taught until students reach mastery (judged by their getting, perhaps, 80 percent of the items correct on a criterion-referenced test). Students who reach mastery move on to new instruction; those not reaching mastery receive more intensive instruction, perhaps with a different approach.

This type of model can adapt to a variety of programs for teaching word recognition skills. The Wisconsin Design for Reading Skill Development (Otto & Askov, 1972) is one example of a system built on a diagnostic-prescriptive model. The Design should be implemented on a school-wide basis to monitor progress of all students through important instructional objectives. (Word attack objectives are listed in Appendix D.)

Similarly, the Crawley Diagnostic Reading Schedule (Cole & Chan, 1981) may help teach individuals who are having difficulty learning word recognition skills. Objectives are provided for reading readiness, sight vocabulary, phonic analysis, and structural analysis. Underneath each objective is a grid, as shown in Figure 7.2.

To use the Crawley Schedule, select from a list of word recognition objectives, such as those in Appendix D, those objectives most appropriate for a given student with reading problems. (A student like Harry is obviously lacking mastery in almost all word recognition generalizations. But you would select only those that he needs to learn first to progress beyond recognition of initial consonants.)

Prepare test materials as specified by the objective. In the example in Figure 7.3 the teacher prepares a list of 20 words, half of which contain $\bar{e}\bar{e}$ and half of which have $\breve{e}$ in the medial position. You would usually prepare more than the number specified in the objective, creating an item pool, so that you could randomly draw items for any test form from the pool.

Next determine the levels required for mastery for each objective in terms of accuracy (proportion correct) and rate (seconds). In Figure 7.3 the mastery level for proportion correct was set at 18/20, recorded in the box next to criterion; the mastery level for rate was set at 20 seconds, recorded in the box next to criterion for seconds.

Given a list of twenty words, ten of which contain the $\bar{e}\bar{e}$ combination in the medial position and ten with a short $\breve{e}$ vowel in the medial position, the learner selects and reads those with the $\bar{e}\bar{e}$.

|  | 1 | 2 | 3 | 4 | 5 | 6 | sessions |
|---|---|---|---|---|---|---|---|
| criterion | $18/20$ | $12/20$ | $14/20$ | $18/20$ | $18/20$ | $18/20$ | proportion correct |
| performance | $7/20$ | $11/20$ | $15/20$ | $18/20$ | $19/20$ | $18/20$ |  |
| criterion | 20 | 60 | 40 | 20 | 35 | 20 | seconds |
| performance | 75 | 55 | 38 | 45 | 30 | 18 |  |

**Figure 7.2** Crawley Diagnostic Reading Schedule; Word Attack Skills (Copyright 1981, Peter Cole and K. S. Chan. Crawley: University of Western Australia. Reprinted by permission.)

Test each student as specified in the objective to gather baseline or pretest data. Write the accuracy, or proportion correct (7/20 in Figure 7.3), and the rate in the number of seconds (75 in Figure 7.3) in the performance boxes underneath the previously specified criterion boxes.

A discrepancy between criterion and performance indicates a need for instruction. The performance shown in Figure 7.3 was considerably below each criterion, so each criterion for the first instructional session was adjusted to be more realistic and obtainable (12 out of 20, or 60 percent, in 60 seconds). At the end of the first instructional session, the teacher readministered the test, again randomly drawing items from the pool. The student's performance improved to 11 out of 20 accuracy in 55 seconds. These scores were recorded in the boxes next to performance.

Since the student's performance improved, the teacher raised each criterion for the next instructional session (although not yet to mastery levels): 14 out of 20, or 70 percent, in 40 seconds. The student can suggest a criterion that might be realistic for the next instructional session. Thus, the teacher and student work together to improve the student's scores.

When using this schedule with a group of students, instruct all those students needing help with a particular skill. Complete the assessment after instruction quickly but individually. You can save time by having the students keep their own records. They should also be involved in goal setting, that is, establishing the criteria for accuracy and rate in the next instructional session. They may display the results on graphs or charts (as shown in Figure 7.3) to provide visible evidence of progress.

You should generally set accuracy levels between 80 and 90 percent (100 percent is usually unrealistic). You can obtain realistic time estimates by having a competent reader of the same age perform the objective. Measuring performance within time constraints is extremely important in building automaticity of skills (see Chapter 8 and La Berge and Samuels, 1976). Many poor readers can apply particular word recognition skills, given ample time, but their levels of skill development have not reached the stage of being automatic. Until automaticity is attained, they are unable to apply the skills fluently in contextual reading.

On the surface it might appear that such intensive diagnostic-prescriptive instruction would become tedious. But you can introduce the element of chance by randomly drawing items for any given test out of an item pool. Students who have failed to learn reading skills do not ordinarily find the repeated tasks boring. In fact, the experience of success gives them the incentive to learn. Remember, success breeds success. Overlearning is necessary to ensure that the student will retain the mastery demonstrated on one or two occasions.

*Since corrective reading programs must be built on the needs of individual students, one program is obviously not appropriate for all students. We are skeptical of claims that any instructional program or materials can be a "cure" for all students' reading programs. Diagnostic-prescriptive instruction at an appropriate level may be a long process for some students. We suggest, therefore, early intervention. Diagnostic-prescriptive instruction enables a teacher to spot problems early and to correct them while they are still minor.*

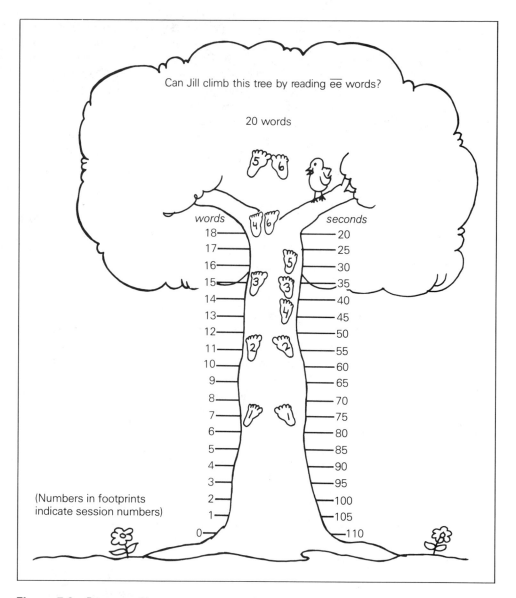

**Figure 7.3** Progress Chart

# Learning Modalities

In spite of good diagnostic-prescriptive corrective instruction, occasionally a student does not learn. It may be necessary to refer that student to a reading specialist or school psychologist for a more complete diagnosis of problems that may be impeding progress.

Some students, however, can learn if taught through a particular modality. The issue of learning modalities is controversial, and evidence of their existence and importance in instruction is in dispute; nevertheless, some students with reading difficulties seem to have a particular modality as a strength through which instruction may best be offered. (A good discussion of the conflicting research studies and implications for instruction may be found in Spache, 1976.) Several tests of learning modalities (for example, Barbe & Swassing, 1979; Mills, 1970) exist, but they measure modalities in different ways and hence may yield different results.

Students who learn well in the auditory modality profit from phonics instruction. They acquire an automatic recognition vocabulary by sounding out words until they have seen the words often enough to recognize them instantly. These students generally have little trouble learning to read.

Students strong in the visual modality can acquire an automatic recognition vocabulary through the techniques described in Chapter 6 under "Sight Vocabulary." While developing other word recognition skills, such as phonics, expand the students' sight vocabulary simultaneously through the strength in the visual modality. Also teach skills in contextual and structural analyses, which depend primarily on the visual modality.

If the student does not appear to learn through either the auditory or visual modalities, approach instruction through the tactile/kinesthetic modality; reinforce the visual approach by having students trace words in a sand or salt tray. (These procedures are similar to those recommended by Fernald, 1943.) The students first copy a word from an index card in a cake pan filled with sand or salt, saying the word while writing. When they can write the word without copying it, they do so in the sand or salt, again saying the word. Finally, the students write the word on paper while saying it. Students may also benefit from tactile/kinesthetic reinforcement in learning structural analysis skills (roots, affixes, common syllables). Since these procedures are slow, try to move students to a visual approach as soon as possible. Tactile/kinesthetic reinforcement can be especially effective with highly distractible or learning disabled students.

Informal observation of a student's approach to recognizing and learning new words may reveal a strength in a particular modality. Although most students do not show much modality preference, some with reading difficulties do show a strong preference. Offering reading instruction through these children's strengths while building up their weak areas seems to make sense as part of the diagnostic-prescriptive process.

## Approaches to Reading Instruction

You have now seen how a teacher can use diagnostic information gleaned from a variety of sources to plan instruction focused on students' word recognition needs. This instruction is carried out within a classroom reading instructional program. Usually you choose an instructional approach, or combination of approaches, that best meets the needs of each reading group. (Occasionally an individual within a group will not respond to your selected strategies. If you cannot find some other approach that works for the individual, then you must call in outside help, such as the reading specialist.)

We present the various approaches to reading instruction by their emphasis—whether on getting meaning or on decoding (as in Figure 7.4). Rarely are approaches kept pure in the classroom; this categorization is for discussion purposes.

| Meaning-getting Emphasis | | Decoding Emphasis |
|---|---|---|
| Language experience (LEA) | Basal reader | Phonics |
| Individualized reading | | Linguistics |

**Figure 7.4**  Approaches to Reading Instruction

We consider these approaches especially as they apply to teaching poor readers. More information on the approaches may be found in various textbooks related to reading (for example, Miller, 1984).

## Basal Readers

Basal readers vary in their emphasis. Some emphasize decoding skills while others stress meaningful context as an aid to word recognition. Usually the teacher's overview to the series indicates the emphasis in a particular basal series.

The problem with basal readers is also an advantage—namely, that they are basic, intended for any child of a given chronological age. This feature makes them easy to use with average learners in a typical setting. They become less satisfactory, however, when used in atypical situations, such as at an Indian reservation school.

Usually a teacher does not have a choice of basal readers. We do know of one school district that adopted two series—one emphasizing decoding and the other emphasizing meaning-getting—in an attempt to accommodate students' various learning needs. This situation is unusual; more often teachers use the officially adopted basal series with average and better readers but use an older, discarded series with poor readers because it is perceived to move at a slower pace.

If you have access to but one basal reading series, you may use readers at different levels in an attempt to provide appropriate reading materials for students at various levels. But consider our fifth-grade students in Chapter 1. How appropriate can a second-grade basal reader be for Tony, who is learning disabled but an otherwise normal fifth-grade boy with eleven-year-old interests? Simply matching the reading level of the basal reader to the reading level of the students is usually not appropriate with severely disabled readers. Basal readers are most appropriate for average readers, those not deviating far in either direction from grade-level placement.

Tactile/kinesthetic learning. (Photo by Ben Chandler)

## Language Experience Approach (LEA)

In using LEA, first introduce some sort of stimulus, perhaps a pet brought from home, a field trip, or a movie. Sometimes an object in the room, such as an aquarium, becomes the stimulus. Discussion following the stimulus is important in bringing out the vocabulary and concepts to be used. The student (or students) dictates a story that recaps the main ideas from the discussion. Record the story on a chart or chalkboard. Because the story is written by the student, he or she has little difficulty with word recognition. Upon encountering an unknown word, the student rereads from the beginning to recapture the flow of the story, usually recognizing the word from the ample clues in the context.

After the student has reread the story several times for several days, select high-utility words from the story to present in isolation and in new contexts. You can also teach word recognition skills using words from the student's story.

*We consider LEA to be a very appropriate instructional strategy with poor readers. Students are usually motivated by their own writing, particularly when their stories are bound together in a "book" to be shared with other students in a classroom library. The teacher can present the word recognition skills needed by the children, not necessarily those presented in a basal workbook.*

Encourage students to do their own writing to record their ideas. Urge them to spell words as well as possible using their word recognition skills. Independence in these attempts is important in helping students apply their skills. Reading and writing complement each other; development of one benefits the other. Daily writing programs, used frequently in some parts of the United Kingdom, Canada, and Australia, seem to improve the development of word analysis skills in reading.

LEA must be supplemented with other readings—written not only by other children in the classroom but by established children's authors. Reading books to the children can stimulate discussion and creation of LEA stories. Reading appropriate books on their own encourages students to apply their growing skills independently. Individualized reading forms a natural follow-up to LEA as children mature in their reading.

## Individualized Reading

Individualized reading, like LEA, emphasizes meaning as a cue to word recognition. Students select their reading material, read at their own pace, and discuss the material in individual conferences with the teacher. This approach works best after readers have reached some proficiency in reading, about a second-grade reading level.

Group students having similar needs for skill instruction. Students may also work together in groups to plan sharing activities, such as a puppet show to depict scenes from a book.

Individualized reading includes students' silent reading, followed by an individual conference at the completion of a book. In the conference, check the student's comprehension through questions and discussion. You might ask the child to read a portion aloud to check application of word-recognition skills. The final step in the conference is selection of another book with guiding questions and prereading motivators (Hunt, 1971).

A variation of this approach is SSR, Sustained Silent Reading (McCracken, 1971). As a supplement to another approach SSR offers students daily opportunities for uninterrupted reading. Students do not necessarily have to make book reports or even discuss their books with others. They simply read at a given time during the day. The teacher might keep a record of the number of books read or time spent reading outside class to encourage further reading. SSR has proven useful in building fluency in application of reading skills. It is based on the premise that students learn to read by reading—"practice makes perfect."

Poor readers, if properly motivated, can become "hooked on books" (Fader, 1976) in an individualized reading approach. As they develop fluency in reading, it becomes less frustrating. They may enjoy one book in a series, which leads them to do further reading in the series. A teacher's efforts are rewarded when students choose reading as a leisure time activity outside school because their interest has been aroused during SSR.

Appendix C contains a list of some fine children's books that you might want to include in your classroom library to support individualized reading and SSR.

*We heartily endorse meaning-getting approaches for the poor readers in your classroom. Because reading has not been pleasurable or easy, poor readers often avoid it. We have found that making reading personally meaningful to students has made them* want *to read. Increased reading time results in improved reading skills.*

## Phonics

Phonics emphasizes the decoding process (refer to Figure 7.4). Basal readers usually employ an *analytic* approach to teaching phonics. Children first learn whole words by sight; after they have learned several words containing the same sound, they are led to generalize about the sound made by a particular letter or letter combination. Some children, especially in special education classes, however, are unable to learn phonics by the analytic approach. These children benefit from *synthetic* phonics programs, in which they learn each letter sound separately and then learn to blend the sounds together.

The difference between these approaches to teaching phonics may be illustrated by the following example. In the synthetic approach children would not learn the word *cat* until they had learned each letter sound separately. They would then be taught to blend "kuh-ă-tuh" by saying the sounds together quickly. By contrast, in the analytic approach children might learn the word *cat* as a whole in association with a picture. After they had also learned such words as *can* and *cow,* their teacher would ask them to conclude what sound is the same in all three words. These words would then become the basis for teaching the *c* sound.

The synthetic approach is deductive—the teacher tells the children the phonics generalization and lets them apply it to new words. The analytic approach is usually inductive—the children draw the generalization after being presented with specific examples. Some children seem to need the structure of the synthetic approach, finding it difficult to draw generalizations on their own. They may also benefit from the more intensive drill and practice of the synthetic approach.

Research (Guthrie, 1977) on the Follow Through program, which followed Head Start children through the elementary grades, indicates mixed results on the various approaches to instruction for these high-risk students. In general, however, a synthetic phonics approach (Distar) produced higher reading achievement. (See Carnine and Silbert, 1979, for more information.) This particular program has become popular for special education children and for children who don't seem to be able to learn to read by any other method. Only a small group of children may be taught at a time and without interruption.

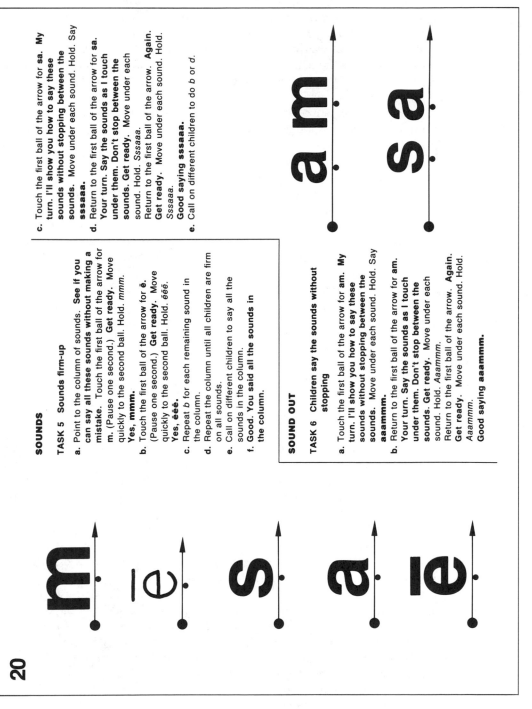

## SOUNDS

### TASK 5   Sounds firm-up

a. Point to the column of sounds.  **See if you can say all these sounds without making a mistake.**  Touch the first ball of the arrow for m. (Pause one second.)  **Get ready.**  Move quickly to the second ball. Hold. *mmm.*  **Yes, mmm.**

b. Touch the first ball of the arrow for **ē.** (Pause one second.)  **Get ready.**  Move quickly to the second ball. Hold. *ēēē.*  **Yes, ēēē.**

c. Repeat *b* for each remaining sound in the column.

d. Repeat the column until all children are firm on all sounds.

e. Call on different children to say all the sounds in the column.

f. **Good. You said all the sounds in the column.**

## SOUND OUT

### TASK 6   Children say the sounds without stopping

a. Touch the first ball of the arrow for **am.  My turn. I'll show you how to say these sounds without stopping between the sounds.**  Move under each sound. Hold. Say *aaammm.*

b. Return to the first ball of the arrow for **am.  Your turn. Say the sounds as I touch under them. Don't stop between the sounds. Get ready.**  Move under each sound. Hold. *Aaammm.*
Return to the first ball of the arrow.  **Again. Get ready.**  Move under each sound. Hold. *Aaammm.*
**Good saying aaammm.**

c. Touch the first ball of the arrow for **sa.  My turn. I'll show you how to say these sounds without stopping between the sounds.**  Move under each sound. Hold. Say *sssaaa.*

d. Return to the first ball of the arrow for **sa.  Your turn. Say the sounds as I touch under them. Don't stop between the sounds. Get ready.**  Move under each sound. Hold. *Sssaaa.*
Return to the first ball of the arrow.  **Again. Get ready.**  Move under each sound. Hold. *Sssaaa.*
**Good saying sssaaa.**

e. Call on different children to do *b* or *d.*

Distar reading instructional materials. (From *Reading Mastery: Distar® Reading 1, Presentation Book A* (p. 126), by Siegfried Engelmann and Elaine C. Bruner. Copyright © Science Research Associates, Inc. 1983, 1974, 1969. Reproduced by permission of the publisher.)

*We recommend that synthetic phonics be reserved for those who seem to be unable to grasp phonics through an analytic approach. These children can usually be identified by the end of first grade. Some schools have successfully used synthetic phonics programs for high-risk students identified in kindergarten.*

Phonics in either the analytic or synthetic form is part of almost every school reading program today. Research in the 1960s, while producing mixed results in terms of the best approach to reading instruction, indicated that early, intensive phonics programs produced higher reading achievement (Chall, 1967). As a result of these research findings most basal reader systems incorporated more phonics instruction earlier in their reading systems. By the time children reach the upper elementary grades they have very likely had quite a heavy dose of phonics.

*We are convinced that some children, because of auditory processing problems or some other factor, are simply unable to learn to read by applying phonics generalizations. The senior author recalls one junior high school (special education) boy who, after one year of synthetic phonics instruction, still said* ah *for the* ă *sound. When his reading teacher switched to a sight approach reinforced by tracing, he not only learned the words in his LEA stories but he also recognized the words in new contexts and retained them the following year. As a rule of thumb, if students have had phonics instruction (as most students today have had) and they are still unable to apply phonics generalizations in attacking new words by the end of fourth grade, we recommend a sight approach, accompanied by tactile/kinesthetic reinforcement.*

## Linguistics

Linguistic approaches to reading have been handicapped by confusion of terminology. Almost every basal reader claims to be "linguistic," or to follow linguistic principles. What is meant is that the materials reflect a knowledge of the structure of our language.

When we speak of the linguistic approach to reading instruction, however, we think primarily of the materials that have been developed on the basis of the work of C. C. Fries (1963). Known as the Merrill *Linguistic Readers,* the materials emphasize decoding rather than meaning-getting in the initial stages, but through the visual modality. Students learn the word *cat,* for example, as a whole word. They also learn *fat, mat,* and *Nat* in the same lesson. Through instruction in the *at* spelling pattern, students learn new words by "minimal contrasts"—that is, by learning new words that differ only in one letter. The sounds are not isolated or taught synthetically. The first lesson from the teacher's edition is shown in Figure 7.5.

After children have mastered the basic decoding skills, the linguistic materials place greater emphasis on meaning. By the end of second grade they appear similar to a basal reader system. They still introduce new word elements by spelling patterns, but they also stress comprehension. By the upper elementary grades the linguistic readers are almost indistinguishable from the other basal readers.

The linguistic approach has been effective primarily with high-risk children and those who have had difficulty with basal readers. It is particularly successful with those children who have difficulty learning phonics or with nonnative speakers, who are

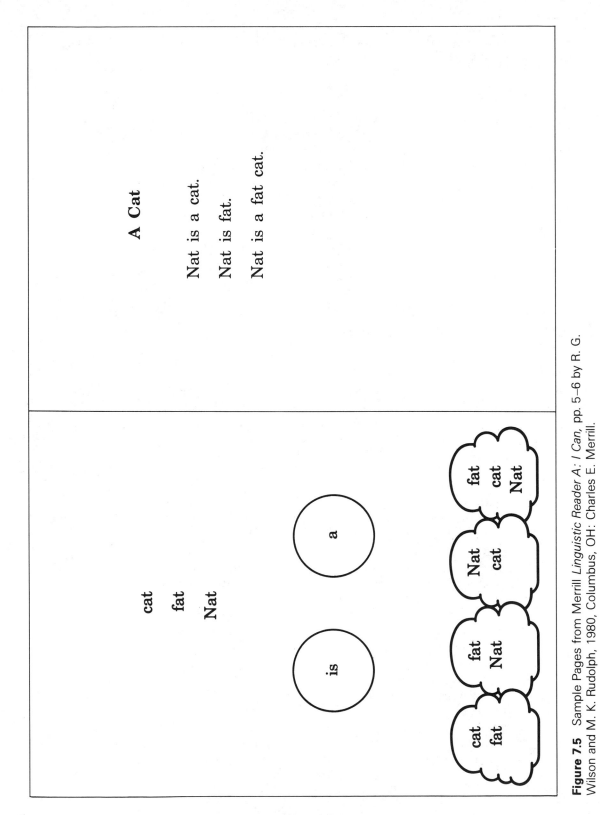

**Figure 7.5** Sample Pages from Merrill *Linguistic Reader A: I Can*, pp. 5–6 by R. G. Wilson and M. K. Rudolph, 1980, Columbus, OH: Charles E. Merrill.

often confused by phonics because the sounds in English are different from those in their native language. Because children easily learn spelling patterns, and hence words following those patterns, they experience some immediate success. It is more structured and controlled than LEA but less meaningful to the individual reader.

Let us sum up this discussion of instructional strategies by saying that most poor readers benefit from some combination of decoding and meaning-getting activities. Basal readers, which have both elements, are popular for teaching average learners but have limited usefulness for teaching poor readers.

*Therefore, we endorse an eclectic philosophy, using anything that works. No single instructional approach works with every child, nor is every teacher equally adept with every approach. Our advice is that you have a variety of approaches to instruction in your "bag of tricks." You must be sensitive to the needs of individuals to decide upon the most effective strategy for each learner.*

# Teaching Word Recognition Skills to Underachievers

Good teachers constantly monitor their students' learning through observing daily written and class work as well as through periodic tests. A teacher working with students with reading difficulties must especially adhere to the principles of effective instruction described in Chapter 17. Underachieving readers need to *see* their progress in tangible ways. It is not enough to tell them that they are "doing a good job." Individual progress charts can fulfill this need.

Underachieving readers perform better if they feel that the corrective process is a "team effort" between the teacher and student. Corrective instruction ought to be done with them, not to them. It is important for poor readers to understand where their problems lie and how they can overcome these problems. They need to understand *why* they are learning this particular skill or doing that particular practice exercise.

Not only should they participate in the decision making as much as possible, but they should also be asked to make judgments about their own reading abilities. Asking them to help set a criterion or goal helps them evaluate their abilities. Of course, some students are unrealistic about their reading abilities; a teacher must help them set attainable goals to prevent further discouragement.

Try to encourage students to monitor their own reading. When a student makes self-corrections in oral reading, these efforts ought to be praised—indeed acclaimed! Self-corrections indicate that the student is monitoring his or her own comprehension. When a student says "This just doesn't make sense," credit that student with realizing that the reading process has somehow broken down.

Similarly, students need to learn to think about which word recognition skills are appropriate in what situations. Encourage them when they use various strategies appropriately. All teachers should have the goal of independent learning in mind as they help students acquire word-recognition skills.

# Summary

While an IRI provides information regarding a student's reading levels, miscue analysis helps a teacher identify a student's strengths and weaknesses in reading. The teacher may also determine whether a student is relying primarily on one cueing system—semantic, syntactic, or graphic—or using all cueing systems appropriately.

Strengths and weaknesses in each of the word recognition skills may be identified with appropriate corrective instruction planned for each skill. Good corrective instruction is based on a diagnostic-prescriptive model with an emphasis on mastery. Reading instruction should be offered through the student's strengths, especially if a learning modality strength or weakness is present, while the weak skills are being developed. Teachers should involve students in decision-making in their instructional programs to encourage growth of self-monitoring and independence.

The various approaches to reading instruction range from a meaning-getting emphasis to a decoding emphasis. The basal reader approach includes both emphases; the language experience approach (LEA) and individualized reading stress meaning-getting; and the phonic and linguistic approaches emphasize decoding.

# References

Barbe, W. B., & Swassing, R. H. (1979) *Teaching through modality strengths: concepts and practices.* Columbus, OH: Zaner-Bloser.

Carnine, D., & Silbert, J. (1979) *Direct instruction reading.* Columbus, OH: Charles E. Merrill.

Chall, J. S. (1967). *Learning to read: the great debate.* New York: McGraw-Hill.

Chall, J. S. (1983). *Stages of reading development.* New York: McGraw-Hill.

Cole, P. G., & Chan, K. S. (1981). *Crawley diagnostic reading schedule; word attack skills.* Crawley: University of Western Australia.

Engelmann, S., and Bruner, E. C. (1983). *Reading Mastery: Distar Reading I, Presentation Book A.* Chicago: Science Research Associates, p. 126.

Fader, D. (1976). *The new hooked on books.* New York: Berkley.

Fernald, G. (1943). *Remedial techniques in the basic school subjects.* New York: McGraw-Hill.

Fries, C. C. (1963). *Linguistics and reading.* New York: Holt, Rinehart & Winston.

Goodman, Y. M., & Burke, C. L. (1972). *Reading miscue inventory.* New York: Macmillan.

Gough, P. B., Alford, J. A., Jr., & Holley-Wilcox, P. (1978). Words and contexts. Paper presented at the National Reading Conference, St. Petersburg Beach, Florida.

Gough, P. B., & Hillinger, M. L. (1980). Learning to read: an unnatural act. *Bulletin of the Orton Society, 30,* 179–196.

Guthrie, J. T. (1977). Research views: Follow Through: a compensatory education experiment. *The Reading Teacher, 31* (2), 240–244.

Hunt, L. C. (1971). Six steps to the Individualized Reading Program (IRP). *Elementary English, 48* (1), 27–32.

La Berge, D., & Samuels, S. J. (1976). Toward a theory of automatic information processing in reading. In H. Singer & R. B. Ruddell (Eds.), *Theoretical Models and Processes of Reading*. Newark, DE: International Reading Association.

Lewkowicz, N. K. (1980). Phonemic awareness training: what to teach and how to teach it. *Journal of Educational Psychology, 72* (5), 686 – 700.

McCracken, R. A. (1971). Initiating sustained silent reading. *Journal of Reading, 14* (8), 521 – 524, 582 – 583.

Miller, W. H. (1984). *Teaching elementary reading today.* New York: Holt, Rinehart & Winston.

Mills, R. E. (1970). *The teaching of word recognition.* Black Mountain, NC: The Mills Center.

Otto, W., & Askov, E. (1972). *The Wisconsin Design for Reading Skill Development; rationale and guidelines.* Minneapolis: National Computer Systems.

Pikulski, J. J., & Shanahan, T. (Eds.). (1982). *Approaches to the informal evaluation of reading.* Newark, DE: International Reading Association.

Shannon, A. (1983). Diagnosis, remediation, and management of reading miscues among children of limited English proficiency. *Reading Improvement, 20* (3), 224.

Spache, G. D. (1976). *Diagnosing and correcting reading disabilities.* Boston: Allyn and Bacon.

Yussen, S. R., Matthews, S. R., & Hiebert, E. (1982). Metacognitive aspects of reading. In W. Otto & S. White (Eds.), *Reading Expository Material.* New York: Academic Press.

# Check Your Reading Comprehension

1. How do the functions of the IRI and miscue analysis differ?

2. What is meant by each of the following statements:
   a. Not all errors are equal.
   b. Good and poor readers differ in respect to the cueing systems they use.
   c. One program of corrective instruction is not appropriate for all students.
   d. Reading instruction should be offered through a child's strong modality (while building up the weak areas).
   e. Corrective instruction should be perceived (by the student) as a "team effort."

3. *Matching Exercise:* Look carefully at each *Problem Statement* and match it with one of the *Possible Solutions.* There is more than one correct answer for some of them. Remember, these are hypothetical situations and you have very little information about the problem. In your own classroom you would have much more background knowledge concerning each child's reading strengths and weaknesses.

*Problem Statements:*

_____**1.** The child's reading is very choppy and lacks fluency.

_____**2.** The child uses initial and final phonic cues but not medial cues. For example, the child substitutes *horse* for *house.*

_____**3.** The child reads well orally but afterward cannot recall information from the selection.

_____**4.** The child's errors show very little use of context cues. For example, the child substitutes *it* for *and.*

_____**5.** The child's errors usually involve the endings of words or syntactic cues. For example, the child substitutes *barked* for *barking.*

_____**6.** The child is extremely nervous when asked to read orally.

_____**7.** The child makes very few errors. The substitutions made show correct use of semantic cues (eg., *house* for *home* ). The child's comprehension skills are also good.

_____**8.** The child stops to "sound out" most words. Very few errors are made but the reading is quite slow and labored.

*Possible Solutions:*

**a.** The child is probably trying to read material that is too difficult. Try easier material and begin to work on all word recognition skills.

**b.** The child should be encouraged to stop often and recall what was just read.

**c.** Activities that emphasize the endings of words would probably help. For example: The (cat, case, cats) moves very quietly.

**d.** The child could practice "echo reading" with a tape recording by the teacher.

**e.** The child could continue in a developmental reading program.

**f.** Activities that emphasize the middles of words could be effective. For example: The d_g caught his b__e and barked happily.

**g.** The child should have prior warning and be allowed rehearsal time.

**h.** The child should be in a program that emphasizes sight vacabulary.

Answers:

| | |
|---|---|
| 4. a,b | 8. h |
| 3. b | 7. e |
| 2. f | 6. d,g |
| 1. a,d | 5. c |

# Energy and Food Chains in the Ecosystem

Birds fly. Rabbits run across a field. Squirrels collect nuts for winter. These animals carry on ~~digestion~~ *direction* and these animals breathe. They do many things to stay alive. They need energy to do ~~these~~ *those* things. This e*sc*nergy comes from food and can be called food energy.

In an ecosystem, food is made by green plants. Green plants are called the pro*sc*ducers. **Producers** can make their own food. They use sunlight, water, and carbon ~~dioxide~~ *divide* to make food.

Animals are called the consumers. **Consumers** cannot make their own food. They must get their food energy by eating ~~other~~ *those* things.

One way for an animal to get food energy is to eat plants. Some animals, like hawks, ~~do not~~ *don't* eat plants. They must get their food energy by eating animals. They are ~~predators~~ *people* of other animals. Some animals, like vultures, do not eat plants and also are not predators. They eat animals that have already died. Animals that eat dead animals are called ~~scavengers~~ *scouts* (SKAV uhn juhrz).

**Decomposers** (dee kuhm POH zuhrz) are living things that feed on dead plants and animals and cause them to decay or rot. Decom*sc*posers are usually ~~protists~~ *Protected*. Decom*sc*posers help to ~~return~~ *give* to the Earth materials that were part of living things. Without

**Figure 7.6** Energy and Food Chains in the Ecosystem. From Sund, R. B., Adams, D. K., & Hackett, J. K. (1980). *Accent on science.* Columbus, Ohio: Charles E. Merrill, pp. 157–160. Reprinted by permission.

decomposers, some needed materials for life would never be returned to the Earth. Materials could not be used again by other living things. Soon there would be no materials left for living things.

Producers and consumers make up food chains. Food energy passed from one living thing to another is a **food chain**. ~~Every~~ Each community has a food chain. **SC** There may be many separate food chains in an ecosystem. Why is the work of decomposers important to food chains?

Trees grow in a forest. A cricket eats some of the leaves on the trees. A frog eats the cricket. A raccoon eats the frog. The raccoon dies and is ~~eaten~~ ate by a vulture. These living things make a food chain. In this food chain, the trees are the producers. The cricket, frog, ~~raccoon,~~ rabbit, and vulture are the consumers. The vulture is a consumer called a scavenger. **SC** Why is the vulture called a scavenger?

The vulture **SC** did not get all the food energy that was in the ~~leaves~~ food the cricket ate. Each animal in the food chain used some of the energy for its life needs. The last living thing in a long food chain gets very little of the food energy made by the producers.

The sun supplies the energy that ~~starts~~ begins all food chains. Plants change this energy into food energy. Without this constant **SC** supply of energy, food chains could not be started.

You are a ~~member~~ Part of many food chains. You are a consumer in these food chains. Name the living things in one food chain to which you belong.

**4.** Imagine that you have had a student read the selection entitled, "Energy and Food Chains in the Ecosystem" (Figure 7.6 on pages 162–63). The material was previously judged to be on the child's instructional level. All substitutions made by the child are indicated. If the child corrected the error, this is also marked (SC). Create a miscue analysis chart like the one in Figure 7.1. Analyze the child's reading. What patterns do you see? What type of word recognition instruction would you prescribe? (Note: To simplify your practice, a shorter selection with fewer errors has been used. In an actual situation, remember that at least 25 miscues should be obtained to make the analysis meaningful.)

**5.** Choose a selection appropriate for one of the poorer readers in your class. Follow the same procedure as in #4. Devise a corrective instruction plan for the child based on the data you have collected.

**6.** In Chapter 10 a variety of study guides are discussed. One is the pattern guide. Complete the following pattern guide summarizing some of the information from this chapter:

| Approaches to Reading Instruction | Emphasis | Characteristics | Advantages | Disadvantages |
|---|---|---|---|---|
| 1. Basal Reader | | | | |
| 2. LEA | | | | |
| 3. Individualized Reading | | | | |
| 4. Phonics | | | | |
| 5. Linguistics | | | | |

# 8

# Words to Meaning: Easing the Transition

The focus in the two preceding chapters (Chapters 6 and 7) is on words—developing word attack skills and strategies. The focus in the next three chapters (Chapters 9, 10, and 11) shifts to meaning—developing comprehension and study strategies and skills. We agree with the position taken by increasing numbers of people who do reading-related research and theory building that reading—particularly learning to read—is a two-stage process. One stage is *decoding*, where the reader attends mainly to converting printed letters to sounds; the other is *comprehending*, where the reader gives more attention to attaching meaning to the spoken or silently decoded words.

We particularly like the way Bateman (1983) gets to the heart of the matter:

True, we read for the purpose of extracting meaning from print. However, to say so overlooks the vital fact that early reading (and some if not all, of later reading) is a two-stage process. In reading an alphabetic language we first convert the print to sound (words) and then we attach/derive meaning from the spoken word or its silently decoded equivalent. Phonics has nothing to do with helping us attach or derive meaning from a spoken word such as "blip." It has everything to do with helping us know that the letters b-l-i-p say "blip" and do not say "pig" or "girl" or "bid" or "lip" or anything but "blip." (p. 111)

*In other words, if you don't get the words, you can't get the meaning.*

Once one accepts the notion of reading as a two-stage process, the implication for corrective teaching is clear: First see to efficient decoding, and then move on to effective comprehending. In the chapters that precede and follow we offer suggestions on doing just that. But in the present chapter we talk about making the transition from decoding to comprehending a smooth one, which is very important to subsequent success in reading.

In her classic book, *Learning to Read: The Great Debate,* Chall (1967) suggested that the facts of beginning reading fit a developmental theory better than a single-process theory. She argued that the data from formal studies and from classroom experience indicate that the first task in learning to read is to learn the relation between sounds and letters—decoding; and the second task is to read for content and meaning. At the time, Chall's position conflicted with the prominent single-process position that, because beginning and more mature reading are essentially the same, meaningful reading is to be emphasized from the start. Now, some 15 years later, the intensity of the great debate has subsided and, whatever the reasons, the position that Chall articulated so eloquently is widely accepted.

*We take our stand with the title of this chapter, "Words to Meaning: Easing the Transition." We think the two-stage theory makes sense in light of the data on children's reading development and that the implications for teaching reading are clear. But we also think that if it is important for teachers to shift the emphasis of their teaching from decoding to comprehending as children progress from stage one to stage two, then it is doubly important to give attention to the transition from stage one to stage two.*

For teachers, the transition mainly involves a shift in emphasis from words to meaning; for children, the transition also involves a shift from oral to silent reading. A reader who fails to make that transition successfully is likely to bog down at a relatively primitive stage of reading development. Our two main purposes in Chapter 8, then, are to put the transition into an overall framework of reading development and to discuss certain requisites of a successful transition.

First, we present and describe Chall's (1983) six stages of reading development in order to place the transition in an overall scheme of reading development. These are briefly listed here:

- *Stage 0. Prereading.* This spans all of a young child's development before formal reading instruction begins.

- *Stage 1. Initial Reading or Decoding.* The beginning reader learns to associate letter forms and letter sounds.
- *Stage 2. Confirmation, Fluency, Ungluing from Print.* The developing reader learns to use decoding skills and to seek meaning from context. This is the *transitional* stage that we stress in the discussion that follows.
- *Stage 3. Reading for Learning the New.*
- *Stage 4. Reading for Multiple Viewpoints.*
- *Stage 5. Reading for a World View.* In the latter three stages the developing reader becomes more and more sophisticated in using reading to seek new information, to meet personal needs, and to reach new levels of understanding.

Next, we describe a method—repeated reading—for easing the transition by helping the student develop fluency. Finally, we discuss some techniques for vocabulary development that are timely and appropriate for aiding the transition to fluent, meaningful reading.

*In stressing the notion that reading—particularly the teaching of reading—is a two-stage process we do not mean to suggest that reading should ever be meaningless word calling. But we do mean to say that the first emphasis should be on decoding; the content should be familiar and comprehensible enough to assure understanding while the reader gives attention to the letters and sounds.*

## The Transition in Perspective

Chall (1983) puts the transition from words to meaning into an overall perspective in her book *Stages of Reading Development.* She suggests a scheme of the six developmental stages of reading we just mentioned. The six stages are essentially an amplification of the two-stage theory mentioned early in the chapter introduction.

We briefly summarize each of Chall's six stages. Our own comments follow each stage. Special emphasis is given to Stages 1 and 2 because that is where the need for a transition from words to meaning is clearly established. Chall suggests the age/grade equivalent for each stage; but she warns that the equivalents are only approximations to be "considered hypothetical, based on current educational achievements and practices" (Chall, 1983, p. 13).

## Stage 0. Prereading: Birth to Age 6

This stage covers the period from birth to the beginning of formal education. The research on reading readiness strongly suggests that many abilities, knowledge, and skill acquired at the prereading stage are substantially related to success in early reading—for example, ability to discriminate and name letters of the alphabet and inclination to "pretend" to read a book.

*Many children who come to need corrective help got pushed into formal reading instruction before they were "ready." But how can a teacher know*

*when a child is ready? Unfortunately, there is no pat answer. There is no such thing as "general reading readiness." But there is such a thing as having the ability, knowledge, and skill to respond to specific instruction. Teachers at all levels must be sensitive to their students' readiness to respond to forthcoming instruction.*

*Harry, one of the children described in Chapter 7, is probably still at Stage 0 in his reading development. He seems to know that printed words can convey meaning, but he has no useful notion of how it happens. His attempts to "read" are attempts to attach spoken words to printed words, but without any appreciation for the clues to meaning that are supplied by the printed letters and words.*

## Stage 1. Initial Reading, or Decoding: Grades 1–2, Ages 6–7

The beginning reader's task at this stage is to learn the letters of the alphabet and to associate them with corresponding parts of spoken words—to associate letter forms with letter sounds. This learning proceeds from an awareness of what letters are for, knowledge of how to decide that "blip" is not "pig" or "boy" or "lip" or "flip," and ability to decide when a mistake has been made. Sometimes new readers' efforts at this stage are disparagingly referred to as "grunting and groaning" or "barking at print" because more attention is given to pronouncing words than to their meaning. But here Chall takes an important position. She argues that Stage 1, where the new reader is "glued to print," is the essential basis for subsequent development.

Chall cites a developmental study by Biemiller (1970), who studied the oral reading errors of first-grade children taught by a sight-word method. Biemiller identified three developmental phases: first, oral reading errors were characterized by word substitutions, most of which were semantically and syntactically accurate; second, there was more nonresponding, more errors with a graphic resemblance to printed words, and loss of some semantic acceptability; and, third, there was continued concern for graphic exactness, but a return to greater semantic acceptability. The pattern implies that the new readers shifted their attention from (a) seeking meaning, regardless of the words, to (b) seeking accurate sound-symbol correspondence, regardless of meaning, and to (c) a balance between seeking both sound-symbol accuracy and meaning.

The premise is that new readers must and will go through the three developmental phases at Stage 1, regardless of the teaching emphasis. In Chall's words, "To advance, to build up skill for making choices, beginners have to let go of pseudo-reading. They have to engage, at least temporarily, in what appears to be less mature reading behavior—becoming glued to print—in order to achieve real maturity later" (Chall, 1983, p. 18).

*Our own observations are in line with Biemiller's phases and Chall's conclusion: New readers must first learn to respond effectively to the symbol-sound code before they can shift their main attention back to extracting meaning from printed passages. Many poor readers seem to be hung up at Biemiller's first phase; they continue to approach a reading task as a guessing game with no systematic or dependable clues. They make their guesses about an author's intended meaning on the basis of available pictures, whatever sight words they may recognize, their memory of what was on the page with the smudge in the upper left corner, and any other cues they can get from their classmates and teacher. They learn to respond to a wide variety of clues, and they may even appear to be doing well for a while. But somehow they do not get the notion that the letters stand for sounds in a very systematic and dependable way, so they do not get the concept that they can seek meaning by attending to the letters and words.*

*Many new readers seem to figure it out for themselves; some have great difficulty with that basic concept. The latter need corrective help. They must be encouraged to become glued to print so they can, in due developmental time, become unglued. Corrective help at this stage amounts mainly to helping the student let go of "meaning" substitutions and attend instead to what words look and sound like.*

*Dick, whose reading is described in Chapter 7, appears to be bogged down somewhere in Stage 1. His miscall of "cannery" for "canary" indicates that he has some sense of letter-sound association, but no real appreciation of the essential facts that (a) one must pay attention to all of the letters to get the word right, and (b) the words, taken together, should make sense. Dick needs to be glued to print before he can set himself free to give all of his attention to seeking meaning from what he reads. Because getting meaning is always an important consideration in reading, it is important that the material Dick reads as he gets glued to and unglued from print be meaningful. We do not favor— except in certain testing situations—the use of nonsense material for teaching reading at any stage of development.*

## Stage 2. Confirmation, Fluency, Ungluing from Print: Grades 2–3, Ages 7–8

At this stage readers consolidate Stage 1 learning by reading widely from what is familiar and already known. Reading is not for learning, but for *confirming* what is already known. Readers develop fluency by reading many familiar books—books in which the stories, the subjects or the structures (such as the predictably familiar structures of fairy stories or folktales) are well-known. Because the content is familiar, each reader's attention can be given to the printed words, usually the most common, high-frequency words. Readers learn to use their decoding skills and to seek contextual clues to meaning that are inherent in the familiar language and the familiar stories and subjects.

     Chall mentions two sources of support for Stage 2. One is data showing that (a) reading achievement scores at the end of grade 3 have much more predictive value than scores at the end of grades 1 and 2 (Kraus, 1973), and (b) students who read substantially below the norm at grade 3, and who do not receive special help, continue to experience failure throughout their school years (Bloom, 1964). The other source is observations that campaigns to increase adult literacy often flounder at Stage 2. Chall's point is that new readers who fail to develop fluency, regardless of their success at Stage 1, are unlikely to become self-sufficient, mature readers. She concludes that "Generally, the greater the amount of practice and the greater the immersion, the greater the chance of developing the fluency with print that is necessary for the difficulty to come—the acquisition of new ideas at Stage 3" (p. 20).

     *Chall's Stage 2 is where the transition occurs from attending mainly to decoding to attending mainly to meaning. Readers who fail to progress through Level 2—who fail to develop fluency—will be stuck at Level 1. There they will continue either to guess at meaning or to concentrate on accurate word calling. Those who have progressed to the phase of accurate word calling are ready for corrective help with the transition. Those still guessing about meaning without regard for the specifics of letters and words need help, first, with Stage 1.*

     *We have observed that teachers are more likely to neglect a need for help with the transition more than a need for help with decoding. The reasons may be an overzealous inclination to teach phonics to students who get off to a slow start in reading, and a disinclination to provide reading time and easy, readable materials for students who seem to be successful decoders. After all, shouldn't kids who know their phonics be able to go it on their own? The fact is that Stage 2 is at least as important, developmentally, as Stage 1. If anything, Stage 2 may be more important in corrective teaching. Poor readers who receive plenty of opportunities to work with easy, familiar materials just might figure out decoding on their own. And they just might benefit more from that than from going through—one more time—a collection of phonics exercises. But since corrective teachers don't need to choose between Stage 1 and Stage 2 development, the preferred strategy is to help students acquire a good Stage 1 foundation.*

*In the remaining stages of Chall's developmental scheme, the focus is on meaning. The assumption is that after a successful passage through Stage 2 readers are prepared to shift their attention to extracting meaning and acquiring new knowledge when they read. The rest of this chapter is a discussion of ways to ensure a successful transition. But first take a look at Chall's last three stages and a few of our brief comments. The stages provide a sensible framework that may help you organize your thinking about how to sequence the focus of corrective teaching.*

## Stage 3. Learning the New: A First Step

At Stage 3 the reader moves from mastering print to mastering ideas—but usually from just one point of view. That is in contrast to Stage 4, where a multiplicity of points of view is expected. Chall suggests that Stage 3 might best be divided into two phases: Phase A, from about grades 4–6 (ages 9–11), when the materials read are essentially child-oriented, or "schoolish"; and Phase B, covering grades 7–8 and perhaps 9 (ages 12–14), when the reader moves closer to materials at the general adult level (local newspapers, popular magazines, and popular adult fiction).

## Stage 4. Multiple Viewpoints:
## High School, Ages 14–18

The essential characteristic of this stage, Chall says ". . . is that it involves dealing with more than one point of view" (p. 23). Stage 4 is acquired mainly through formal schooling, where layers of facts and concepts are added to those learned earlier.

## Stage 5. Construction and Reconstruction—
## A World View: College, Age 18 and Above

The reader who reaches Stage 5 knows what to read and how to read it to suit his or her own purpose. The reader also knows what not to read. As Chall suggests, whether all people can reach Stage 5, even after four or more years of college, is open to study.

*Notice that specific and systematic teaching is called for at Stage 1. After that, particularly after successful passage through Stage 2, learning becomes more self-generative. Chall suggests that both children and adults with severe reading problems tend to be either hung up at Stage 1 or bogged down at Stage 2. The invitation to provide corrective help is clear.*

# Automaticity Through Repeated Reading

Children who experience reading difficulties typically do take longer to make the transition from decoding (Stage 1) to confirmation and fluency (Stage 2). Our own observations tell us that. The children seem either to be glued to the print or to be inclined to guess widly; they take a long time to become comfortable with even the simplest books. Chall (1967 & 1979, p. 51) notes that the difficulty of the transition was also recognized by many of the early investigators of reading disability, such as Gray, Gates, Orton, and Fernald. And, more recently, Samuels (1977, 1979, & 1983) and his associates have given considerable attention to gaining a clearer understanding of the processes involved and to effecting a successful transition by helping new readers develop *automaticity,* or "automatic" decoding.

## The Concept of Automaticity

Samuels and his colleague, LaBerge, (LaBerge & Samuels, 1974) introduced the concept of automaticity in an article titled "Toward a Theory of Automatic Information Processing in Reading." In that article the authors present a model, or theory, of the reading process that is based on their beliefs that (a) getting meaning from printed symbols requires sequential stages of information processing, and (b) to focus attention on getting meaning, the reader must first attain automaticity in processing "the visual code" (decoding printed symbols). The sequential stages identified in the LaBerge-Samuels model are as follows:

- *Acquisition.* The beginning reader's attention is directed to decoding, associating the proper sounds with printed symbols.
- *Accuracy.* The reader's attention is directed to accurate recognition of words. The developing reader is able to recognize many words but must continue to devote much attention to the decoding process.
- *Automaticity.* Word recognition is quick and accurate. Because little attention is required for the word recognition task, the reader is free to direct attention to getting meaning.

The model acknowledges changes in readers' abilities to attend to different aspects of the reading task as they acquire the component skills of successful reading.

*Don't be confused by the fact that LaBerge and Samuels talk about three stages of reading development and Chall talks about six stages. Chall is concerned with reading development from infancy to adulthood; LaBerge and Samuels are describing the early stages of learning to read. Both models stress the importance of making a smooth transition from the* acquisition *of decoding skills to the* application *of these skills in fluent, automatic decoding. See Samuels (1983) and Otto (1983) for elaboration and commentary on the LaBerge-Samuels model.*

The developmental steps that Samuels and LaBerge describe suggest a sequence similar to Chall's move from Stage 1 to Stage 3. Both models highlight shifting the focus of instruction as the reader moves from the acquisition of decoding skills to the application of skills and strategies to get meaning.

Samuels (1979) has described an instructional procedure for helping readers move from mere "barking at print" (acquisition and accuracy) to giving full attention to comprehending the message (automaticity). Repeated readings can help the new reader or the reader who is hung up on decoding make the transition from decoding to comprehending.

## The Method of Repeated Reading

Samuels' description of the method is very straightforward. He says it "consists of rereading a short, meaningful passage several times until a satisfactory level of fluency is reached. Then the procedure is repeated with a new passage" (Samuels, 1979, p. 404). To explain why it works, he offers an analogy of the reader being like an athlete or a musician, who is "given a small unit of activity and this unit is practiced over and over until it is mastered" (p. 407). Samuels also offers empirical evidence that the method improves both accuracy and speed (fluency), not only for the practiced passages but for new ones as well.

Samuels does not claim to have "invented" the method. He suggests that teachers have always used it—although, presumably, in a naturalistic, atheoretical way—and acknowledges that it resembles techniques described by Chomsky (1978), Heckelman (1969), Hollingsworth (1970), and Hoskisson (1975a, 1975b). We cite Samuels because his use of the method is in line with the transition discussed in this chapter, and his description of the method is unpretentious and clear.

Reading speed and the number of errors are recorded for each reading. Samuels suggests that the "short, meaningful passage" be a selection of 50 to 200 words from an easy story, chosen by the child. The procedure goes like this: (a) the child orally reads the chosen passage, (b) the teacher records speed and errors, (c) the child practices rereading the same passage alone until his or her next turn to read aloud for the teacher, and (d) the routine is repeated until a criterion of accurate, fluent oral reading is met.

Repeated reading would be a promising technique for helping John, one of the children described in Chapter 1. John seems to have some understanding of phonics principles in isolation; but he is unable to apply them efficiently. He is "glued to print" and is likely to remain stuck at that stage of development unless he has opportunities to develop automaticity.

Repeated reading allows a child to develop fluency. (Photo by Strix Pix)

## Modifications for Group Instruction

Lauritzen (1982) has suggested two slight modifications in the procedure that permits use of the method with a large group of children. She says that keeping individual records may be too demanding of the teacher's time and that some children may find solitary rereading dull or mechanical.

First, the teacher should choose reading selections that have the "sing-it-again" quality that children love. Lauritzen suggests four features that contribute to this quality.

- *Definite rhyme*—a rhyme scheme that is predictable and appealing.
- *Strong rhythm*—a steady beat to support fluent reading. Many poems and

songs have the jump-rope-rhyme sort of rhythm that has a heavy beat; stories with repeated sentence patterns may also be good.

- *Compelling sequence*—an easily identified story sequence that makes for clear expectations and certain fulfillment to help "pull the readers through the passages."
- *Oral literature patterns*—structural patterns typical of oral literature, which include link wording, repeated words, repeated syntax, and cumulative structure. These patterns appear in folk tales such as Henny Penny, The Three Pigs, Gingerbread Boy, and The Three Bears.

Second, the teacher should depend on the appeal of the reading material rather than record keeping and individual progress reports to keep students motivated for rereading. Lauritzen offers a number of suggestions for presenting a well-chosen selection so as to hold the readers' attention. She says the teacher should first read the entire selection to the children while the children follow the print, which the teacher has already written either on a chart or on the chalkboard. Next, the children echo read a line, a sentence, or a paragraph at a time, depending on the type of selection. (In echo reading, the teacher leads in pace and volume; and the readers follow, a word or so behind.) Then the teacher and students read the entire selection in unison. After that, the children may read individually, in pairs, or in small groups, as many times as they wish.

The unison reading can be repeated for several days. It is critical that the teacher present a fluent model for the children to imitate. If the teacher records the initial reading on tape, the children can continue to compare and to echo read for practice. Occasionally, the children can "show off" their good performance to parents, the principal, or children from another classroom.

## Oral to Silent Reading

For the teacher, the transition we are talking about is mainly a matter of shifting the emphasis of instruction from *decoding* to *comprehending*. It may be difficult to develop a good sense of when a student is ready for the shift, but familiarity with Chall's developmental stages should help. For the student, the transition is, as we suggested earlier, largely a matter of shifting from *oral* to *silent* reading. In general, "reading" at the decoding stage usually culminates in some sort of oral response. But reading for meaning, mature reading, is usually silent.[1] Schreiber (1980) argues very convincingly that the main reason why the method of repeated reading works so well is that the practice permits the reader to develop alternatives to the prosodic cues of oral language.

---

[1] Our purpose here is not to reopen any historical debates about the proper role of oral and silent reading in the reading curriculum. We tend to agree with Taylor and Connor (1982) that (a) in general, teachers should focus on silent reading instruction, and (b) they should use oral reading instruction "rationally for purposes appropriately served by oral reading" (p. 443). The fact is, though, that new readers' responses to print tend to be oral, whether oral responses are called for or not. Our intent is simply to acknowledge a developmental fact and to examine its place in the developmental sequence.

*Prosody* is the stress and intonation patterns of spoken language. Schrieber contends that "... the acquisition of fluent reading competence crucially involves the beginning reader's tacit recognition that s/he must learn to compensate for the absence of prosodic cues in the written signal by making use (or better use) of the cues that are preserved" (1980, p. 1978). In other words, the student learns that prosodic cues are not systematically preserved in writing, but that other kinds of signals occur, such as function words, inflected endings, punctuation, and syntactic structures. Schreiber admits that exactly which written clues are most important is not known, but he is convinced that the crucial first step between LaBerge and Samuels' second and third stages comes with the reader's realization that "... parsing strategies other than those which rely on prosody or its somewhat haphazard graphic analogues are required in order to read with sense" (1980, p. 183).

In fact, Schrieber goes a step beyond Samuels' method of repeated reading to develop fluency. He suggests the importance of a good model of fluent oral reading, by the teacher or some other competent reader. Having heard a fluent reader's appropriate phrasing of the sentences in a passage, the student should have less difficulty imposing such phrasing and, therefore, more easily grasp the character of the task at hand.

A sensible sequence of instruction designed to help a reader move from painstaking decoding to efficient silent reading, then, would involve some quite straightforward steps:

1. Selection of a short, easy-to-read passage on a familiar topic.
2. Expressive, fluent oral reading of the passage by the teacher while the student follows the print.
3. Repeated oral reading of the passage by the student, individually or, at least some of the time, as part of a group activity. Tape recordings of an individual's oral performance can demonstrate progress. A tape recording can also be used (a) initially to provide a model of fluent reading, and (b) repeatedly, as a model for the reader to follow in a read-along fashion. The essential point is that the student must have the opportunity to rehearse and improve oral reading; and the teacher must check to see that there is progress toward the criterion of accurate, fluent reading.
4. Repetition of steps one, two, and three with a variety of short, easy-to-read passages. Step four should be repeated until the student is able to read passages accurately and fluently without the rehearsal of repeated readings.
5. Silent reading of similar short, easy-to-read passages followed by a comprehension check. (Since the purpose is to help the student with the transition from labored oral reading to fluent silent reading, this step is needed to demonstrate success and to assure application.)

Multiple exposures to fluently read stories permit readers to become aware of and familiar with things like phrasing, verb endings, and tense variation. Because both the language and the topics of the passages are familiar, the reader can predict fairly well what is coming next in the passage. The reader is thus free to devote attention to and to develop an appreciation of the patterns and flow of the language. The reader has opportunities to develop the automaticity and fluency that are the bases for reading with understanding and for moving on to more mature reading behaviors.

Also involved in a smooth transition from decoding to comprehending are *vocabulary development* and increasing *metacognitive awareness.* In the sections that follow we discuss, first, some experience-based approaches to vocabulary development and, second, the concept of metacognition in reading and how to nurture its development.

# Vocabulary Development

In Chall's schema, Stage 2 is where the reader develops fluency by reading familiar material. Because the content is well-known, the reader is free to devote attention to the printed words. The reader learns to use decoding skills in real-life reading situations. The reader is also free to seek contextual clues to meaning that are inherent in the familiar language, stories, and subjects. The conditions are right for beginning to attend to vocabulary development. Rapid expansion of vocabulary will, of course, come at Stage 3 where the main purpose for reading shifts from confirmation of the known to introduction and exploration of the new. Nevertheless, the conditions at Stage 2—where the conceptual demands of the reading task are light and the reader is relatively free to seek contextual clues to meaning—are ideal for easing into vocabulary development. Besides, easing in at Stage 2 could spare a new reader who is making slower-than-normal progress (one who needs corrective help) some of the trauma that may come with the heavier demands for vocabulary development at Stage 3 and beyond.

## Exploiting Experiences

Over a decade ago, Manzo and Sherk (1971 – 1972) reviewed the literature on vocabulary development and concluded that any technique that draws attention to word parts or word meaning is likely to have a positive effect on vocabulary development. As they put it, "if we think of word learning as an extension of basic language learning, teaching vocabulary may be a relatively simple matter of exploiting experience as a means of teaching vocabulary, and exploiting and using vocabulary as a means of getting the most from experience" (p. 88). "Exploiting experience" as a way of teaching vocabulary is hardly a new idea. Over the years, educators have stressed the importance of relating children's experiences to vocabulary concepts when teaching new vocabulary. But it is interesting to note that since the Manzo and Sherk review there has been a marked shift in the way that many researchers and educators view the role of vocabulary in comprehension. (See Toms-Bronowski, 1982, for a more complete discussion. We are indebted to her for much of the substance of the present discussion of vocabulary development.)

Historically, the inclination has been to examine vocabulary development from either an *instrumentalist* or an *aptitude* position. Simply put, the instrumentalist position is that word knowledge *enables* comprehension; therefore, *how* vocabulary development proceeds is less important than the belief that any increase in word knowledge will help the reader understand text. The aptitude position is that some persons are better able to understand text because they have superior verbal ability; therefore, increased verbal fluency should be associated with increased comprehension. The two positions stress individual word meanings and verbal ability, respectively, and they are the bases for instructional strategies designed primarily to increase word knowledge and to enhance word acquisition (phonic analysis, structural analysis, use of dictionary, drill on word meanings, study of word lists).

More recently, there has been increasing inclination to approach vocabulary development from a *knowledge* position. The knowledge position is in line with the notion of "exploiting experiences" when it assigns a major role in comprehension to "building bridges between the new and the known"; that is, it assumes that to be learned, new concepts must be related to known concepts. (Pearson & Johnson, 1978, p. 24). The position draws on recent information-processing theories that stress the importance of prior knowledge and the way it is stored and retrieved. Without denying the importance of traditional vocabulary-teaching techniques, the knowledge position switches emphasis away from the instrumentalist and aptitude positions. The underlying premise is that (a) prior knowledge is crucial for understanding text, and (b) it is not merely individual word meanings that are important, but the entire conceptual framework elicited by the word meaning. In other words, an individual's general knowledge, not just specific word meanings, interacts with text to enable that individual to "comprehend."

Toms-Bronowski (1982) suggests three vocabulary-teaching strategies consistent with the knowledge, or "exploiting experiences," position. Each one is in line with what we have said about vocabulary development at Chall's Stage 2 and what we will say about the importance of prior knowledge in the following chapter on techniques for developing comprehension (Chapter 9). The strategies are (a) contextual analysis, (b) semantic mapping, and (c) semantic feature analysis.

## Contextual Analysis

Words derive meaning from the context they are in. The strategy of contextual analysis involves the reader in searching for the semantic, syntactic, or graphic cues that may surround an unknown word in order to (a) reduce the possibilities of what the word may mean and (b) associate known facts and concepts with the word. Teaching the strategy is largely a matter of creating a mind set whereby the reader expects to derive meaning for an unknown word from an understanding of the words and phrases that surround the unknown word. Toms-Bronowski (1982, p. 34) offers this example: "in the sentence 'My uncle, an *itinerant* preacher, traveled constantly and was always on the road' the words 'traveled' and 'on the road' help a reader to discern the meaning of the word 'itinerant.' "

The types of words or phrases that convey contextual clues have been categorized in a variety of ways; but three categories seem to be most popular and to have the greatest commonsense appeal:

1. Direct Explanation. For example, "The spacecraft was enormous, so big that it blocked the view from my second-story window."
2. Appositive. For example, "An enormous spacecraft, a gigantic flying saucer, landed outside my window."
3. Comparison/Contrast. For example, "The enormous spacecraft towered over the cars in the street."

*We believe that the most effective technique for teaching contextual analysis, at the Stage 2 level, is simply to point out the common types of context clues when they occur, to discuss their function in the context, and, when appropriate, to ask the reader to respond with a word or phrase from his or her own experience.* (See Chapter 9 for additional comments on contextual analysis.)

## Semantic Mapping

Semantic mapping involves asking students to relate new words to their own experience and prior knowledge in graphic form. An instructional sequence for semantic mapping could go like this:

1. Select a word of general interest or need, such as a word central to a story to be read.
2. Write the word on the chalkboard.
3. Ask the group to think of as many words as they can that are in some way related to the target word and to jot them on paper in categories. (The mapping strategy probably works best with a group because the pool of words is likely to be larger. But the strategy can be useful with an individual, as a strategy for tapping into the individual's store of related prior knowledge.)
4. Have individual students share the words they have written and, as they do, write the words on the board and attempt to put them into categories.
5. Discuss the words and categories.

Student discussion is essential to the success of the strategy. Through discussion students can discover the meanings and uses of new words, including the target word, and new meanings for known words. They may also see old words in a new light and begin to see relationships among words.

Figure 8.1 shows a very simple semantic map for the word "environment."

## Semantic Feature Analysis

Semantic feature analysis focuses on ways that words related to a topic are alike and different and, through discussion, relates their meanings to prior knowledge. We give an example of a completed semantic feature analysis grid in Figure 8.2. The instructional sequence for creating a semantic feature analysis grid could go like this:

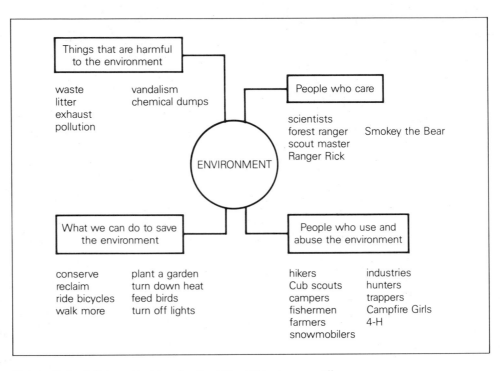

**Figure 8.1**  A Semantic Map for the Word "Environment"

1. Select a topic (word).
2. List, in a column at the left, some words that relate to the topic.
3. List in a row along the top features shared by some of the words in the column.
4. Have the students put pluses or minuses in the grid to indicate whether or not each word that is listed in the column shares each of the features that is listed across the top.
5. Encourage the students to add more words and features. (Again, the strategy works best with a group because there can be more suggestions and more discussion. But, like the other strategies, it can be a good way to tap into an individual's store of prior knowledge.)
6. Have the students complete the extended matrix with pluses and minuses.
7. Conduct a discussion about the uniqueness of each word as reflected by the pluses and minuses on the grid.

Notice that vocabulary is presented in a orderly, logical way. Discussion of the pluses and minuses in the grid can help to display relationships among words and to clarify finer nuances among concepts.

| ENVIRONMENT | | | | | | |
|---|---|---|---|---|---|---|
| Examples of Acts That Help the Environment | | | | | | |
| Acts That Help The Environment — Stay within limits when fishing | Drain a swamp for farmland | Save fuel by turning down heat and wearing sweaters | Irrigate a desert | Be careful when camping | Help animals | Drive 55 |
| Conserve | | | | | | |
| + | − | + | − | + | + | + |
| Limit | | | | | | |
| + | − | + | − | + | − | + |
| Reclaim | | | | | | |
| − | + | − | + | ? | − | − |
| Restore | | | | | | |
| ? | − | − | − | − | + | − |
| Preserve | | | | | | |
| − | − | + | − | + | + | + |
| Recycle | | | | | | |
| − | ? | − | ? | + | − | − |
| Produce | | | | | | |
| + | + | − | + | − | + | − |

**Figure 8.2**  A Semantic Feature Analysis Grid for the Word "Environment"

## Focus on Prior Knowledge

The specific strategies just discussed are only a sampling from the many strategies being suggested for activating existing memory structures and processes (prior knowledge) to enhance word knowledge and comprehension. Some of the strategies may turn out to be more effective for enhancing general vocabulary development while others may be more effective for text-specific vocabulary development—that is, to teach the specialized words associated with a specific topic or likely to be found in a subject area textbook. Which strategies are in fact most effective and for what purposes remains to be determined through careful research. Meanwhile, there has been a shift in vocabulary studies from a general understanding of vocabulary acquisition (trying to find the best teaching method for most words) to an emphasis on teaching strategies (trying to find effective ways to help students use what they know to learn more from text). A recent study by Beck, Perfetti, and McKeown (1982) illustrates well the latter emphasis.

*We believe that the direction of the shift is positive. Vocabulary development strategies that build on prior knowledge are more likely to have a positive effect on both general reading comprehension and acquisition of specific word knowledge. While definitive research support for this commonsense belief remains to be demonstrated, it seems safe and sensible to proceed in the manner we have suggested.*

# Metacognitive Development

Babbs and Moe (1983) describe two types of students likely to be found in any classroom: "Some reread purposefully when meaning is unclear, raise questions in order to clarify an assignment, and flexibly use reading as a tool for learning and pleasure. Others never reread, have little or no awareness of an occasional lack of understanding, do not realize the need for exact understanding when reading directions, and have not learned to use reading as a versatile tool either for learning or for pleasure" (p. 422). To a certain extent such a contrast in behaviors could be explained in terms of differences in students' general ability, background experiences, general knowledge, word recognition skills, vocabulary development, and overall motivation to read with understanding. But what if the students are able to perform equally well under the teacher's direct supervision? Babbs and Moe suggest that the first type of student displays *metacognition* and the second type does not: "If all other reading-related factors are equal, then a difference in metacognitive development may account for the difference in their independent reading performance" (1983, p. 422).

*We believe that metacognitive development is indeed an important aspect of overall reading development. And because differences in metacognitive development can and often do account for striking differences in students' independent reading performance, we believe that the development of metacognitive awareness should be a consideration in the transition from words to meaning.*

## Metacognition and Reading

The study of metacognitive development has received much attention from developmental psychologists in the last decade. According to Flavell (1976) metacognition amounts to "knowledge concerning one's own cognitive processes and products or anything related to them . . . Metacognition refers, among other things, to the active monitoring and consequent regulation and orchestration of the processes . . . usually in the service of some concrete goal or objective" (p. 232). Brown (1978) puts it more simply when she says that metacognition is "knowing about knowing" and "knowing how to know."

The research of Flavell, Brown, and others suggests that beginning learners have difficulty managing their attempts to learn and monitoring their performance in learning. For example, beginning readers—or, more generally, readers who frequently fail to understand their reading tasks—have difficulty judging the success of their efforts to read with understanding. They tend to ignore inconsistencies within the text, they are unlikely to reread when they fail to understand, and they have no good sense of when they are ready to attempt recall. (See Yussen, Mathews, and Hiebert, 1982, for a review related particularly to metacognition in reading.)

Metacognition: Knowing how and why. (Photo © C. Quinlan)

The literature on metacognition has important implications for reading. Mangano, Palmer, and Goetz (1982) explain it like this: "Metacognitive analysis of the reading task stresses the active role of the reader in constructing a sensible, coherent representation of the meaning of the text. The reader must be flexible and adaptive, modifying the reading process to fit his or her purpose for reading and the characteristics of the text being read. Comprehension monitoring, the assessment of one's own understanding, is a crucial process . . . Developmental research with elementary-age children suggests that they have serious difficulties monitoring their own understanding and learning" (p. 366).

Any astute reading teacher can confirm the suggestion from a growing body of research that failure to successfully monitor understanding or to apply appropriate corrective strategies virtually assures failure to comprehend. Poor readers tend to read as if they neither expect nor care that the text makes sense (Ryan, 1981); they do not monitor their understanding. Unlike successful readers, they have no reason to employ corrective strategies when they fail to understand.

*We are convinced that a successful transition from words to meaning depends heavily on the reader's success in developing metacognitive awareness. "Ungluing from print" involves, among other things, a growing awareness of the conventions of printed material and of the clues that are provided to aid understanding; and developing vocabulary involves, among other things, a growing awareness of the availability and utility of prior knowledge in deriving meaning from and extending the meaning of words in context.*

Metacognition is not something to be "added on" to reading instruction. Successful readers' metacognitive development seems to parallel their cognitive development in reading: They learn *how* and *why* at the same time. They know reading and they *know about* reading. When they engage in the cognitive act of reading they also know what the process involves or what influences it—they have developed metacognition (Yussen, Mathews, & Hiebert, 1982, p. 190).

Poor readers' metacognitive development may lag behind cognitive development related to reading. Then you observe behavior like that described by Babbs and Moe at the beginning of this section. Or lack of metacognitive awareness may even stand in the way of normal cognitive development. A reader who stays "glued to print," for example, may lack metacognitive understanding of what "reading" is really all about. An important aspect of corrective teaching, then, is to consciously and overtly assist the development of metacognitive awarenesses. This is best done by (a) teaching students specific skills and strategies for extracting meaning from printed materials, and (b) providing many opportunities for the students to practice applying the skills and strategies for specific reading purposes. (We talk more about skills and strategies and their application in Chapter 9.)

## Development of Metacognitive Awareness

In the growing literature on metacognition there are many suggestions for instruction. (See, for example, Babbs and Moe, 1983, and Mangano, Palmer, and Goetz, 1982, for specific discussions related to reading instruction.) We are, however, struck by the fact that most of the suggestions are very similar to the ones for helping students improve their reading comprehension. If there is a difference, it is more a matter of emphasis than of fact. Suggestions for "teaching" metacognition tend to emphasize the need for explanation, for making clear the *why* as well as the *how* when introducing and developing comprehension skills and strategies.

In Chapter 9 we suggest a number of skills and strategies for improving reading comprehension. We suggest that the specific skills you teach should be the ones that are taught in the developmental materials—in most instances, the basal readers—that you use. Then we suggest some more general "strategies" that readers need in order to seek and extract meaning from printed material. Specifically, the strategies we suggest are (a) establishing a purpose, (b) using prior knowledge, (c) attending to or imposing organization, and (d) monitoring understanding. These strategies are very similar to a list of "processes leading to comprehension" suggested by Yussen, Mathews, and Hiebert (1982) in a discussion of metacognitive aspects of reading. Their list includes (a) reading with a purpose, (b) searching for main ideas, (c) being sensitive to characteristics of the text, and (d) monitoring one's understanding. The words differ slightly, but the concerns are virtually identical.

We do not mean to suggest that the concept of metacognition is pointless or redundant insofar as reading instruction is concerned. To the contrary, the recent work related to metacognition has served to underscore important differences between successful and unsuccessful reading behavior. The work has made reading educators much more aware of the need to help readers go beyond cognition of processes to metacognition, knowing *about* knowing.

We do want to suggest that corrective teachers should not consider adding a unit or a series of lessons on metacognition to their curriculum. "Teaching metacognition" amounts to *direct teaching* as we describe it in Chapter 3 and to using the techniques we describe in Chapter 9. It amounts to sharing your views as an expert reader with the novice readers you teach.

## Summary

Reading—particularly learning to read—is a two-stage process. At the first stage the words are the main focus of attention. The reader attends mainly to converting printed letters to sounds; and instruction is primarily a matter of helping the new reader become proficient at the task. At the second stage the meaning of printed words is the main focus of attention. The reader attends mainly to attaching meaning to printed material; the focus of instruction is on helping readers acquire the skills and strategies to read with understanding.

The transition from stage one to stage two is extremely important to the development of reading proficiency. Readers whose development hangs up at stage one turn out to be severely disabled readers, unable to cope with the reading tasks they encounter in and out of school. The chapter is devoted to (a) a rationale for giving the transition the instructional attention that its importance demands, and (b) suggestions for helping students make the transition smoothly and effectively.

## References

Babbs, P. J., & Moe, A. J. (1983). Metacognition: A key for independent learning from text. *Reading Teacher, 36,* 422–426.

Bateman, B. (1983). A commentary on Johns's critique of Gurren and Hughes's study: Measuring the effects of intensive phonics vs. gradual phonics in beginning reading. In L. M. Gentile, M. L. Kamil, & J. S. Blanchard (Eds.), *Reading Research Revisited.* Columbus, OH: Charles E. Merrill, pp. 105–111.

Beck, I. L., Perfetti, C. A., & McKeown, M. G. (1982). Effects of long-term vocabulary instruction on lexical access and reading comprehension. *Journal of Education Psychology, 74,* 506–521.

Biemiller, A. (1970). The development and use of graphic and contextual information as children learn to read. *Reading Research Quarterly, 6,* 75–96.

Bloom, B. S. (1964). *Stability and change in human characteristics.* New York: Wiley.

Brown, A. L. (1978). Knowing when, where, and who to remember: A problem in meta-cognition. In R. Glaser (Ed.), *Advances in instructional psychology.* Hillsdale, NJ: Lawrence Erlbaum.

Chall, J. S. (1967). *Learning to read: The great debate.* New York: McGraw-Hill.

Chall, J. S. (1979). The great debate: Ten years later with a modest proposal for reading stages. In L. B. Resnick & P. A. Weaver (Eds.), *Theory and practice of early reading* (vol. 1). Hillsdale, NJ: Lawrence Erlbaum.

Chall, J. S. (1983). *Stages of reading development.* New York: McGraw-Hill.

Chomsky, C. (1978). When you still can't read in third grade: After decoding what? In S. J. Samuels (Ed.), *What research has to say about reading instruction.* Newark, DE: International Reading Association.

Flavell, J. H. (1976). Metacognitive aspects of problem solving. In L. B. Resnick (Ed.), *The nature of intelligence.* Hillsdale, NJ: Lawrence Erlbaum.

Heckelman, R. G. (1969). A neurological impress method of reading instruction. *Academic Therapy, 4,* 277–282.

Hollingsworth, P. M. (1970). An experiment with the impress method of teaching reading. *The Reading Teacher, 24,* 112–114.

Hoskisson, K. (1975). The many facets of assisted reading. *Elementary English, 52,* 312–315. (a)

Hoskisson, K. (1975). Successive approximation and beginning reading. *Elementary School Journal, 75,* 442–451. (b)

Kraus, P. E. (1973). *Yesterday's children: A longitudinal study of children from kindergarten into the adult years.* New York: John Wiley and Sons.

LaBerge, D., & Samuels, S. J. (1974). Toward a theory of automatic information processing in reading. *Cognitive Psychology, 6,* 293–323.

Lauritzen, C. (1982). A modification of repeated readings for group instruction. *The Reading Teacher, 35,* 456–458.

Mangano, N. G., Palmer, D., & Goetz, E. T. (1982). Improving reading comprehension through metacognitive training. *Reading Psychology, 3,* 365–374.

Manzo, A. V., & Sherk, J. C. (1971–1972). Some generalizations and strategies for guiding vocabulary. *Journal of Reading Behavior, 4,* 81–88.

Otto, W. (1983). A commentary on LaBerge and Samuel's retrospective analysis of the theory of automaticity in reading. In L. M. Gentile, M. L. Kamil, & J. S. Blanchard (Eds.), *Reading research revisited.* Columbus, OH: Charles E. Merrill, pp. 57–61.

Pearson, P. D., & Johnson, D. D. (1978). *Teaching reading comprehension.* New York: Holt, Rinehart and Winston.

Ryan, E. B. (1981). Identifying and remediating failures in reading comprehension: Toward an instructional approach for poor comprehenders. In T. G. Waller and G. E. MacKinnon (Eds.), *Advances in reading research* (vol. 2). New York: Academic Press.

Samuels, S. J. (1977). Introduction to theoretical models of reading. In W. Otto, N. A. Peters, & C. W. Peters (Eds.), *Reading problems.* Boston: Addison Wesley, pp. 7–41.

Samuels, S. J. (1979). The method of repeated readings. *The Reading Teacher, 32,* 403–408.

Samuels, S. J. (1983). A critique of a theory of automaticity in reading: Looking back: A retrospective analysis of the LaBerge-Samuels reading model. In L. M. Gentile, M. L. Kamil, & J. S. Blanchard (Eds.), *Reading research revisited.* Columbus, OH: Charles E. Merrill, pp. 39–55.

Schreiber, P. A. (1980). On the acquisition of reading fluency. *Journal of Reading Behavior, 12,* 177–186.

Taylor, N. E., & Connor, U. (1982). Silent vs. oral reading: The rational instructional use of both processes. *The Reading Teacher, 35,* 440–443.

Toms-Bronowski, S. C. (1982). *An investigation of the effectiveness of selected teaching strategies with intermediate grade children.* Doctoral dissertation. University of Wisconsin, Madison.

Yussen, S. R., Mathews, S. R. II, & Hiebert, E. (1982). Metacognitive aspects of reading. In W. Otto and S. White (Eds.), *Reading expository material.* New York: Academic Press.

# Check Your Reading Comprehension

1. In what ways does the two-stage concept of reading carry implications for corrective reading?

2. How does this two-stage model relate to Chall's six-stage model?

3. Consider the following statement from this chapter:
   > Notice that specific and systematic teaching is called for at Stage 1. After that, particularly after successful passage through Stage 2, learning becomes more self-generative.

   Argue both the *pro* and *con* sides of this issue.

4. Matching exercise:

   _____**1.** Stage 1 (Chall)

   _____**2.** Stage 2 (Chall)

   _____**3.** Automaticity

   _____**4.** Repeated Readings Model (Samuels)

   _____**5.** Exploiting experiences

   _____**6.** Metacognition

   **a.** A perspective for vocabulary development that emphasizes building bridges from the known to the new.

   **b.** Fluent, accurate word recognition, or decoding; little attention required for decoding.

   **c.** Initial reading or decoding stage.

   **d.** Knowledge concerning one's own cognitive process and products.

   **e.** Conformation, fluency, ungluing from print stage.

   **f.** Rereading a short, meaningful passage several times until a satisfactory level of fluency is reached.

Answers:

6. d

5. a

4. f

3. b

2. e

1. c

5. Look over the selection entitled "Energy and Food Chains in the Ecosystem" in "Check Your Reading Comprehension" for Chapter 7. Choose three terms that might need to be clarified if you were actually using this selection. Prepare a mini-lesson for each word. With one, use the *contextual analysis* approach. With another, use the *semantic mapping* approach. With the last, use the *semantic feature analysis* approach.

6. Choose either the individualized or group approach to repeated readings. Following the guidelines in this chapter, select an appropriate passage. Prepare a tape to demonstrate fluent reading of the passage. Try the tape and the method in your classroom.

7. Choose the vocabulary development approach with which you feel most comfortable. Prepare a lesson to be used in your classroom.

# 9

# Helping Students Understand Their Textbooks

**Dr. Donald J. Richgels, Assistant Professor at Louisiana State University, wrote sections of this chapter and provided comments throughout.**

Our main focus in this chapter and the two chapters that follow is on ways to help students understand their textbooks. Although students learn from many other sources, the fact is that schools continue to rely on textbooks as a basic curriculum resource. This is true throughout most students' entire school experience. Typically, students begin to read from basal reader texts almost as soon as they begin to read at all; they continue to read from basal readers and from a wide range of content area texts and textbook-like materials throughout their elementary school years. After formal reading instruction ends, they continue to read from textbooks and textbook-like materials through their formal schooling. The textbook is, and will probably remain for the foreseeable future, a prominent reality for most students.

It does make sense to look for alternatives to the textbook as a main information source for readers with severe problems. No amount of teacher direction or coaching is likely to enable a student who lacks basic decoding skills to read and understand a 10th-grade history text. On the other hand, it makes very little sense to abandon the text—or in so doing to abandon the reader—when the problem is the reader's partial or inadequate understanding of the text. A more realistic and productive approach is to provide the help students need to understand their texts through corrective teaching. In this chapter and the two that follow we discuss techniques and procedures that will help you do just that.

In Chapter 9 we identify and discuss some of the skills and general strategies that readers employ to extract meaning from the materials they read. Of course, it is a truism that teaching students to read with understanding involves more than teaching a collection of discrete skills and strategies. But it is also true that the successful teachers we know regard specific skills and strategies as the "enabling behaviors" that permit readers to interact with printed materials in ways that make comprehension possible.

Too often reading skills and strategies are taught in relative isolation from meaningful reading tasks, and too few opportunities are given for their application. Students learn skills and strategies in the context of workbook exercises and contrived activities in reading classes. They are too seldom encouraged to apply their well-practiced skills and strategies in any systematic way when they read textbooks and other materials. In this chapter we suggest two techniques for encouraging the application of skills and strategies. One is a time-tested classic: the directed reading-thinking activity. The other is a new application of an old technique: gloss.

*We want to reiterate that teaching skills and strategies is necessary but not sufficient for helping students understand their textbooks. All students need to know how to apply the skills they learn. But especially students who are having trouble comprehending their textbooks can benefit from corrective teaching that stresses systematic application of skills and strategies.*

# Comprehension Skills[1]

Reading with understanding requires an interaction between the reader and text. For the interaction to be productive, the reader must bring certain capabilities to the reading task. We believe that facility with certain specific skills is one of these essential capabilities. Our conviction is based in part on our experience in identifying relevant skills and in helping teachers teach them (Otto & Askov, 1974) and on the classroom observations of our colleagues (Kamm & White, 1979). It is also based on the scholarly work that brings Downing and Leong (1982) to the conclusion "that psychological research findings on skill acquisition in general can be applied with confidence to the specific skill of learning to read" (p. 28).

In *learning-to-read* situations, students usually receive some type of skill instruction, and in many instances they are required to demonstrate competence with reading-learning skills on criterion-referenced tests, norm-referenced tests, or both. In *learning-from-text* situations, however, merely "having" a skill in one's repertoire is not sufficient. The successful reader must be able to appropriately apply the skills in a variety of contexts. We have found that students do not usually apply skills spontaneously. "Application" must be demonstrated and nurtured in content-area reading as students use their skills to learn from text.

---

[1] The discussion of comprehension skills and strategies and of the glossing technique in this chapter borrows freely from a theoretical paper by Otto, White, Richgels, Hansen, and Morrison (1981).

Robinson (1978) defines skills, with a content area classroom perspective, as "individual components that appear to be essential tools for contending with the writer's message . . ." (p. 24). As we have suggested, a command of reading-learning skills and the ability to apply these skills appear to be essential for a productive interaction between a reader and a text. Furthermore, the nature of a specific reading task, particularly in content area reading, determines what particular skills are needed. Several skills might be required for one task while one particular skill might be sufficient for another. Instruction in the content areas, then, ought to make provision for the application of appropriate skills in content reading tasks. Students must practice and apply reading skills in whatever combination a particular task requires with the expectation that the skills will help the reader get meaning from the text.

We have identified several skills that seem both *teachable* and *applicable* for students who are reading for understanding. We state each skill in terms of an instructional objective (review Chapter 3 if necessary) and cluster the objectives according to *function* (skills for getting meaning from words, from sentences, and from selections) and *type* (skills that deal with word parts, with context clues, and so forth).

## Skills for Getting Meaning from Words

***Word parts.*** The learner recognizes that an affix can modify the meaning of a base word and help identify the grammatical function of the base word. Example:

> *sense + less = senseless,* that is, without sense; *admire + ation = admiration,* allowing *admire* to work as a noun, as in *John had much admiration for his teacher.*

The learner determines the meaning of a compound word by applying knowledge of component words. Example:

> *saw + dust = sawdust,* that is, dust from sawing.

***Context clues.*** The learner uses explicit context clues (for example, synonym definitions, equivalent phrases, summary) to determine the meaning of an unfamiliar word in context. Example:

> In "Jerry is thinking about being a reporter someday. He is very good at writing intelligibly, that is, clearly and understandably," intelligibly means clearly and understandably.

The learner determines the meaning of an unfamiliar word in a context that contains implicit clues (for example, cause/effect, contrast, example, modifying phrase). Example:

> In "Jerry is thinking about being a reporter someday. He is working at writing intelligibly, since a reporter's writing must be clear and easy to understand," intelligibly means clearly and understandably.

The learner uses explicit and implicit context clues to determine the obscure meaning of a familiar word in context. Example:

> In "Because it has a crop, in one dive the pelican can catch more fish than it can eat at once," crop means pouch in the throat of a bird.

## Skills for Getting Meaning from Sentences

***Paraphrase.***    The learner restates sentences by rearranging the order of words in the sentence and/or by substituting for one or more words. Example:

> "News of the coming blizzard was put in the afternoon paper, since Pineville had never had snow" is paraphrased as "Because snow had never fallen in Pineville, the approaching storm was talked about in the newspaper."

***Detail.***    The learner attends to details of syntactic relations within sentences. Example:

> In "The policeman was warned by the boy," the boy is the one who did the warning.

The learner attends to details of semantic relations within sentences. Example: In "The dog and rabbit ran and hopped across the field," the dog is identified as the runner and the rabbit as the hopper.

## Skills for Getting Meaning from Selections

***Main idea.***    The learner identifies the main idea of a selection that includes a topic sentence and contains only information that is relevant to the main idea or central thought.

The learner generates a statement of the main idea of a selection that (a) includes both relevant and irrelevant details with reference to the central thought, and (b) may or may not include a topic sentence.

Paraphrasing helps students get meaning from sentences.

*(Notice that learning to identify main ideas is at least a two-stage process. Discussion and examples of a sequence of main-idea skill development appear later in this chapter.)*

***Relationships and conclusions.***    The learner identifies relationships that are described in a selection, such as cause-and-effect, part-to-whole, and equivalence relations. *(The relationships may be stated explicitly; or the learner may have to infer them from information provided.)*

The learner draws conclusions based on described relationships.

***Sequence.***    The learner determines where a specific event occurs within the framework of a series of events. *(Again, the sequence may be stated explicitly, as in "First . . . second . . . then . . ."; or the learner may have to determine the sequence from implicit clues.)*

The preceding skills are examples of specific comprehension skills stated as instructional objectives. We will refer to them again in the discussion of the glossing technique. You should understand, though, that you should choose skills for corrective teaching from the specific comprehension skills taught in the context of a reader's developmental program of instruction. The main thrust of corrective teaching must be to help the reader both perceive the function of specific skills in extracting meaning from printed materials and become adept at applying the skills that are introduced and practiced in developmental instruction. If a basal reader series is the primary source for developmental instruction, that series should be your prime source for specific skills. If you have a comprehensive reading program (see Chapter 2), the program itself would be your main source.

The essential point here is threefold. First, specific comprehension skills are in fact taught in virtually all classrooms. Second, many students successfully "learn" comprehension skills, but they have difficulty using them to extract meaning from their textbooks. Third, an important function of corrective teaching is to help students apply the skills through direct, systematic teaching.

You might decide to make direct use of the preceding skills. This would be appropriate if (a) they reflect the specific skills content of your developmental program, (b) you are unable to determine which, if any, skills are already in a given reader's repertoire, or (c) you make a deliberate decision to introduce and develop an "independent" set of comprehension skills. If you decide to use the skills given you must be aware that the objectives are stated as relatively long-term goals. You will need to identify more explicit, short-term objectives for day-by-day instruction. (Review Chapter 3 if necessary.)

# Comprehension Strategies

Getting meaning from printed material requires the application of certain general strategies as well as more specific skills, such as the ones just discussed. Individual readers employ many different strategies in their quest for meaning, but a few strategies seem to be widely and consistently used by successful readers.[2] We have selected four that are frequently described by good readers and that appear to have high utility for discussion in this chapter. They are (a) establishing a *purpose* for reading, (b) relating what is being read to *prior knowledge,* or what one already knows, (c) attending to the *organization* provided by a text or imposing organization on both new information and prior knowledge, and (d) *monitoring* one's own comprehension.

Many traditional study skills or study techniques—for example, Robinson's (1961) well-known SQ3R technique and its many variations—are primarily concerned with what the student does *before* or *after* reading (Baker & Brown, in press). The reader first "surveys," "questions," and "anticipates" and then "recites," "reflects," and "reviews." The strategies that follow have much more to do with what the student does *during* reading to facilitate understanding and learning. What the student does during active processing is likely to have a more profound effect on understanding than any preliminary or follow-up activity.

In the discussion of each strategy we first discuss its characteristics and then suggest some ways to go about teaching it.

## Establishing a Purpose

Establishing a purpose may be either initiated by the teacher or self-imposed by the student. Robinson (1978) suggests that the only strategy that is as effective in improving study-reading is having the teacher establish purposes for reading is having students identify their own purposes. Robinson goes on to suggest that once a purpose is set, a reader can initiate other strategies for comprehending that relate to that purpose. This is in line with the phases of productive purpose-setting identified by Morrison (1980): (a) once a purpose has been set by the students or the teacher, (b) the students are in a position to develop questions relevant to their purpose, and (c) then the students can determine and adjust their reading speed in view of the purpose.

The important strategy of establishing a purpose must be developed systematically. A well-defined purpose goes beyond "gaining understanding" to identifying specific goals and reasons for reading. One way to help students develop their purpose-setting strategy is to provide activities that deal specifically with the three phases identified by Morrison.

First, set purposes *for* the students. Move gradually toward having them identify and establish their own purposes for reading. *(Be sure the students realize that when they do assigned reading, they usually do not have the luxury of setting truly personal purposes for reading. Even if their teacher's purposes for assigning specific reading are unstated and only implied, students can learn to set purposes for reading based on expected course outcomes—as demonstrated, for example, by the tests that are given, or by the content of class discussions.)*

---

[2] The basis for this statement is a large and expanding body of research and theory (see, for example, Otto & White, 1982) and direct experience with students (Camperell, 1980; White & Camperell, 1980) and teachers (Morrison, 1980).

Second, as the students are learning how to identify and establish purposes, help them develop the skill of asking questions that they would hope to answer while reading the text for a specific purpose. In the beginning, you should provide model questions for them; but it is essential that you give them guidance in generating questions of their own in line with their purpose for reading.

Third, help the students adjust their reading rate in accordance with their purpose for reading. Again, in the beginning you could suggest appropriate rates; then students should be led to set their own rates in line with the purposes they identify. *(Remember that an individual's rate of reading is a highly personal matter. Suggestions about appropriate rates must be handled on a very personal basis. Take your cues from the student's success in finding answers to the purpose-directed questions that are raised.)*

## Using Prior Knowledge

Recent studies by cognitive psychologists underscore a fact that good teachers seem to have known intuitively for a long time: what is already known affects one's understanding of new material. Kintsch (1982), puts it more strongly when he says that "The meaning of a text . . . is defined only for a particular comprehension episode, and depends as much on the reader's background and goals as on the characteristics of the text itself." In other words, the reader's purpose and prior knowledge combine to shape the meaning that a given reader takes from a given text at a given time.

Interview studies with students (Camperell, 1980; White & Camperell, 1980) suggest that students do, indeed, try to use their prior knowledge to gain understanding in at least three ways: (a) by *relating* the new information in a passage to ideas they have read in preceding passages, (b) by *contrasting* the information they are reading to their prior knowledge and experience, and (c) by *comparing* the information they are reading to their prior knowledge and experience.

Smirnov, a Russian psychologist, also points out the importance of using prior knowledge to comprehend texts. He says, ". . . the greater the knowledge with which the new is correlated, the more it is connected with it, and the more recognized are their connections, the deeper is comprehension" (1973, p. 143). Subjects whom Smirnov interviewed said they engage in the following actions when they try to understand a text: (a) compose a plan, (b) correlate the text with existing knowledge, (c) correlate the content of various parts of the text, (d) utilize images, and (e) translate the content of the text into their own words. *(Notice that "compose a plan" could involve setting a purpose and that "translate the content" is an application of the paraphrasing skill we identified earlier. There is considerable overlap among the skills and strategies we discuss.)*

Smirnov concluded that unless correlating the various parts of a text goes on constantly there can be no comprehension of the text as a whole. One of Smirnov's subjects put it well: "While reading I often stopped in order to emphasize in my mind what had been read, comparing it with what had been said earlier about bacteria" (Smirnov, 1973, p. 143).

It seems clear that using prior knowledge involves two processes: relating text content to existing knowledge and correlating the content of various parts of the text. To develop the strategy, then, students must learn how to relate what they are reading to (a) what they already know and to familiar experiences, and (b) information they have just read in a previous passage of the same text. A teaching sequence should start with *direct teaching* that involves explanations as to what information within the text and within the students' experience is related and in what ways. Later, practice activities should guide students' efforts to correlate existing knowledge with new information. The glossing technique, which is described presently, is particularly well-suited for practice activities.

## Attending to or Imposing Organization

Most of the content area teachers in Morrison's (1980) survey said that students need to develop the strategy of attending to the organization of material to comprehend their textbooks. But they also must actively organize what they are reading in relation to what they already know. In other words, students must learn to seek out and make use of the organization cues provided in their books and, at the same time, devise and improve their own organization of how new information relates to what they already know.

Herber (1978) says that students must learn to be aware of both *internal* and *external* organizational clues in textbooks. Internal organizational patterns include cause-effect development, comparison-contrast, and simple patterns for listing facts. External clues involve *format* (for example, the formulas and problems of math texts and the typographic conventions characteristic of poetry and drama) and *physical features* (such as graphic aids, tables of contents, chapter headings, and subheads).

If a text does not provide a consistent, easy-to-follow organization, students must impose meaningful organization. In addition, they must organize the information they gain in their day-to-day reading in relation to their prior knowledge. The task is not an easy one; and dealing with it must, of course, always be a highly personal matter, for it involves each individual's personal background of experience. Smirnov (1973) found that the people he interviewed had evolved a plan whereby they would break up new material into parts, group related thoughts, and isolate meaningful points. The interviewees seemed to be consciously and actively imposing organization to improve their comprehension.

Teachers can help students develop their strategies for attending to the organization of text through direct teaching (and, as we explain presently, the use of gloss notations). Explicit examples and explanations will help students recognize and make use of the different text formats and external features of text, such as headings and subheadings, and the different internal organizational schemes or "text types" that authors use to organize information. Some of the more common internal organizational schemes are cause-effect, comparison-contrast, sequential order, simple listing, definition, and classification. You can teach students to recognize and make use of all of these schemes as they seek understanding. Begin by (a) pointing out the common organizational schemes as they are actually used in texts, and (b) discussing with students how each of these schemes can serve as an organizational framework for relating prior knowledge to new information.

Consider a well-organized social studies textbook passage titled "Actual Union Operations," which has several subheadings. The teacher can prepare an outline for the passage using the subheadings and discuss each as follows:

| Outline | Discussion |
|---|---|
| A. Collective Bargaining | This section tells about the main function of labor unions. After reading, you should be able to describe collective bargaining, who is involved, and what issues they consider. |
| B. 1. Mediation<br>   2. Voluntary Arbitration<br>   3. Fact Finding | The three subheads identify other methods to use when collective bargaining fails. Compare the three methods and know what is different about each one. |
| C. 1. Presidential Influence<br>   2. Injunction and Seizure | These two sections discuss powers imposed by the president or US government. Why does the president have influence? What are injunctions and seizures? |
| D. Compulsory Arbitration | This section reports on a method that is rarely used. Can you find a relationship between the term *compulsory* and the fact that compulsory arbitration is rarely used? |

## Monitoring Comprehension

Baker and Brown (in press) characterize comprehension monitoring as a metacognitive[3] activity, which "entails keeping track of the success with which one's comprehension is proceeding, ensuring that the process continues smoothly, and taking remedial action if necessary." A reader who is operating at the metacognitive level is aware of the alternative strategies available for tackling different comprehension tasks, and actively chooses the best alternative for a given task. That reader (a) constantly checks to see that the meaning is clear, (b) seeks assurance that the specific purpose for reading is being met, and (c) makes appropriate adjustments as needed—for example, adapting the rate of reading, checking to see that the organization of the text is clear, shifting attention from details to main points, and rereading to clarify certain points.

Comprehension monitoring may seem quite complicated because it requires the reader to apply simultaneously all three of the strategies we just discussed, but it must be developed—as are the other comprehension strategies—from simple, teacher-directed activities to more complex, self-directed acts. Comprehension monitoring begins when the reader notes that a point or concept is not clear and looks for sensible organization in whatever is being read. At the earliest stage, monitoring is largely a matter of responding to questions asked by the teacher and getting clarification

---

[3] Metacognition in reading is defined and discussed in Chapter 8. Review that discussion if necessary (pp. 184–87).

Monitoring comprehension.

through discussion of inadequate answers. The questioning must, of course, be guided by an established purpose.

Ultimately, comprehension monitoring calls for the active, self-directed involvement of the reader. The reader must select the skills and strategies that will be most effective in fulfilling the purpose set for a given reading task. In other words, the reader must not only recognize when problems occur but also be able to select those skills and strategies that are most appropriate for dealing with a given task, and know how to apply the proper strategy or skill to overcome a specific problem.

## Two Techniques for Teaching

We have identified several comprehension skills, which—if they are skills taught in your students' developmental reading program—would be appropriate for corrective teaching. We have also pointed out four comprehension strategies that good readers frequently use. While we are confident that students learn such skills and strategies in reading classes, we are concerned about the difficulty students experience in applying them outside reading class. We now present two techniques that you, the corrective teacher, can use to help students who are not fully comprehending their textbooks, techniques that encourage students to apply skills and strategies in their content-area reading. The two techniques are the *directed reading-thinking activity* and *gloss*.

In the pages that follow we describe each technique. We provide guidelines for inplementation and our own examples of their use with specific elementary textbooks.

## Directed Reading-Thinking Activity

The directed reading-thinking activity (DRTA) was described and popularized by Stauffer (1969) as a means of developing readers' critical thinking abilities. It was originally designed for use in reading class as an alternative to the standard teacher's-edition approach to basal reader selections. Its combination of the teacher's directing and students' thinking makes it well-suited to application of comprehension skills and strategies. The emphasis is on developing students' critical thinking. Stauffer contends that using DRTA with expository material "makes it possible to develop cognitive processes at a much higher level than is otherwise possible (1975, p. 55). He provides examples of "directive questions" that promote involvement with topics in history, geography, and economics, rather than mere memorization of facts (1975, pp. 54–66).

Otto, Rude, and Spiegel (1979) have outlined three steps for using DRTA. Examples are interspersed to show an application of DRTA to a selection from a fifth-grade science textbook.

***Step one: Setting a purpose.*** Otto, Rude, and Spiegel (1979) have identified this first step, developing purposes for reading, as the most important part of the DRTA.

> During this portion of the lesson, students, at first with teacher direction and later by themselves, establish their reasons for reading. You might think of this as the "what are we reading for" section. Accordingly, questions such as "What do you think the title of this story means?" or "Why do you think the girl is holding the dog the way she is?" may be asked of the group. The teacher's job is to elicit a number of *diverse* responses. The greater the number of responses, the more chance there is of student involvement when the story is read. Once a sufficient number of plausible answers have been given, the group is ready to move on to the next step. (p. 242)

Setting a purpose is as important when students read content area textbooks as when they read a basal reader selection. You can use DRTA by substituting the same open-ended questions suggested in the preceding paragraph for the factual, content-specific questions suggested in the teacher's editions of textbooks. Again, your goal is to elicit a number of diverse responses from your students.

Many units or smaller sections of content area texts have subheadings and pictures that you can use to stimulate students' predictions about what the purpose or theme of the entire selection is. The title of a unit of a fifth-grade science textbook (Holmes, Leake, & Shaw, 1983), for example, is "New Sources of Energy"; its sub-headings include "Using geothermal energy," "Garbage power," "Energy from the sun," "Using wind energy," and "Energy from atoms;" and it has pictures of a geyser, a garbage dump, a solar collector on a rooftop, a space satellite's solar battery panels, windmills, and an array of fuel rods for a nuclear power plant. You might tell students the titles even before giving them their textbooks and ask them to speculate about possible "New Sources of Energy." Or you might ask, "What do you think 'Garbage power' is?" before they read the section of the unit bearing that subheading. You might ask, "Why is there a picture of a spacecraft?" or "What does a bunch of ordinary-looking long metal rods have to do with energy?" Remember that you want to stimulate student involvement by getting a large number of responses.

**Step two: Thinking.**     This step gives the activity its name: reading-thinking.

> In this portion of the lesson, the students silently read the selection, relating both personal and vicarious experiences to the story. While the students read, some of their earlier expectations will be rejected, and others will be confirmed. Students are asked to stop reading at selected spots in the story and to conjecture about what might happen next. By following this procedure, students actively engage in a search for evidence to confirm their earlier expectations (Otto, Rude, & Spiegel, 1979, p. 242).

Stauffer (1975, p. 43) suggests varying the amounts of information students may use before predicting what the plot of a basal reader story will be. You might ask your students to predict based on a title only, on first page clues, or on information given in the first half or even five-sixths of a story.

Again, the approach also works well with many selections from content-area textbooks. At well-chosen stopping points throughout a selection, ask questions about the material just read to stimulate students' checking or revising their predictions about what the purpose or theme of the entire selection is. For example, you might stop students after they have read the section "Garbage power" and before they read "Energy from the sun" and ask what they now think is the point of "New Sources of Energy." As they get farther through such a well-organized and appropriately sub-headed unit, they should be able to predict more easily the gist of the unit or the authors' purpose for presenting such diverse subtopics.

**Step three: Testing hypotheses.**     Otto, Rude, and Spiegel (1979) stress that this last step of the DRTA is intimately linked with the other two steps.

> At this point students present the evidence that supports or rejects their earlier conjectures (Stauffer, 1961). It is not really important that some of the hypotheses will be retained and others will not. In the DRTA "right" answers are not the ultimate goal. Instead, the teacher encourages students to explore why some hypotheses might be more acceptable than others. Furthermore, students will learn not to be afraid of supplying more than one answer to questions that have been raised. (p. 242)

If you use the DRTA teaching strategy with "New Sources of Energy," you are concerned not just about your students' scores on the chapter review provided at the end of the unit. That review's ten matching items and six fill-in-the-blank items focus on specific facts (for instance, that atoms are split in nuclear reactors). Even three of the four "Think and Write" questions in that chapter review are narrowly focused. Using DRTA, you would also be concerned about whether your students can use the text to confirm or reject their earlier predictions about the authors' purposes for writing about "Garbage power" or for showing a windmill. Ask your students to share evidence to support or refute earlier predictions and to compare predictions. Which were able to stand up to the evidence? Which ended up having little to do with this text but are nevertheless good ideas that might make sense in light of other information available to your class? You might compare the text's "Review the main ideas" section with the conclusions your class came to about the authors' theme. Alternative themes (such as conservation of existing sources of energy) may be raised or reviewed in light of relevant information from this unit (for instance, that new sources are only in early stages of development—solar energy—or have hazardous side effects—nuclear energy).

There are opportunities throughout this three-step process for you to ask questions that encourage application of comprehension skills and strategies. Directing and questioning in the first step can follow the same suggestions we gave for the strategy of establishing a purpose (pp. 198–99). Students' stopping, conjecturing, and searching for evidence in the second step and testing hypotheses in the third step can—with teacher guidance, especially in the beginning—include their attending to organization, relating prior knowledge, and monitoring their own comprehension. The students might also discover the appropriateness of using specific comprehension skills from their developmental reading program.

The success of DRTA to encourage application of skills and strategies requires that your questioning be guided both by a familiarity with the test (and its skill and strategy demands) and by a knowledge of your students' level of skill and strategy ability. At the same time, you must keep in mind the goal of encouraging critical, divergent thinking. To do that you must respect students' contributions to the reader-text interaction and allow for their reading with many possible purposes in mind and with many possible hypotheses to test. Once purposes are set and hypotheses formed, encourage application of skills and strategies as a means of using the text efficiently and honestly, interacting with it completely to be open to all the evidence it may provide—both in support of and in contradiction of a given hypothesis.

## Gloss

"Gloss" or "glossing" is a procedure that has been around at least since medieval times, when theologians wrote gloss to elucidate scriptures. We suggest a new application of gloss as a technique for improving students' understanding of textbooks. It was developed primarily with secondary students in mind, to teach them the four comprehension strategies described earlier in this chapter and to help them apply skills already learned in elementary school to their subject area reading tasks (Otto, White, Richgels, Hansen, & Morrison, 1981). It is easily used with young children as well; and introducing it in elementary school avoids an artificial and undesirable division of the school years into periods of "learning to read" and "reading to learn."

We describe ways of writing gloss to direct students' attention to places in texts where the application of specific comprehension skills and strategies are appropriate. While gloss notations may be thought of as marginal notations, our procedure involves writing not actually in the margins of texts but on separate sheets of paper and then keying numbered notations to the text with numbered brackets. These brackets appear on the edge of the gloss sheet. When the gloss sheet is placed next to the text page, the brackets set off sections of text to which the gloss notations refer (see Figure 9.1).

The development of gloss was motivated by the belief that comprehension skills and strategies can be taught and by a concern that students need help in making the transition from learning skills to applying them when they read content-area materials (Otto, White, Richgels, Hansen, & Morrison, 1981). In other words, content and process are inseparable; if students are to gain new knowledge from their reading of textbooks, they must be skillful at the reading process.

Gloss is similar to traditional study guides for secondary content-area reading. But, by providing help *during* the reading of the text, gloss is more highly focused than traditional study guides. It focuses on specific parts of texts and on the skills and strategies most useful for understanding those parts.

Think back to our discussion in Chapter 2 of three categories of readers: appliers, tacit appliers and nonappliers. Very briefly, appliers are successful readers; they can see the purpose for a specific reading task and they know how to proceed in view of their purpose. They seldom need corrective help with their reading. Nonappliers seem to have acquired certain skills but they are unable to apply them in a systematic, useful way. In general, they need extensive corrective—possibly remedial—help to become adept appliers and fluent readers. Tacit appliers seem to be able to use the skills they have learned in productive reading, but they do not seem to have any real understanding of how they apply the skills or why.

Tacit appliers would be likely to benefit most from working with glossed materials. As appliers of decoding skills they tend to be fluent readers; but because they lack awareness of their own abilities, their performance and their ultimate progress is limited. Gloss notations can help them to better understand the connection between the acquisition and the application of reading skills and techniques.

Before they can benefit much from gloss notation, nonappliers need to develop sufficient fluency to decode both text and gloss with reasonable ease and comfort. Until decoding comes easy to them, nonappliers are likely to view gloss notations more as a difficult additional task than as helpful hints.

***Guidelines.***    The purpose of glossing is to make easier the reader-text interaction; if you are planning to gloss a text, you ought to know well both the text and your students. In addition, you ought to begin with a specific list of skills and strategies in mind. Any of the comprehension skills presented earlier in this chapter could be an appropriate focus for gloss notations.

*Remember, though, that the skills you stress in corrective teaching should always be the same as the skills that you teach in your developmental reading program—in most instances your basal reader series—even though the resulting list of skills may be different from the ones we listed. That will keep your students from being confused by too many skills or by skills that seem to change from one lesson to another. (You need not be so concerned about the four general strategies we described. Those are —or should be —embodied in any sound program of comprehension instruction. Teaching them is not likely to conflict with the wording or the intent of most basal reader programs.)*

You should then examine the text to determine which of the skills and strategies on your list would be required most for a successful reading of the text. For example, a text whose paragraphs often lack topic sentences may demand a high level of skill at determining main ideas.

The following gloss notation was written to help develop the skill of determining the main idea of a single paragraph in a chapter of a social studies text about families in various cultures:

> The *main idea* of a section of text tells about the *topic* of the section, or what the section is about. This section tells something about families. Look for a word that is used often in this section and that tells about families. The topic of this section is _____ families.

Note that this gloss notation takes the first step in what would be a sequence of steps designed to help readers understand what a main idea is and how to identify one in a variety of contexts. This particular gloss notation defines *main idea* and *topic* in preparation for other gloss notations that would guide the reader's development from identifying topics of paragraphs to identifying topic sentences to, finally, inferring main ideas in the absence of specific topic sentences (see the sequence of main-idea skills given earlier in this chapter, p. 196). Note also that the gloss notation suggests a strategy for identifying the topic of the glossed paragraph so that readers can successfully fill in the blank.

At a later point in the sequence of developing the main-idea skill, a gloss notation like the following would be appropriate:

> Sometimes the *main idea* of a section is not given by any one sentence in the text. The topic of this section is the *dowry system,* but there is no *topic sentence* to tell you the main idea. To get the main idea of this passage you must combine ideas found throughout it. Reread the passage and then complete this telling of its main idea: "The dowry system is illegal and is opposed by females, but _____ _____ ."

The preceding examples were prompted by the demands of a particular text, one requiring a high level of skill at determining main ideas because it often lacks topic sentences. It is equally important to consider the demands or needs of your students. Consider what degree of mastery your students have already shown with the required skills and strategies. Continuing with the example given above, those students who lack a high level of skill at determining main ideas will especially need notations to guide them toward discovery of main ideas not explicitly stated in topic sentences. You should also consider how much prior knowledge your students have of the text's subject matter. Gloss notations may remind readers of past experiences with the subject matter or may simply provide relevant information that the author of the text assumes the reader has.

Another guideline to consider as you write gloss notations is that you should be sensitive to the physical and personal realities of your classroom and your students.

How much time is available for your students to read gloss notations and perform accompanying activities? Are you working with small or large groups, homogeneous or heterogeneous groups? (Unless you are working with individuals or homogeneous groups, it will be difficult to write gloss with students' prior knowledge and prior process ability in mind.) You may even have to consider whether you have enough ditto paper to run multiple copies of gloss sheets.

Finally, you should begin modestly. Concentrate on only a small section of text at one time—for example, a part of a unit—and on only a few skills or strategies with which students need help and that are called for by the strengths and weaknesses of the text.

***Examples.***     We now provide a detailed illustration of gloss written for a selection from a fourth-grade social studies textbook, *Windows on Our World: The Way People Live* (Branson, 1976). (See Figure 9.1.) The text is described, and where necessary quoted, and a hypothetical group of students is described so that you can see the importance of knowing well both your text and your students.

A ten-page section, "Lesson 1" of a unit about language, is entitled "You, Your Language, and Culture." The teacher's edition of *Windows on Our World: The Way People Live* tells that this lesson focuses on how individuals learn language and develops the ideas that language is learned without formal teaching and that speakers accept their own language as "natural" or "right." There is an introduction under the title, "You, Your Language, and Culture." There are six sections: "Homo Sapiens: The Talking Animal," which tells how widespread speech is among humans; "You Discover Language," "You Begin to Learn," and "You Make Progress," which outline an individual's learning to talk; "Language and Culture," which includes the subsections "Everyone Has a Native Language" and "Culture Needs Language" (reproduced with gloss in Figure 9.1); and "Hear It for Yourself," which suggests that students carefully observe and record the speech of younger children, age two to four.

This text is obviously well-organized. The subheadings are descriptive of subsections' content and emphasize the ideas that the teacher's edition had said would be developed. Lists of important facts and pertinent examples and use of direct address and direct questions help the reader to deal with a difficult, fairly abstract subject.

"Language and Culture" (see Figure 9.1) explains, or teaches, more about language than about culture. The text of that section makes some reference to prior knowledge: "Language does many things for human beings. You learned some of those things earlier in this book (page 51)." The text assumes, however, that by now readers know what culture is; no definition of culture is provided; no reference to a previous development of the concept of culture is given; in fact, the word "culture" appears only once. Nowhere does the text say—though it is implied in the first sentence of the last paragraph—that a language is actually a principle artifact of a culture. A final weakness of this subsection is that the last sentence raises an important new subtopic, which is not further developed.

The gloss shown on the right side of Figure 9.1 was written with the preceding observations about *the text* in mind. In addition, in accordance with the guidelines for gloss given earlier in this chapter, the writer of that gloss was guided by a list of skills and strategies (those presented in the first half of this chapter) and a knowledge of the reading ability and prior content knowledge of *the students* who would use that gloss. In the past those students have had difficulty using context to discover word meanings; they depended on previous teachers' supplying a study guide that simply gave new vocabulary and definitions. The students have never paid attention to the organization of the text; in individual conferences, they have tended to read from the beginning of a text when searching for an answer to the teacher's question, rather than going to a subsection whose subheading suggested that it might provide the answer. Despite previous treatment of the concept of *culture,* students have difficulty understanding it. They have associated some of a society's artifacts (language, art, music, literature, even tools and some behaviors, such as how subgroups like women, children, and men are treated) with culture; but it remains a fuzzy, abstract concept for most of the students.

Notation 1 takes advantage of this text's good external organization and helps students learn the strategy of attending to that organization. Notations 2 – 4 are intended to help students apply the skill of using context clues to determine the meaning of a new word. Notations 5 and 6 help students learn the strategy of using prior knowledge. Notations 6 and 7 should help the students overcome the text's assumption that they already have a thorough enough concept of culture to make necessary inferences about language and culture. Notation 8 picks up on a new theme that is only mentioned and not developed in the closing sentence of the text.

The preceding guidelines suggest ways of *writing* gloss. It is important, as well, to consider ways of *using* gloss. Our experience tells us that when students first work with gloss notations they need a careful introduction from the teacher. They need to be informed about the mechanics of gloss—what it is and how it works—and to be encouraged to do the extra reading and writing that the gloss requires. Teachers who have used gloss have reported several ways to motivate their students; (a) by explaining the purposes of gloss notations (that the gloss will help students apply reading skills and strategies where they need them most, in their subject area texts), (b) by demonstrating how the gloss notations and activities may be used in preparing for class discussions and tests, and especially (c) by ensuring that students' initial experience with gloss is pleasant and rewarding. To ensure initial success you must provide careful step-by-step guidance—in person—to the readers. We envision later stages in the use of gloss in which readers will be able to use it more independently, and in which the gloss notations will function less as tools of instruction and more as reminders to the reader to apply appropriate skills and strategies.

# Summary

This chapter describes techniques and procedures that should enable you to help students understand their textbooks. Comprehension skills, which students must learn to apply as they read their textbooks, are stated in terms of instructional objectives. Remember, though, that your corrective teaching ought to be guided by your own list of skills and objectives drawn from your students' developmental read-

## LANGUAGE AND CULTURE

At least 3,000 different languages are spoken in the world today. That may seem like an enormous number of languages. But linguists say there are about 700 African languages alone. No person, however, including you, decided *which* language he or she would learn to speak as a baby.

### Everyone Has a Native Language

Every child is born into a particular group or society. As the child grows, he or she learns to speak the language of the people around him or her. That language is the child's native language or native tongue.

Say that a baby girl is born to French parents in France. And for some reason they give the child up soon after her birth. She is adopted by an English-speaking American couple. While she is still just a few months old, her American parents take her to the United States. She grows up there. Why is her native language English, not French?

Every language seems natural and easy to those who have heard it since their birth. The words which your own society gives to objects seem "right" to you.

For example, if you grow up among English-speaking people, you think a dog should be called *a dog*.

If you have Spanish-speaking parents, you would call a dog *un perro* (oon PAIR'roh).

And if you grew up in a German family, you would think of that animal as *ein Hund* (ine HOONT').

Below you see the words for "dog" in some other languages:

Swahili: *mbwa*
Japanese: *inu*
Russian: *sobaka*
Hebrew: *kelev*

### Culture Needs Language

*Which* language you learned to speak as a baby is not as important as the fact that you *did* learn to speak a language. Language does many things for human beings. You learned some of those things earlier in this book (page 51). Language enables human beings to tell about the past and share hopes and plans for the future. With language people can pass on their experience to other people. And language also makes it possible for human beings to work together.

These things can all be summarized by saying that language is the chief way by which human beings learn about the rest of culture. Language gives every one of us a sense of belonging to the group in which we grow up and live. Language differences can also create problems, however, between people who don't understand each other's way of speaking.

(Text)

1. Titles and subheadings in the text can help you understand how this section is organized. The title of this section is "Language and Culture." There are two subheadings, "Everyone Has a Native Language" and "Culture Needs Language." The texts under those subheadings explain two ways that language is related to culture. Decide which subheading matches which of the following questions (each question can be answered by reading under the right subheading):
   a. Why do a group of people need a language to be able to share their culture?
   b. Why is English your native language?

2. To understand what *native language* means, you must remember the second sentence of this paragraph. That sentence talks about what a native language is, even though you don't see the words "native language" until the last sentence. Reread the second and last sentences of this paragraph and complete this sentence:

   Your _____ is the language you learn from the people around you as you are growing up.

3. This paragraph contains an example of what native language means. Notice that it doesn't matter which society you are born into; what matters is which society you grow up in. In this example, why is the baby girl's native language English, not French?

   _____

4. Here are more examples of what native language means. Where would you have grown up if you always thought a dog should be called *inu*? _____

5. This tells you that you already read about something to do with culture and language. Find two things from page 51 that language does for people and write them here:

   _____

   _____

6. To understand this section, you must know what *culture* means. A group of people share a culture if they have the same kind of music, art, and literature. But other things they make and share are also part of their culture—even things like tools and ways of acting, such as ways of raising their children. In fact, all that they make and share are parts of their _____. MacDonald's is part of our culture. So is PacMan. And so is our language—we make and share it.

7. But language is a special part of our culture because it helps us make and share the other parts of our culture. That is what this sentence tells you. Without language, it would be hard for you to know about MacDonald's or PacMan. Tell something else you might miss out on in our culture without language: _____

   _____

8. You may need an example to help you understand this sentence. Here is an example of how differences in languages may create problems:

   English has only one word for snow. The Eskimo language has several words for many different kinds of snow. Suppose that you have an Eskimo friend who has learned to speak English. What would happen if you phoned him or her and said, "We had a terrible storm last night; there's a lot of snow on the ground"?

   _____

(Gloss Sheet)

**Figure 9.1** Gloss notations for pages from a fourth-grade social studies text. (From *Windows on Our World: The Way People Live*, pp. 259–260, by M. S. Branson, 1976. Boston: Houghton Mifflin. Reprinted by permission.)

ing program. Four comprehension strategies are commonly used by many good readers. The four strategies—establishing a purpose, relating to prior knowledge, attending to organization, and monitoring one's own comprehension—are more general behaviors that you can teach with confidence regardless of which specific skills you teach in the developmental program. The directed reading-thinking activity (DRTA) and gloss are two techniques you can use to encourage students to apply comprehension skills and strategies when they read their textbooks.

# References

Baker, L., & Brown, A. L. (in press). Metacognitive skills of reading. In D. Pearson (Ed.), *Handbook of Reading Research.* New York: Longman.

Branson, M. S. (1976). *Windows on Our World: The Way People Live.* Boston: Houghton-Mifflin.

Camperell, K. (1980). *Identification of seventh grade students' insights about the strategies they used to study and understand an expository text* (Technical Report No. 566). Madison: Wisconsin Research and Development Center for Individualized Schooling.

Downing, J., & Leong, C. (1982). *Psychology of Reading.* New York: Macmillan.

Holmes, N. J., Leake, J. B., & Shaw, M. W. (1983). *Gateways to Science.* New York: McGraw-Hill.

Herber, H. L. (1978). *Teaching Reading in Content Areas.* Englewood Cliffs, N.J.: Prentice-Hall.

Kamm, K., & White, S. R. (1979). *A description of the procedures used in implementing an objective-based reading program in four schools* (Technical Report No. 503). Madison: Wisconsin Research and Development Center for Individualized Schooling.

Kintsch, W. (1982). Text representations. In W. Otto & S. R. White (Eds.), *Reading Expository Material.* New York: Academic Press.

Morrison, B. (1980). *The identification of reading skills essential for learning in seven content areas at postelementary levels* (Technical Report No. 528). Madison: Wisconsin Research and Development Center for Individualized Schooling.

Otto, W., & Askov, E. (1974). *Rationale and guidelines for the Wisconsin design for reading skill development.* Minneapolis: National Computer Systems.

Otto, W., Rude, R., & Spiegel, D. L. (1979). *How to teach reading.* Reading, MA: Addison-Wesley.

Otto, W., & White, S. R. (Eds.) (1982). *Reading expository material.* New York: Academic Press.

Otto, W., White, S. R., Richgels, D., Hansen, R., & Morrison, B. S. (1981). *Part I: A technique for improving the understanding of expository text: Gloss; Part II: Examples of gloss notation* (Theoretical Paper No. 96). Madison: Wisconsin Research and Development Center for Individualized Schooling.

Robinson, H. A. (1978). *Teaching reading and study strategies: The content areas.* Boston: Allyn and Bacon.

Robinson, R. P. (1961). *Effective study.* New York: Harper & Row.

Smirnov, A. A. (1973). *Problems of the psychology of memory.* New York: Plenum Press.

Stauffer, R. G. (1969). *Directing reading maturity as a cognitive process.* New York: Harper & Row.

Stauffer, R. G. (1975). *Directing the reading-thinking process.* New York: Harper & Row.

White, S. R., & Camperell, K. (1980). *Investigations into students' understanding of the reading process and their perception of ability to read content material* (Working Paper No. 302). Madison: Wisconsin Research and Development Center for Individualized Schooling.

# Check Your Reading Comprehension

1. Why are specific skills and strategies described as "enabling behaviors?" Why should these be presented in context?

2. The authors described two reading situations: *learning-to-read* and *learning-from-text.* How are these situations different? How are they similar?

3. What are the four comprehension strategies commonly used by good readers?

4. What should be the main thrust of a corrective reading program?

5. How should a teacher choose the skills to emphasize in a corrective reading program?

6. Imagine that you are a ninth-grade teacher. You decide to use the DRTA strategy with the passage entitled "Consumer Choices" (Figure 9.2). You begin by having the students suggest purposes for reading. List three possible statements/questions your students might offer.

   a.

   b.

   c.

   After reading the passage, you should help your students test their hypotheses. Find evidence (in the selection) that either supports or rejects your earlier statements/questions.

   a.

   b.

   c.

# CONSUMER CHOICES

Consumers in the United States are free to use their disposable (after tax) incomes as they wish. Most people's incomes are not high enough to allow them to buy everything they want. They must make their decisions on the basis of opportunity cost. **Opportunity cost** is the value of whatever is given up when an economic choice is made. When a society makes a decision to use resources to produce one thing over another, the opportunity cost is the value of what might have been produced instead. When a person decides to go to law school, the opportunity cost is the value of what might have been done instead—getting a job, for example. When a person decides to buy a new car, the opportunity cost is the value of other things that could have been done with the money.

Each consumer tries to choose the combination of goods and services that will have the greatest utility or usefulness. The right combination is the one that will bring the most personal satisfaction to the consumer. One person may choose to spend a large part of his or her income on a fancy car. Another may choose to spend the same amount of money on clothes. One way that consumers make these decisions is according to the principle of marginal utility. **Marginal utility** is the extra usefulness or satisfaction that the consumer gets from one more unit of any product. Usually, the more the consumer gets of any one good or service, the less marginal utility it has. The first piece of pie has great utility to someone who is hungry. The second piece gives somewhat less satisfaction. But the third or fourth piece of pie may have no marginal utility at all.

The decisions of an individual consumer are influenced by many things, such as personal tastes, family background, the opinions of others, and education. A major influence is advertising. Businesses compete to sell their products by buying time on radio and television and space in newspapers and magazines to advertise. A single company may spend millions of dollars a year on advertising. Much advertising attempts to make people want things they never wanted before. Advertising can be helpful

**Figure 9.2** Consumer Choices. (From *Urban Communities,* pp. 213–215, by I. Cutler, P. Senn, J. Zevin, and M. Branson, 1982. Columbus, OH: Charles E. Merrill. Reprinted by permission.)

A hundred years ago, the consumer had fewer choices of things to buy. Chances were that the buyer and the seller knew each other and lived in the same area. The rule of the day was "let the buyer beware." This meant that buyers had to watch out for their own interests. If they were cheated, it was their own fault.

As our society became more industrialized and more urbanized, the variety of goods available greatly increased. Technology and specialization of labor made it almost impossible for individual buyers to protect themselves. They could not always know who made a product, or how it was made, or what went into it.

Now the federal government has taken over a large part of the responsibility for protecting consumers. Many federal agencies, such as the Food and Drug Administration, enforce consumer protection laws. Private organizations of consumers work to educate people and to get more consumer protection laws passed.

Consumers may decide to save part of their incomes rather than spend all they have. A person who puts money in a savings account is lending money to the bank and receives interest on the account. Putting money into pension plans, credit unions, life insurance, stocks, or bonds are some other ways of saving. Savings by individuals and businesses become an important source of money capital for investments. Banks and other financial institutions use part of the money they are holding as savings to make loans. People borrow this money to buy homes, businesses borrow to expand, and governments borrow to meet their everyday expenses. If people and businesses did not save, money for these loans would not exist.

to consumers by giving them truthful information about what products are available, what they do, and what they cost. Some advertising, however, is misleading. The consumer must be careful to separate facts from other methods of persuasion. For example, an advertisement may appeal to the feelings of vanity or fear that most people have, by suggesting that a person who does not use the product is not good-looking, or not respectable, or not popular.

## 15-3 Three Points

Imagine that the ice on an ice rink never ends. In geometry, the idea of a never-ending flat surface is called a **plane.**

A photographer at the ice rink uses a tripod having three adjustable legs. For the tripod to stand, the tips of the legs must *not* be placed in a straight line.

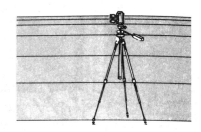

For any three points not in a straight line, there is exactly one plane which contains the three points.

Suppose you connect the tips of the tripod legs with line segments as shown below.

The resulting figure is called a **triangle.** This triangle can be referred to as triangle *ABC* and symbolized as △*ABC*.

The three angles in the figure are ∠*ABC*, ∠*BCA*, and ∠*CAB*. The angles also can be named as ∠*B*, ∠*C*, and ∠*A*.

The line segments are called the **sides.** One side is $\overline{AB}$. Name the other two sides.

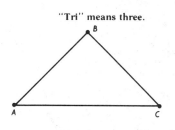

"Tri" means three.

*Complete the following.*

1. A pane of glass is a model for part of a plane. Name three other models of parts of a plane.

2. In your classroom, find three models of points. Be sure that the points are not in a line. Imagine a triangle formed by these points. How many planes can include the points of the triangle?

3. Think of three points on a line through the spiral of a notebook. Think of the pages as planes. How many planes can include the three points?

4. Imagine four points not all in one plane. By choosing three points at a time, how many planes can you find?

5. Is it easier to make a 3-legged stool or a 4-legged chair steady? Explain.

6. Name the angles of △*DEF* and the line segments that form △*DEF*.

**Figure 9.3** Three Points. (From *Mathematics of Everday Life,* p. 324, by J. Price, O. L. Brame, M. Charles, and M. L. Clifford, 1982. Columbus, OH: Charles E. Merrill. Reprinted by permission.)

7.  Imagine that you are a seventh-grade teacher. You decide to use the glossing strategy with the passage entitled "Three Points" (Figure 9.3). You plan to use glossing to identify and develop vocabulary. Write the gloss notations you feel are appropriate.

8.  Choose a selection from one of the textbooks you are using with your class. Develop a DRTA lesson based on the selection.

9.  Choose a selection from one of the textbooks you are using with your class. Develop a set of gloss notations to be used with the selection.

# 10

# Guiding Students' Reading and Study Skills

Gloss, as presented in Chapter 9, is a very effective technique for ensuring comprehension while a student reads. It enables interaction between the text, teacher, and reader during the reading process. Sometimes, however, gloss is not practical, for example, while doing independent research in the library. Study guides offer a different kind of aid to comprehension.

You may be wondering how gloss and study guides differ. Gloss focuses to a greater extent on the processes of reading. Study guides, on the other hand, tend to emphasize content rather than processes. You must assess the needs of your students to determine whether you will use gloss or a study guide for a particular reading assignment. If comprehension of the reading material requires knowledge of new organizational writing patterns, for instance, gloss might better help students comprehend the material. Otherwise, a study guide might be equally effective.

Since variety in any study technique is important in maintaining interest and motivation, we present several types of study guides. The nature of the material to be read greatly determines which guide is most appropriate. After we consider study guides, we present some study skills that are particularly useful to underachieving readers.

# Study Guides

Some study guides are intended for use as the students read, as is gloss. Others are to be used following the reading. You, the teacher, must be sure that students understand the intended procedure.

The first step in creating a study guide is a careful analysis of your objectives in assigning the reading material. What do you want the students to learn from reading the material? Do you expect all students to attain equal mastery of all the objectives? In other words, can you realistically expect similar comprehension of the material by all students?

*Obviously not; it is unrealistic to expect that able readers and disabled readers will be able to comprehend a piece of reading material, especially textbook material, equally well. So your objectives in assigning the material may actually differ for the different types of readers.*

For the best readers you may intend the assigned reading material as a general introduction to a topic and plan to have them pursue more reading on the topic afterwards. With the average readers you may use the reading material as the major resource for their study of the topic. Gloss or a study guide may help to guide the average reader's comprehension. You know that the disabled readers need more assistance in reading the selection than the average and very able readers. You also know that much of the conceptual background—the content about which they are reading—may have to be filled in through sources other than reading, such as films, audiotapes, and class discussion. Your expectation for these readers is to have them grasp the main ideas from the reading selection, knowing that it is unrealistic to expect more from them.

Having determined the objectives for reading the material, next analyze the text to determine what types of assistance might be most effective for the different types of readers. Since you have various options, including numerous types of gloss and study guides, it is important to study the reading selection to see if any pattern or organization exists that the readers must detect to comprehend the selection. This step is particularly important for the underachieving readers.

Also consider the levels of thinking that you want to promote. The level of thinking is usually encouraged by the kinds of questions you ask. If the objective in reading a selection is to learn factual information about a subject, then literal-level reading comprehension is appropriate. Questions about facts and clearly stated main ideas encourage literal comprehension. If you want students to be able to make inferences beyond what is stated, then study guide questions should encourage inferential thinking by probing beyond what is specifically stated in the text. If you want students to be able to make critical or evaluative judgments—for example, comparing two accounts of the same event in history—then create some questions to promote critical thinking. We recommend that teachers try to include all three levels of questioning in study guides if their objectives and evaluation include these levels of thinking. Barrett's *Taxonomy of Reading Comprehension* (1972), based on Bloom's *Taxonomy of Educational Objectives* (1956), suggests some questions appropriate for each level.

After creating the guide, again check it against your objectives for reading. Also check the guide against the evaluation to be used at the completion of study of the topic. You should be able to see a clear correspondence between objectives, guide, and evaluation. For example, if the evaluation emphasizes understanding of the main ideas, then the objectives and study guide should similarly stress the main ideas of the material.

You can give advance organizers (Ausubel, 1968), or prompts, to students before they read to alert them to what is important in an assignment. Advance organizers can effectively promote reading comprehension when they appropriately reflect the instructor's objectives and evaluation. Gloss and study guides are types of advance organizers that help the reader—especially the underachieving reader—sort out what is to be learned from a reading selection.

## Guide for Underachieving Readers

The first guide we present is intended for poor readers who are unable to read a textbook without help. The study guide in fact tells them what to read and what not to read. Most content area textbooks contain descriptive details that embellish the main ideas. Poor readers usually get lost in the details, "unable to see the forest for all the trees." This type of guide enables a reader such as John in Chapter 1 to read a textbook that is actually at his frustration level. Figure 10.1 gives an example of a study guide that directs disabled readers in what they should read. They use it while they are reading an assigned reading selection.

## Category Guide

Another type of study guide effective with underachieving readers requires them to organize information by filling in a chart. This type of guide is particularly useful for a child like Allison in Chapter 1 who does not actively read for meaning. The guide forces her to think about the material.

First the students read the material, which does not contain many descriptive details, but which they would not comprehend without assistance. Upon completion of the reading selection, they fill in a chart requiring categorization of information. Because they have to arrange the material into categories, they are more likely to

---

1. Read the last paragraph. This summarizes the selection.
2. Read paragraph 1. Write the main idea: _____
   _____ .
3. Skip paragraph 2.
4. Read the first sentence of paragraph 3. How does this help you understand the main idea in the first paragraph?
   _____ .

**Figure 10.1**  Sample from a Study Guide for Disabled Readers

| Explorers | Route | Destination | Discovery | Date |
|---|---|---|---|---|
| DeSoto | | | | |
| Marquette | | | | |
| Lewis and Clark | | | | |
| Balboa | | | | |

**Figure 10.2**   Category Guide for Disabled Readers

remember the content. Figure 10.2 shows an example of a guide intended to accompany a social studies textbook. The textbook material described the routes of explorers. Recording important details in the correct category helps the students remember them. This type of guide is also useful if students are reading a variety of materials on the same topics. They know what types of information they must seek from either assigned materials or library research.

## Common Questions for Multiple Reading Materials

A related type of guide that is effective with alternative materials is simply a common set of questions to guide students in their reading. To accommodate differences in reading abilities, you may sometimes assign different reading materials of various difficulty levels on the same topic of study. Rather than creating a separate study guide for each set of materials, provide a common set of questions for the students to answer as they read, regardless of the materials they are using.

Similarly, you might allow choice of topics and reading materials within a unit of study. Guide the students in matching reading materials to their reading abilities. If sixth graders were researching life in different countries of their choice, for example, you could give them a common set of guide questions for studying each country. Questions would pertain to such topics as transportation, food, shelter, and trade products. One question might be "Describe the major industries in your country; why did these develop?" Regardless of which reading materials they were using, the students would search for answers to that same question. Design the common set of questions to tap the main ideas. The students thus grasp the important concepts of the unit of study by using the study guide.

## Pattern Guide

Pattern guides (Estes & Vaughn, 1978) can help teach students to recognize the patterns of cause-effect or comparison-contrast in a selection. Because underachieving readers often invest so much effort in simply decoding words they fail to see the organization of the text. A pattern guide can help them see the structure. The example in Figure 10.3 is based on a science book on planets.

---

### The Planets

There are many planets in our solar system. As you read, you will be learning some interesting facts about the planets. You will be learning some things that make the planets *alike* and some things that make them *different*.

The first planet that you are going to read about is *Mercury*. You will be comparing facts about Mercury with facts about Earth. See if you can find out how these two planets are alike and how they are different.

Below are two lists. List A tells you some interesting facts about Earth. Read these to yourself. Now you will need to complete List B. Fill in the facts about Mercury that match the facts about Earth using your science book. Number 1 has been done to help you. Read pages 3–10 to find out about Mercury.

| List A | List B |
|--------|--------|
| 1. Earth is the third planet from the sun. | 1. Mercury is the first planet. It is the planet nearest the sun. |
| 2. The earth is 93 million miles from the sun. | 2. |
| 3. The earth is a medium-sized planet. | 3. |
| 4. It takes the earth 365 days to *revolve* or go around the sun. | 4. |
| 5. It takes the earth 24 hours to *rotate* or spin around one time. | 5. |
| 6. The earth gets just enough heat from the sun to let us stay alive. | 6. |
| 7. The coldest temperatures on the earth get down to 125 degrees below zero. If the earth were further from the sun, everything would freeze! | 7. |
| 8. The earth's surface has many different coverings. It has mountains, valleys, lakes, and oceans. | 8. |

---

**Figure 10.3** Pattern Guide. Prepared by Sarah D. Weidler, State College (PA) Area School District

## Problem-Solving Guide

Word problems in math often are troublesome for underachieving readers. Teachers complain that these students can do the problems only if they are given simple procedures to follow. The students seem to lack knowledge of how to attack word

---

### Mathematics Problem-Solving Guide

Directions to students: The following six statements or questions are designed to help you solve the thought problems on this worksheet. Before you read each problem, number your scrap paper from one to six and leave extra room for number one and number five. After you have numbered your paper, come back to this worksheet, read the six questions, and follow any directions given. Each thought problem should have the six steps outlined on your scrap paper before you write your answer on the blank beside the problem. Good luck!

1. Read the problem quickly to form a picture in your mind and draw that picture on your paper beside number one.
2. Reread the problem to understand what you are to find out and write what you are to find beside number two. For example, if the problem asks that you find bananas, then write the word "Bananas" beside number two.
3. Reread the problem for a second time to find out exact figures and values and write them beside number three on your paper.
4. Make up a formula to fit the problem and write the formula beside number four on your paper.
5. Solve the problem beside number five on your paper using your formula and the exact values from the problem.
6. Read your answer and the problem again to see if your answer makes sense. If it makes sense, go on to the next problem. If your answer does not make sense then go back and look at each of the steps to see if you can find a mistake. If all else fails, ask me or one of the student helpers for some help.

### Thought Problems

A. What is the speed per hour of a jogger that runs 20 miles in 4 hours? _____
B. At 13 miles an hour how far can Judy run in 23 hours? _____
C. How many hours will it take Sam to go 399 miles if his sailboat travels at a rate of 21 miles per hour? _____
D. Juan and his mother jogged one week and ran the following number of miles each day: 14 miles, 9 miles, 17 miles, 15 miles, 18 miles, 20 miles, and 12 miles. What was the average number of miles they ran per day? _____
E. Dan Beppu flew 2,944 miles in 16 hours to visit his grandfather. What was the average rate of speed per hour of the plane he flew in? _____
F. A health food store manager sold 560 jars of wheat germ at $3 per jar. After paying $892 for a used car, how much money did he have left from his sale of wheat germ? _____

---

**Figure 10.4**    Problem-Solving Guide for Math Word Problems. Prepared by Rodger Smith, Mifflin County, PA, School District, from *Content Area Reading* (pp. 197–198) by M. M. Dupuis and E. N. Askov, 1982. Englewood Cliffs, N.J.: Prentice-Hall. Reprinted by permission.

problems. Some math teachers (following suggestions by Earle, 1976) outline a step-by-step process that may be taught to all students. Sometimes it helps to place these procedures on a chart or bulletin board for the students' reference. In devising the problem-solving guide presented in Figure 10.4, the teacher required poor readers to

---

## Answers

A.
1.
2. speed of the jogger
3. runs 20 miles in 4 hours
4. $\dfrac{\text{miles}}{\text{hours}} = \dfrac{\text{distance}}{\text{time}} = \text{rate/speed}$
5. speed $= \dfrac{20}{4} = 5$ miles per hour
6. yes

B.
1.
2. distance run
3. runs 23 hours at 13 miles an hour
4. $d = rt$
5. $d = 23 \times 13 = 299$ miles
6. yes

C.
1.
2. number of hours
3. 399 miles; 21 miles
4. $\text{time} = \dfrac{\text{distance}}{\text{rate}}$
5. $\text{time} = \dfrac{399}{21} = 19$ hours
6. yes

D.
1.
2. average miles per day
3. 14, 9, 17, 15, 18, 20, 12 miles; 7 days
4. $\text{average miles} = \dfrac{\text{total miles}}{\text{number of days}}$
5. average $= 14 + 9 + 17 + 15 + 18 + 20 + 12 = \dfrac{105}{7} = 15$ miles per day
6. yes

E.
1.
2. average rate of speed per hour
3. 2,944 miles; 16 hours
4. $\text{rate} = \dfrac{\text{distance}}{\text{rate}}$
5. $\text{rate} = \dfrac{2{,}944 \text{ miles}}{16 \text{ hours}}$
6. 184 miles per hour
6. yes

F.
1.
2. How much money is left over?
3. 560 jars at $3 per jar; $892 for a car
4. jars × price = income
   income − car = leftover
5. $560 \times \$3 = 1680$
   $\$1{,}680 - \$892 = \$788$ leftover
6. yes

fill in each step of the guide (the six questions) as they worked through each thought problem.

As stated in the beginning of this chapter, variety in study guides is important to avoid tedium. If you use the same type of guide repeatedly, students tend to ignore it or else copy the answers from another student simply to get it finished. A bit of humor throughout helps lighten the task. Since you know your students better than a textbook publisher, you can tailor your guides to your students in ways that questions at the end of a chapter cannot. We advise looking at textbook questions and exercises carefully. In our experience, often these questions require either rote recall or such high-level inferential/creative thinking that even the teacher is unsure of the desired answer! You can incorporate textbook questions that do seem valuable into a study guide that includes other items of your own devising.

# Study Skills

Next we consider the study skills that disabled readers need to know in order to "survive" academically in content area subjects, especially as they enter junior high school. Unfortunately, without guidance in reading and without important study skills, many disabled readers do not make it through high school. This waste of human resources can be prevented if teachers find appropriate alternative materials, offer guidance in reading, and teach the basic study skills.

Study skills are the important learning-how-to-learn skills. They enable a person to continue learning independently after completing school experiences. They enhance school learning by making reading and study more efficient and effective.

Study skills are especially important for those students who are having difficulty learning how to read. These skills help students improve their reading comprehension and retain what they have read. Askov and Kamm (1982) recommend that study skills be taught as part of content area studies to ensure transfer of the skills to realistic reading tasks. Incorporating study skills instruction into content area studies also helps students learn the content subject.

Here we are concerned with five study skills that are particularly useful for the underachieving reader. Coverage of additional study skills may be found in Askov and Kamm (1982).

## Test-Taking Skills

Test taking is important for all students, regardless of reading abilities. But test-taking skills can especially help poor readers. Because these children have trouble reading the test as well as the material on which they are being tested, they are often unable to demonstrate on the test what they do know about the material.

Not only the teacher, but also the students, should be able to see the correspondence, shown in Figure 10.5, between objectives for instruction, instructional processes, and test questions.

Teachers should objectively examine their test questions to see if the questions accurately reflect the instructional objectives and learning strategies employed. For

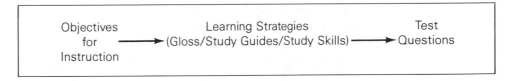

**Figure 10.5** Flowchart for Analyzing Instruction

example, a science unit may present information on the forms of matter (solids, liquids, gases) and on how physical changes occur to elementary children. The objectives for instruction may include knowledge of this information and application in children's lives. Learning strategies may include reading textbook materials with a study guide plus classroom demonstrations of physical changes. Test questions should appropriately assess understanding of this information and application in the children's lives. If test questions require the student to know material that has not been taught, they are not appropriate.

Test questions should also assess the type of reading that has been required. If a study guide has stressed only the main ideas found in reading materials, assessing comprehension of details would not be appropriate. On the other hand, some teachers like to give a "thought question" on a test that requires students to make inferences beyond the materials studied. This is appropriate if it has been included in the objectives for instruction and encouraged by instruction.

Assuming that you are able to see this correspondence between objectives, learning strategies, and test questions, the next step is to be sure that this correspondence is communicated to students. Be sure to inform students of their objectives for instruction as well as the importance of these objectives to their lives. Unless students understand the objectives before study and see their relevance, only the very able students, motivated by other reasons, will learn the material (Anderson & Armbruster, 1982).

One teacher we know, before a unit of instruction in social studies, shows his objectives for instruction and his unit test questions to all students. He points out how the test questions measure mastery of his objectives. Although students have no further access to the test questions during study, they have a better idea of what the teacher considers important in the unit. They realize whether he is interested primarily in their learning main ideas or whether details, such as names and dates, are also important. They see the type of test—whether it is multiple choice, completion, essay, or something else. He works especially closely with the disabled readers to show them study techniques that help them prepare for the unit test.

The advantage of such a procedure is that the students learn how to prepare for different types of exams. If they receive no guidance, they may spend study time learning only factual details while the test may require that they grasp main ideas and concepts.

*Another advantage of this approach is that it keeps a teacher honest, so to speak. If you wait until the night before the test date to dash off some quick test items, your test may not really measure what you believe is important in the material and what you have been stressing in instruction.*

Another approach to teaching test-taking skills is to encourage students to analyze test items after an examination while working in small groups. The procedure goes like this:

1.  After the exams are scored, assign the children to small groups to analyze the test content.
2.  Put the objectives for instruction on the chalkboard with the numbers of the test items that relate to each objective.
3.  Have the students discuss each item—why a particular answer is correct or incorrect.

Be sure to include in each group at least one child who did well on the exam and who can talk about his or her choices if necessary. (This role is sometimes good for gifted children who may need leadership experience.)

Through analysis of test items you are laying the foundation for later work on test-taking skills. As students learn how you construct tests to measure particular objectives for instruction, they also learn how to study to prepare for those types of tests. When they are in high school they can learn more sophisticated test-taking skills, such as elimination of distractors from multiple-choice items. Disabled readers particularly benefit from test-item analysis because often their study is inefficient and ineffective. Because they do not know how to read appropriately, they also do not know how to study appropriately for a test. Unfortunately, by the time they reach junior or senior high school, many have simply given up because their past efforts have not been successful.

The following study skills will not only help students prepare for tests but also enable them to learn content concepts more easily and independently.

## Independent Study Technique

One reason to use gloss and study guides is to help students comprehend content material independently—to show them how to read. Because students cannot always depend on having their teacher's guidance, however, they need to learn how to guide their own reading to achieve good comprehension as they ultimately will have to do in the upper grades and once they are out-of-school.

The earliest and probably most widely known technique for independent study is SQ3R (Robinson, 1961), which is an abbreviation for Survey, Question, Read, Recite, and Review. Other similar formulas have been devised to prompt students to remember steps in the studying process. The initials are relatively unimportant; what is important is teaching students the process, which applies to short selections or whole books. We outline the independent study technique in the following paragraphs.

***Surveying, or previewing, the material.***    Quickly read through the major headings as well as the introductory and summary paragraphs to get an overview of the selection. In a book, this involves reading the table of contents and prefatory material that explain what the intent and audience of the book are. In this step the material may be deemed acceptable or rejected as inappropriate for the reader's intended purpose. This survey process is essentially the same as skimming.

***Formulating questions.*** Based on the survey, the reader formulates questions that he or she expects the reading material to answer. The reader may do this by converting headings or chapter titles into question format. The reader should write down questions, leaving space for answers.

***Reading the material.*** Now the student is able to read purposefully because of the questions set forth. It is easier to grasp the main ideas and see the relative importance of supporting details.

***Answering questions.*** The student writes answers to the questions set down in the second step, also jotting down other important details. If the questions have identified the main ideas of a selection, then in essence answering them becomes similar to the process of outlining. The reader should write notes in his or her own words to insure that they are meaningful.

***Studying.*** At a later point the student should review the notes to recall the main ideas and important details. Because the student has gone through the process of actively reading the material—by formulating and answering questions—the notes should be meaningful. In fact, rereading notes should be more meaningful than reading the material itself.

Teach these steps using content area reading materials. First, demonstrate the steps with a reading assignment in class. Next, assign the students to groups (again including at least one able reader in each group) and have each group go through the steps of the independent study technique in writing. Finally, ask the students to turn in as an assignment the written steps of the independent study technique. Continue to require these written steps throughout the school year for assigned reading material not accompanied by a gloss or study guide. Doing so will reinforce the students' learning technique.

Teaching students to use the independent study technique corresponds to the view, presented in Chapter 8, that the preparation and background a reader brings to reading material is crucial to comprehension. Using the directed reading-thinking activity, gloss, and study guides, the teacher guides students through the material and helps them identify important points. Through the use of the independent study technique, the reader guides himself or herself through the task of reading. By anticipating what will be said, the reader becomes actively involved in the reading task. The reader who is comprehending is not just passively processing the writer's words, but is actively engaged in the problem-solving task of trying to answer anticipated questions. The strategy is particularly helpful for readers like Allison in Chapter 1 for whom reading is a process of merely saying the words but not grasping meaning.

Students usually do not readily accept the extra work involved in using independent study techniques. Passively reading and rereading material is easier than actively trying to anticipate what the author is saying. Therefore, you must require students to formulate and answer questions. You must check the answers, as you would a study guide, until the process becomes truly independent. Effective independent study habits may indeed be the most important learning that students can take away from content area study.

One caution, suggested by Anderson and Armbruster (1982), is in order. Sometimes a student's questions tend to be trivial if the textbook headings do not adequately state the main idea of the section. For example, if a heading in a social studies textbook were labeled "The Louisiana Purchase," a student might convert that heading to "What was the Louisiana Purchase?" While an answer stating the date, extent of territory purchased, and amount of money paid might be appropriate in some instances, the important point may actually be the impact that the Louisiana Purchase had on the eventual development of the United States. Therefore, students should be aware that a heading may not always form the best question; the material may very likely go beyond the scope suggested by the heading.

## Organization of Study Material

Most elementary and junior high school students have trouble in organizing notes and other papers. The senior author's son, when a sixth grader, was known to sigh, "Oh, if only I could get organized!" Usually desks, book bags, and textbooks are crammed with assorted papers with no apparent order. Teachers complain that students are not

Someday I'll get organized!

even able to copy information from the chalkboard accurately—for example, that they copy solutions to math problems down the page instead of across the page in the logical sequence of steps shown on the chalkboard.

This situation is exacerbated for a poor reader, particularly a learning disabled student who has general organizational and sequencing problems anyway. Solutions are not easy, but sometimes teachers can help students organize materials.

Because students need to take notes in class, the first step may be to provide composition books to students for each content area. If the school budget does not permit this expenditure, another alternative is requiring students to purchase either a ring binder notebook with dividers or separate spiral bound notebooks for each subject. Make it clear to students that they should do all notetaking in these notebooks, not on loose sheets of paper. They should leave the notebooks at school and use them for no other purpose.

Some teachers have found weekly assignment sheets (on ditto paper) to be helpful. The usual weekly assignments, such as spelling, reading, social studies, writing, and so forth, are listed in the left column with the days of the week listed across the top of the page as column heads. Vertical and horizontal lines are drawn to create boxes. The students enter the dates that the various assignments are due. When students have organizational problems, the assignment sheet becomes a communication device between teacher and parents so that progress may be monitored at home. Rewards for completing assignments on time, such as participation in a special activity or bonus points, may provide incentives. Students should also be informed of the realities of high school—that late assignments lose points and lost assignments receive no points.

## Notetaking

Content area materials, even for first grade students, are often written in the narrative form so children can more easily understand them. By third grade, however, most children are expected to read expository content materials. Many children have difficulty at this point for two reasons. First, they can no longer rely on the familiar "story" organization, for presentation of main ideas with supporting details characterizes expository organization. Second, the content may not be as familiar as in the narrative stories. In fact, the purpose of content reading materials is to introduce new information. Vocabulary terms become increasingly harder as familiar background concepts are extended and new concepts introduced. Students must learn to take notes to deal with the new information and the unfamiliar method of presentation.

The study guide requires a form of notetaking when used with young children. The teacher, however, is directing the students to the important aspects of the material. Because study guide questions are often rewordings of the headings used in the material, students learn to read the headings to help them identify the main ideas. Therefore, teaching the use of study guides is a good way to begin teaching notetaking.

As students become accustomed to study guides, they need opportunities for independent notetaking. You can help students by alerting them to what is important for them to remember from the material. If not guided, they may try to write down everything, or they may record very little. A teacher's directions, while not as explicit as study guide questions, help students learn to pick out what is important in the material.

Eventually, students must take notes independently. At that point they must have clearly in mind the purpose for their notetaking. They must know whether they are reading the material to prepare for a test, to pursue a research project, or to achieve some other end. You can help by establishing the purpose for reading.

Students' notes, of course, should reflect that purpose. If you have directed students to read for the main ideas, then their notes should contain the main ideas of the content materials. As a part of teaching notetaking, check students' notes to see whether they have recorded the proper type of information.

Students should learn to use note cards to prepare for a research project. You might require that a certain number of note cards be filled out in response to specified questions about the subject to be researched. One sixth-grade teacher helped a student devise three questions about Charles Lindbergh to be used as a guide to notetaking in an individual research project. The questions related to Lindbergh's contributions to aviation, his role in World War II, and the circumstances of his child's kidnapping. The student was to gather information from the research only about these questions. Different aspects of each question were to be recorded on separate note-cards. In preparing an outline for the research report, the student was then expected to organize the note cards first by the questions, then by the topics under each question.

The senior author has observed the same procedure being used at Benchmark School, a private school for children with learning difficulties near Philadelphia. Even primary-grade children use this notetaking technique as a means for organizing their writing. Through writing a research report for social studies, they also learn how to read content materials as they gather information from written sources. (The relationship of reading and writing will be discussed in Chapter 12.)

One final suggestion about notetaking is that students be required to paraphrase. Simply writing down an author's words does not help a student remember the material well. "Translating," or rewording, forces the student to think about meaning. The active thought process or "depth of processing" is what aids comprehension (Anderson & Armbruster, 1982).

Some students underline as a study technique. *We have reservations about this technique because underlining does not force the reader to rework, rephrase, and think about the material. In our opinion, students can use underlining effectively only if they have already mastered the processes of notetaking and outlining. Then underlining may be more than mere rote underscoring. It may include designation of importance of ideas, listing by numerals which details fit under a main idea, and marginal notes. We regard underlining as a study technique more appropriate for the college student who has already learned to take notes effectively.*

Having students write a summary of assigned material is another way to check their ability to grasp main ideas. Encourage students to create summaries *in their own words* in addition to notes that they take. The summary expresses only the main ideas; notes, on the other hand, express both main ideas and important details.

## Outlining and Mapping

Outlining while reading is a specialized form of notetaking. The objectives in teaching outlining are to help students see relationships while reading and to organize their own ideas in preparing a written or oral report. Outlining is probably more useful for the second purpose—that of helping students organize their own ideas for presentation to others. Nevertheless, teachers often use outlining of reading material to teach students the process of outlining. In other words, the first step is to learn to outline written material; the next step is to create an outline of one's own ideas to present to others.

Students can learn to outline material in the upper elementary grades by completing partial outlines. You might provide the main headings and some supporting details, requiring students to fill in most of the subheadings that represent the important details. Figure 10.6 provides an example of a partial outline.

---

### Nature Changes Rocks

I. Weathering
    A. What is it? _____
    B. When does it happen? _____
II. Water changes rocks
    A. Fast water picks up sediments
        1. _____
        2. Sediments chip off small pieces of rocks.
    B. Rocks may have cracks.
        1. _____
        2. When water freezes, ice _____
        _____
        3. _____
    C. Water soaks into rocks
        1. Minerals leave rocks when water moves out
        2. _____
        3. Rocks break apart
    D. Erosion
        A. What is it? _____
        B. When the water slows down, sediments _____
III. Wind changes rocks
    A. Wind blows sediments against rocks.
    B. Wind can cause _____ and _____
IV. Living things change rocks.
    A. _____
    B. _____
    C. People use machines to break rocks.

---

**Figure 10.6** Sample Outline: Nature Changes Rocks. Based on *Accent on Science,* pp. 198–205, by R. B. Sund, D. K. Adams, J. K. Hackett, and R. H. Moyer, 1983. Columbus, OH: Charles E. Merrill. Reprinted by permission.

We are not overly concerned about formal outlining in notetaking. In formal outlining each heading and subheading should be presented in the same form class, or part of speech. In other words, all headings and subheadings should consist of either noun phrases or verb phrases, but the two constructions should not be mixed. While formal outlining may be of some value in teaching logical thinking and organization, it does not seem necessary when outlining is used as a form of notetaking.

Outlining shows the logical relationships when main ideas and supporting details are clearly presented. A newer system, mapping, may be more effective in illustrating relationships when the organization does not consist of main ideas and supporting details.

Mapping is a visual representation of the relationships in a passage. Since it can become quite complex and time-consuming to try to show all relationships within a passage, we recommend using mapping only when a visual representation is particularly helpful in understanding the meaning of a passage. If the intent of a passage is to describe a concept or idea, then mapping can show the relationship of descriptive characterizations to that concept.

In mapping we usually place the main idea in the center with relationships to other concepts represented visually. For example, the characteristics of amphibians are represented in Figure 10.7; the visual picture helps students see relationships and thereby aids retention.

Many representations of the same material are possible. Encourage student creativity in devising visual representations of important material. Students remember the material better not only because they have a visual representation in mind but also because they have spent time and effort thinking about the relationships expressed to be able to portray them in a map. Because mapping does require considerable time and effort, it ought to be used only for significant passages, those developing important

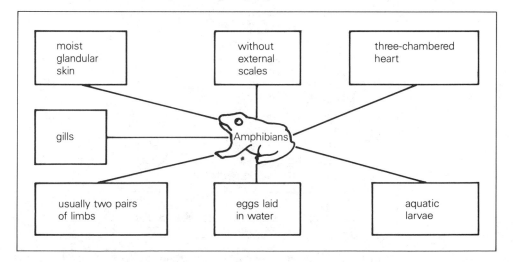

**Figure 10.7**   Mapping. From *Study Skills in the Content Area,* p. 67, by E. N. Askov and K. Kamm, 1982. Boston: Allyn & Bacon. Reprinted by permission.

concepts for the content area study. Sometimes a map can help a disabled reader understand relationships that otherwise are too abstract to be grasped immediately.

This treatment of study guides and study skills has been included to emphasize the importance of independence in learning. Unfortunately, many underachieving readers, because they are unable to read the materials appropriate for their grade level, tend to become dependent upon their teachers, parents, and other students. As a result, they lack confidence in their abilities to function independently. Unless they have access to appropriate materials so that they can have successful learning experiences, their dependence upon others may become a major problem in itself.

*We regard study skills as enabling skills that increase independence. Your objective in using gloss and study guides and in teaching study skills should be to move students, including disabled readers, gradually toward independent learning. You are teaching the life-long learning skills that enable students to continue learning in adulthood.*

## Summary

Various types of study guides help students comprehend content area textbooks. Your choice of a study guide depends upon the organization of the text and your purpose for the reader. While gloss and study guides enable you to provide direct guidance, students also need to learn how to learn independently. Study skills are taught as part of the content area studies to help students arrive at independent learning. Five aspects of study skills—test taking, independent study techniques, organizing study material, notetaking, and outlining and mapping—are particularly useful to underachieving readers in attaining more independence in learning.

## References

Anderson, T. H., & Armbruster, B. (1982). Reader and text-studying strategies. In W. Otto & S. White (Eds.), *Reading expository material.* New York: Academic Press, p. 219–239.

Askov, E. N., & Kamm, K. (1982). *Study skills in the content areas.* Boston: Allyn & Bacon.

Ausubel, D. (1968). *Educational psychology: a cognitive view.* New York: Holt, Rinehart & Winston.

Barrett, T. C. (1972). Taxonomy of reading comprehension. *Reading 360 Monograph.* Lexington, MA: Ginn.

Bloom, B. S. (Ed.). (1956). *Taxonomy of educational objectives. Handbook I: Cognitive Domain.* New York: David McKay.

Dupuis, M. M., & Askov, E. N. (1982). *Content area reading: an individualized approach.* Englewood Cliffs, NJ: Prentice-Hall.

Earle, R. A. (1976). *Teaching reading and mathematics.* Newark, DE: International Reading Association.

Estes, R. H., & Vaughn, J. L., Jr. (1978). *Reading and learning in the content classroom.* Boston: Allyn & Bacon.

Robinson, F. P. (1961). *Effective study* (rev. ed.). New York: Harper & Row.

# Check Your Reading Comprehension

1. What is the goal of instruction in study skills?

2. If you decide to invest instructional time in study skills, how should you decide which strategy or technique is most appropriate?

3. Matching Exercise:

_____ **1.** Guide for Disabled Readers

_____ **2.** Category Guide

_____ **3.** Pattern Guide

_____ **4.** Problem-Solving Guide

_____ **5.** SQ3R

_____ **6.** Teachers can help students build *test-taking skills* by allowing them to . . .

_____ **7.** Teachers can encourage *organizational skills* by having students . . .

_____ **8.** Teachers can help students develop *note-taking skills* by . . .

_____ **9.** Teachers should emphasize *outlining skills* so that students learn to . . .

_____ **10.** Teachers should emphasize *mapping skills* so that students learn to . . .

**a.** Use separate composition books, divided notebooks, or weekly assignment sheets.

**b.** Analyze test items after taking an examination (as a small group activity).

**c.** A guide that might be useful in emphasizing cause-effect and comparison-contrast relationships.

**d.** A guide that points out what to read and what not to read.

**e.** A guide emphasizing step-by-step math processes to be used with word problems.

**f.** Giving students practice in learning to "translate," or paraphrase, reading material.

**g.** An independent study technique (Survey, Question, Read, Recite, Review).

**h.** A guide that requires students to organize information by filling in a chart.

**i.** Create a visual representation of the relationships within a selection or passage.

**j.** See relationships while reading and organize their own ideas in preparing a written or oral report.

Answers:

| | |
|---|---|
| 5. g | 10. i |
| 4. e | 9. j |
| 3. c | 8. f |
| 2. h | 7. a |
| 1. d | 6. b |

4. Imagine you are an eighth-grade teacher. Use the selection entitled "Paleozoic Era" (Figure 10.8) to develop a study guide for your disabled readers.

5. One helpful way to give students practice in outlining skills is to provide the headings and subheadings. The students must decide the appropriate placement of these items. The following are details and subheadings from the selection "Paleozoic Era" in Figure 10.8 (pages 238–239). Place them in outline form.

   - Known as the age of fishes
   - Permian Period
   - Silurian Period
   - Climate became drier and colder
   - First fish-like vertebrates began to appear
   - Many marine animals without backbones (eg. trilobites, brachiopods, and cephalopods)
   - Major coal fields date from this period
   - Cambrian Period
   - First land plants began to appear
   - First amphibians began to appear
   - Carboniferous Period
   - Much volcanic activity
   - Large parts of continents covered by shallow water
   - Large plants were very plentiful
   - Many amphibians and all trilobites died out
   - Great limestone, oil, and natural gas deposits were formed
   - Devonian Period
   - Fossils from this period are found in coal
   - First air-breathing land animals began to appear
   - Ordovician Period

6. Choose a passage from one of the textbooks you are using with your class. Develop a study guide for poor readers who must nevertheless read the passage.

7. Choose an appropriate study skill for your class. Write an objective to define the skill. Develop a lesson that emphasizes that skill. Provide a few sample items of a criterion-referenced test assessing mastery of the skill.

## Paleozoic Era

The Paleozoic Era began about 570 million years ago and lasted for 345 million years. At times, shallow seas invaded the land, then receded.

Although climates tended to be mild, they varied at times from humid tropical in some regions to desert in others. There were large numbers of plants and animals. Therefore, the sedimentary rocks of the Paleozoic age contain many fossils.

During the closing stages of the Paleozoic Era, very high mountain ranges were formed, including the Appalachians and the Alps. Glaciers also formed in Australia, Africa, India, and South America.

The Paleozoic Era has been divided into six time periods. Each time period is marked by the appearance of new plant and animals forms.

The *Cambrian* (KAM bree un) *Period* began about 570 million years ago. During the Cambrian Period, large parts of the continents were covered by shallow seas. Great numbers of marine animals without backbones lived in these waters. Fossil traces of trilobites, jellyfish, sponges, brachiopods, snails, and cephalopods have been discovered. All of the plant fossils found in the Cambrian rocks are seaweeds.

Trilobites were the most plentiful forms of sea life. Some were only a fraction of a centimeter long and others were as long as 68 cm. Trilobites had segmented bodies with a tough outer skeleton. They were somewhat like today's lobsters and crayfish.

The *Ordovician* (ord uh VIHSH un) *Period* followed the Cambrian period. In the first part of this period, much of the land was still covered by shallow seas. There was a wider variety of marine life than existed in the Cambrian Period. The first fishlike vertebrates began to appear. Great limestone, oil, and natural gas deposits were formed.

The *Silurian* (suh LOOR ee un) *Period* had much volcanic activity. In some areas, lava and ash were deposited to depths of 1200 to 3000 m. Seas disappeared from parts of the continents. Fossils of the first land plants were found in the Silurian rocks of England and Austria. The first air-breathing land animals, the scorpions, also left fossils in Silurian rocks

**Margin questions:**

Why do sedimentary rocks of the Paleozoic age contain many fossils?

Name a major characteristic of the Cambrian Period.

During which period did fish-like vertebrates begin to form?

During which period did the first land plants and the first air-breathing land animals appear?

**Figure 10.8**   Paleozoic Era. From *Principles of Science: Book One,* pp. 206–209, by C. H. Heimler and C. D. Neal, 1983. Columbus, OH: Charles E. Merrill. Reprinted by permission.

## Paleozoic Era (continued)

The *Devonian* (dih VOH nee un) *Period* had a wide variety of fish, including the first backboned fish. This period is known as the "Age of Fishes." Land plants growing as tall as 12 m were plentiful. The first amphibians appeared. At least 700 kinds of brachiopods have been found in the rocks of this period. Trilobites, once so plentiful, were slowly becoming extinct. The first fernlike seed-bearing trees appeared.

Which period is known as the "Age of Fishes?"

The *Carboniferous* (kar buh NIHF rus) *Period* followed the Devonian Period. Major coal fields date from the Carboniferous Period. The term Carboniferous refers to these coal deposits.

The coal beds in Carboniferous rocks tell much about the earth during this time. Coal was formed from the carbon in plant matter. Thus, conditions during Carboniferous time must have favored plant growth. The land was low in many parts of the world. The climate was moist and warm. These conditions were ideal for the formation of swamps filled with giant plants. Several thousand species of plants that lived at this time have left their fossil traces. Most of the species were ferns and cone-bearing plants.

What geologic period was most favorable to plant growth?

Coal is formed in the following way. Large deposits of plant matter build up in an area. Much of the vegetation is preserved in the swampy environment. The area slowly sinks down and sea water flows in to cover it. Layers of sand and gravel are deposited at the bottom of the sea. Through millions of years, the sediment layers build upward. Intense heat and pressure change the sediments to rock and the vegetation to coal. Petroleum deposits were also formed during the Carboniferous Period. Petroleum, like coal, is a fossil fuel.

The *Permian* (PUR mee un) *Period* followed the Carboniferous Period. During this period climates became drier and colder. The land began to rise from below the sea. Because of the dry climate, the plants present during the coal ages could not survive. Flowering plants replaced the ferns that had been the main plant life for so long. All trilobites and nearly all the amphibians died out during this period.

# 11

# Content Area Reading

Recall the fifth-grade children introduced in Chapter 1. You may remember that the children with special needs all had difficulty with grade-level textbooks in social studies and science. Some students could do well in these subjects, but they are thwarted because they cannot learn by reading. Tony, for example, was mainstreamed from an LD room. He could grasp science concepts by watching a film, but he couldn't understand the same content in a textbook.

Joe, on the other hand, mainstreamed from an EMH room, is functioning below his age peers. Regardless of the method of presentation, Joe cannot grasp concepts mastered by average fifth graders unless the content is simplified. Like Tony, he cannot learn the content by reading a grade-level textbook.

How do you, the classroom teacher, confront these obstacles? Even gloss, as described in Chapter 9, is not helpful with those students for whom the textbook is much too difficult. Likewise, study guides are not effective with students reading far below grade level.

Figure 11.1 presents some alternatives. Experiment with these to determine which are feasible for which students. Combinations of approaches offer variety. With any of these alternatives, use a Directed Reading-Thinking Approach, as described in Chapter 9.

Use of the unmodified text supplemented by gloss or study guides requires less of your effort and time, so try these strategies first. If they don't work, you may need to modify the textbook—or particularly difficult parts of it.

*We do believe students should be required to learn by reading. Even media presentations (films, filmstrips, audio- and videotapes, and microcomputers) involve reading, sometimes above grade level. For example, while the captions on a filmstrip may not be lengthy, their vocabulary, sentence structure, and concepts may be more difficult than those in a grade-level textbook. Students not required to read may get the false impression that reading is not important. You must teach them not only how to read content materials at an appropriate level, but also that they have the ability to do so.*

# Modified Textbook Strategies

If you decide that a particular group of students—those like Tony and Joe—cannot learn by reading the grade-level textbook, even aided by gloss or study guides, the next step is to find alternative routes to learning. Many teachers prefer to modify the textbook. Students like Tony may only need a modified reading level; students like Joe may also require simplified content, particularly concepts.

## Alternative Reading Materials

An obvious alternative, although not necessarily an easy one, is to use other reading materials. You may be able to locate textbooks or supplementary materials intended for use with younger children, covering the same content. Ask the librarian and reading specialist to help you find alternative reading materials. As long as the material is not too childish, it may be exactly what learners like Joe need in terms of ease of reading and simplified content. Learners like Tony may read it easily and acquire greater depth of content and concepts through other media and class discussion.

Rough estimates of reading level may be obtained by applying readability formulas such as the Fry Graph for Estimating Readability (Fry, 1968, 1977), shown in Figure 11.2. To use the Fry Graph, count the number of syllables and sentences in each of at least three 100-word passages taken from the beginning, middle, and end of the textbook. Average the numbers of syllables and sentences and plot them on the Fry Graph; this yields an approximate grade level of reading difficulty. The assumption is that the longer the words and sentences, the more difficult the material.

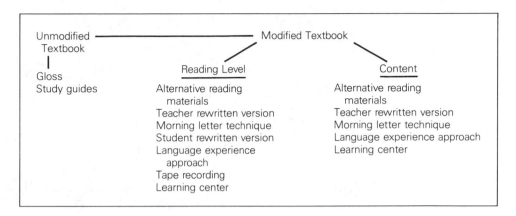

**Figure 11.1**  Alternatives to Textbooks

This approach to determining readability has appeal in its simplicity. But long words and long sentences are not the only factors contributing to reading difficulty. As discussed in Chapter 8, lack of familiarity with the content and concepts can make reading difficult. *(Consider for a moment the difficulties you might encounter reading a nuclear physics or medical textbook. Your lack of familiarity with the content might cause you to associate the wrong meanings with mutliple-meaning words. You would also be unfamiliar with technical vocabulary, and glossary definitions might not be of much help.)*

The concept load, or the difficulty of the concepts, is a related problem. Sometimes even relatively simple language can convey sophisticated concepts that are difficult for elementary school children to understand. Because students do not understand the concept of democracy, for example, their comprehension of textbook material relating to democracy is inaccurate or distorted to fit what they do know (Hildyard & Olson, 1982).

Other factors, such as typeface and text aids, also affect readability. A textbook with headings and subheadings in different size typefaces helps students understand the organization of material. Guide questions can help students direct their attention to the main ideas in a selection. Although maps, graphs, tables, charts, and diagrams may cause problems for students who do not know how to read them (Askov & Kamm, 1982), they can present content more clearly.

Therefore, we recommend that you apply readability formulas, such as the Fry Graph, very cautiously to estimate reading levels.

Another better method for determining the suitability of alternative reading is to have each student individually and privately read aloud to you as a type of informal reading inventory. If the student can read fluently and understand the material, then it is a suitable alternative to the textbook. Another quick means of determining suitability of reading materials is to devise a cloze test, as described in Chapter 5. You can administer it to a group of students, score it according to the guidelines, and quickly know for whom the material is appropriate (those scoring at the instructional and independent reading levels).

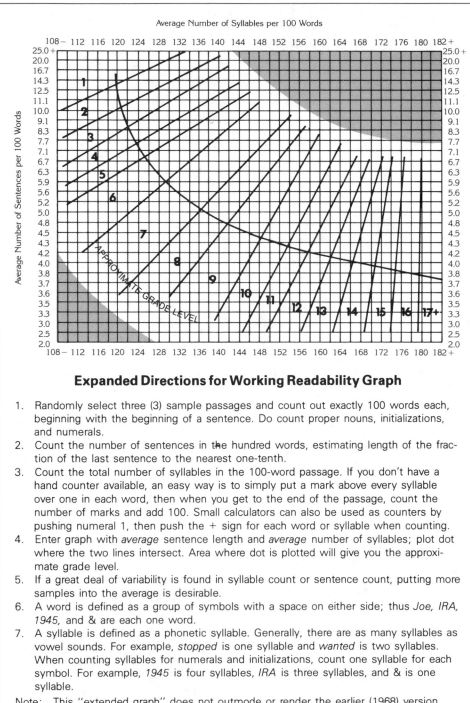

## Expanded Directions for Working Readability Graph

1. Randomly select three (3) sample passages and count out exactly 100 words each, beginning with the beginning of a sentence. Do count proper nouns, initializations, and numerals.
2. Count the number of sentences in the hundred words, estimating length of the fraction of the last sentence to the nearest one-tenth.
3. Count the total number of syllables in the 100-word passage. If you don't have a hand counter available, an easy way is to simply put a mark above every syllable over one in each word, then when you get to the end of the passage, count the number of marks and add 100. Small calculators can also be used as counters by pushing numeral 1, then push the + sign for each word or syllable when counting.
4. Enter graph with *average* sentence length and *average* number of syllables; plot dot where the two lines intersect. Area where dot is plotted will give you the approximate grade level.
5. If a great deal of variability is found in syllable count or sentence count, putting more samples into the average is desirable.
6. A word is defined as a group of symbols with a space on either side; thus *Joe, IRA, 1945,* and & are each one word.
7. A syllable is defined as a phonetic syllable. Generally, there are as many syllables as vowel sounds. For example, *stopped* is one syllable and *wanted* is two syllables. When counting syllables for numerals and initializations, count one syllable for each symbol. For example, *1945* is four syllables, *IRA* is three syllables, and & is one syllable.

Note: This "extended graph" does not outmode or render the earlier (1968) version inoperative or inaccurate; it is an extension.

**Figure 11.2** Fry Graph for Estimating Readability—Extended. By Edward Fry, Rutgers University Reading Center, New Brunswick, NJ. Reproduction permitted. No copyright.

## Teacher Rewritten Version

You may decide to rewrite the textbook in addition to or instead of using alternative reading material. Since this is no easy task, we recommend rewriting only crucial portions of the textbook for which no suitable alternative reading material exists.

To simplify the text, substitute easier words for difficult vocabulary, usually decreasing the length of the words. But remember that students do need to learn some technical terminology. For example, it is hard to talk about photosynthesis without using the word. *Photosynthesis* is a long word, although not necessarily a difficult one, once the students learn the word parts. Therefore, identify and teach the key vocabulary words that are also concept labels—words essential to teaching the concepts—*before* assigning the reading material so that students will not have difficulty reading these words. Eliminate or replace other difficult words that are not essential to the content.

Likewise, reduce sentence length where possible. Replace complex sentences with simple sentences, but be sure to retain connectives with meaning. For example, a sentence might state, "Because John was sick, he left school." Simplifying this complex sentence into two simple sentences ("John was sick. He left school.") would do away with the notion of causality. Short, choppy sentences, in fact, are more difficult to understand (Pearson, 1974). Reducing sentence length does not guarantee more readable material. We suggest that you modify only very long sentences containing several clauses. A sentence with a dependent clause between the subject and verb, as demonstrated by this sentence, should be rewritten. (The clause "as demonstrated by this sentence" interrupts the flow of thought between the subject and verb.) The passive voice, in which the subject is acted upon (as in this and the previous sentence), should also be avoided. (Restated in the active voice: "We should avoid the passive voice.")

Try to keep the sense of the whole paragraph or section in mind, when you rewrite, instead of rewriting sentence by sentence. Doing so will help you to better restate the main ideas in very simple language.

Figure 11.3 shows a passage from an upper-grade social studies textbook and a rewritten version to be read by underachieving readers. Note in the textbook passage that phrases and clauses sometimes interrupt subject and verb (for example, the last sentence in the first paragraph) and verb and complement (for example, the first sentence in the first paragraph). The passive voice is used occasionally, especially in the last paragraph, where the subject, or "doer," of the action is unclear. (". . . then these laws are usually found invalid . . ."; ". . . then they are allowed to stand. Every citizen is asked to obey them.")

The rewritten version distills the main ideas and states them as simply as possible. The quotation from Abraham Lincoln was deemed to be enrichment that even average readers find difficult to read and understand. Therefore, the whole second paragraph was eliminated. But the last sentence of the first paragraph retains the idea that governments have always been needed (even in Lincoln's time).

While most of the sentences are shorter than in the textbook, the second sentence in the first paragraph is long. The list (police, schools, and so forth) in the

## Limited Powers

At one time the United States was, for the most part, thinly populated, rural, and agricultural. Today it is urban and industrial, with a large population living closely together in cities. Large numbers of people in a complex urban environment need a government to provide community services and to enforce the laws which keep the community running smoothly. To this end, cities and towns, suburbs and villages create police forces to protect their citizens. They also create schools, fire departments, health clinics, libraries, and many other services. But first the people who live in urban areas must create a government to manage and develop the services that are demanded.

The need for some form of government has always been apparent. Government holds a nation, state, or city together. According to Abraham Lincoln, the purpose of government is ". . . to do for the community of people whatever they need to have done but cannot do at all, or cannot do so well, for themselves in their separate and individual capacities [abilities]."

Law and government are closely connected. Governments follow the rule of law, the basic principles of which are found in the United States Constitution. Governments create new laws and make decisions based on old laws. The American court system, local, state, and federal, supervises our complicated political system by testing laws. Sometimes laws are approved (upheld) by courts and other times laws are disapproved (denied). Approval or disapproval must be based on sound reasoning and Constitutional principles. If urban, state, or federal lawmakers create new laws that go against the basic law of the land, the Constitution, then these laws are usually found invalid and overturned or cancelled. If new laws fit the basic principles, then they are allowed to stand. Every citizen is asked to obey them.

## Limited Powers, Rewritten

Today the United States has many people. We need a government to provide police forces, schools, fire departments, health clinics, libraries, and so forth. We have always needed a government to provide services.

Governments run by obeying laws. Governments also make new laws. New laws must not go against the basic law of our country, the Constitution. The court system tests new and old laws to see whether they uphold the basic principles.

**Figure 11.3** Sample Textbook Selection with Rewritten Version. (From *Urban Communities,* pp. 239–240, by I. Cutler, P. Senn, J. Zevin, and M. Branson, 1982. Columbus, OH: Charles E. Merrill. Reprinted by permission.)

textbook was retained because it helps students understand what services governments do provide.

You can check rewritten versions for readability level by applying a readability formula such as the Fry Graph. Even better is observation of underachieving readers actually using a rewritten version to see if the new version has eliminated difficulties.

## Morning Letter

A technique called the morning letter has been used for many years in the State College, Pennsylvania, Area School District. Because social studies and language arts are taught together as a block in the elementary grades in that school district, the teacher uses the morning letter both to present content and to teach reading skills. The technique involves writing on the chalkboard or chart a message to the students that introduces the content to be studied. The letter contains key vocabulary and concepts that the teacher wishes to introduce. Reading of the morning letter is followed by reading skill instruction using the words in the letter as examples. The students each have their own morning letter booklets; they usually also keep a daily journal pertaining to the content of the morning letters. The students read other sources of information about the content, such as library books or textbooks. They may incorporate information gleaned from these sources into their journals and research reports.

An example is shown in Figure 11.4, a part of a social studies unit on Japan. The morning letter conveys information about everyday life that the teacher wants her

---

_____, 19__

Dear _____,

    Japanese homes are small and built close together. _____ in the city have tiled roofs; homes in the country have thatched _____.

    The rooms in Japanese houses do _____ have much furniture. There are _____ chairs, couches or beds. Square, flat cushions are _____ on the floor beside a low table for eating or drinking tea. At night thick comforters, or futons, are spread out on the _____ to make beds. During winter months an iron pot called an hibachi is _____ in the middle of the room in a pit to help keep the people _____.

    In one corner of the main _____ is a raised platform where a flower arrangement or other art work is displayed beneath a long hanging scroll picture.

    Most Japanese homes _____ gardens, which are also works of art. These _____ are very quiet and peaceful areas. The house is often built around the _____ so that everyone inside can _____ it from all the windows. The garden might have flowers and _____ tiny cherry trees. Water might drop down _____ some rocks.

    The kitchen is a small _____. It does have _____ electric stove, a sink, _____ a refrigerator.

    These _____ homes are small and quite simple. They are _____ attractive though for these people in this island country.

                             Your teacher,

                             Mrs. Yendol

---

**Figure 11.4** Morning Letter from a Social Studies Unit. (Written by Maureen Yendol, State College, PA, Area School District.)

fourth-grade students to learn. She has used a cloze format, described in Chapter 5, to stimulate active comprehension. The students will comprehend the selection better if they must think about the omitted words. Note that the deletions are irregularly spaced, rather than every fifth word as in a cloze test. The deleted words are those that the student should be able to supply if they are comprehending the letter. The teacher has used some enrichment words, such as *futon* and *hibachi,* but has not deleted these words. Comprehension questions following the letter focus on the main idea, inferences, and vocabulary. These constitute the skill development aspects of the morning letter strategy.

You might use a morning letter as an introduction to new vocabulary and concepts for all students. For the disabled readers the morning letter might become the sole text (if it is placed on a ditto master) supplemented by other activities, such as learning centers and media presentations, while the better readers read the text-book or other more difficult reading materials.

## Student Rewritten Version

You might also use student rewritten versions of the textbook with underachieving readers. Asking the average and better readers to summarize important selections from their reading material is an excellent way to enhance their reading comprehension (Anderson & Armbruster, 1982); it also helps you determine which students can restate main ideas in their own words. The students, individually or in groups, write their paraphrased version on ditto masters, which are then duplicated for use with the poor readers. You may want to retain these versions to use with next year's disabled readers. While you do have to spend time checking the student rewritten versions, you save time by having students to the rewriting. The greater reward is that the under-achieving reader can read the summaries rather than the textbook to learn the content.

## Language Experience Approach

The language experience approach (LEA) is often thought of in terms of beginning reading, but the principles and procedures also apply to content area reading (Askov & Lee, 1980). Briefly, LEA involves group discussion of some type of stimulus or group experience. Afterward the students dictate the main ideas as you write them down on chart paper. Students are able to read the material written on the chart because it is written in their own words. If they forget a particular word, they can usually remember it by rereading the sentence.

In using LEA in content area studies, the most important consideration is finding an appropriate stimulus. Since the LEA is to replace the textbook for the disabled readers, the stimulus should contain the essential content, concepts, and vocabulary. Sometimes a film, audiotape, demonstration, or guest speaker may provide the stimulus for group discussion. After discussion, ask the students to state the main ideas in their own words. Record these on a chart, which may later be transcribed on a ditto master. The dictated selection can act as a rewritten version of the textbook for the underachieving readers. They will be able to read it because they helped write it. The better readers may read the textbook version for greater depth and description.

An example of an LEA dictation as part of a science class is shown in Figure 11.5. The teacher has been careful to elicit from the children during dictation the technical vocabulary *(photosynthesis, germinate, experiment)* necessary to understanding the content study. Even though the teacher might have to suggest that the students use one of their new words (such as *germinated* instead of *broke open* ), the dictation consists of the students' words; the poor readers will be able to rely on the familiarity of content and language in reading. This dictation followed an experiment conducted over the period of a week. Each student had planted beans in two pots (milk cartons) and placed their pots in the sunlight to germinate. After the plants had sprouted, each student placed one pot in a dark closet, leaving the other pot on a window sill. Each day for one week the students measured their plants and recorded the growth in a table. Then they created a line graph showing the growth progress of both plants.

## Tape Recording

Another technique, which we would not endorse as the sole technique for presenting content, is tape recording textbook material. The disabled readers during independent study time may listen to the material in the library or at a listening post in the corner of the classroom. Some suggestions are in order:

1. Select only the most essential portions of the textbook for taping. Usually some paragraphs within a section can be omitted. Have the students follow the teacher's (or volunteer's) oral reading in their textbooks.
2. Especially direct their attention to graphic material, such as maps, graphs, and tables, that may help them understand the content.
3. Provide a study guide to accompany the tape. Students need to respond to the material whether they read it or listen to it.

Younger students usually accept this technique without difficulty. Sometimes older students, especially at the junior high school level, dislike having to study in such

---

### Photosynthesis

We learned about photosynthesis in our experiment last week. First, we planted bean seeds in pots. After the seed germinated, we put half the pots in a dark closet. The bean plants on the window sill grew about two inches in one week. The bean plants in the closet stopped growing.

We watered all our plants every day. But the plants in the closet began to die. Plants need sunlight to change the water into food. This is called *photosynthesis.*

---

**Figure 11.5** LEA Dictation in Science

an overtly different way from their peers. Teachers who have used this technique with older students report that students often abuse the time at the listening post or in the library. They do not want to be singled out as being disabled readers, and they resent the time it takes to listen to the material.

*The elimination of the need to read when using this technique troubles us. For this reason we recommend using oral reading either on a tape recording or in class by teachers only in small doses on occasion.*

## Learning Centers

Learning centers work well in conjunction with the other techniques. You might introduce key vocabulary words and important concepts in a morning letter. The able readers might next read the assigned content area textbooks, perhaps accompanied by gloss or a study guide. The disabled reader might go directly to a learning center, which would present the content through games or other media. Able readers, upon completion of their reading assignment, might do portions of the learning center as follow-up activities to reinforce and extend the textbook material.

Students should be able to use learning centers independently, freeing you to circulate and provide individual help or to offer small group instruction. The instructions should be simply worded or presented on a tape recording at the center. The activities should involve self-checking or peer checking. If teacher checking is necessary, do this soon after a student has completed an activity to provide immediate feedback.

Learning centers need not be large; often they fit on a window sill or inside a large shallow box. Rotate different centers often throughout the year for variety. A colorful backboard poster adds attractiveness and interest.

Learning centers should consist of more than a series of worksheets, especially those designed for disabled readers. Students like John learn best when manipulating materials, if only sorting index cards with names of living beings into appropriate phyla or piles for a science class. Other media, such as audio- and videotapes, may be incorporated into the learning centers. Usually students work through a series of activities within the learning center. The number of activities designated for a particular student depends upon the needs of the student. John, for example, might work through all activities in a center on animals while more able readers might do only the most difficult activities.

Writing activities can also be built into learning centers, requiring students to state their new learning in new ways. For example, a science center activity on pollution might require students to express their thoughts about pollution of a local stream by industry in a "letter to the editor."

Sample learning centers intended for junior high school students as part of content area studies may be found in Dupuis and Askov (1982). An example is to have students manipulate vocabulary cubes and strips to create new words using roots and affixes related to a social studies unit. Even though some of the combinations of roots and affixes might be whimsical (such as "monomanualology"), the students must

Learning center for developing vocabulary related to a social studies unit. (Photo by Joseph B. Bodkin)

create definitions and sentences using their new words. ("Monomanualology" might be defined as "the study of one hand!")

Figure 11.6 shows one station of a learning center designed to teach the concept of the main idea to young readers. The teacher who developed it finds it particularly useful for those students who have comprehension difficulties. She is using the content area of poetry as a vehicle for teaching the reading skill of grasping the main idea. The poetry used in the station is concrete poetry printed in the shape of the object that is the topic of the poem. The poetry should be rich in imagery, short in length, and easy to read, and should develop a single idea. The other stations in the center require the student to work with increasingly difficult poems and to write summary statements rather than check statements that are correct.

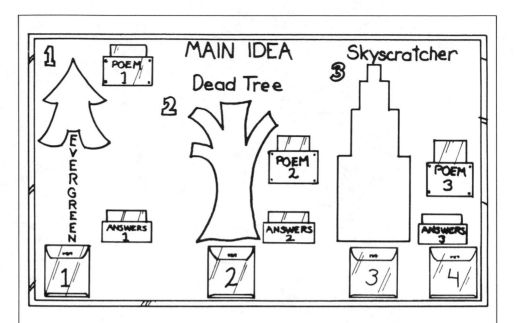

Instructions to students (tape recorded and printed):

1. Look at shape number 1. A poem has been written about this title and shape and has been placed in an envelope.
2. Go to the large envelope under shape number 1. Take out a green paper with some ideas on it.
3. Read all the ideas. Place a check next to all the ideas that tell what a poem with this shape and title could be about. Place the green paper in envelope number 4.
4. Read poem 1.
5. Go to envelope number 1 again. This time, take out a yellow piece of paper. Read all the ideas and check the ones that tell what poem 1 is about.
6. Check your answers by reading the answer key next to poem 1.
7. If you think your answer is better, write why. Place your answer on the line below the idea you think is correct.
8. Place finished work in envelope number 4.
9. Do steps 1 through 8 for shapes 2 and 3.

Poems:
Froman, R. (1971). Skyscratcher. *Street poems.* New York: McCall. p. 4.
Froman, R. (1974). Dead tree. *Seeing things.* New York: Thomas Crowell. p. 9.
Merriman, E. (1973). Evergreen. *Out loud.* New York: Atheneum. p. 38.

**Figure 11.6** Learning Center for Teaching the Main Idea. (Prepared by Phyllis Belt-Beyan, Doctoral Candidate at The Pennsylvania State University.)

As it is probably becoming apparent, no one technique for modifying content area reading works all the time. In fact, variety is important to maintain interest and enthusiasm. The techniques presented in Figure 11.1 may be used in various combinations. You can retain materials that you or your students create for use in future years. Over a period of time you can accumulate learning centers as well as simplified versions of the textbook that have been written by the teacher, students, or both, such as in using the language experience approach. The unit approach encourages growth over a period of time. Each time you use a particular unit, you can add activities to expand the range of opportunities for learning for all readers.

# Unit Approach[1]

Instruction in a content area, such as science or social studies, can be organized into units of study. We have assumed in the preceding discussion that the teacher has a textbook that he or she must use. In some school districts this is indeed the case. In most districts, however, the teacher may not necessarily use the textbook as long as the curriculum is followed. How to present the curriculum is left to the teacher's discretion.

Some teachers assume that their textbook equals the curriculum. Although this assumption may appeal to "lazy" teachers because they have to present only what is in the textbook, they quickly run into difficulties. Approximately a third of the students in a heterogeneous classroom (that is, a classroom with students of various levels of ability) are unable to read the textbook with adequate comprehension. Use of gloss and study guides helps some of these less able readers, but for others the textbook is clearly inappropriate. We have already presented alternatives to using the textbook; now we need to consider the steps for teaching content area studies using the textbook as a *tool,* not as the curriculum. The step-by-step process follows.

## Steps in Teaching Content Area Studies

First, consider your *objectives for instruction* in the content area. Instead of the objective being "cover Chapter 1," the objective(s) should identify the major concepts to be learned. Base objectives on the district curriculum, not on the textbook.

The second step is to apply *diagnostic techniques* to this unit. Information on the class is essential: informal reading inventories, cloze procedures, and the like provide specifics about reading levels. You also need to know the students' prior knowledge of the content to be covered. This step may cause you to revise unit objectives, but more likely the information gathered will help you determine how to present the unit.

Once you have identified the important objectives for instruction and know students' skill levels, the next step is to decide what *learning strategies* might best be

---

[1] This section on the unit approach was written by Dr. Mary M. Dupuis, Associate Professor at The Pennsylvania State University.

used. You might pretend that the textbook does not exist, to free your mind to think of other alternatives, such as guest speakers, learning centers, independent research, role playing, and small group projects. Sometimes it helps to develop a block plan listing the objectives for instruction on the left side of the page with the correspond-ing activities filled in beside each objective. (See the Week Three Outline in Figure 11.7 as an example.)

Only in the fourth step in this process should you consider the *selection of materials*. Determine what materials can be used to carry out the objectives through the learning strategies planned in the third step. Identify these materials and write them beside the objectives. When content area studies are structured in the unit approach, you can more easily use a variety of materials. Since students are all using various sources of information, including reading and other media, it does not matter that some students may use the textbook less frequently than others. When the textbook is the curriculum, on the other hand, stigma may be attached to not using the textbook.

Within the selection of materials should be a variety of reading levels. The textbook may indeed be a source of information for those who can use it successfully. If good alternative reading materials and other media exist, make these available for underachieving readers. (Similarly, the best readers should be challenged with addi-tional materials beyond the textbook.) The unit approach is the framework that permits management of a variety of learning strategies and materials.

The fifth step is to establish *student evaluation* procedures for each objective. The evaluation may range from quizzes and tests to written reports to classroom discussion and teacher observation. A careful unit plan allows you to use many forms of evaluation during a unit to be sure that students are not penalized by the use of only one type.

Figure 11.7 is part of an actual unit for fifth-grade social studies by a Jersey Shore, Pennsylvania, teacher. She has combined U.S. geography content and map reading skills. Once students have mastered basic map skills, she moves them into the regular text to study the regions of the United States. Students use study guides for each region along with the text. Underachieving readers use easier reading materials with their own study guides. One culminating activity for the unit is a series of group projects on U.S. regions consisting of both written and oral reports. Each student takes part in a group activity, regardless of reading level, though their participation may differ. Students also take a final test on the unit content, once they have finished the oral group projects. Week Three of this unit (Days 11 – 15) involves the first group work of the unit so the teacher must set up the groups and their tasks, then review group progress with them. At the same time she must deal with vocabulary and with map worksheets related to U.S. regions. Finally, she provides a study guide related to the map skills of the unit, including latitude and longitude and topographical features relating to the U.S. regions. Finally, her students develop a dictionary of geographical terms within their groups.

Such a unit provides the teacher with many forms of evaluation on each student's performance: oral, written, group participation. It also allows the teacher to put students into situations that fit their capabilities in reading, interest, and participation

*Sample Objectives for Map Skills* (including evaluation)

A. Given ongoing instruction in map reading skills, the student will become a fluent reader of maps used in our unit. This fluency will be demonstrated by completing map reading exercises with the degree of accuracy specified within each exercise.

B. Following a teacher-led discussion on the need to develop a vocabulary that is functional for the unit, the student will meet this objective in the following ways:
   1. Completion of a vocabulary worksheet (see Day 14—Activities) with 100 percent accuracy.
   2. Participation in preparing a group dictionary, with a grade of *S* (satisfactory) or *U* (unsatisfactory) being assigned by other members of the group according to the level of the individual's participation in this project.
   3. Completion of a vocabulary test (see Day 23) with no less than 85 percent accuracy.

C. Students will increase their knowledge and understanding of conditions in at least one region of the United States by fulfilling reading assignments, participating in group and individual research, and completing other related activities. Evaluation of this objective will be ongoing and both formal (worksheets, reports, tests, etc.) and informal (teacher observation, student discussion, etc).

D. Students will demonstrate their ability to function as effective group members, with regard to cooperation, attitude, responsibility, and other related factors. Fellow group members will assign grades of *S* or *U* to each group member on the Group Work Checklist.

E. After completing a specific reading assignment, the student will complete a study guide with no less than 85 percent accuracy.

### Week Three Outline

| Day | Objectives | Activities | Reading/Materials |
|-----|-----------|------------|-------------------|
| 11 | A, C, D | Discuss group activities and assign groups<br>Distribute folders on regions and unit work | Text<br>Chart paper, regional charts<br>Dictionary handout |
| 12 | A, C, D | Meet in groups on regions<br>Map worksheet | Classroom resource materials (library, newspapers, filmstrips, etc., for group use)<br>Map worksheet |
| 13 | D | Map worksheet completed and turned in<br>Group work; plans for presentation completed | Classroom resource materials |
| 14 | B, C, D | Vocabulary worksheet related to regions (dictionary, worksheet)<br>Group work; teacher reviews plans with each group | Classroom resource materials<br>Vocabulary handouts |
| 15 | C, D, E | Distribute and discuss study guide<br>Groups discuss study guide; teacher meets with each group | Classroom resource materials<br>Study guides |

**Figure 11.7** Map Skills of Regions of the United States: A Fifth-Grade Social Studies Unit. (Prepared by Beverly Porter, Jersey Shore, PA, School District.)

level. Underachieving readers are not segregated from other students, except in their reading activities. Heterogeneous groups work on projects together. It is possible in units such as this one to challenge students while making it likely that all of them can succeed.

## Structured Overview

One way to organize unit content for students is to develop a structured overview. Figure 11.8 shows Mrs. Porter's overview, which gives some of the critical vocabulary for the unit and indicates its relationship to the five regions being studied. The center of this overview includes the two central concepts of the unit: climate and terrain. Each region is graphically connected to vocabulary items related specifically to it.

Such a structured overview can provide students with a cognitive map of the unit content. Presented at the beginning of the unit, it helps students organize their ideas and their study of the unit materials. The structured overview is an example of an advance organizer (Ausubel, 1968), a critical component of effective concept teaching. Mrs. Porter's overview was developed from the vocabulary lists she generated for each of the five regions. Her lists include terms from the text, alternative reading materials, and the map she uses as examples.

## Evaluation

Units need not be lengthy. Most extend for three to five weeks with some sort of culminating activity to give students a sense of closure. Usually teachers require an examination or some sort of project at the end of the unit to make students accountable for acquiring a given body of knowledge. As long as students are responsible for the same objectives, although attained through different strategies and materials, they may be assessed through the same examination. Be sure that disabled readers are not penalized on an exam because they have not used the textbook. Base the exam on the objectives, not on the textbook.

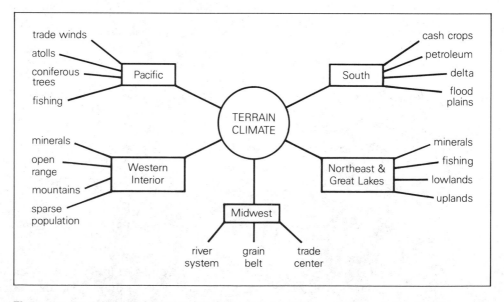

**Figure 11.8**   Geography of U.S. Regions. (Based on the unit prepared by Beverly Porter, Jersey Shore, PA, School District.)

Projects created as part of a fourth grade unit on medieval times.
(Photo by Joseph B. Bodkin)

Culminating activities may involve fun activities as well, such as creating a diorama, putting on a puppet show, writing a play, or building a model. Some selection by students enhances their motivation. If they are encouraged to plan their culminating activity and occasionally to select others with whom to work, they are more likely to be interested in what they are studying.

At the completion of the unit, evaluate the unit itself, especially considering the learning of the underachieving readers. Did the students attain the objectives set forth? Were the selected learning strategies and materials appropriate? If the disabled readers did not do well on the examination, was it because they did not learn the content or were they unable to read the test? Check the examination for the match between the test items and the objectives. Were the objectives being measured by the test items? Did the students understand what was expected of them? Were they informed of the objectives of the unit before instruction began?

Seek evaluative feedback from your students; ask them what was successful and what needs modification. Students enjoy having some say in the instructional process.

Although teachers often neglect evaluating their own teaching, feeling that it is like "flogging a dead horse," the evaluation process can be very useful. Effective teachers continually modify what they are doing. Evaluation is the feedback system that leads to constant tinkering with units of instruction.

# Contracts

Within a unit plan, or even without the unit approach to content area studies, contracts can be effective with all types of readers, especially underachieving readers.

Contracts are individual or group agreements between student and teacher for the accomplishment of a specified amount of work. Contracts, if used with the whole class, can be especially beneficial to underachieving readers in content area studies. Just as you can contract with the best students to extend their reading assignments, the disabled readers can contract for reading material appropriate for them. The contracts are private, permitting individualization of content area instruction. A sample of a completed contract is shown in Figure 11.9.

The teacher created the photosynthesis booklet that John was assigned to read from an old science textbook. It was selected because it explained photosynthesis in simpler language. The teacher had found the textbook, which had previously been used in a lower grade, while rummaging through some discarded books stored in a cupboard. Because the textbook was old and not as attractive as more modern text-books, the teacher cut it apart, retaining the parts that pertained to topics of study in the science units. Students covered, bound, titled, and decorated these selections during an art project. Even though only one copy of the photosynthesis booklet existed, the teacher could rotate it among the underachieving readers through the contract system. While John might use the booklet on April 14, Jill, another under-achieving reader, may have signed a contract stating that she would use the booklet beginning April 15.

Groups of students may work together in completion of a contract, perhaps to read a particular play and build a model of a stage showing a particular scene. Or a group may contract to study a particular topic—such as transportation, within a unit pertaining to state history. The group members use different reference sources, which you suggest in accordance with reading levels. But the group members all contribute to the development of a map, for example, and accompanying report.

Provide rewards for contracts that are completed satisfactorily on time. The teachers in one school known to the authors designated Friday morning as enrichment study. Those students who completed their contracts for work during the week could choose to study a topic of interest from a wide variety offered on Fridays. The teachers, and sometimes students with special talents, conducted the Friday workshops. Topics changed each week but included such activities as studying rocks, cooking, playing the guitar, writing poetry, and experimenting with electricity. Those few students who did not complete their contracts during the week had to spend the enrichment time in a

---

Student's Name _____ *John* _____

Week of _____ *April 15* _____

We agree that _____ *John* _____ will complete the work outlined as follows in studying science. This work will be completed by _____ *April 19* .

| Work | Initial Conference Date | Final Conference Date | Evaluation of Progress |
|---|---|---|---|
| 1. Read pp. 50–55 in photosynthesis booklet | 4/13 | 4/15 | o.k. |
| 2. Complete gloss for those pages | 4/13 | 4/15 | good |
| 3. View photosynthesis filmstrip and do study guide | 4/13 | 4/19 | o.k. |
| 4. Take daily measurements of bean plant kept in dark closet | 4/13 | 4/19 | o.k. |
| 5. Complete all activities at learning center | 4/13 | 4/19 | good |

Signed _____ *John* _____
(Student's Name)

_____ *Ms Weidler* _____
(Teacher's Name)

**Figure 11.9**  Sample Contract for Science

study hall completing their contracts. Needless to say, most students completed their contracts before Friday!

Usually contracts are drawn up on a weekly basis during a private conference between the teacher and student (or students, when using a group contract). A few students, however, need more direction than is afforded by weekly individual conferences. Children who are extremely distractible may require daily conferences and daily contracts. These children are not necessarily those with reading problems, although reading problems often accompany difficulties in attention span. If you must use daily contracts and conferences, try to extend the time period gradually as students learn to become responsible for their work.

Keep progress charts for individuals in private folders rather than on a wall chart showing all children's names. Competition is usually fierce in the middle grades and may backfire if the poorest students become discouraged rather than motivated by a chart. Progress charts showing successfully completed contracts may prove useful if kept in individual student folders.

## Summary

As a classroom teacher you have various options for dealing with the inevitable range of reading abilities in content area materials. While you can use gloss and study guides without modifying the textbook, other approaches modify or replace the grade-level textbook so that underachieving readers are able to read content reading assignments. We have offered the unit approach as a means of organizing content study that uses a variety of reading materials at various difficulty levels. Whether or not you follow a unit approach, first consider the important objectives for instruction of the content area. Only then should you consider learning strategies and materials.

## References

Anderson, T. H., & Armbruster, B. B. (1982). Reader and text-studying strategies. In W. Otto & S. White (Eds.), *Reading Expository Material.* New York: Academic Press, pp. 219–242.

Askov, E. N., & Kamm, K. (1982). *Study skills in the content areas.* Boston: Allyn & Bacon.

Askov, E. N., & Lee, J. W. (1980). The language experience approach in the content area classroom. *The Journal of Language Experience, 2* (1), pp. 13–20.

Ausubel, D. (1968). *Educational psychology: a cognitive view.* New York: Holt, Rinehart & Winston.

Dupuis, M. M., & Askov, E. N. (1982). *Content area reading: an individualized approach.* Englewood Cliffs: Prentice-Hall.

Fry, E. (1968). A readability formula that saves time. *Journal of Reading, 11* (7), pp. 514–515.

Fry, E. (1977). Fry's Readability Graph: Clarifications, validity and extension to level 17. *Journal of Reading, 21* (3), pp. 242–243.

Hildyard, A., & Olson, D. R. (1982). On the structure and meaning of prose text. In W. Otto & S. White (Eds.), *Reading Expository Material.* New York: Academic Press, pp. 155–184.

Pearson, P. D. (1974). The effects of grammatical complexity on children's comprehension, recall and conception of certain semantic relations. *Reading Research Quarterly, 10,* pp. 155–189.

## Check Your Reading Comprehension

1. Why should students be required to learn by reading?

2. Why is it important to use a variety of techniques in presenting content area material to students?

3. Reading materials may be too difficult in terms of reading level or content. What are some techniques you could use to compensate for either situation?

4. What techniques could you use to assess the appropriateness of a particular textbook for a student or group of students? What are the advantages and disadvantages of each? Try using some of these techniques; then write an analysis of the textbook.

5. Matching exercise:

| | |
|---|---|
| _____ **1.** Alternative reading material | **a.** Method for presenting content and teaching reading skills through a written message to the students. |
| _____ **2.** Rewritten material | **b.** Individual or group agreements between students and teacher for the accomplishment of a specified amount of work. |
| _____ **3.** Morning letter | |
| _____ **4.** LEA | |
| _____ **5.** Tape recording | **c.** Textbooks or supplementary materials that are written several levels below grade level. |
| _____ **6.** Learning centers | **d.** A technique for independent learning that makes use of games and media. |
| _____ **7.** Unit approach | |
| _____ **8.** Contract | **e.** A technique in which students dictate material to the teacher, who writes it down. |

Answers:

|   |   |   |   |
|---|---|---|---|
| 1. c | 2. h | 3. a | 4. e |
| 5. g | 6. d | 7. f | 8. b |

**f.** An organizational plan that allows the teacher to determine how to present the curriculum.

**g.** A technique that may help some disabled readers during independent study time. Should be used sparingly.

**h.** Simplified version of a textbook, written by the teacher or other students.

6. Imagine you are a seventh-grade teacher. Rewrite the passage entitled "The Importance of Good Health" (Figure 11.10) so that your disabled readers will be able to read it independently.

7. Imagine you are a fifth-grade teacher. You are teaching a unit on the history of your state. Write a morning letter for your disabled readers that presents one of the concepts you wish to emphasize.

8. Choose one of the textbooks you are using with your class. Devise a language experience lesson to be used to teach one of the concepts in that text.

9. Devise a contract for one week's work in social studies for your disabled readers. Try to balance realistic reading and nonreading activities in learning.

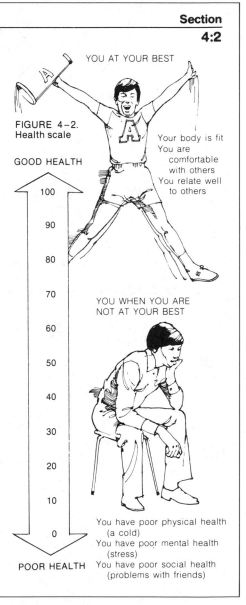

### The Importance of Good Health

You were born with certain genes that influenced your development. These genes were transferred to you from your parents. Heredity is the transfer of genes from one generation to the next. Your heredity makes you different from others. No one else is just like you. That means your health is unique (yoo NEEK). You are **unique** because you have a combination of qualities others do not have. No one else functions as you do. No one else has exactly the same potential as you do. Your **potential** is your future abilities which are not yet developed.

Look at the health scale. It is divided into units that range from zero to one hundred. When you are at 100, you are at your best. You are able to work toward your full potential. This is another way that we can define good health. Good health is being at your best physically, mentally, and socially.

Sometimes you do not have good health. When you are at the lower numbers on the health scale, you are not able to reach your potential. **Disease** can be viewed as anything that blocks you from being at your best. Did you think that having a disease always means that your body is sick? Disease can be physical (having a cold), mental (not able to think clearly), or social (having problems with your friends). Disease is the improper functioning of a body part or process.

Make a list of ten things that you really want to do. How will your health influence your ability to do these things? Why is it important to have good health? What are you doing about your health?

FIGURE 4–2.
Health scale

GOOD HEALTH

YOU AT YOUR BEST

Your body is fit
You are comfortable with others
You relate well to others

YOU WHEN YOU ARE NOT AT YOUR BEST

You have poor physical health (a cold)
You have poor mental health (stress)
You have poor social health (problems with friends)

POOR HEALTH

**Figure 11.10**   The Importance of Good Health. (From *Health: Focus on You,* p. 51, by L. B. Meeks and P. Heit, 1982. Columbus, OH: Charles E. Merrill. Reprinted by permission.)

**10.**   Choose one of the topics you teach in your class. Begin to build a unit emphasizing that topic. Remember, a unit is open-ended; it is never finished. Materials and activities can always be added, deleted, or changed. Perhaps you will want to include one or more learning centers as part of your unit.

# 12

# Integrating Reading and Writing

**Written by Dr. Carol T. Fishel, formerly of The Pennsylvania State University.**

Let's return to the fifth-grade class introduced in Chapter 1. By now you are making some progress in meeting the reading needs of your different students. Your large group of fifth graders is no longer a mass of faces but a collection of individuals whose reading and learning needs you are trying to fulfill. Nevertheless, you realize that you need more instructional time to help students develop their own comprehension strategies.

John, for instance, needs more practice reading simplified material. The rewritten materials in science and social studies and the guides and glosses for other materials are certainly helping, but it is difficult to supply enough appropriate reading materials for John. You sense his need but feel swamped by all your other responsibilities.

You want your students to deal with written language successfully and independently. They must develop strategies to deal with a variety of written material—textbooks, stories, reports, and poetry—to say nothing of the other language arts skills—speaking, listening, and writing. You realize you are not meeting your goal of integrating reading, writing, speaking, and listening in meaningful activities. How can you find the time to teach all the language arts?

When you share your concerns over a cup of coffee with Jim, a fellow teacher, he smiles knowingly and asks, "Why don't you use writing to develop reading comprehension?" You begin to explore reading and writing as part of language development.

# Oral Language

Language is a complex process involving skills in listening, speaking, reading, and writing. Listening and speaking, the oral language skills, develop early in childhood. In the home, children quickly learn to use language to obtain what they want, to control others, to interact with other children and adults, to express feelings, to question, to describe the world, and to create new worlds of imagination (Smith, 1977). As children experience oral language in all these ways, they learn the power and efficacy of language. By age five, they have mastered the basics of oral language.

# Written Language

Later, the child encounters written language—reading and writing. Although similar to spoken language in many ways, printed language is detached from the immediate concrete situation. Written language has three general functions.

First, written language is used to *describe* the world. Writers construct verbal pictures of people, places, and things we cannot directly experience. Through the mind's eye we "see" these worlds. Second, written language is used to *explore and explain* the world. Most books are written to explore relationships and explain how the world operates. Successive generations build and shape society based on written knowledge from prior generations. Third, written language can be carefully chosen to create works of art. The whole creates feelings and impressions greater than the sum of the individual parts. For example, a poem may use very few words, and even these may be simple, yet the impact of the poem may be great because of the artistic choice of words.

Written language is often more precise and developed than is oral language because the written words must provide all the cues necessary for meaning to form in the reader's mind. There are no concrete situations or nonverbal gestures to provide meaning. Allowing language alone to touch the knowledge and memory and recreate meaning requires complex thinking skills. The reader must see the organizational patterns of written language to understand it. The roles of writer and reader are reciprocal: the writer creates meaning and the reader (ideally) recreates that intended meaning.

## A Reading/Writing Model

Trosky and Wood (1982) have developed a detailed theoretical model of the relationships between reading and writing as ways of processing. We briefly consider an adapted form of this model to see how writing exercises can affect reading skills.

Reading involves abstracting the main ideas and supporting details and understanding the sequential development of material. Beyond this literal level, the reader makes inferences—constructs meaning, analyzes the author's point of view, and draws conclusions. Finally, the reader evaluates the appropriateness or effectiveness of the material.

Writing involves similar mental processes. A writer selects, names, and organizes material on the literal level. The author chooses a point of view suited to a particular audience and makes many stylistic choices to accomplish certain purposes. These choices are often made consciously or unconsciously during the actual drafting. Finally, a writer edits, checking for style, proper sequence, clarity of ideas, and realization of purpose.

Reading may be viewed as a reverse process of writing in which the reader recomposes, reflects, and reacts (Trosky and Wood, 1982). Figure 12.1 illustrates this process. Recomposing means attending to the type and organization of the literal information. Reflecting means analyzing the author's purposes and stylistic choices. Reacting involves evaluating and integrating the material into one's own cognitive structures.

Research has shown that students' reading and writing skills are correlated (Hammill and McNutt, 1981) and that good writers spend significantly more time rereading their own writing than do poorer writers (Emig, 1971). Good writers know how to take the role of reader to evaluate their own writing.

## The Effects of Writing Development

Writing development seems to follow a specific pattern in children. At first, they are very much concerned with handwriting, spelling, and grammatical conventions (Calkins, 1980; Graves, 1982). Later awareness of topics and detail grows. Finally writers become aware of the *options* available to them and the tentativeness of choices (Calkins, 1980; Graves & Giacobbe, 1982).

Writing gives children new reasons to connect with reading. Calkins (1983) found from several case studies of young readers/writers that progress in writing was coupled with a new perception of books. As writers who were aware of the options they exercised, the children were able to evaluate their choices (Calkins, 1983; Boutwell, 1983; Hansen, 1983).

Writing in the classroom can be helpful in three ways. First, writing seems to require the same kinds of mental processes as reading. Second, the writing process provides opportunities to integrate the other language arts skills of reading, speaking, and listening. Third, writing activities produce ample amounts of meaningful, appropriate material for classroom reading.

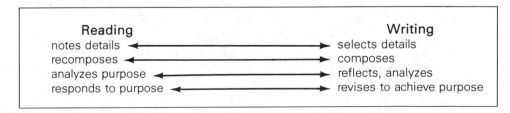

**Figure 12.1**  Reading and Writing as Reciprocal Process

> Combining reading instruction with different kinds of writing activities may help to teach reading comprehension in possibly the most meaningful way—and it may be the missing link in reading comprehension instruction. (Stotsky, 1982, 338)

### Integrating Reading and Writing

Children who have reading problems usually exhibit even greater difficulty with writing (Gaskins, 1982). Reading requires a student to see the choices made by the author, but writing requires an even greater level of skill—making choices that communicate an intended meaning. How, then, can you effectively use writing to develop reading comprehension, especially with poor readers?

Early and frequent exposure to writing helps children to become aware of how written language works (Boutwell, 1983; Calkins, 1983). Introduce writing in the early elementary school through the language experience approach (LEA), described in Chapter 7. As they see language captured in the form of letters, children begin to understand the relationships between oral language and print. Those who have developed some conception of the roles of printed language are ready to write as well as to read. At this point, students can begin to keep a journal, in which they can express both their feelings and their knowledge about the world. Journal writing is an excellent way to introduce writing as a process.

# Writing as a Process

Writing can be thought of as a three-part process—prewriting, drafting, and revision. During prewriting the writer builds up a store of ideas and words about a topic. Reading, writing, and talking help to create a store of "inner speech" and possible approaches to the topic. After "priming the pump" through prewriting activities, the writer actually drafts thoughts on paper. The last step is revision. The writer takes the role of a reader, checking to see what needs to be added, removed, or moved to another position to fulfill the purposes of writing. The emphasis during revision is on the relationships of ideas and their clarity rather than on proofreading. After revising ideas, the writer polishes the writing by proofreading for spelling and grammatical errors. Other readers can also participate in the revision process. Revision makes the writer scrutinize his or her own thinking and writing (Calkins, 1980).

The writing process is similar to all other creative acts. Four fairly distinct stages are involved—preparation, incubation, illumination, and validation. Interviews with professional writers indicate that they go through similar stages in which they read, talk, and think about the topic (preparation), allow some time for ideas to take shape (incubation), draft their thoughts (illumination), and then revise based on their own responses and the responses of others (validation) (Britton, 1970). Figure 12.2 illustrates writing as a creative act.

Writing in the classroom should follow the same stages. Structure activities to allow students to maximum amount of thinking, reading, and writing.

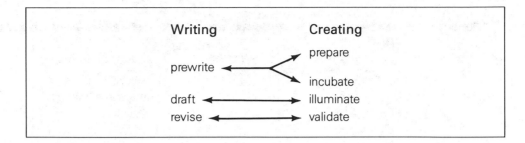

**Figure 12.2** Writing as a Creative Act

## Journal Writing

Journal writing illustrates the writing process. It can be organized in several ways, but the scheme provided has proven effective even with children who have reading and writing difficulties (Gaskins, 1982).

With your students, brainstorm possible topics, about which students may know as much or more than you. Students who do not succeed academically often have interests or skills that can be used in writing. For example, Joe in Chapter 1, who was mainstreamed from an EMH room, could offer his experiences helping at his uncle's service station. Jot topics on the board and have students write as many of them as possible on the backs of their journals.

Students themselves should next learn to conceive of writing as a three-part process consisting of prewriting activities, drafting, and revision. Emphasize reading as an integral part of each step. Remember, writing and reading support each other.

***Prewriting*** For the prewriting stage, students learn different ways of "creating" information about a chosen topic. They can discuss their topic with other students or with adults, or they can interview someone who is an "expert" about the topic. Two techniques that help recall and organize information are (a) naming and categorizing and (b) clustering. For the topic "camping," children might generate a list of terms and then categorize them in different ways, as shown in Table 12.1. The key is to know why terms are best categorized in a particular way.

Clustering also teaches children to tap their meanings and to show relationships. See the example for camping in Figure 12.3. Notice how clustering could generate different terms and new ways of grouping them. It is important that students learn to group terms logically. They need to see the choices involved in writing.

Students might also read materials about camping or a camping story, such as *Kids Camping* (Paul, 1973). Or you might read camping stories aloud to the class. The students then share their own experiences with camping. Initially, you should lead students through prewriting activities, but later they should begin to choose those topics of interest to them and complete prewriting activities outside class. Parents can be helpful if made aware of the pattern of the journal writing and the activities children should complete at home.

**Table 12.1**  Naming and Categorizing Information

| Terms | Equipment | Weather | Around the Fire | Environment |
|---|---|---|---|---|
| tent<br>forest<br>bear<br>campfire<br>rain<br>marshmallow<br>pegs<br>guitar | tent<br>pegs | rain | campfire<br>marshmallows<br>guitar | forest<br>bear |

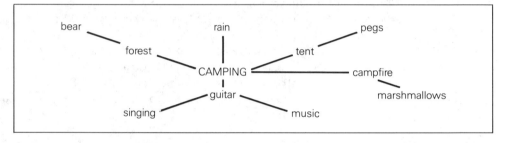

**Figure 12.3**  Clustering Information

***Drafting.***    Each day children should write a page in their journals and put a check-mark on the back of their journals next to the topic they have written about. Children who have difficulty with spelling should write the first letter of the troublesome word and then draw a line about as long as they believe the word to be or spell the word phonetically, as it sounds.

You must provide help and conferences as students need them. In a conference you may have to write on the line above the child's writing the word(s) the child wants to say (Gaskins, 1982). It is crucial that you discern and respond to what the child is saying even though his or her control of the language is imperfect.

Graves and Giacobbe (1982) suggest some questions to help children become conscious of writing:

1.  How did you go about writing this?
2.  What are you going to do next with this piece of writing?
3.  What do you think of this piece of writing?

Your response to students' writing should include praise for specific parts of journals that work well, questions about organization and details, and help with editing.

You might try interactive journals—responding with written comments to students' journals. Your written responses reinforce writing as a communicative process. In addition, students are practicing reading skills.

***Revising.*** Students must learn to revise their writing. Careful rereading for ideas provides a foundation for revision; then peer response can provide multiple sources of feedback. Students should share much of their work with each other (as well as with the teacher) since they are usually less threatened by each other (James, 1981).

Lyons (1981) has developed a method of balanced criticism. Students learn to "PQP" the work of others. Praise (P) involves noting what they really liked about the work and why they liked it. Questioning (Q) includes probing ideas or phrases that are not clearly expressed. Polishing (P) involves making suggestions about grammatical and spelling problems that should be corrected to produce a finished product. Through the PQP method students learn to see revision as a process. Teaching this method in three general steps builds students' confidence in writing and keeps them from directing their attention primarily to gross errors in grammar and spelling. Children should have some choice in revision of their own writing. Every piece of writing does not have to be completely revised.

Gaskins (1982) lists several guidelines for managing journal writing in the classroom:

1. Students must not sharpen pencils or engage in nonwriting activities during the writing time.
2. No student should interrupt when the teacher is in conference with another student.
3. Students should not wait over ten seconds for help. They should count to ten with hand raised; then they should ask another student, try to solve the problem, or skip over it.
4. Each student should proofread alone or with a friend when writing is finished.
5. Students should choose topics and do prewriting activities at home.
6. Students must listen and respond to the writing of others.
7. Each student should notify the teacher when a conference is needed.
8. Students should prepare for a conference by carefully rereading their writing and by putting checks where there are problems.
9. Students should always write on every other line.

# Content Writing Activities

As students become more experienced writers and editors of journals, they can expand their topics to content-based assignments. They gradually move from personal expression in writing to more public uses of writing to represent knowledge and transmit it effectively. At this point instruct them in such often used patterns of textual organizations as problem and solution, pro and con, cause and effect, and parts to the whole. Using these organizational patterns in writing about content-based materials should lead students to better understand textual material.

We now look at other writing activities, besides journal writing, that meet the comprehension needs of different kinds of students and that can be based on content materials.

## Dictation

Dictation is more widely used in other countries than in the United States but it is growing in acceptance (Stotsky, 1982). Dictation helps prevent the separation of spoken and written language and makes students more aware of spelling, punctuation, and capitalization when they are expressing thoughts. Dictation can also enlarge speaking vocabularies.

A good source of dictation material is introductory content material that repeats key vocabulary. The dictation process can thus function as a prereading organizer in the directed reading-thinking activity (DRTA) described in Chapter 9. The pattern for content material dictation follows:

1. Read the passage (usually a paragraph) aloud to students all the way through to build a background of meaning.
2. Read it a second time in phrases for the actual dictation process. List difficult vocabulary on the board and give punctuation orally; however, do not repeat phrases.
3. Read the passage again at a normal speed for students to make a final check.
4. Direct students to compare their passage with the one in the book and to correct any mistakes they find. Students lose points for mistakes not corrected.

Dictation may help train students to pay attention to detail, to listen carefully, and to develop memory strategies for syntactic units. As students' skills improve, enlarge the syntactic phrasing, as illustrated by the following examples.

Example 1:
You were/ born with/ certain genes/ that influenced/ your development./ These genes/ were transferred/ to you/ from your parents./ Heredity is/ the transfer/ of genes/ from one generation/ to the next./ Your heredity/ makes you different/ from others./ No one else/ is just/ like you.

Example 2:
You were born/ with certain genes/ that influenced your development./ These genes were transferred/ to you from your parents./ Heredity is the transfer/ of genes/ from one generation to the next./ Your heredity makes you/ different from others./ No one else is/ just like you.

Dictation helps students learn to read and write. (Photo by Jean Greenwald)

Example 3:

> You were born with certain genes/ that influenced your development./ These genes were transferred to you/ from your parents./ Heredity is the transfer of genes/ from one generation to the next./ Your heredity makes you different from others./ No one else is just like you.

Dictation is especially good for students who use English as a second language because the relationships between inflectional meaning and punctuation are explicit.

The meaning of punctuation marks in written language thus becomes clearer and more precise.

## Paraphrasing

Paraphrasing is an excellent reading comprehension activity that involves writing. Give students a passage and ask them to paraphrase it, or write it in their own words (Stotsky, 1982). Students process the reading material, integrate it, and reproduce it in writing. Paraphrasing hones attention to details, helps identify main points, and expands vocabulary.

One of the most useful ways to assess reading comprehension is to have students explain something in their own words (Anderson & Armbruster, 1982). Certainly, paraphrasing builds both comprehension skills and organizational skills.

## Summary Writing

Summary writing is another writing activity that is also an effective comprehension activity (Stotsky, 1982). Give students long content passages and ask them to summarize them in a paragraph or two. Limiting the number of words forces students to become more analytical and precise. Summary writing demands more synthesis of meaning than does paraphrasing. Provide examples of summary writing from summaries in textbooks, at the ends of chapters or sections.

Research with elementary school students has shown that students who wrote summaries of materials they had read scored significantly higher on reading comprehension tests than did students who used study guides, students who discussed the material they had read, or students who had no guidance (Taylor and Berkowitz, 1980). Both paraphrasing and summary writing help prepare students for essay tests in secondary school.

# Interest-Building Writing Activities

Although the preceding writing activities are particularly effective when using content materials, other writing activities in the classroom may be more effective in building student interest in language skills.

## Letter Writing

Although letter writing is often taught in language arts, students usually practice only a sample letter or two and then proceed to the next exercise. But letter writing can be a vital, ongoing activity with concrete results. Students may write letters to friends, relatives, penpals, famous personalities, newspapers, television or radio stations, and government officials. The United States Postal Service publishes various booklets that help students write letters to real audiences. Students can search magazines for offers of free booklets or materials, which they can request in a letter and then share with the class. Many informational booklets can thus become part of the classroom library.

## Class Newspaper

Another interesting writing activity is producing a class newspaper to be read by students and friends. The newspaper can include letters to the editor, cartoons, news articles, classified ads, and display advertisements. Even students with poor writing skills can contribute. Newspapers might have themes, such as Ancient Greece, the Future, or Colonial America. Themes help students organize their world view and often produce humorous, educational newspapers. This activity builds upon regular reading assignments and produces new reading material for students.

## Informational Booklets

Another favorite writing activity of older elementary students is writing a booklet that introduces their community to newcomers or composing a local history booklet to supplement their social studies text. These projects can involve reading newspapers and booklets for background material, interviewing knowledgable people, and working together in writing/editing groups. During the process, students build such reading skills as summarizing and interpreting material. The resulting publications, which can include photographs, sketches, or pictures, provide interesting, meaningful reading material.

## Search Project

Another interest-building activity for writers is a "search" project (Macrorie, 1980). Students pick a topic of interest, write what they already know about the subject, and then formulate questions about what they want to know. They then interview resource persons and read various materials. Finally they write a draft and revise it with the help of a writing partner.

For example, older elementary school children are often interested in different occupations. A search project on occupations can involve reading (at various levels of difficulty) and practicing oral language skills in interviews. Final versions, along with any pertinent photographs or drawings, can be bound in a book for the classroom library. Younger elementary school students may enjoy search projects on pets, relatives, or favorite recipes. Students should follow the pattern of tapping their own memory, formulating questions, and seeking information for writing. They can revise materials for a simple book with the help of writing partners and you, the teacher.

## Clay Activity

A writing activity that appeals to children of all ages is the "clay activity" (Catroppa, 1982). Each child forms a figure from a lump of clay and then writes a description of the figure. A partner reads the description and discusses both the figure and description with the author. Each writer then adds more details as desired. Place the descriptions on a ditto master and duplicate them so that each student can have a copy of every description. Then place all clay figures on a table and distribute the written descriptions (without identifying the figures). Each student reads a description and locates the matching clay figure, circling the clues that identified the figure. At this point, discuss with the class the use of details, clarity, and audience. Students begin to see writing and reading as reciprocal processes.

# Developing Spelling Conventions

Teaching writing can be discouraging, especially with younger children. Actual development in communication seems slow as elementary school students struggle to master basic writing conventions. Handwriting, spelling, and usage absorb their attention. But as students begin to master the motor skills along with acceptable writing conventions, they are able to direct more attention to the issues of topic and information (Graves, 1982). Later, young writers struggle with the problems of adding, deleting, or reorganizing to make writing accomplish its desired effect. As a teacher, you must be aware of the possible problem areas. Is a student most concerned with basic conventions, topic selection and development, or revising (adding, deleting, reorganizing)? Appropriate help from you is crucial to a child's progress in writing.

## Phonetic Spelling

The development of writing conventions, particularly spelling, is important in the early elementary school years. To learn to spell, most young students must grasp the alphabetic principle as a major cue. The latest research on spelling indicates that children look for patterns of alphabet/sound correspondence and that the majority of words do evidence this letter/sound correspondence, within certain general rules of construction (Hodges, 1982).

Phonetic, or invented, spelling—spelling words as they sound—can help students eventually learn conventional spelling. Students say the word, listen to it, and write it as best they can. Most students are able to distinguish clearly the consonant sounds and can learn the letter/sound correspondence. After the consonant sounds, the long vowel sounds are most easily grasped. When writing words, young writers may leave blanks for missing letters or parts of words. In invented spelling, *work* may be written as *wrk* or *guys* as *gis* (Hodges, 1982; Wood, 1982). These invented spellings seem to be a clear indication that the child is developing a conscious knowledge of how sound is expressed in print.

One way to check for deviant spelling is to have children read their work orally. Children who are deviant spellers are still in the stage of using random letters to stand for a word or part of a word and consequently cannot reread their writing at a later date. If writers can decipher their spelling and if they have repeated most constructions (always using *wrk* for *work*), they have developed knowledge of basic relationships between oral words and written words. Through invented spelling, children learn that speech can be recorded.

Invented spelling is a learning stage through which many children may go in developing conventional spelling. As children edit their work, have them compare invented spellings to conventional spellings to see how the two spellings are alike and how they are different.

Most children also develop a base of visual cues from reading. Some may rely more on visual cues and others more on phonetic cues (Hodges, 1982). Combining speaking, reading, and writing instruction allows students to draw upon a variety of cues.

## Spelling Activities

Students should keep personal spelling lists of words they have not yet learned to spell in their writing. Each student should have a writing partner test him or her in writing the unknown words weekly. Students must learn that once they are taught the standard spelling of a word, they are responsible to use it, relying on both sound and visual cues.

A class can produce a classroom dictionary of commonly used words with pictures and meanings. Have them insert large cards, each with a single word on it, in a two-ring notebook. The children can quickly learn to use the simple "dictionary" to look up needed words. They can easily add new words. The habit of using letter/sound cues to find conventional spelling in a dictionary is an important skill to develop.

In addition to invented spelling strategies, personal spelling lists, and dictionary work, children should learn basic spelling generalizations. The following seem to be most helpful in elementary school and can be reinforced through learning centers (Ley, 1982):

1. dropping the final *e* (rate/rating),
2. doubling the final consonant of one-syllable root words (drop/dropped),
3. doubling the final consonant of multiple-syllable root words (permit/permitted),
4. determining whether to use *ei* or *ie*,
5. using prefixes and suffixes (un + tie, joyful + ness)
6. using contractions (can not/can't).

All spelling should be grounded in a rich base of speaking, reading, and writing to provide contexts and to build a variety of cues (Hodges, 1982). Spelling is important to writing; "faulty spelling inhibits writers, confuses readers, and infuriates the public" (Ley, 1982, p. 25).

# Developing Handwriting

Children must write legibly to communicate with others. Most school systems promote a standardized, prescriptive approach to both manuscript and cursive handwriting. Children in kindergarten through second grade learn manuscript writing using circles, half circles, and straight lines. In late second or early third grade, they learn mastery of curved lines in cursive writing.

Handwriting is a developmental process and varies from child to child. In the classroom you should encourage children to improve their skills, but expect individual differences. The intent in this chapter is to discuss handwriting only as it relates to the writing and reading processes. See the summary of handwriting research in the *Encyclopedia of Educational Research* (Askov & Peck, 1982) for further information on handwriting development.

## Handwriting Activities

Handwriting is usually taught through direct instruction coupled with a multitude of practice sheets; however, writing activities can provide more meaningful practice time than worksheets can. After introducing students to all the letters, have them create alphabet books. Animal alphabet books are popular with students; so are books on "My World," which list items at home and school to illustrate the letters of the alphabet. Drawing, coloring, and writing names reinforce motor skills while students review alphabetic principles.

Simple story writing provides opportunities to develop different skills. After reading and discussing stories written by others, students write their own stories, which they illustrate. Although at first they may simply string actions together, children soon learn to recognize story structure and are later able to reproduce it. Creative writing of stories provides meaningful handwriting practice, even in first and second grade. Writing time reinforces handwriting and spelling as necessary skills for communication.

# Evaluating Writing

Teachers often avoid writing assignments because they believe that evaluating writing is too time-consuming. On the other hand, they realize that students need a great deal of writing experience to become proficient writers. You can resolve this dilemma: don't read everything that students write! Although someone should respond to each student's writing, that person does not have to be the teacher. A writing partner, peer groups, and parents can respond to writing.

## Evaluation by Others

A writing partner selected by each student can help in the evaluation process. Once the piece of writing is ready for the revising step of the writing process, the writing partner can assist by reading it critically for ideas, organization, and mechanics. The writing partner can check the writing again after revision to see if improvements have been made. Although you need not directly evaluate the piece of writing, you ought to supervise the writing partners to be sure that the relationship between partners is positive and productive.

Team or group evaluation can also be effective. Each team of students checks for only one type of error, such as spelling, punctuation, capitalization, or run-on and fragmented sentences. The team approach is particularly useful in checking for errors in writing mechanics. Form the teams to include good and poor readers/writers so that underachieving students may learn from the more capable ones. Teams function most effectively when given guidelines or checklists to assist them in evaluation.

Writing partners. (Photo © Richard Khanlian)

Students can rotate through the various teams so that they gain experience in evaluating writing for different kinds of errors.

Parents can assist their children in the revising process if a good working relationship exists between them. You should show parents, perhaps at parent conferences or in a class newsletter, how to help their children. Again, checklists can assist parents in evaluating relevant items. You might want to ask parents to evaluate their children's writing for only one type of error, such as punctuation. Of course, you should have already provided direct instruction on punctuation so that the parents are simply checking their child's application of the instruction.

## Teacher Evaluation

You can score writing in a variety of ways. To evaluate only the level of writing competence without providing feedback to the students, rank writing using a holistic system of *1* to *4* with *4* being the highest level and *1* the lowest. Each category is characterized by the level of language use in four areas: originality, organization, grammar, and spelling. For example, a *4* could be characterized by the following:

- Strong controlling ideas supported by convincing details or arguments.
- A clear beginning, middle, and end with adequate transitions.
- Varied word choice and sentence structures.
- No errors or few errors in spelling, punctuation, and grammar.

By contrast, a *1* would be characterized by the following:

- Sketchy and poorly supported ideas.
- Writing that seems to be associative rather than logically organized.
- Predictable and unvaried word choice and sentence structure.
- Lack of use of language conventions in spelling, punctuation, and grammar.

These examples provide an idea of how to set up your own holistic scoring categories. The emphasis in holistic scoring is on recording a general impression of quality immediately after reading. Familiarize yourself with the characteristics of the four categories and then score student writing after a quick reading.

Holistic scoring is appropriate for assignments that have already undergone extensive evaluation and revision. You might score students' writing holistically several times during the school year to determine whether improvements are being made in general writing competence.

Often, however, you will want to provide students with evaluative feedback. Traditionally, teachers have used a grade and written comments. This approach can be inconsistent, depending upon the teacher. One way to provide feedback in a balanced format to students is to use a scoring criteria chart based on the primary traits of good writing, as illustrated in Table 12.2. Note how this chart weights the quality of ideas and organization much more heavily than spelling or handwriting. When reinforcing conventions in the early grades, you may wish to modify the scale and weight them more heavily.

This scale provides consistent feedback so that students can see which areas need improvement. You could also use this scale to evaluate students' paraphrases or summaries of reading assignments.

**Table 12.2** Scoring Based on the Primary Traits of Good Writing

|  | Low |  | Middle |  | High |  |
|---|---|---|---|---|---|---|
| Clarity of Ideas | 1 | 2 | 3 | 4 | 5 | (__ × 6) = _____ |
| Organization | 1 | 2 | 3 | 4 | 5 | (__ × 4) = _____ |
| Language Usage | 1 | 2 | 3 | 4 | 5 | (__ × 4) = _____ |
| Punctuation | 1 | 2 | 3 | 4 | 5 | (__ × 2) = _____ |
| Spelling | 1 | 2 | 3 | 4 | 5 | (__ × 2) = _____ |
| Handwriting | 1 | 2 | 3 | 4 | 5 | (__ × 2) = _____ |

Finally, you can evaluate students' writing on a selective basis. Indicate what is being evaluated at the top of the paper. For example, you may want to score students on the *amount* written, awarding an *S* or *U*. This scoring method is most appropriate for journal writing or other fluency-building writing assignments. Sometimes you will evaluate writing for the content or ideas. This type of evaluation is appropriate especially if other students have already evaluated the writing for mechanics.

# Summary

Language is a complex process that the children begin to master early in life. By the time they reach school, they have learned the power of language. Written language is more precise, organized, and developed than oral language. Reading and writing seem to be parallel ways of processing written language and are important, related skills.

Writing development moves from concern with writing conventions to awareness of the choices made in effective communication. Writers develop more critical perceptions of books. Writing activities in the classroom can integrate the language arts skills of reading, writing, speaking, and listening and can provide appropriate, interesting reading material to meet students' needs. Writing may be the missing link in reading instruction.

Writing as a process involves three main stages—prewriting, drafting, and revision—which parallel the creative thought processes. Prewriting activities include categorizing, clustering, and talking and reading about a topic to create a store of "inner speech." Drafting of thoughts follows. Finally, revision involves attention to adding, moving, or removing material to make ideas clear and organized. Regular journal writing is a good way to introduce writing as a process.

Students can also develop comprehension of written language through dictation, paraphrasing, and summary writing, which help them develop (a) memory for language structural units and (b) skills in noting and remembering main ideas and their relationships in text material. Interest-building writing activities include letter writing, "book" writing, search projects, and classroom newspapers.

Students develop control of spelling through phonetic and visual clues, often progressing from invented to conventional spelling. Writing provides a reason for learning to spell. Handwriting development can also be fostered by written activities.

You can score writing by holistic scoring, primary trait scoring, or selective scoring. Writing assignments can also serve as reading comprehension assessments. Reading and writing are complementary processes important to integrating the language skills of reading, writing, speaking, and listening.

# References

**Anderson, T. H., & Armbruster, B. B.** (1982). Reader and text-studying strategies. In W. Otto & S. White (Eds.), *Reading Expository Material.* New York: Academic Press, pp. 219–242.

Askov, E. N., & Peck, M. (1982). Handwriting. In H. E. Mitzel (Ed.), *Encyclopedia of Educational Research* (5th ed., Vol. 2) New York: Macmillan, pp. 764 – 769.

Boutwell, M. A. (1983). Reading and writing process: A reciprocal agreement. *Language Arts, 60* (6), 723 – 730.

Britton, J. (1970). *Language and learning.* London: Penguin Press.

Calkins, L. M. (1980). Children's rewriting strategies. *Research in the Teaching of English, 14* (4), 331 – 341.

Calkins, L. M. (1983). Making the reading-writing connection. *Learning, 12* (2), 82 – 83, 85, 86.

Catroppa, B. D. (1982). Working with writing is like working with clay. *Language Arts, 59* (7), 687 – 695.

Emig, J. (1971). *The composing processes of twelfth graders.* Urbana, Illinois: National Council of Teachers of English.

Gaskins, I. A. (1982). A writing program for poor readers and writers and for the rest of the class, too. *Language Arts, 59* (8), 854 – 861.

Graves, D. (1982). How do writers develop? *Language Arts, 59* (2), 173 – 179.

Graves, D., & Giacobbe, M. E. (1982). Questions for teachers who wonder if their writers change. *Language Arts, 59* (5), 495 – 503.

Hammill, D., & McNutt, G. (1981). *The correlates of reading.* Austin, Texas: Pro-Ed.

Hansen, J. (1983). Authors respond to authors. *Language Arts, 60* (8), 970 – 976.

Hodges, R. E. (1982). On the development of spelling ability. *Language Arts, 59* (3), 284 – 290.

James, F. (1981). Peer teaching in the writing classroom. *English Journal, 70* (6), 48 – 50.

Ley, T. C. (1982). Teaching spelling without spelling books. *English Journal, 71* (8), 22 – 25.

Lyons, B. (1981). The PQP method of responding to writing. *English Journal, 70* (3), 42 – 43.

Macrorie, K. (1980). *Searching writing.* Rochelle Park, NJ: Hayden.

Paul, A. (1973). *Kids camping.* New York: Doubleday & Co.

Smith, F. (1977). The uses of language. *Language Arts, 54* (6), 640.

Stotsky, S. (1982). The role of writing in developmental reading. *Journal of Reading, 25* (4), 330 – 339.

Taylor, B., & Berkowitz, S. (1980). Facilitating children's comprehension of content materials. In *Perspectives on Reading Research and Instruction* (Twenty-Ninth Yearbook of the National Reading Conference). Washington, D.C.: National Reading Conference.

Trosky, O., & Wood, C. (1982). Using a writing model to teach reading. *Journal of Reading, 26* (1), 34 – 40.

Wood, M. (1982). Invented spelling. *Language Arts, 59* (7), 707 – 717.

# Check Your Reading Comprehension

1. Why should writing be integrated with reading? How can writing activities be helpful in teaching reading?

2. Matching Exercise

_____ **1.** Oral language skills

_____ **2.** Written language skills

_____ **3.** Prewriting skills

_____ **4.** Drafting

_____ **5.** Revision

_____ **6.** Stages of creative acts

_____ **7.** PQP

_____ **8.** Invented spelling

_____ **9.** Holistic system

_____ **10.** Primary trait system

**a.** Reading and writing.

**b.** A stage in which the writer takes the role of a reader, checking to see what needs to be added, removed, or moved to fulfill the purposes of writing.

**c.** Preparation, incubation, illumination, and validation.

**d.** Listening and speaking.

**e.** A technique in which students spell words as they sound.

**f.** A stage in which the writer builds up a store of ideas and words on a topic.

**g.** A method of evaluating writing based on a general impression of quality immediately after reading.

**h.** A stage in which the writer actually writes thoughts on paper.

**i.** A method of balanced criticism (praising, questioning, polishing).

**j.** A method of evaluating writing using a scoring criteria list to minimize inconsistency of feedback.

Answers:

| | |
|---|---|
| 1. d | 6. c |
| 2. a | 7. i |
| 3. f | 8. e |
| 4. h | 9. g |
| 5. b | 10. j |

**3.** Imagine you are teaching a fifth grade class. You ask your students to pretend they are traveling with Lewis and Clark. Choose one event from their explorations. Use either the categorizing or clustering technique to guide your class through the prewriting stage.

**4.** Paraphrasing and summary writing can be especially helpful with content area texts. Prepare either a paraphrased or summarized version of the selection entitled "The Importance of Good Health" from the activities at the end of Chapter 11.

**5.** In Chapter 7 you learned about different approaches to teaching reading. Obviously, writing can easily be integrated with LEA. What about the other approaches? How might you integrate writing with a basal approach? a linguistic approach? a phonics approach (either analytic or synthetic)? an individualized approach?

**6.** Several interest-building activities were described in this chapter (letters, class newspaper, search project, etc.). Which do you feel would be most appropriate for your class? Why?

# 13

# Affective Factors in Corrective Teaching

Written by Dr. Joyce Lee, Reading Specialist, State College, PA, Area School District and Affiliate Assistant Professor, The Pennsylvania State University; Dr. Eunice N. Askov, Professor of Education, The Pennsylvania State University; and Linda Merchant, Reading Specialist, Grier School, Tyrone, PA.

Let's consider once again the children we met in Chapter 1. You have worked diligently to help John and Allison improve their comprehension skills by developing the skills of reading for meaning. You have helped Maria to build her vocabulary and to develop meaningful background concepts. Although Tony and Joe still receive special reading services, they depend on you for instruction in content area materials and related reading skills.

Although each of these children has special individual needs, there seems to be a common ingredient that is missing in the way they approach the reading process. When you stand back and observe these children at work, you realize that their attitudes are negative toward their work and achievement in reading. They don't appear to be enthusiastic about reading. They seldom choose to read for pleasure or enjoyment. As these thoughts pass through your mind, you become aware that you must carefully build an affective component into your reading program. Concern only for reading skills and achievement is not enough.

The primary focus of the preceding chapters is on the cognitive factors essential to corrective teaching. In this chapter we consider the affective elements that have an enormous impact on students' achievement in reading—specifically self-concept, attitude, and motivation. We show how these affective components of the curriculum can be intricately woven into the cognitive dimension of a corrective reading program. We also show

how to use parents, peer tutors, and community volunteers in an effective reading program.

# Self-Concept

Reading disability can have disastrous consequences for the learner. Underachieving readers confronted with one frustrating reading experience after another may develop negative self-concepts as well as poor attitudes toward reading. It is difficult to evaluate completely the effects of self-image on learning, but a low self-concept often leads to academic difficulties, especially in the area of reading.

*Consider for a moment those activities that you enjoy doing in your leisure time. List at least five on a sheet of paper. On another sheet of paper list the things that you do well. Chances are that your two lists contain overlapping activities. Likewise, activities that you do not enjoy are probably those that you do not do well. The senior author of this book, for example, does not like to ice skate, and she does not skate well. Therefore, she elects to stay inside by the fire with a good book while others choose to go skating. Because she does not skate, she does not improve her skating performance. Similarly, children who do not read well generally avoid reading. Reading, like any other skill, requires practice for improvement.*

Research on children's self-concepts has shown that students who feel good about themselves and their achievements are the ones who succeed in academic endeavors. Conversely, students who fail to achieve are usually the ones who perceive themselves negatively (Purkey, 1970).

The total of all the perceptions individuals have of themselves makes up what is called the global self-concept (Quandt, 1972). Subcategories of this global self-concept appear to exist: self-concept of appearance, self-concept of general ability, and self-concept of specific ability, such as in reading or mathematics. We learn self-concept through rewards and punishments, successes and failures, and the reactions of other people (Quick, 1973).

We are concerned here with the relationship between self-concept and reading achievement. Individuals who believe that they cannot succeed in reading have a poor or low reading self-concept. They may exhibit behaviors that contribute to poor achievement, thus becoming victims of a self-fulfilling prophecy. Poor self-concept interferes with learning to read and the resulting reading disability reinforces the poor self-concept. Initial difficulties in reading may also have negative effects on self-concept; the student expects to fail rather than succeed.

On the other hand, if individuals perceive themselves as capable readers, they develop positive reading self-concepts. They continue to read and improve their skills, become more capable, and thus are praised for their improvement. The reading self-concept is enhanced, and the individual chooses to read as a school and leisure activity.

## Assessment of Self-Concept

Although it is impossible to actually walk in another person's shoes to see and feel the concept we call self, we can infer the self from: self-report inventories, or individuals' statements about themselves, and from observations of individuals' behaviors. Rogers (1951) believes that self-reports are reliable sources of information about the self and that individuals have the right to be believed when they report feelings about themselves. When relying on observations to infer self-concept, the observers must try to free themselves from subjective inferences and remain objective.

Self-report inventories are widely used to infer self-concept as they give some insight into the way individuals see themselves and their worlds (Quandt, 1972). Although assessment of self-concept is difficult, these inventories can provide strong clues for diagnosis. Quandt (1972) provides lists of published and unpublished inventories for the assessment of self-concept.

Informal teacher observations also provide valuable information about self-concept. Quandt (1972) lists five behaviors that can illustrate students' self-concepts.

1. Students' comments about themselves or about their reading
2. Students' reactions to reading instruction or reading tasks, including facial expressions, body movements, gestures, and verbalizations
3. Students' interactions with peers, such as avoiding working with others, engaging in attention-getting behaviors, and receiving ridicule from others
4. Students' degree of willingness to volunteer during discussions, including avoiding participation altogether or offering inappropriate answers
5. Students' level of confidence exhibited during decision-making or problem-solving activities

## Enhancement of Self-Concept

Teacher expectations of student achievement are crucial, as illustrated through the research of Rosenthal and Jacobson (1968). According to Quick (1973), the Rosenthal study involved giving teachers the names of students who were expected to make intellectual gains in the year ahead. The children had actually been randomly selected. Teachers when working with the students revealed tendencies of preferential treatment to those who were said to be bright. Tone of voice, touch, facial expressions, and posture projected the teachers' expectancies to the students. The Rosenthal experiment indicated that the children from whom teachers expected gains showed such gains because of teachers' positive attitudes toward them.

Problem readers often confront one frustrating reading activity after another. The teacher comes not to expect the student to succeed and the student usually doesn't. As we have noted, unsuccessful reading experiences impede future progress and reinforce negative self-concepts. Your task, then, is to provide alternatives to the methods, techniques, and materials that have been unsuccessful. You must study the student's work closely to know how to provide successful experiences. You must also expect success once appropriate materials and strategies are used.

Noland and Craft (1976) discuss the program initiated at the Auburn University Reading Clinic, which has proved successful with remedial readers ages 7 through 16. Elements of this model could easily be adapted to a school setting. Clinicians are encouraged to establish a close confident relationship with their students, emphasizing a humanistic approach to learning. Because reluctant readers often believe that they cannot read, it is important to insure success by beginning at a low level of difficulty. Lessons center around high-impact materials that the student selects. The student and clinician together set short-range goals that can serve as motivators when they are achieved. Students keep their own progress charts and records; conferences are held to update records and establish realistic goals. The Auburn model can be characterized as student-centered with emphasis on the affective as well as the cognitive domains of learning.

Arvanities (1980) and Hettinger (1980) have found that lessons based on real-life experiences improved reading achievement and self-concept. They suggest relevant materials keyed to students' interests and attitudes instead of more traditional curriculum materials.

# Attitude

While self-concept refers to one's feelings toward one's self, attitude toward reading may be defined as "a system of feelings related to reading which causes the learner to approach or avoid a reading situation" (Alexander & Filler, 1976, p. 1). Attitude toward reading is affected by self-concept, specifically the student's self-concept with regard to reading.

How can a teacher know which children have positive attitudes toward reading? While it is possible to infer by observation, other techniques may be useful, especially at the beginning of the school year when the teacher does not yet know the students well.

The *Primary Pupil Reading Attitude Inventory* (Askov, 1972, 1973) is useful for assessing reading attitudes of students through the third grade. (The complete inventory is in the Instructor's Manual but samples are in Appendix E.) The inventory measures attitude toward recreational reading, rather than in-school reading, to determine how beginning readers feel about reading in general rather than the specific reading instructional program. The primary child must choose between pairs of pictures of recreational activities, some of which depict reading. A total score indicates how many times reading was selected as a favorite activity.

Instruments for use with older children include the San Diego County Inventory of Reading Attitude (1961), which requires *yes* or *no* answers to questions probing attitudes toward reading. Items are scored differentially, yielding a total score that indicates how positive or negative a child's attitude is. Sample items include

yes   no      Do you think you are a poor reader?
yes   no      Is reading your favorite subject in school?

Alexander and Filler (1976) describe the Heathington Primary and Intermediate Scales in detail. The primary child is asked to rate questions such as "How do you feel when you go to the library?" on a five-point scale consisting of five faces that range from sad to happy. The intermediate child rates statements such as "You feel uncomfortable when you're asked to read in class" on a five-point scale from *strongly disagree* to *strongly agree*.

Another approach is to provide students with incomplete, teacher-devised sentences, such as the following:

On Saturdays I like to _____.
When I read, I feel _____.
I like to read _____.
If I had a million dollars, I would _____.

Observation accompanied by a checklist of behaviors associated with positive attitude can help determine students' attitudes toward reading. You can note on the checklist which children go to the library voluntarily, which read the most books, which use spare time in the classroom for reading, and so forth.

Alexander and Filler's book *Attitudes and Reading* (1976) provides further information on assessment techniques and research relating to attitude toward reading.

# Motivation

Motivation is a third affective factor, closely associated with self-concept and attitude. While motivation cannot be directly measured, it can be inferred from observation of behavior (Ball, 1982).

Factors related to motivation are often classified as internal or external. Internal motivation, or self-motivation, is preferred because "needs, desires, interests, and loves that come from within a person trigger far more learning than other influences" (*Practical Applications of Research,* 1982, p. 2).

External motivation pertains to forces outside the individual that influence behavior. While rewards can be effective external motivation, they can become ends in themselves and perhaps even drive out internal motivation (*Practical Applications of Research,* 1982). You must therefore be careful in using behavioral modification schemes as a form of external motivation.

Although the research findings related to motivation are difficult to present simply, especially as the implications relate to reading instruction, Ball (1982) has identified some practical applications for education.

1. Children are differently motivated. What works with one student may not work with another. . . .
2. Students are more likely to work without extensive supervision if they have an internal locus of control—if they see themselves as responsible for their own behavior.
3. Teachers should lead students to attribute successful performance to ability, or, if relevant, to long-term effort. However, teacher educators should lead teachers to see that external socioeconomic factors are not under the student's control.
4. Competitive learning situations compared to cooperative learning situations increase self-punitive reactions to failure and greater self-esteem after success. Care has to be exercised in dealing with competitive learning situations, especially when involving less able students.

5. Efforts to make children feel that they are the origins of their own behavior and not simply pawns pushed by external forces can be fruitful. . . . [A classroom climate should encourage individual student initiative.]

6. Getting rid of anxiety in the classroom may make students feel more at ease but is not likely to improve academic performance. Mild anxiety levels may enhance learning, but teachers must be aware that high anxiety is counterproductive. . . .

7. For humanitarian reasons teachers should try to enhance the way students see themselves. . . . Teachers probably should concentrate on specifics—such as making students feel confident about their achievements in [reading]—rather than trying to enhance the vaguely defined "self-concept."

8. Curiosity in the classroom requires the presence of novel stimuli. . . . Teachers who want their students to be curious have to give students the privilege of exploring. Overstructured classrooms inhibit curiosity. Teachers can constructively baffle students by presenting problems, giving a few clues, and then letting student curiosity take over. This process might take longer than a routine teacher lecture, but it certainly adds more positive affect to the classroom experience.

9. Educators should consider the incentive system that operates in their sphere of influence (classroom, department, school). Are the right behaviors being reinforced? Is the noisy child getting too much attention? Is the independent and hardworking child being wrongly ignored? Does the teacher who complains most get the fewest duties? . . . Remember that incentives include social attention and token rewards, but each person has his or her own set of preferred reinforcements. (p. 1261)

Some students are able to read but are not motivated to do so by the traditional reading instructional program (Farr, 1981). Drilling students on isolated reading skills and using materials about which students have little prior knowledge and background tend to obscure the fact that reading is getting meaning from print. Use reading as a tool and integrate it with the other language arts.

A thematic or unit approach to teaching reading can help reading skills within the context of meaningful application. As described in Chapter 11, the unit theme becomes the focal point of study. Reading skills develop within the context of study relating to the theme rather than as a result of isolated skill instruction. Motivation is usually high because of interest in the topic of study. Students read not for the sake of reading but as one of many sources of information.

*You may at this point be feeling a bit overwhelmed. How can you attend to all these affective factors—self-concept, attitude, and motivation—as well as develop cognitive skills in teaching reading? How can you cram all reading instruction into an hour and a half each day? In fact, you can't!*

*The remainder of this chapter focuses on how one classroom teacher integrates both the cognitive and affective aspects of reading instruction throughout the school day. He employs motivational techniques that also enhance self-concept and attitude toward reading, especially among those students having trouble learning to read. He also uses parents, peer tutors, and community volunteers in an effective reading program. In essence, he knows how to give reading top billing in a busy school day.*

## Reading: Priority Number One

A familiar lament at faculty meetings is, "How can we find time to teach reading with all the other things we're expected to include in the curriculum?" No wonder that reading sometimes appears to take the back seat, getting lost in the exhaustive effort to "do it all" in days already crammed with lunch counts, library periods, fire drills, assemblies, special service pullout programs, and the creation of a positive affective learning environment. Let's take a look at just how reading, especially for the under-achieving readers in a regular classroom, can become and remain priority number one.

We are going to study how Mr. Jackson, a second-grade teacher, has integrated both the cognitive and affective elements of reading instruction into his classroom. He is intended as a model of good pedagogy; we hope you will not be "turned off" if he seems a bit too good to be true. We are trying to show that a good teacher can become a better teacher by implementing these strategies over a period of years. Even Mr. Jackson couldn't do all we talk about during his first year of teaching!

Time management experts have long suggested ways to increase efficiency when no increase in time is available. A frequently suggested strategy is compiling detailed

Mr. Jackson, our model teacher.

"to do" lists and then placing them in order by priorities. At regular intervals during the school year, you, the classroom teacher, need to compile this detailed list of *all* the items you are expected to include during a given time period, such as a week, month, report card period, or semester.

Most educators and parents would agree that reading ought to appear near or at the top of any teacher's priority list. Easily said, yes. Easily done, no, unless you carry time management one critical step further by applying the techniques of "combining."

| | TO DO |
|---|---|
| PR | Daily lunch count. |
| PR | Daily attendance count. |
| PR/I | Daily announcements. |
| PR | Nutrition miniunit on fruits and vegetables. |
| PR/I | Making valentines for parents. |
| PR | Valentine's Day party. |
| PR/I | Bus safety. |
| PR/I | Washington's birthday. |
| I | Daily basal reader lessons. |
| | Writing PTA Open House invitation to parents. |
| PR/PL | Daily silent reading time. |
| PR | Justice awareness. |
| PR/I | Daily math period. |
| | Lincoln's birthday. |
| | Handwriting. |
| | Creative writing. |
| | Discuss Groundhog Day. |
| PR/PL | Focus on self-concept, attitude, and motivation. |
| PR/PL | Book Buddies. |
| PR/PL | Bookworm program. |
| | Read-aloud. |
| PL | Family Thinking Night. |
| PR | Let's Read to Find Out! |

**Figure 13.1**    Mr. Jackson's "To Do" List for February

Busy people have long recognized the wisdom, indeed necessity, of doing two or more things at once. A careful analysis of Mr. Jackson's list in Figure 13.1 yields invaluable insights into how a seemingly overwhelming number of things "to do" can be cut down to manageable size by combining.

Let's see how you can effectively combine reading as the top priority with almost, if not every, item on Mr. Jackson's February "to do" list in Figure 13.1. Note how he has penciled in three subcategories of reading: *I* for instruction, *PR* for practice, and *PL* for pleasure. A review of the February "to do" list clearly indicates that while the month demands an incredible number of "add-ons" to an already full second-grade curriculum, Mr. Jackson intends that reading will indeed be an integral part of most of the activities.

Just what does Mr. Jackson mean when he notes that reading for practice (PR) is part of the item "daily lunch count," or that reading for both instruction (I) and practice (PR) will be taking place during "bus safety"?

Mr. Jackson has indicated in the right-hand column of Figure 13.2 just how reading might best be incorporated into the first few items on his "to do" list. He plans to have children read the daily school menu each morning during attendance and announcement time, one child assigned by monthly "lottery drawing" to a particular day's lunch possibilities. Note that Mr. Jackson has combined the lunch count with attendance by having the same child who reads the daily menu read the class list and mark the office record, another practice reading activity squeezed into the crowded day.

Next to the bus safety item, Mr. Jackson notes that he plans to read aloud a pamphlet provided by the local police and then have the class dictate the suggested

| Activity | Implementation |
|---|---|
| Daily lunch count. | Use "lottery" system to assign each child a date for which he or she is responsible for reading that day's menu offerings to rest of class. |
| Daily attendance count. | Same child in charge of reading attendance and making slip for office. |
| Daily announcements. | Include these in letter to whole class that appears on board each morning. |
| Nutrition miniunit on fruits and vegetables. | Each day's letter on board will include mention of the day's cafeteria fruit and vegetable items with new or reinforcing information about nutritive value. |
| Making valentines for parents. | Instruction in following directions will precede activity. Students will follow a written set of directions in making valentines. |
| Bus safety. | Class will dictate for chart, which will be reread occasionally during daily announcements. |

**Figure 13.2** Implementation of Mr. Jackson's "To Do" List for February

safety rules for a language experience chart. This chart is to be posted and reread aloud occasionally during morning attendance and announcement time.

Mr. Jackson has managed to change a list of activities that initially appears to *preclude* much reading instruction into a month's plan of activities that *emphasizes* reading instruction. Reading emerges, not as a back-burner agenda item, but in its proper place, priority number one.

Let's look more closely to see how our model teacher, Mr. Jackson, has set about creating a highly motivating classroom environment that says clearly to his students, and to their parents, that reading *is* priority number one.

The children arrive in September to find bulletin boards proclaiming various promotional activities that Mr. Jackson has planned for the year, all clearly focusing on developing skill in, and love for, reading. One display announces the kickoff of Mr. Jackson's annual Book Buddy program featuring "The Little Engine That Could"—a colorful drawing of Watty Piper's famous "Little Engine" above a giant bar graph listing every child's name. Another bulletin board display features this year's storybook character, Paddington Bear, who will serve as the classroom "mascot" and will promote Mr. Jackson's annual Bookworm program. Those children who attended first grade in this school the previous year are already aware of the schoolwide enthusiasm generated each year by Mr. Jackson's "mascot." They may have been eagerly awaiting this opening day of school to discover which one of their many beloved children's literature characters would be joining them as they progress through second grade. They recall that last year's second graders entertained, and were entertained by, Winnie the Pooh, whose picture appeared all over the school throughout the year and who made a personal appearance in the auditorium on Awards Day in the Spring. These children already know of Mr. Jackson's love of children's literary favorites and enter the classroom with a positive mind set, which should give them a good start toward assimilating the intensive reading focus that will characterize their year with Mr. Jackson.

# Classroom Strategies

Now let's take a close look at precisely how Mr. Jackson orchestrates his task of motivating second graders to read and read and read during the school year. Careful examination of Mr. Jackson's "to do" list (Figure 13.1) with implementation plans (Figure 13.2) allows us to extract those items that represent ongoing motivational activities specifically intended to promote good self-concept and positive attitudes among his students. In other words, we can identify those specific items that Mr. Jackson is likely to include on *each* month's "to do" list.

## Daily Letter

Each morning as the children arrive in Room 6, they check their individual mailboxes for messages. Mr. Jackson uses these mailboxes, made from half-gallon milk containers glued together to form a mini–post office, for individual reminders about unfinished work, for messages commending jobs well done, and for other special information.

The primary function of the mailbox system is, of course, to focus on each child as an individual. Finding occasional "just for you" notes from Mr. Jackson in their very own mail slots appears to contribute substantially to the children's positive self-concept, as evidenced by the enthusiasm with which they enter the room each day and check their boxes.

Whether there is a "just for you" note in the mailbox or not, each day there *is* in each child's slot a letter prepared by Mr. Jackson before school that morning. Each child knows that this daily letter represents the first major task of the day. Anyone observing the children in Room 6 at the start of each school day is likely to find 26 children already intensely involved in a highly motivating and instructionally rich language arts activity.

The letter varies in length and content from day to day but always reflects a number of common emphases. First, while the letter is prepared on a ditto or duplicated on the office copier, Mr. Jackson always takes the time to personalize each letter by writing a child's name after the greeting word, *Dear,* before placing the letter in that child's mail slot. Second, the letter always begins with a low-key "social" paragraph about a topic of current interest to all the children: perhaps a brief reference to a funny incident of the day before or an anecdote about Mr. Jackson's life outside the classroom. Occasionally, too, this opening paragraph might focus on a special event concerning one particular child in the classroom, thus creating a "spotlight" for that child, an especially useful technique for a child experiencing academic, social, or emotional difficulties. Mr. Jackson has observed that even his poorest reader eagerly reads this part of the daily letter, especially when his or her name appears in the first paragraph.

A third element common to each day's letter is the use of the cloze procedure to insure each child's active construction and reconstruction of language, both important facets of the reading comprehension process. Mr. Jackson always carefully chooses what words to leave as blanks to reinforce skills he is hoping to build in other parts of the curriculum.

The daily letter deletions generally fall into three categories: (a) structure words, which demand that the children utilize syntactic language cues for prediction, (b) high-frequency content words, which demand semantic cue processing, and (c) content words peculiar to topics currently being considered in the classroom and therefore likely to be readily retrieved in the prediction process. Mr. Jackson wants to be certain that this important first activity of the day emphasizes that reading is primarily acquiring meaning, not just decoding words. He tries to make the content of each day's letter interesting enough that the children will be eager to search out meaning as active participants in constructing and reconstructing language.

One critical factor in Mr. Jackson's management of the daily letter involves his technique for accommodating the wide range of reading abilities in his classroom. While the letter is written at a level most of the children in the room can read independently, it is usually beyond the capabilities of his poorest readers. Occasionally Mr. Jackson has the time to prepare a separate, easier version of the day's letter that these youngsters are able to read with minimal teacher assistance. But he usually gives each child the same letter and then provides for a special kind of help for each child he knows will be unable to read the letter independently.

Over the years Mr. Jackson has made good use of peer tutoring in a variety of ways. This year he is using in-class tutors for the daily letter activity. Early in the year he carefully pairs each of his least able readers with a classmate. He pairs students on a very personalized basis, making certain that each peer-tutor match will be comfortable and beneficial in some way to both children. Pairings are flexible and change as the children's needs and performance change; but each morning in Room 6 the children reading below grade level can be seen working with a partner to complete the daily letter, thus relieving a great deal of pressure that Mr. Jackson would otherwise experience if he had to help each poor reader with this first activity of the day.

The sample in Figure 13.3 demonstrates some of the ways in which Mr. Jackson utilizes the daily letter strategy. Note that he attempts to provide a stimulating reading activity for the morning's initial task while at the same time he manages to cover a number of important instructional objectives. This strategy is similar to the morning letter presented in Chapter 11 as a vehicle for the teacher to present content concepts, knowledge, and vocabulary to students unable to read the textbook.

---

### Watch for a Missing Comma in Today's Letter!

Feb__ary 8, 198_

Dear _____

      Happy birthday, Amanda! We'll have a special birthday snack for _____ after recess this morning. The snack is a food from the _____ and vegetable group.

      The school lunch today _____ a peanut butter sandwich. There will also be green beans and an orange _____ the lunch trays. Oranges are full of vitamin _____!

      First, do your _____ order. Next, do your letter work. Please be ready _____ go to the library _____ 9:40. Do _____ want to look for a _____ book today?

Your friend,

_____ Jackson

### Today's Questions

1. Today is Tuesday.   Yes   No
2. How many paragraphs are in today's letter? _____
3. Amanda's birthday snack may be cupcakes.   Yes   No
4. The vegetable in today's school lunch is _____.
5. Today is music day.   Yes   No
6. Did you find the missing comma?   Yes   No
7. I hope Amanda's snack will be _____.

**Figure 13.3**  Sample Daily Letter

## Book Buddy Program

Mr. Jackson was introduced to the Book Buddy program several years ago when a similar program was developed by the remedial teacher in his building. Each fall for several years this teacher read aloud to all the second-grade remedial readers in her program that children's literature favorite, *The Little Engine That Could* by Watty Piper. She then challenged the children to be "Little Engines" that try to meet what seemed an impossible goal: reading one hundred books between September and June! All one hundred books were to be read to various volunteers during school time and charted on a special bulletin board. Those children reaching the magic one hundred mark before the end of the school year would receive special recognition at the annual school awards assembly.

Mr. Jackson was so impressed by the success of the Book Buddy program that when the remedial program was severely cut back because of budget reductions, he suggested that he take over the Book Buddy program, with some modifications to insure that those poor readers assigned to him would get additional daily practice reading easy-to-read books, so critical for sight vocabulary development in the early stages of reading.

Thus, during the first week of the school year, Mr. Jackson always reads aloud to his whole class *The Little Engine That Could,* asks all his children if they think they can read one hundred books before the end of school, and then explains how he will help make it possible for all of them to become as successful as Piper's famous little blue engine with its admirable power of positive thinking.

Over the years Mr. Jackson has put together a very large collection of books appropriate for second graders. These books range in difficulty from picture books and very easy-to-read short storybooks to longer books of above second-grade difficulty. He has sorted these books into various bins, color-coding each bin and each book (using small colored labels) according to difficulty. He has put together three sets of one hundred books, with some overlap between sets so that in fact the entire collection consists of less than three hundred books. Each set represents a different level of difficulty, the easiest set intended for that group of children reading below second-grade level, the next, more difficult set intended for his average readers, and the third set, the most difficult books, intended for his small group of children already reading above grade level.

As early as possible in September, Mr. Jackson completes his assessment of the children in his room, using an informal reading inventory, and tentatively forms three reading groups. He knows that the composition of his groups will change during the year as some children make faster progress than others. A child can easily move from reading books in one set to those of greater or lesser difficulty in another set. As he has his initial meetings with his groups, he shows the children the Book Buddy bins and explains which books he would like the children in each group to read during the year. He points out each child's name on one of the three charts on the "Little Engines" bulletin board. The three charts, one for each set of one hundred books, list each title in the left column with the same color-coded label appearing next to a title as that appearing on each book in the appropriate bin. Across the top of the charts the children's names appear; vertical and horizontal lines form a matrix. As a child reads a book, he or she places a star in the column under his or her name in the row beside the particular book title.

Next, Mr. Jackson meets with his lowest achieving reading group to explain how the "buddy" part of the program works. He has arranged with the fourth-grade teacher to team up one fourth grader with each of his poorest readers. Each morning as soon as the fourth-grade "buddies" arrive at school and take care of their routine tasks, such as lunch count and putting away coats, they come to Mr. Jackson's room to listen to their second-grade "buddies" read the easiest books in Mr. Jackson's collection. If there is enough time before the day's opening exercise period, each of the poorer readers might well be able to place a star on the "Little Engine" chart and be one book closer to that one hundred mark!

In addition to the fourth-grade "buddies," Mr. Jackson has managed to recruit a number of volunteers from both inside and outside the school. These volunteers include the school custodian, who occasionally visits Room 6 during his lunch break to listen to children read; several senior citizens, who drop in once or twice a week to be Book Buddies; and a small group of students in a service sorority from a nearby college who spent part of one week in Mr. Jackson's room. Regardless of when these various volunteers arrive, Mr. Jackson sees to it that someone is available even if it means excusing a child for a short time from another activity, such as math or music class. Mr. Jackson's commitment to providing this important practice reading time for poorer readers clearly reflects his belief that reading is top priority.

Those reading on grade level and above no longer appear to need the daily intensive sight word practice that characterizes the Book Buddy program. Instead, these children are ready for, and capable of, longer and longer periods of silent reading. Therefore, when Mr. Jackson initially meets his "middle" and "high" reading groups, he explains that he expects them to try for the goal of one hundred books more or less on their own. He encourages these children to select books from the appropriate bins and to read these books any time they complete an activity early and during the daily scheduled silent reading period.

Thus, Mr. Jackson provides each child an equal opportunity to reach the "Little Engine" goal of reading one hundred books; but he still accounts for individual differences, particularly the special needs of those children having difficulty in the beginning reading stage. Carefully planned attention to self-concept, attitude, and motivation is indeed the cornerstone of the Book Buddy program.

*We hope you can see in this brief description of the Book Buddy program how the three emphases of this chapter (self-concept, attitude, and motivation) emerge as the underlying rationale. The "buddy" system, a form of peer tutoring, becomes a vehicle for enhancing the self-concept of both the fourth-grade listeners and the second-grade "engines." Consistent progress toward a goal made visually evident through charting and frequent classroom reinforcement is intended to foster positive attitudes toward reading. Mr. Jackson's careful management of the program and frequent reference to the accumulation of stars serve as motivational factors for the children. We hope you'll agree that such a program, with modifications made to suit particular classrooms, is a worthwhile model to replicate.*

## Listen and Read

Because of federal budget cuts, the remedial program in Mr. Jackson's school no longer includes all of the children in his class who could benefit from it—those with relatively severe reading problems. Thus, it is critical that Mr. Jackson accommodate the special needs of this group of students.

The Book Buddy program provides for daily practice reading of independent level books, particularly for those children needing repeated exposures to high-frequency sight words. Mr. Jackson also makes special provision for these children during "Daily Letter" time by assigning them each a more capable reader to help complete each day's letter. Mr. Jackson's Listen and Read strategy is yet another way of providing for those reading below grade level.

Listen and Read Center. (Photo by Strix Pix)

Children having trouble learning to read often miss out on an important part of the curriculum: silent reading of high-interest children's literature. Many popular titles, targeted for specific age or grade levels because of content, are beyond the reading capabilities of many children. For example, Judy Blume's *Tales of a 4th Grade Nothing* may be too difficult for fourth graders to tackle on their own unless they are proficient readers.

Mr. Jackson has chosen to adapt the familiar strategy of taping difficult books for children. He has selected a number of books that good second-grade readers have chosen in the past as special favorites. Over the summer he has tape-recorded these books in much the same way he might read them aloud, stopping occasionally to explain a difficult concept, define a new word, or ask a question to encourage critical thinking or develop prediction skills. He has attractively packaged each book with its tape and displayed them in the Listen and Read Center.

Over the years Mr. Jackson has simplified and shortened each story in the form of a small booklet, duplicated so that any number of children might have a copy to keep. Each booklet contains carefully controlled vocabulary Mr. Jackson is reasonably certain his below grade level readers will be able to read independently with a high degree of success. He has left a space above the simplified text for the children to draw a picture of what is being said. A sample from a simplified book is shown in Figure 13.4.

Mr. Jackson encourages the poorest readers in his room to use the Listen and Read tapes during the sustained silent reading period he schedules each day for the 20 to 25 minutes following lunch. (At this time each day the children in his room are expected to read self-selected books as soon as they have finished eating.) Once he has introduced the Listen and Read tapes and rewritten booklets to the children for whom they are intended, Mr. Jackson can feel confident that most of his children are engaged for a time each day in what most reading authorities agree is a critical component of the developmental reading process—silent reading of self-selected material. His underachieving readers can enjoy high-interest (but hard-to-read) children's literature through the listening mode and then follow this experience with silent reading of the same stories written at a difficulty level they can successfully handle.

Thus, Mr. Jackson has once again put a priority on affective factors (self-concept, attitude, and motivation) considered critical for *all* learners, but particularly for those progressing at a slower-than-average rate. When they have listened to a tape and then successfully read their own version of the story, their attitude toward "hard" books might be more positive, and their self-concept regarding what they *can* do should be at least a notch higher.

# Parent Involvement Activities

Mr. Jackson is very aware of the close correlation between success in school and positive parental modeling at home. He makes his plans with this thought in mind and as much as possible includes frequent opportunities for parent-school interaction. In

> Up, up, up. . . .
> Faster, faster, faster . . .
> Up to the top of the tall
> mountain! The toys smiled. The
> little blue engine smiled and said,
> "I thought I could, I thought I
> could, I thought I could!"

**Figure 13.4** Simplified Literature for the *Listen and Read Center.* (Adapted from *The Little Engine That Could* by W. Piper, 1961, New York: Platt & Munk.)

Figure 13.5 a parent is helping students decorate a hallway in preparation for a program for both students and parents that culminates a unit of study. Let's look at specific examples of how the parents of children in Mr. Jackson's room might become closely involved in the learning process.

## Monthly Newspaper

Like any other teacher, Mr. Jackson sends home lots of handouts, sometimes several in one day, ranging from announcements of PTA meetings to information on how to obtain free or reduced lunch tickets. He often wonders (and worries) about whether

**Figure 13.5**   Students benefit when parents get involved in school activities. (Photo by Joseph B. Bodkin)

or not all those papers the children clutch as they race for the buses at 3:00 actually get home and, if they get home, whether they are attended to by busy moms and dads preparing hasty suppers, supervising homework, and otherwise juggling harried schedules.

Mr. Jackson is fairly certain that one set of papers taken home is welcomed—and read—by most of his students' families. The monthly class newspaper, now a long-standing tradition, has become a popular and successful part of his parent involvement program.

A key to the success of the Room 6 newspaper is that the children help in its preparation. Each September the children select a title for their newspaper and begin work on their contributions. An ongoing task, beginning the first day of each school year, is the gathering of news items to include in the next issue.

The content of the newspaper depends largely on what the children are studying and what activities are going on in the school and community. Because Mr. Jackson includes a great deal of writing in his language arts curriculum, his students quickly discover that any writing assignment might well form the basis of an item for their paper. A child in this classroom always knows that a particularly well-done writing lesson might be selected for publication with a by-line. The thrill of seeing one's name in print is hard to equal. (Mr. Jackson makes sure that everyone contributes at least once during the year.)

All the students are encouraged to submit at any time items they would like to have considered for the paper. Mr. Jackson urges the children, especially those with reading difficulties, to write brief descriptions of special experiences they have had, "news releases" about new pets, new brothers or sisters, amusing family anecdotes, and so forth. Initial submissions need not be polished products; instead, Mr. Jackson promises to take a look at each contributor's rough draft or brief outline and then lets the child know whether or not the idea is okay to continue developing into finalized form.

Children become accustomed to Mr. Jackson's frequent suggestion that they put into writing various ideas they bring to daily sharing time. This often serves a dual purpose. Some children have a difficult time limiting their verbal "show and tell" experiences; Mr. Jackson can quite diplomatically stop these children when he feels they have used up a reasonable amount of time, asking them to tell the rest in writing. Further, as any teacher knows, sharing time is never long enough to allow all who wish to share the opportunity to do so. Inviting those children who don't get the chance to share to put it down on paper lets them know that their contributions have equal value. Mr. Jackson has in fact reserved a special column in the class newspaper for the children's sharing. The children and their parents eagerly look forward to reading this "sharing sheet" each month.

Mr. Jackson makes it a policy to keep himself out of the newspaper as much as possible. Instead of writing up a feature article telling how the spelling program is progressing or describing a new procedure he plans to follow, Mr. Jackson assigns various "reporters" to write these items. He encourages these children to conduct brief interviews to obtain the necessary information or to read about the assigned topic. Thus, in each month's edition, families read articles written by the children themselves.

The only exception to Mr. Jackson's policy is his monthly Editor's Message column, in which he shares with parents various observations he is making about the children and comments on the way the year is progressing. A very popular part of each month's Editor's Message is Mr. Jackson's emphasis on one of his favorite parent involvement programs, Family Thinking Night, described in the next section. Each month's column includes suggestions for helping families develop the habit of "thinking together" on a regular basis. Mr. Jackson also shares tips from the International Reading Association's newsletters for parents.[1]

A unique feature of Mr. Jackson's class newspaper is his use of "parent reporters." From the beginning of the year, he sends home notices asking parents to contribute to the paper. He asks for brief descriptions about how families handle common problems such as sibling rivalry, homework, and home chores. He also

---

[1] International Reading Association, 800 Barksdale Road, P.O. Box 8139, Newark, DE, 19714.

requests recipes for nutritious snacks, ideas for inexpensive birthday gifts for friends, and suggestions for special family activities.

One very important parent contribution to each edition is the actual preparation of the paper; Mr. Jackson always manages to recruit two or three parent volunteers who come in the last week of each month to type the material on dittoes, run off copies in the office, and collate and staple the pages. The popular "Room 6 Review" is then ready to be sent home!

## Family Thinking Night

For many years Mr. Jackson, who has taught at almost every grade level from kindergarten through eighth grade, has wrestled with the problem of parents and homework—more specifically, how parents might best help their children at home to be more successful at school. Year after year he found himself counseling parents about setting reasonable time limits for schoolwork, about the importance of setting aside special times and places for doing homework, and about creating a comfortable, nonpressured environment for children studying at home.

Mr. Jackson began making a point of asking parents to describe specifically what transpired during homework time on the previous night. He compiled a most enlightening file of anecdotes, only a few of which described really productive home learning situations. Parents frequently reported time spent "trying to keep my daughter working on her assignment," "explaining how to do the day's math problems," "helping my son rewrite a report," and "arguing about why you shouldn't try to do a reading assignment in front of the TV." Mr. Jackson was distressed to discover that what he and most teachers would envision as a positive, accepted daily routine turned out to be, in too many homes, a very negative, stressful situation. Homework time appeared to be a counterproductive activity for too many children, especially those with learning difficulties.

Out of Mr. Jackson's disillusionment came the Family Thinking Night. Mr. Jackson investigated research literature in the area of home and school involvement to discover how best to help parents make productive use of the time they are willing to invest in their children's at-home education. Mr. Jackson began implementing his idea by meeting with parent groups on various occasions such as PTA meetings. He suggested a regular shared time at home for modeling the thinking/learning process.

Mr. Jackson began each parent session with his own modeling strategy, inviting parents to role play with him how such an at-home thinking activity might be managed. Once parents had actually participated in a simulated Family Thinking Night, they were generally more receptive to ideas about how to get such a project underway in their own homes.

Mr. Jackson suggested that parents set up one period of time each week when all family members can be present and are unlikely to be interrupted. He assured parents that the time period need not be long and should, in fact, last only as long as all family members are able to remain stimulated and "on task." (Most families who establish the Family Thinking Night routine find supper time, perhaps once a week, the ideal time to set aside.)

Mr. Jackson suggested a number of ideas that might be used for this at-home activity, always urging parents to focus on only one or two at a time to ensure quality time invested in developing children's thinking skills. Over the years he has created a packet of "idea sheets" he shares with interested parents. He is always on the lookout for new ideas and urges parents to share ideas they have discovered. All these new ideas find their way, of course, into the monthly newspaper in Mr. Jackson's "Editor's Message" column.

Another way new ideas are shared with both parents and children is on the bulletin board right inside the classroom door, which is labeled "You Have to Think to Learn!" Throughout the year Mr. Jackson updates this "thinking board" with motivating items that force children to use logical thought processes. Depending, of course, on the grade level he is teaching that year, the items he selects for the thinking board represent a wide variety of difficulty. When he taught fifth and sixth graders, for example, they found on the board each day one of those popular "equation puzzlers" such as "60 = S. in a M." (60 seconds in a minute); "26 = L. of the A."; "11 = P. on a F.T."; or "30 = D.H.S.A.J. and N." These children often found a new "Wacky Wordy" such as "late ne v er" ("better late than never"); "lines reading lines"; or "agb" posted on the thinking board. They were encouraged to try to figure out these puzzlers and were urged to copy them, take them home to use during their Family Thinking Nights, and create their own versions to add to Mr. Jackson's collection. (Are you stumped? You'll find the answers to these and the following puzzles in Figure 13.6.)

A really popular item on the thinking board over the years has been Mr. Jackson's seasonal sports quiz. Each baseball season, for example, he posts one or two disguised team titles, such as "fought in the Civil War" (New York Yankees); "terrors to ships at sea"; and "workers in a Spanish church." During hockey season, children might find "are raked up in the fall"; "help cardinals fly"; or "keep you warm" posted on the board for them to contemplate.

Children in Mr. Jackson's classes have always enjoyed Rhyme Thyme items, and both parents and children have contributed dozens of additions to his collection. They include "747 puppy" ("jet pet"); "thin bird"; "evil preacher"; "path for frogs"; and "chocolate dropped on a beach." Because Mr. Jackson has been teaching younger children for the past several years, he has been focusing on thinking activities more appropriate for this age level but clearly structured so that the same kinds of language stimulation occur. For example, he has devised an extensive set of multiclued riddles for posting on the second-grade thinking board starting in September. The children might find on Monday, next to a large blank sheet of art paper, the clue "I'm long and yellow." Children write their guesses and place them in the "riddle box" under the bulletin board. On Tuesday a second clue appears, "I have many wheels." By the end of the week most children have figured out that the week's "mystery riddle" is a school bus, and Mr. Jackson asks someone to draw a picture of a school bus on the blank piece of art paper. In the monthly newspaper, he explains how the "mystery riddle" works and urges parents to incorporate this idea into their Family Thinking Night. He also suggests that parents try setting up a thinking board in their kitchens and encouraging all family members to contribute challenging items, such as word games, riddles, startling newspaper articles, or headlines, and thought-provoking pictures, riddles, jokes, and so forth.

Mr. Jackson has always urged parents to consider incorporating read-aloud time into Family Thinking Night. Believing strongly in the modeling theory, Mr. Jackson points out to parents the importance of having children see adults actively engaged in and enjoying reading on a regular basis. (The read-aloud program is described in the next section.)

He urges parents and children to select something to read as part of Family Thinking Night, perhaps a collection of famous short stories, humorous children's poetry, or a book from his many lists of suggested titles families have reported enjoying together over the years. Many of his parents begin each week's Family Thinking Night with one family member reading a favorite Shel Silverstein poem from *Where the Sidewalk Ends,* or with the reading aloud of one chapter from a book such as E. B. White's *Charlotte's Web* or Kjelgaard's *Big Red.*

Gradually families who have a Family Thinking Night come to see this special shared time as a valuable contribution to children's success in school. Perhaps laughing together over Silverstein's "Sarah Cynthia Sylvia Stout Would Not Take the Garbage Out" and working together to solve the equation, "30 = D.H.S.A.J. and N." doesn't get a child's math homework finished or a composition proofread, but the time invested in exercising thinking skills is likely to be the time that reaps the greater dividends. Parents and children work together in problem-solving and learning; reading skills are reinforced by application. This spirit of cooperation carries over to the nightly homework assignments, especially for those with learning problems.

## Read-aloud Program

Many parents do not realize the importance of reading aloud to their children. Some who read aloud to their preschoolers stop this practice when their children reach

---

| | |
|---|---|
| 26 = L. of the A. | 26 letters of the alphabet |
| 11 = P. on a F. T. | 11 players on a football team. |
| 30 = D.H.S.A.J. and N. | 30 days has September, April, June and November |
| | |
| lines reading lines | reading between the lines |
| agb | mixed bag |
| terrors to ships at sea | Pittsburgh Pirates |
| workers in a Spanish church | San Diego Padres |
| are raked up in the fall | Toronto Maple Leafs |
| help cardinals fly | Detroit Red Wings |
| keep you warm | Atlanta Flames |
| thin bird | narrow sparrow |
| evil preacher | sinister minister |
| path for frogs | toad road |
| chocolate dropped on a beach | sandy candy |

**Figure 13.6**  Puzzler Key

school age, assuming that it is somehow wrong to read aloud to a child who is capable of reading even to a limited degree.

Because Mr. Jackson has encountered many parents who do not read aloud to their children—even to their preschool children—he has instituted a read-aloud program, which he explains to parents at the first PTA meeting.

He includes in the classroom newspaper descriptions of good read-aloud books that would be appropriate for the age levels of his children. He encourages parents to share good books that they have read aloud to other children. He works in close cooperation with the public and school librarians, who inform him of new books that would be appropriate. He also suggests follow-up activities and discussion for particular books.

Why does Mr. Jackson think it's so important that parents read aloud to their children, even school-age children? Why does he read aloud in school? A preschooler learns while sitting on the parent's lap listening to a story that reading is a meaningful and important activity. The squiggles on the page have meaning and result in a

Read-aloud program. (Photo by Ben Chandler)

pleasant experience for both parent and child as they enjoy Dr. Seuss or nursery rhymes together. The preschooler learns to pay attention for a period of time while the parent is reading. The youngster develops readiness skills, such as visual discrimination, by studying pictures and following along with the words as the parent reads aloud.

When this preschooler goes to school, he or she knows how to sit still and listen to a story that the teacher reads. Furthermore, the child enjoys this experience and participates in follow-up activities. Mr. Jackson has seen better reading comprehension result from listening comprehension activities such as students predicting what will happen next, telling why they like one book better than another, or justifying a character's actions.

Mr. Jackson uses read-aloud time to expand vocabulary. When he reads a new word, he stops at the end of the paragraph and asks the students for a definition based on the context in which the word was used. (He also tries to incorporate the new word into his lessons and conversation to reinforce its meaning.) He frequently stops to ask students to visualize what they are hearing—to see a character or scene in their mind's eye.

Mr. Jackson also uses oral reading as a means of developing background concepts for content area studies, such as social studies and science. For example, he read aloud one of the Laura Ingalls Wilder's books in connection with a social studies unit on the Westward Movement. The book would have been too difficult for many of his students to have read alone, but it provided a sense of the struggle of pioneer families that could not be conveyed by a social studies textbook. The book also provided important conceptual background to make their study of the Westward Movement more meaningful to the children. Conceptual background—what a reader brings to the reading process—is often lacking in weak readers because their poor reading ability has prevented them from reading widely.

Mr. Jackson knows that the students who struggle most with reading in school benefit the most from parents who read aloud to them. He also realizes that many of these students come from homes where reading is not a valued activity. He has observed that some of his students' parents have poor literacy skills themselves. Yet many of these parents want to help their children in any way they can.

Mr. Jackson carefully assesses the home situation before recommending to individual parents that they read aloud to their children on a daily basis. Sometimes an older sibling can receive valuable practice in reading aloud to a younger child, relieving the parent of the embarrassment of inept reading. Or the parent may feel more comfortable reviewing a set of flashcards with the child rather than reading aloud.

To the parents who are capable readers, however, he urges reading aloud on a daily basis (or at least a regular basis). Bedtime is often selected as a good time, providing a "wind-down" time as well as a chance for parent-child communication. Parents need not feel guilty if they cannot maintain this routine every night, but it should take priority over an extra TV program.

As children's reading skills improve, parents may want to use the read-aloud time to entice their children into new books. The parent might read the first few chapters of a book to ensure that the child understands the setting, characters, and so forth and then encourage the child to continue reading, informing the parent of new events in the story. Some reluctant readers can be encouraged by alternating pages in reading aloud, as described in the next section.

## Bookworm Program

*We've saved the best for last, not to diminish the importance of the other parts of Mr. Jackson's "master plan" for the year, but to insure that you are left with a clear reminder of the essential message of this chapter: motivating children to read demands careful attention to attitude and self-concept. We've illustrated ways in which specific classroom activities, such as the Book Buddy program and the daily letter, contribute to building and maintaining positive self-concepts and attitudes among children, particularly those having difficulty learning to read. We've also pointed out the importance of involving parents in their children's learning and have suggested the classroom newspaper, home read-aloud time, and Family Thinking Night to encourage this involvement. Now we describe for you one other kind of parent-child activity that has proved successful in a variety of classroom settings. Note the high degree of flexibility inherent in Mr. Jackson's popular Bookworm program; with a few changes dictated by your particular teaching situation, the Bookworm program can become one of the most successful ingredients for motivating children to read in any classroom!*

The Bookworm program in Mr. Jackson's room has become such a popular tradition over the years that, as noted early in this chapter, many children return to school in September eager to see which storybook character will serve as the mascot for Room 6 during the new school year. Children in Mr. Jackson's room have in the past found giant-sized pictures and stuffed replicas of such favorites as A. A. Milne's Winnie the Pooh, Michael Bond's Paddington Bear, and Norman Bidwell's Big Red Dog waiting to invite them to participate in the year's at-home reading program.

The Bookworm program is based on the premise that mastering any skill requires practice. Attaining reading proficiency requires as much direct classroom instruction as possible accompanied by as much practice reading as can fit into each day's busy schedule. As we have seen, Mr. Jackson has attempted to incorporate practice reading in a variety of ways in each day's activities.

Every child in Mr. Jackson's room receives direct instruction in both specific and generalized reading skills during the daily reading lesson in her or his assigned small group. During this time, each child engages in reading at the instructional level, reading selections that are challenging enough that a teacher's close guidance and assistance are likely to be required. Mr. Jackson explains to parents that this daily direct instruction parallels their own experiences in learning any new skill—such as skiing, golf, sailing, or photography. Each learning experience demands that a qualified instructor show the learner what to do through direct instruction, whether in a weekly adult evening class or through an illustrated manual of instructions. Then the learner needs to invest some time practicing each new skill and combining mastered skills with newly acquired ones.

When Mr. Jackson leads parents to compare their personal experiences in learning new skills to what their children are facing in learning to read, they are usually receptive to establishing directed reading practice time at home. Mr. Jackson presents this information at the annual "Back-to-School" night scheduled for parents each September as part of the PTA agenda. Once he has explained why children need to practice at home the skills they learn in school, he hands out the current year's Bookworm program brochure and invites parents to share with their children the most popular and motivating part of the year's planned activities.

Perhaps the easiest way to describe how the Bookworm program operates is to present excerpts from Mr. Jackson's brochure for this year. He revises this brochure each year, adapting the program to fit the levels of the children assigned to him and making changes dictated by experiences the past year. Over the years many other teachers have used ideas similar to those in the Bookworm program, making changes in parent-child requirements, bookkeeping procedures, and the reinforcement reward system to reflect their personal goals and management styles. The responses to some of the questions in the brochure should suggest to any classroom teacher the degree of flexibility inherent in such an at-home program.

## Why a Bookworm Program?

The Bookworm program involves parents and children reading together on a regular basis. We tell the children that people who love to read and find enjoyment in reading are called "bookworms" because they often seem to have themselves hidden in a book. We tell them that they can become bookworms by reading to or with someone at home on a regular basis.

## Why Should Our Children Need to Practice Reading at Home?

We believe we can provide during school time all the materials and the instruction necessary for your child to be sufficiently exposed to how to read. We can also provide *some* of the critical practice your child needs to apply what we have taught. But we cannot provide *enough* practice in a busy school day.

The at-home shared reading experiences we suggest for the Bookworm program can provide this essential extra practice reading your child needs.

## How Does the Bookworm Program Work?

We will explain the program to your children in school, but it is important that you talk about it at home and support our efforts to get your child involved. The Bookworm program suggests that you and your child agree on sharing something to read each school day and once over the weekend. Your child must read the selected material and provide some proof of comprehension. When you are satisfied that she or he has read and understood the material, you or your child fill out one day's coupon provided at the end of this booklet (shown in Figure 13.7). When you complete each weekly coupon sheet, send it to school with your child on Monday morning.

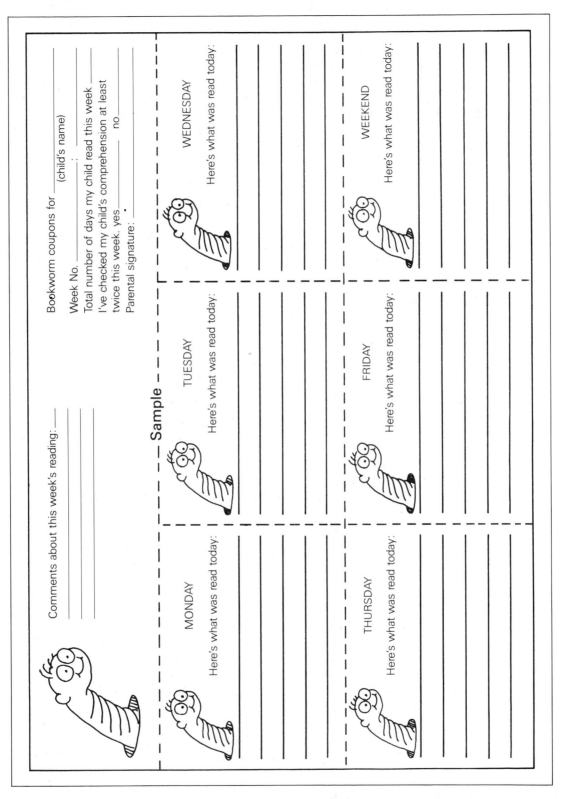

**Figure 13.7** Bookworm Weekly Coupon Sheet

Comments about this week's reading: _____

Bookworm coupons for _____ (child's name)

Week No. _____ :
Total number of days my child read this week _____
I've checked my child's comprehension at least twice this week. yes _____ no _____
Parental signature: _____ .

— Sample —

MONDAY
Here's what was read today:

TUESDAY
Here's what was read today:

WEDNESDAY
Here's what was read today:

THURSDAY
Here's what was read today:

FRIDAY
Here's what was read today:

WEEKEND
Here's what was read today:

For each weekly coupon your child receives a colorful circle of construction paper to staple to his or her Bookworm, which is on display in the classroom. Each circle becomes a part of the Bookworm's body. As the Bookworm grows in length, your child has a visual record of at-home practice reading. When the Bookworms reach a certain length, we will display them on our Super Bookworm wall and begin another bookworm for the child.

Any child who completes at least one Super Bookworm will be eligible to receive an official Bookworm certificate at our spring ceremony, to which parents and other family members are invited. Special awards will be presented to the most regular participants. Again this year a very special prize will be awarded to those children able to maintain perfect, "6 times a week" records throughout the program.

## Does the Child Have to Read a Whole Book Each Day?

It is not always necessary for the child to read a whole book, though many children will want to do so. It is okay to divide a long book into sections or to have the child select one story from a basal reader or collection of stories. Your child then reads one section, chapter, or story per bookworm session, and this is marked on the coupon.

## Does the Child Have to Read from a Book to Qualify for a Bookworm Circle?

Many children will resist "book" reading but might respond to reading from other sources. The important consideration is that you see that the child reads *something* with you on a regular basis. Try these alternatives:

- a recipe
- a baseball or football card
- a sign in the grocery store
- parts of a menu
- directions for a game or for putting a model together
- an article, story, or poem in a magazine
- any part of the local paper's "Mini-Page"
- a letter from someone
- a note you write for the child to read
- a game that requires some reading
- any booklets, letters, or worksheets brought home from school
- the school lunch menu
- a cereal box
- Sunday School worksheets or Bible verses

Substituting some of these alternative reading experiences occasionally for any child will vary the daily routine and maintain enthusiasm for the Bookworm program. Use your imagination in helping your child decide how to qualify for Bookworm circles.

## How Can I Tell if Reading Material Is of the Appropriate Difficulty?

The books children select for this program should be "easy reading" books. That is, the child should be able to read these books comfortably without having to stop frequently for help with words.

Have your child read the first few pages to you. If the child hesitates or stumbles over every few words, the book is probably too difficult. In school we urge children to use the "rule of hand" when selecting a book to read at home. We tell them to read one page, folding down one finger for each word they have trouble with. If all the fingers on one hand are folded down by the end of the page, we tell them to try another.

When your child reads at home, you should not have to help sound out words. This can make practice reading a painful process and can create a tense situation between parent and child that is not likely to help the child become a better reader. It is probably best to tell the child unfamiliar words so that he or she can get on with reading.

## How Long Should At-Home Practice Reading Sessions Last?

These sessions should only be long enough to keep the parent-child relationship comfortable and the idea of sharing a reading experience a pleasant one.

## How Can I Check My Child's Understanding of What Is Read?

This is a critical part of the Bookworm program. While it is important that the child read something with you regularly, it is even more important that you check for understanding. There are lots of ways for you to check your child's comprehension. The most common way is to ask your child to retell the story. You can also ask several questions, one of which requires the child to tell you why or how something occurred. But don't require children to read and answer questions each time. Children (and parents!) quickly tire of this routine. Other ways to check comprehension are to have your child:

- make some illustrations for the story; put a caption with each one
- write a sentence or paragraph about the story
- make a book cover or jacket that is different from the one on the book
- think of another good title for the story and draw a book jacket or cover pictures to illustrate this title
- make a diorama (using a shoe box or other small box) that illustrates the child's favorite part of the story

- make paper bag or sock puppets for one or more characters
- make a poster advertising the book or story
- write an answer to a question that requires some real thinking
- stop before the end of the story and write or tell about how it will probably end
- write another ending for the story
- write about why the story couldn't really have happened
- list *in sentences* three things that happened in the story in order of occurrence
- write about the favorite (or least favorite) part of the story
- write about one new thing learned from the story

Let your child help decide how to establish that the reading has been understood. Remember, we want to make reading enjoyable. Shared reading experiences for Bookworm coupons should be pleasant moments together; don't kill the enthusiasm with dull, dreary questioning sessions. Why not just talk about what has been read? This is, after all, the best way for anyone to share reading.

## May the Child Read More Than One Book or Story Per Session?

Yes!

## May the Child Read The Same Book or Story More Than Once?

Yes! Particularly at the very beginning levels of reading, it is very important for a child to read a story or book several times. Rereading a familiar book increases confidence among less able readers and helps reinforce word recognition. You will have to judge whether rereading a book or story is providing valuable practice or is being used as an excuse to avoid selecting something harder. If you feel that the child really loves a book, by all means let him or her enjoy it.

## Should the Child Read Out Loud or Silently?

While one of the important goals of the school reading program is effective silent reading, many children do not feel that they have really shared a reading experience unless they have read a story aloud. Particularly beginning readers benefit from reading aloud to you at least part of each selection. You might try having your child read aloud all but the last few pages and then answer questions on what was read silently.

One of the important benefits of our Bookworm program is the time shared by parent and child. This very often becomes the primary benefit. Reading aloud may be what makes this such a special time of sharing. Why not combine your read-aloud time with your child's daily Bookworm reading? You might read a page or so to your child and then have your child read the next page, continuing to alternate this way until you finish the story, chapter, or book.

### Must It Be a Parent with Whom the Child Shares a Reading Experience?

No. It's okay for the child to share reading with some other older person. How about an older brother or sister? An aunt or uncle? Babysitter? Grandparent? Neighbor? Family friend?

### How and When Will the Bookworm Program Begin?

Your child will be invited to participate in a special "kick-off" celebration the first week in October. At this celebration the children will be introduced to this year's mascot, Paddington Bear, and will hear the first installment of this year's read-aloud selections from the collection of stories about this lovable, clumsy bear from Peru. The children have already seen lots of Paddington Bear pictures, posters, and books around our room, so they are eager to get acquainted with Paddington and find out how he will help them in reading this year.

The children will learn that their parents have had the Bookworm program explained to them and have a brochure at home that should answer their questions. They know that they are expected to read at home every day for a short period of time. They should help you keep track of their reading by using the weekly coupons attached to the back of the parent brochure.

When your child comes home with a pinned-on tag proclaiming, "Please help me be a Super Bookworm this year!" it's time to begin helping build the bookworm habit. Good luck!

---

A Bookworm program like the one just described is a monumental undertaking for any teacher. It involves a commitment to continuous high-level motivation throughout the year to insure its success. It means close interaction with parents. It demands carefully planned management so that weekly record-keeping does not get out of hand. For these reasons, many teachers make large-scale changes as they adapt the Bookworm program idea.

Many teachers choose to run a Bookworm program for a limited period of time, such as one report card marking period, in the hope that this will be enough time to get parents and children into an at-home reading habit that will continue even when the formalized program ends.

The management of a Bookworm program can become a burden unless you devise an easy system for processing coupons. Mr. Jackson relies heavily on one of the office aides or a parent volunteer each Monday when coupons are returned. The aide or parent checks to see that each coupon is correctly filled out and records in a log the number of times each child has read that week. This same person then adds the appropriate number of circles to each child's Bookworm. Parents and children are recruited to cut out all the circles, thus eliminating another time-consuming teacher task.

Any of a variety of motivational rewards might be given at the end of the program. Mr. Jackson tries to come up with a new idea each spring, always focusing on something related to the children's literature character he has chosen as mascot. The Super Bookworms whose mascot had been Winnie the Pooh, for example, each received their own copy of one of the original hardbound editions in the A. A. Milne series. The year Mr. Jackson used Big Red Dog as the theme character will best be remembered for the end-of-year presentations of red, furry dog-shaped pajama storage bags made by volunteer mothers.

When Mr. Jackson used Paddington Bear, the children never tired of hearing the original Michael Bond stories read aloud throughout that school year. They became so enchanted with Paddington's adventures many other classroom activities became integrated with this read-aloud and Bookworm theme.

When the children discovered, for example, that their favorite bear loved marmalade, not honey, one of the cooking projects planned as part of their mininutrition unit was to make marmalade. That year's Bookworms will never forget the day they baked whole wheat bread and made their own orange maramalade to serve all the primary children in honor of Paddington's birthday!

At the conclusion of that year's program, 19 of the 26 children in Mr. Jackson's room stepped forward on the school stage to shake the paw of an authentically costumed bear and to receive hand-crocheted stuffed Paddington Bears!

No, Mr. Jackson did not crochet 19 bears. Instead, early in the school year he advertised by word-of-mouth, the local newspaper, the school newsletter, and PTA gatherings his desire to find senior citizens and handicapped and unemployed persons able to crochet and follow a simple pattern. He was gratified by the response to his plea and located more than a dozen eager crocheters. By spring, he had a wheelbarrow full of magnificent Paddingtons—and, needless to say, 19 delighted Super Bookworms!

# Summary

Affective factors are crucial to reading, especially for students with reading difficulties. We presented guidelines for promoting a positive self-concept, a good attitude toward reading, and motivation to read.

Through the activities planned by Mr. Jackson, our model teacher, we described affective strategies that also enhance the reading program, both in the classroom and for parental involvement at home. Parents, important forces in the elementary child's life, can play an essential role in complementing the teacher's efforts in teaching reading. Underlying the descriptions of specific activities for parents is the assumption of communication and trust between teacher and parents.

# References

Alexander, J. E., & Filler, R. C. (1976). *Attitudes and reading.* Newark, DE: International Reading Association.

Arvanities, M. (1980). The effects of a series of lessons based upon real-life experiences for improving self-concept and reading achievement of seventh and eighth grades. *Dissertation Abstracts International, 41,* 2051A.

Askov, E. N. (1972). *Assessment of attitudes toward reading in primary pupils* (Tech. Rep. No. 206). Madison: Wisconsin Research and Development Center of Cognitive Learning.

Askov, E. N. (1973). *Primary pupil reading attitude inventory.* Dubuque, IA: Kendall Hunt.

Ball, S. (1982). Motivation. In H. E. Mitzel (Ed.), *Encyclopedia of Educational Research* (5th ed., Vol. 3). New York: The Free Press, pp. 1256–1263.

Farr, B. P. (1981). Building language experiences for reluctant readers. In A. J. Ciani (Ed.), *Motivating Reluctant Readers.* Newark, DE: International Reading Association, pp. 3–12.

Hettinger, C. S. (1980). The effect of grade level utilization on the achievement, self-concept, and attitude toward reading of problem readers in the junior high. *Dissertation Abstracts International, 41,* 2230B.

*Improving reading instruction: an inventory of reading attitude* (Monograph No. 4). (1961). San Diego: Superintendent of Schools, Department of Education.

*Practical Applications of Research* (Vol. 5, No. 1). (1982). Motivation. Bloomington, IN: Phi Delta Kappa's Center on Evaluation, Development, and Research.

Noland, R., & Craft, L. (1976). Methods to motivate the reluctant reader. *Journal of Reading, 19* (5), 387–391.

Purkey, W. W. (1970). *Self-concept and school achievement.* Englewood Cliffs, NJ: Prentice-Hall.

Quandt, I. (1972). *Self-concept and reading.* Newark, DE: International Reading Association.

Quick, D. M. (1973). Toward positive self-concept. *The Reading Teacher, 26* (5), 460–471.

Rogers, C. (1951). *Client-centered therapy.* Boston: Houghton Mifflin.

Rosenthal, R., & Jacobson, L. (1968). Teacher expectations for the disadvantaged. *Scientific American, 218* (4), 19–23.

# References for Further Professional Reading

Canfield, J., & Wells, H. C. (1976). *100 ways to enhance self-concept in the classroom: a handbook for teachers and parents.* Englewood Cliffs, NJ: Prentice-Hall.

Ciani, A. J. (Ed.). (1981). *Motivating reluctant readers.* Newark, DE: International Reading Association.

Larrick, N. (1975). *A parent's guide to children's reading* (rev. ed.). New York: Doubleday.

Lundsteen, S. W. (1979). *Listening: its impact on reading and other language arts* (rev. ed.). Urbana, IL: National Council of Teachers of English.

Moffett, J., & Wagner, B. J. (1976). *Student-centered language arts and reading, K–13* (2nd ed.). Boston: Houghton Mifflin.

Rutherford, R. B., Jr., & Edgar, E. (1979). *Teachers and parents: a guide to interaction and cooperation.* Boston: Allyn and Bacon.

Trelease, J. (1982). *The read aloud handbook.* New York: Penguin Books.

## References to Children's Literature

Bidwell, N. (1963). *Clifford the big red dog.* New York: Scholastic Book Services.

Blume, J. (1972). *Tales of a 4th grade nothing.* New York: Dutton.

Bond, M. (1958). *A bear called Paddington.* New York: Dell.

Kjelgaard, J. (1956). *Big Red.* New York: Holiday House.

Milne, A. A. (1926). *Winnie the Pooh.* New York: Dutton.

Piper, W. (1961). *The little engine that could.* New York: Platt & Munk.

Silverstein, S. (1974). *Where the sidewalk ends.* New York: Harper & Row.

White, E. B. (1952). *Charlotte's web.* New York: Harper & Row.

Wilder, L. E. (1935). *Little house on the prairie.* New York: Harper & Row.

## Check Your Reading Comprehension

1. Consider the following statement:
   ". . . the affective components of the curriculum can be intricately woven into the cognitive dimension of a corrective reading program."
   Argue both the *pro* and *con* side of this issue.

2. Matching exercise:

   _____ **1.** Self-concept

   _____ **2.** Measurement of self-concept

   _____ **3.** Enhancement of self-concept

   _____ **4.** Attitude

   _____ **5.** Internal Motivation

   _____ **6.** External Motivation

   **a.** Strategies such as self-report inventories and observations

   **b.** A composite of all the perceptions individuals have of themselves

   **c.** Forces outside the individual that influence behavior

   **d.** Forces within the individual that influence behavior

   **e.** Strategies such as democratic classroom atmosphere, modified teacher's expectations, and relevant materials

   **f.** A system of feelings related to a situation that causes the learner to approach or avoid that situation

   Answers:

   3. e    6. c
   2. a    5. d
   1. b    4. f

**3.** Consider the nine guidelines concerning motivation given in this chapter. Which do you think is the most important? Defend your choice.

**4.** How do the time management suggestions of "to-do lists" and "combining" relate to corrective reading? Give some examples.

**5.** Develop a *Daily Letter* that you could use with your class. How will you handle the children who cannot read your letter? Why did you choose this approach?

**6.** Choose a story or book that would be interesting to your class. Prepare tapes and activities to be used by those children who cannot read it independently. Follow the *Listen and Read* suggestions.

**7.** Imagine that you are contemplating a *Read-aloud Program* with your class. Compile a list of books appropriate for meeting the various interests of your students—books on animals, sports, and so forth. Taking one of these books as a sample, develop strategies for teaching vocabulary words used in the book. Decide which comprehension skills you will emphasize as you read the book aloud to the students and how you will teach them.

**8.** Adapt the Primary Pupil Reading Attitude Inventory (see Appendix E) so that it can be used in a multicultural setting. Or get a copy of the Inventory from your instructor and administer it to your students. Compare the results with other assessments of attitudes and interests.

# 14

# Adapted Teaching for Slow Learners

*Question:* When is a child who performs below grade level not an underachiever? *Answer:* When that child is working up to his or her own capacity.

Some children who achieve below grade level are *slow learners.* Because they have a limited capacity for learning it is unrealistic to expect grade-level performance from them. Corrective or remedial instruction, the goal of which is to overcome difficulties and to read at or above grade level, is likely to be misdirected. Slow learners need instruction that is adapted in two important ways. First, the *pace* is slowed to the personal pace of the learners. Proper pacing is important for all learners, but for slow learners it is essential. The regular developmental instruction in the classroom is confusing because it moves too fast. Second, *expectations* are in line with each learner's abilities. For example, a slow learner in fourth grade might be doing well to perform at third-grade level. It would be unrealistic, then, to expect performance at grade level.

Adapted teaching is designed for pupils who can't keep up in the classroom but who are not likely, for reasons we will discuss, to be good candidates for corrective or remedial groups. To be effective adapted instruction must not only be part of a comprehensive plan for reading instruction, (see Chapter 2), but it must be offered by teachers who are sensitive to the special characteristics and needs of slow learners.

This chapter is organized to help you consider the slow learner in terms of program planning, personal characteristics, and instructional needs. First, we consider slow learners in the reading program by contrasting their reading behaviors with those of remedial readers and learning disabled readers. We then examine slow learners in the classroom, particularly their general characteristics and specific behaviors that interfere with learning. Finally we make suggestions for teaching the slow learner in the regular classroom.

We offer this chapter with more than a little trepidation, and for good reason. When we try to define "slow learners" we tend to use terms like "capacity" and "grade level" quite glibly. By now you know that estimates of capacity are generally based on scores from IQ tests and that grade level is usually defined by scores from reading achievement tests. You also know that the scores from such tests have many limitations—they need to be taken with grains of salt. Furthermore, when we say why slow learners need adapted rather than corrective or remedial instruction, we try to show how slow learners differ from other children who are experiencing reading difficulties. But we all know that human beings never fit neatly into categories. Again, you'll need to take the categories with a grain of salt.

*Why, then, do we offer a chapter on slow learners and adapted instruction, since it would seem to be built on a pillar of salt? The answer is that we prefer to confront reality as best we can, even if that reality cannot be neatly pinned down. We think it is better to try to meet the special needs of students present in substantial numbers in most classrooms than to absorb children with those needs into groups where the needs are different and the expectations are unrealistic.*

*We don't want you to reject all that we've said about the limitations of tests or what we say in the following chapters about the dangers of categorizing children. We do want you to see that any use of test scores and labels must always be tempered with good sense.*

## The Slow Learner in the Reading Program

Classroom teachers confront a substantial group of children with reading difficulties. "This," say Downing and Leong (1982), "is not surprising in view of the heterogeneity of these children and the diverse reading problems they exhibit" (p. 300). A teacher should not be surprised to find a wide range of reading performance in a classroom of children with a wide range of biological and experiential attributes. Children's reading performance is certain to be as varied as they are. But how many children in a given classroom are likely to need special help in reading?

There is general agreement that in English-speaking countries about 10 to 15 percent of *nonretarded* children experience substantial reading difficulties. Estimates vary because definitions of what constitutes "substantial reading difficulty" vary. Nevertheless, Downing and Leong reflect the general agreement when they say that, for whatever reasons, 10 to 15 percent of nonretarded children are at ". . . the lower end of the reading performance continuum whatever our criteria of reading are" (1982, p. 300). The picture is clouded, though, by the use of the term nonretarded. Downing and Leong arbitrarily place the cutoff at an approximate IQ of 84–85 (one standard deviation below the mean on the *Wechsler Intelligence Scale for Children (WISC)* or some acceptable alternative). In the classroom, however, there are multiple criteria; and the IQ criterion for classifying a student as mentally retarded is likely to be substantially lower. The criteria vary from state to state, but in general the IQ cutoff is a score of 68–70 (*two* standard deviations below the mean on the *WISC* or some acceptable alternative). In other words, "nonretarded" tends to be defined one way by researchers (one standard deviation below the mean) and another way in the schools (two standard deviations below the mean). The latter definition includes not only more below-average individuals, but also individuals whose deviance is more substantial.

The picture is clouded even more by the operational definition of the severity of reading disability in terms of deviance from grade level. That is, a fourth grader who reads at second-grade level is considered more disabled than one who reads at third-grade level. Most educators would claim to know that grade level is merely a statistical artifact and that half of the children in a given grade should read above it and half should read below it. Nevertheless, grade level continues to be a standard for judging individuals' reading performance; students who read below grade level are assumed to have reading problems.

We can conclude that estimates of the number of children who need special help in reading are muddled by imprecise definitions and by certain folkways. In general, the estimates that 10 to 15 percent of children have substantial reading difficulties ignore the differences in children's intelligence levels. Furthermore, "grade level" sets a standard that is inherently unattainable by about half of the children in a classroom. Of course, many names have been proposed for both the broad group and for the subgroups of children who experience reading difficulties. (See Downing and Leong, 1982, Chapters 14 and 15, for a lucid discussion of the terms.) But in the classroom there are just two main classification questions: (a) Who can be helped in the classroom and who should be referred for special help? (b) Who has the potential to perform at or above grade level and who does not? You can begin to answer those questions by considering the attributes of three groups of below grade-level readers:

- *Remedial readers,* who have relatively uncomplicated problems that can usually be overcome with corrective or remedial help.
- *Learning disabled readers,* who have more severe and complex problems that require intensive and prolonged treatment.
- *Slow learners,* from the lower end of the classroom IQ distribution, who need instruction that is adapted in terms of pace and expectations.

In an ordinary classroom you could expect about a third of the children to fall into the three categories combined.

## Remedial Readers

"Remedial" is a somewhat imprecise term commonly used to describe readers who manifest varying degrees of difficulty in reading, ranging from minor problems with a few skills to lagging behind in overall skill development. All these students have two things in common. First, their general ability (their IQ scores) is better than their achievement, so there is reason to expect them to overcome their difficulties. Second, their reading errors are the same as the errors made by good readers, so there is no reason to suspect underlying sensory, perceptual, or physical problems. They make more errors than good readers, but the difference is in numbers, not in kinds, of errors.

Simply stated, *remedial readers can't read because they don't know how.* The problem may be attributable to inappropriate teaching, prolonged absence from school, or some combination of these and other experiential and motivational factors. Whatever the causes, reading development has gotten out of phase with the instruction and the demands related to reading. These children need corrective help in the regular classroom; or, in certain instances described in Chapter 2, they may be referred for remedial help if a remedial reading teacher is available.

We have been talking mainly about remedial readers and how to teach them in all of the preceding chapters. They have difficulties with reading because their performance is out of line with the mainstream of instruction in the classroom. They need carefully focused "catch-up" instruction. Once they get it they can usually return to the mainstream of developmental reading instruction quite quickly.[1]

*We don't mean to pass lightly over the discussion of remedial readers. But we are firmly convinced that the first hypothesis a teacher should have when a child experiences reading difficulties is that the child is not reading up to expectations because he or she does not know how. Classroom teachers are better trained to test that hypothesis than any other.*

Some children with average or better general ability have much more complex problems that interfere with their reading performance. We call them learning disabled readers. They need the kind of intensive special help that is best provided by specialized teachers. As a classroom teacher you would ordinarily refer children with learning disabilities for work with a specialized teacher. The discussion in the next section, then, is mainly to help you decide when to make a referral.

---

[1] Now we seem to be in danger of getting caught in our own definitional trap. We stated in Chapter 2 that the main purpose of corrective and remedial teaching is to help a student perform at his or her own capacity level. Technically, then, a slow learner would be eligible for remedial instruction if not performing at capacity. But practically, it is probably more important to acknowledge a need for *adapted* instruction and then to provide it than to look for additional classifications. The following discussion should clarify the issue somewhat, although, unfortunately, conflicting or overlapping federal, state, and local definitions may becloud it.

## Learning Disabled (LD) Readers

"Learning disability" defies neat definition, but Kirk and Gallagher (1979) offer one that suits our purposes:

> A specific learning disability is a psychological or neurological impediment to spoken or written language or perceptual, cognitive, or motor behavior. The impediment (1) is manifested by discrepancies among specific behaviors and achievements or between evidenced ability and academic achievement, (2) is of such nature and extent that the child does not learn by the instructional methods and materials appropriate for the majority of children and requires specialized procedures for development, and (3) is not primarily due to severe mental retardation, sensory handicaps, emotional problems, or lack of opportunity to learn. (p. 285)

A learning disabled reader is like a remedial reader in that reading achievement is lower than general ability. But the learning disabled reader's problem is not simply one of "not knowing how" but also one that requires specialized methods and materials to enable learning. Students who have problems in math as well as reading are likely to wind up in an LD program.

*The term "dyslexia" often shows up in discussions of LD readers. Properly used, the term refers to severe learning disability with neurological implications. "Dyslexics" are only one small subgroup of LD readers. Unfortunately, the term has been misused so often that, for practical purposes, it is virtually meaningless. So if somebody refers to "dyslexia" and "dyslexics," look for a contextual definition. They could be talking about anything from disinterest in reading to severe neurological impairment.*

The diagnosis of children with learning disabilities should be left to special educators, but classroom teachers need to be able to screen children with reading difficulties to (a) separate the remedial readers and slow readers from the learning disabled readers, and (b) refer the latter for special help. The following are some specific problems that learning disabled readers may have.

***Difficulties with visual configuration.*** Children who have this problem have a poor memory for the visual gestalt, or configuration, of letter forms and of whole words—they have trouble remembering what letters and words look like. By third or even fifth grade they may still have trouble remembering how to print or write various letters. They may be able to read words and word lists at or near grade level only by sounding them out very painstakingly, letter by letter. They may be able to plow through long, unfamiliar words phonetically, but be completely stumped by short, familiar words that are spelled nonphonetically. A child with visual configuration problems might be able to tackle a word like *hippopotamus* but go nowhere with *flight, phone,* or even *the.*

***Overapplication of sounding.*** This problem may be closely related to the preceding problem: Overreliance on sounding may develop to compensate for poor memory of the visual conformation of words. Students with this problem are likely to spell words as they sound—*pikcher* for *picture, nashinalite* for *nationality.* Their handwriting may be barely legible, due in part to poor memory for letter forms. Additional phonics instruction may do more harm than good, at least until after the student has had some help with visual memory for letters and words.

***Overreliance on sight words.***    Some children are able to recognize words only by sight and have no sense of sounding. They remember whole words and read by the "look" of words or series of words. Because they rely on their memory of whole words and have no word attack skills, they have no way to deal with unfamiliar words. As their sight vocabularies grow, words with similar configurations become confusing. Longer words like *apparition* and *apparatus* are only a small part of the problem; shorter, more common words like *them/then, and/end,* and *brink/drink/trunk* are a big part. Spelling errors are likely to be frequent and to border on the bizarre. Known words might be spelled correctly; short, frequent, nonphonetic words are likely to be spelled incorrectly; known words may be substituted for similar-looking but unknown words; and known words may be substituted for unknown words with a similar meaning, such as *dog* for *puppy.*

***Lack of visual configuration and sounding.***    Still other children are not able to remember the configuration of words or to sound words phonetically. They have neither a sight vocabulary nor word attack skills. They may learn a few isolated words through repeated exposure or drill, but they are unlikely to be able to read connected words.

***Referral.***    Because all of these problems may also occur among remedial readers, your decision to refer a child for LD instruction must involve consideration of the persistence and the severity of the problem.

We can determine *severity* more easily because it has a legal—though arbitrary—definition. Students can be classified learning disabled if the discrepancy between their academic achievement and their other abilities and achievements is great enough.[2] A rule of thumb is to look for reading achievement that is 50 percent or less than what is expected for a given grade placement. In other words, first-grade performance by a second grader or third-grade performance by a sixth grader would qualify. But you must exclude learning difficulties that could be explained by mental retardation, auditory or perceptual impairment, emotional disturbance, or lack of opportunity to learn. So you can make a referral if the problem is severe enough and if it appears not to be caused by one of the conditions for exclusion.

*Persistence* is a more informal consideration; but it may weigh heavily in a decision to refer. If any of the problems we listed previously persist after the best available corrective/remedial help is provided, then make a referral.

---

[2] In general, a student must have an IQ score of 89 or better to be classified *learning disabled.* Remember that a student must have an IQ score of 69 or less to be classified *mentally retarded.* Students whose IQ scores are in the 70 to 88 range, then, are technically not eligible for either program. For practical purposes, they are *slow learners* and they remain in the regular classroom.

*In other words, if you know you've given the problem your best shot and it still persists, try to get some help.*

## Slow Learners

So far our definition of a slow learner is an individual whose reading performance and general ability are below average. Slow learners' scores on reading achievement tests and tests of academic aptitude (or IQ tests) fall in the range of one to two standard deviations below the average. Even when the limitations of test scores are considered, some children reading below grade level may be reading at or near their capacity level. They need instruction adapted to their needs and capabilities.

Slow learners have historically been the "hard core 20 percent" who have always lagged behind and been a source of great frustration for teachers who expected everyone to learn from the same text and at the same rate. In the recent past, many slow learners were directed to various special programs, often with a false hope that they would overcome their difficulties and learn to perform at grade level. Currently, though, slow learners are being kept in the regular classroom in the belief that their needs can best be served in a more heterogeneous setting.[3]

Meanwhile, back in the classroom . . . slow learners are likely to continue to be a source of great frustration to teachers who perceive them unrealistically and teach them inappropriately. It does little good to label slow learners "underachievers" and lump them together with remedial and learning disabled readers. Instead, both instructional pace and expectations must be adapted to slow learners' particular learning characteristics and aptitudes.

# The Slow Learner in the Classroom

Although slow learners may not learn differently from other children, they do learn at a different rate. They may also exhibit certain disruptive behaviors. First we discuss general characteristics that tend to be associated with the slower pace and then we discuss slow learners' interfering behaviors.

## General Characteristics

Some slow learners' rate of learning may be as low as half that of other children. This means that, even though they learn in the same manner as other children, the slowest learners in a classroom may routinely take twice as long to learn specific skills and concepts. The difference is usually not so dramatic, particularly when instruction is at the appropriate level; nevertheless, slow learners take substantially more time to

---

[3] Slow learners may be candidates for certain compensatory education programs offered by many school districts. For example, Chapter 1 (formerly Title I) programs, commonly staffed by reading teachers or reading specialists, are often available to supplement classroom programs. Because program specifics vary greatly from district to district, we will not attempt to generalize about them. Teachers should make themselves aware of local resources and criteria for inclusion. See Calfee and Drum (1979) for a good review of compensatory programs.

understand and to carry out most tasks. They have difficulty following the presentation of new material—be it fact, skill, concept, or activity—and have trouble doing what is assigned. They may look puzzled or bored or simply drift away into daydreams. Or they may begin a task only to give up in disgust moments later. They are slow in every subject, not just reading, so they are almost always in the "slow" groups, they almost never finish their work on time, and they may even be the last ones out to recess.

It is important for you to remember that most of the time slow learners aren't just trying to "get your goat." They may be trying very hard to follow; but they just do not have the ability to keep up. It is hard to sustain interest for a whole period when you have been lost almost since the beginning. Slow learners need to have tasks broken down into finer bits and to have them explained in greater detail than do other children. They also need more time to complete their assignments. No amount of motivation will enable them to keep up with the rest of the class. They take longer to understand and they work more slowly. They are slow learners.

Slow learners have difficulty with abstractions. Illustrations, such as charts and tables, are as likely to confuse as to enlighten. These children may learn facts relatively readily but may be unable to apply them. For example, they may be able to verbalize phonics facts or principles but be unable to use them effectively. Slow learners often need to experience things in more than one modality. They may need to see, hear, and touch to grasp a meaning. Silent reading may be meaningless, but hearing and seeing the words—sometimes even pointing at or tracing them—may enhance understanding.

A final thing to remember is that some slow learners are well-behaved and charming. They may suffer for their good behavior while disruptive children get attention by making their feelings known. Quiet children may simply blend into the group and be neglected. Children who seem "cute but dumb" may slip through their entire school experience without learning much of anything at all.

## Interfering Behaviors

Many slow learners, however, manifest a variety of disruptive behaviors that can interfere with their own and the whole class's learning. Some of the behaviors appear to have a physical basis;[4] others seem to be psychological reactions to the failure and frustration that many slow learners experience in the classroom. Whatever the cause, disruptive behaviors are likely to get the teacher's attention. The danger is that the behavior will seem willful and perverse, thereby increasing the teacher's frustration and negative feelings toward the child.

A slow learner may exhibit some or most of the following behaviors. Notice that some of the behaviors overlap with behaviors of LD children, discussed more in depth in Chapter 15. Some of the behaviors are also commonly exhibited by children

---

[4] The best treatment for certain physically based behavior problems may be medication, which must be prescribed by a physician. If a child's interfering behaviors are persistent and extreme, the child ought to be referred for evaluation. Ordinarily, teachers should not take it upon themselves to make direct referrals to physicians or to urge parents to seek medication.

classified as educable mentally retarded (EMR) and taught in special classrooms. What all of the children in these groups are likely to have in common is a feeling of frustration in the classroom. Many of their behaviors may be, at least in part, manifestation of that feeling. Being aware that the behaviors are "normal"—or at least common—may not make them easier to cope with; but it may help you to look beyond the behavior to the child who needs understanding and help.

***Short attention span and distractibility.*** The clock clicks before the minute hand moves, and Marvin wheels around to gaze at the clock. . . . Misty drifts away from her reading assignment and listens to the reading group in the back of the room. . . . No sound or movement is too trivial to capture the attention of the child who is easily distracted. Distractibility is associated with a short attention span, and it destroys the continuity of learning or independent activities. Slow learners generally need short work sessions and lots of teacher direction.

***Hyperactivity and impulsiveness.*** Hyperactivity involves motor activity that goes far beyond what the stimulus calls for. Abdul squirms and shouts answers no matter to whom questions are directed; Joyce joins the wrong group leaving the room; Roger jabs Jane with a pencil because she brushed his arm. The impulsive behaviors of hyperactive children may be physically harmful as well as distracting. It is hard for others to take, but hyperactive behavior may be beyond the individual's control.

***Perseverative behavior.*** This involves actions that continue long after they have lost meaning. Lance underlines the target word in a workbook exercise and then continues to underline every word on the page. Peggy draws a circle around a speck on her paper and continues to draw circles until the page is filled. Zach laboriously sounds out a word, letter by letter, and then sounds through again and again. While a bit of repetitive behavior may be nothing more than a sign of boredom, perseverative behavior seems to be almost beyond control. It stops only when someone intercedes, and the stopping may cause upset or even crying.

***Motor awkwardness.*** This may be manifested in relatively fine motor activities— such as nervousness and grimacing while writing, coloring, or cutting with a scissors—and in more gross motor activities—like meandering from one wall to the other when walking down the hall or flapping the hands when engaged in activities involving the feet. Clumsy movement is likely to attract the attention, and sometimes the scorn, of other children. Aside from being disruptive, "bull in a china closet" behavior is likely to be hard on books and other learning materials.

***Gullibility.*** Slow learners tend to have a trusting nature that makes it easy, and tempting, for other children to get them into trouble. Telling Harvey that it's okay to do what is prohibited can be a popular indoor sport . . . and can cause unpleasant encounters with other students, teachers, and even the law. Combined with impulsivity, a gullible nature can get a person into lots of trouble.

What? Me read? (Photo by Strix Pix)

Slow learners may manifest disruptive behaviors.

***Inability to adjust.***    Slow learners often have difficulty with changes that are taken in stride by their classmates. Children who perform quite well with their regular teacher may be completely unable to adjust to and accept a substitute teacher. A fire drill, a field trip, a visit from Bobo the Clown—anything that disrupts the schedule or the routine—may set off totally inappropriate behaviors.

***Inability to delay rewards.***    Even tangible rewards like gold stars, smiling faces, or special privileges are likely to be separated by some time lapse from the acts that earn them. Most children learn to expect and accept delayed gratification, but slow learners may want their rewards *now*. Unless or until a child learns to delay gratification, the teacher must take care to give rewards simultaneously with the desired behaviors. A reward must be seen as a reward to serve any useful purpose.

***Other behaviors.***    The behaviors we have discussed so far may be associated with or even engender other disruptive behaviors. Slow learners are likely to be poorly organized in doing their classroom work. They can't follow directions; they lose their place; they lose their papers; they seldom "get done." They are likely to be very demanding of their teacher's attention and time; and they may be oblivious of the fact that the teacher and the other children are reacting negatively to their demands. Slow learners may also be irritable and may overreact to actions of their teachers or classmates. They may be unaware of subtle cues that signal unacceptable behavior: a raised eyebrow, the wide-eyed look of surprise, or even the palms-up gesture of total exasperation.

Of course, any child in a classroom may exhibit any of the behaviors just described. None is a sole characteristic of slow learners. The point is that some, or all, of the behaviors are common among slow learners and that the behaviors are likely to interfere with learning. Performance related to reading and reading instruction is usually affected in a number of ways.

Test performance is likely to be uneven and unreliable. Taking tests is difficult for slow learners not just because of limited ability. Short attention span, distractibility, impulsivity, and perseveration all lead to poor test performance. Resulting test scores are unlikely to reflect true abilities. Poor comprehension of what one reads and hears is almost certain to limit opportunities to practice and apply reading skills. Limited ability to generalize from one situation to another limits the transfer of skills and strategies learned in reading class to other situations. Thus, the new learner may get involved in a chronically deteriorating sequence where poor performance can only be followed by poorer performance. Finally, the slow learner often has difficulty differentiating good performance from poor. Work that is handed in may be inferior to work that was crumbled and thrown away. Inferior performance by a classmate is as likely to be taken as a model as is acceptable performance.

## Teaching the Slow Learner

There is no special "bag of tricks" for teaching slow learners. While they learn more slowly than other children, their learning patterns and styles do not differ in ways that require special methods or materials. The main consideration in teaching slow learners is to create positive learning situations so they can make appropriate responses and earn the attention and recognition they want and need. All of the following characteristics of a positive learning climate are appropriate for teaching all your students; but they are *essential* for teaching slow learners. (See Chapter 17 for suggestions on how to organize and manage instruction in your classroom.)

### A Positive Personal Style

Individual teaching styles range from relaxed and informal to rigid and formal. An individual's style usually reflects a basic personality type, which could be hard to change very much. Fortunately, whether a personal style is formal or informal is less important than that it be *positive*. Certain teaching behaviors can be modified to convey a positive personal style.

A teacher who takes a formal, by-the-book stance can promote a classroom climate that is as positive and nurturing as that of a teacher who is laid back and informal. What is important is the prevailing teacher-student relationship, often indicated by the way a teacher handles wrong answers. When a child gives a wrong response, is the teacher's response ridicule? A firm "That's wrong"? Much worse, "That's wrong; Mary Sue, what is the right answer?" Or a probe or prompt that might cue a correct response? Teachers can learn to be positive and encouraging no matter what their personal style.

*If you are wondering about your own style, ask someone to observe your teaching and to take note of (a) how and when you pose questions, and (b) how you handle wrong, or only partially correct, responses. The observations will permit you to take an objective look at your own teaching and, if necessary, to modify your actions.*

A teacher's questioning style is not the only gauge of classroom climate, but it may be the most important one because of the message it conveys to students. Some teachers never say anything positive to children; they only let them know that answers are right or wrong. Some only call on children who are likely to give the expected

Develop a positive personal style. (Photo © Jack Hamilton)

answer. They do not explain *how* one would go about getting a right answer. The message that comes through is that the teacher values only right answers—and the people who give them. Such teacher behaviors can be changed fairly readily, to the benefit of the slow learners and everyone else. The direct teaching model described in Chapter 3, for example, presents questions and explanations in a positive light.

A bit of humor can also contribute a great deal to a positive personal style. If Kenny drops a book and then knocks all the books off Susy's desk as he scrambles to catch it, a smile and a remark like "We'll help you clean it up when you're through" would get things settled faster than a threat to pack poor Kenny off to the principal's office. Of course, humor can never be at anyone's expense if it is to have a positive effect. A remark about clumsy Kenny's big feet might get a few laughs, but it would only tend to alienate Kenny.

## Model Behavior

Teachers should provide positive models of the behaviors they want their students to emulate by acknowledging those behaviors. Praising Sally's completion of a tough task not only rewards Sally's effort but also calls attention to the model behavior. When Kenny is working quietly a comment like "I like to see Kenny getting his work done" can accomplish the same things.

Needless to say, the same child should not always be singled out as the model. The behavior of a "teacher's pet" is more likely to be rejected than imitated. Everybody does something right once in a while, even "clumsy" Kenny. It is important, too, to praise the whole group when their behavior is exemplary. "You've really been working hard" or "I liked the way you talked with Ms. Lovejoy (the reading specialist) this morning" gets everybody into the act and lets the children know that you noticed.

You yourself can provide a model for the children to emulate. We know some reading specialists who have not read a novel or biography since they took their last English course in 1958. They aren't very convincing when they talk about reading for pleasure, and they certainly aren't very good models during times set aside for recreational reading. Teachers who want students to value reading should themselves read. If you want students to be interested and enthusiastic about any task you must be interested and enthusiastic when you introduce and monitor the task.

## Interactions

Children must learn to be responsible for their own behavior. As long as they depend on their teacher for direction and evaluation, they will not be inclined to learn or work independently or to give much thought to how well they're doing. Teachers who *react to* instead to *interact with* their students foster dependency because they make themselves the focus of control. The teacher says what is to be done, when to do it, when to stop, and—most importantly—whether the product is good or bad, acceptable or unacceptable. The student may get little information about why the task is important, how it is to be pursued, what direction it should take, and what the outcome should be like. So even if the teacher judges the task to have been successfully completed, the student may have learned very little about how to proceed independently. Slow learners are particularly unlikely to generalize, on their own, from a teacher-directed to a self-directed activity.

You must interact with your students to let them know that you expect them to assume responsibility for their own learning and for their own behavior. You can do so by implementing the direct teaching model described in Chapter 3. Most important, you should monitor students' attempts to carry out their assignments and to apply what they learned in other settings. Monitoring amounts to (a) seeing that the students understand the task, (b) volunteering help when problems arise, (c) responding to questions or requests for clarification, and (d) discussing appropriate and inappropriate applications. The students thus have a chance to discuss any hang-up they may experience during initial learning, practice, and application. You have a chance to convey that the reason for learning a skill, strategy, or concept is to be able to use it when the occasion demands.

## Simple and Direct Assignments

If you recall the first time you asked for street directions while driving in a new place, you may better appreciate some of the problems children have with directions. If you are like us, you could follow the directions through the first two or three turns; but then you had to ask again because you forgot what came next or because things were not unfolding quite as expected. Small wonder, then, that children—particularly slow learners, who tend to be inattentive, impetuous, impulsive, and distractible—have trouble following directions and carrying out assignments.

Directions to slow learners must be simple and direct. Because slow learners have limited memory spans, you may have to give them directions in stages: Be sure they understand and carry out one stage before proceeding to the next. Use appropriate vocabulary. Unless each word you use evokes the appropriate meaning, a single, key word can cause a misunderstanding and a breakdown in performance. Distractible children may fixate on a single word and tune out everything that follows. Direct students' attention. Most busy classrooms are active, fairly noisy places. So when giving directions to an individual or group, make certain that all concerned are paying attention.

## Consistency

Nobody tolerates inconsistency very well. Look at any newspaper and you will see inconsistency decried: Congress freezes military salaries but gives itself a pay boost; a teenager tells Ann Landers that his alcoholic father forbids him to go to a concert where somebody might smoke a joint; the state police crack down on private autos and ignore trucks that exceed the speed limit. Inconsistency almost always causes bad feelings, often raises protests, and sometimes precipitates revolution.

Slow learners may not be in a position to protest inconsistency eloquently or effectively, but their learning is likely to be negatively affected by what might seem to be minor inconsistencies. Because they lack ability to organize themselves and their environment, they depend on others to be organized and consistent.

Effective teachers know that consistency in the classroom ranges from established daily routines to threats and promises being carried out. Nothing undermines a teacher's credibility and destroys the classroom order as quickly and thoroughly as failing to follow words with action. Children see inconsistency when a teacher promises a special privilege to students who complete a task well and on time, and then rewards the entire class because he or she can't bear to disappoint anyone. Slow learners handle disappointment better than inconsistency. *(Of course, it is up to you to set tasks that can be successfully completed by slow learners. Even a game isn't fun if the same people always lose.)* Children see inconsistency, too, when a teacher threatens punishment for a forbidden behavior and then either punishes the whole class when a few transgress or fails to carry through at all. *(At times you might not want to carry through because to do so would attract unfavorable attention from a principal or parents. That could be a good reason! But it would be better, then, not to have made any threats in the first place.)*

Most children seem to function best in a predictable environment. They want to know what they can expect if they perform in certain ways; and they want to be assured that somebody cares enough to pay attention. Slow learners need the attention because it provides a kind of structure that they are unable to bring to most situations.

## Reinforcement

Consistency is closely related to reinforcement because the consistent (or inconsistent) signals that teachers give to children are almost always forms of positive (or negative) reinforcement. Exactly what is reinforcement? A psychology textbook will discuss classical and operant conditioning and consider such things as the unconditioned stimulus, the conditioned stimulus, and the unconditioned and the conditioned response. On the other hand, some of the fairly recent education literature may give one the impression that reinforcement is a matter of dispensing chocolate candies. The first approach tends to be too technical to be practical and the second is too simplistic. In the classroom, reinforcement is mainly a matter of rewarding desired behavior so it will be repeated.

What constitutes a reward and when should you give it? As we have said, slow learners want their rewards immediately. In general, reward desired behaviors without delay so that the slow learner will be able to see the relationship between the behavior and the reward. Exactly what constitutes a reward for an individual is harder to determine. Depending on their prior experiences and expectations, some children are satisfied to know an answer is right; others need a pat, a smile, or a more lasting picture of a smiling face; still others may demand a tangible and explicit reward, a piece of candy or a special privilege. The ultimate goal is to make successful learning its own reward, but it may be necessary to approach that goal through stages of more tangible rewards.

## Summary

Slow learners need adapted instruction. You must adapt *expectations* to slow learners' limited ability; do not expect them to "catch up" and to perform at grade level. You must adapt *pace of instruction* to their slower rate of learning; they may take up to twice as long to perform academic tasks as other children in the classroom. To provide appropriate instruction and to make appropriate referrals, you must be able to differentiate slow learners from remedial readers, learning disabled readers, and children who are mentally retarded.

Slow learners often exhibit certain disruptive behaviors that interfere with their learning and distract other children. These behaviors are often reactions to the frustration they experience with learning. While slow learners do not require special techniques or materials for reading instruction—other than an adapted pace—they do need a positive learning environment. We discuss how to provide a learning environment that encourages the appropriate responses that earn slow learners the attention and recognition they want and need to sustain learning.

# References

Calfee, R. G., & Drum, P. A. (Eds.). (1979). *Teaching reading in compensatory classes.* Newark, DE: International Reading Association.

Downing, J., & Leong, C. K. (1982). *Psychology of reading.* New York: Macmillan.

Kirk, S. A., & Gallagher, J. J. (1979). *Educating exceptional children* (3rd ed.). Boston: Houghton Mifflin.

# Check Your Reading Comprehension

1. What is meant by adapted instruction? How does it differ from corrective or remedial instruction?

2. What are some of the problems involved with identifying children as slow learners?

3. In this chapter you were introduced to the terms *remedial readers, learning disabled readers,* and *slow learners.* Read each following description and identify the group of students to which it refers.

   a. Children from the lower end of the IQ distribution who need instruction that is adapted in terms of pace and expectations. _____

   b. Children who have varying degrees of difficulty. Characteristically, their ability is higher than their achievement and their errors are of the same type as (though more numerous than) those made by good readers. _____

**c.** Children who have more severe and complex problems that require intensive and prolonged treatment. _____

**4.** Matching Exercise:

_____**1.** Interfering behaviors

_____**2.** Positive personal style

_____**3.** Model behavior

_____**4.** Interactions

_____**5.** Simple and direct assignments

_____**6.** Consistency

_____**7.** Reinforcement

**a.** A nurturing, acceptive classroom climate is essential for the slow learner.

**b.** Teachers should pay particular attention to these because slow learners tend to be inattentive, impetuous, impulsive, and distractible.

**c.** The teacher must determine what constitutes a reward and when to give it to a particular child.

**d.** These are necessary to help the slow learner move from teacher-directed to self-directed activities.

**e.** These activities and behaviors disrupt the learning environment (distractibility, hyperactivity, perseverative behavior, etc.)

**f.** This is important to slow learners, who often lack the ability to organize themselves and their environment; they, therefore, depend on others to be organized and predictable.

**g.** Teachers should provide examples of, and reinforcement for, the behaviors they expect.

Answers:

| | |
| --- | --- |
| | 4. b |
| 3. g | 7. c |
| 2. a | 6. f |
| 1. e | 5. d |

**5.** Imagine that you are a sixth-grade teacher. In your class of 25 students you have several who are slow learners. What provisions will you make for them in your comprehensive reading program?

**6.** In Chapter 11 you worked on a unit for use with your class. Are there strands of activities for your slow learners? Some of these activities could be designed especially for the slow learners; others could be designed so that these students could share with others. Perhaps you could add some activities for the slow learner to your unit.

# 15

# Exceptional Children

**Dr. Roger Eldridge, Assistant Professor, East Carolina University, prepared the draft version of Chapter 15.**

In this chapter you learn how to help the exceptional children in your classroom participate in learning-to-read activities. We discuss what these children are like and how their needs are special.

As you enter your classroom in September, you're thinking of your "ideal" class. You may be expecting to have 20 to 25 students in a classroom; to use a basal reader with all students; to form three reading groups to differentiate instruction; and to use the suggestions from the teacher's manual of a basal reader. Many of us have had these preconceived notions, but they seldom hold in the reality of the classroom. You may, for example, enter a classroom with as many as 30 to 35 students. You may find, too, that their reading abilities range from as low as two or three grade levels below to as high as three or four grade levels above the chronological grade. Furthermore, the students' knowledge of specific reading subskills is likely to be just as diverse. In addition, three or more of the students are likely to exhibit any of a variety of exceptionalities. Such students may have been mainstreamed into the classroom as a result of the Education for all Handicapped Children Act (Public Law 94-142). You must teach reading to these students, too.

We are not trying to alarm you. But you should be prepared for the realities of teaching reading today. This chapter focuses on how to work with the educable mentally handicapped, learning disabled, emotionally handicapped, visually handicapped, hearing impaired, and gifted.

Remember, though, that the characteristics of real children often overlap several categories of exceptionality, while the hypothetical children we discuss do not. We suggest certain strategies for working with specific categories of exceptional students, but you will want to employ these techniques with other types of exceptional learners as well.

There is no "bag of tricks" for teaching these children to read. You cannot sprinkle a magic dust or wave a magic wand to turn them into instant readers. Rather, we've found that modifying the same techniques we use to teach average children is often the best strategy. At this point the main thing to remember is that teaching exceptional children to read requires hard work, planning, and patience.

## Assistance from the Special Teacher

In the 1950s and 1960s some educators suggested that the teacher was not as important to the learning-to-read process as either the method or the materials used. (Chall, 1967). But more recent classroom-based studies have shown that teachers' actions and decisions during reading instruction are very important. (Duffy, 1983; McDermott, 1976; Borko, Shavelson, & Stern, 1981).

As a classroom teacher, you must address a number of questions: How should I determine the membership of my reading groups? Do I form three groups, or four, or more, or fewer? Do I assign all my students to read from basal readers? Should I plan to use other materials such as games, kits, and library books to teach reading? How do I assess my students' reading abilities? What reading skills do my students

Magic wands are for friendly witches.

already know? How can I begin to meet the individual needs of my students? Similar questions need to be asked about instruction in mathematics, social studies, and other subjects.

Fortunately, no teacher is expected to take on singlehandedly all of the educational challenges offered by the exceptional learners in a classroom. Other professional school personnel such as speech therapists and learning specialists are specifically trained to teach these students on a daily basis. You and the specialist need to exchange any relevant information about the student's ability to learn and to use language in a school setting. Both of you must agree upon the expectations and goals set for the student, because contradictory expectations only confuse the learner and inhibit learning. An exceptional student mainstreamed into a regular classroom may receive reading instruction from you as well as from a specialist outside of the classroom setting. Only by sharing what each knows about the student can you and the specialist plan an appropriate reading program. You must work as a team.

*Specialized teachers are available to assist you; but it is unlikely that they will come to you. We urge you to make a concerted effort to identify and seek out the*

Seek help from specialists.

*specialists who can help you. Communication leading to complementary efforts is most likely to produce the desired results.*

# General Teaching Practices

In this section we present suggestions for teaching exceptional students in the regular classroom. Remember, although the suggestions concern specific categories of exceptionality, in most instances you can effectively apply them in other categories. As we have said, the characteristics of different exceptionalities may overlap. An educable mentally handicapped student may also be hearing impaired or visually handicapped. An emotionally handicapped student may also be gifted. Techniques for teaching reading often work equally well with students possessing different exceptionalities.

We have drawn our list of teaching practices from the works of several reading educators (Bond & Tinker, 1973; Kirk, Kliebhan, & Lerner, 1978; McGinnis & Smith, 1982; Otto & Smith, 1980; and Richek, List, & Lerner, 1983). Although some of the ideas appear elsewhere in this book, we reiterate them here to emphasize their importance when teaching exceptional students, particularly those with an impairment. Some of our suggestions, such as modeling and providing the student with sufficient opportunity to use newly learned skills, also apply to gifted readers.

***Plan small steps.*** Exceptional learners may be unable to learn, assimilate, and apply new reading skills at one sitting. You must take care to identify and to explain thoroughly all the parts of the skill process. For example, teaching an exceptional student the two sounds of consonant *c* (/k/ and /s/) during one lesson might be overwhelming and cause the learner to confuse the application of the two sounds. Instead, present the generalizations for identifying one sound of *c* during one instructional session. Then provide the learner with practice identifying and pronouncing words containing the one sound, using "real" materials, such as a teacher-constructed story or a library book containing examples of words with the one *c* sound.

At another instructional session thoroughly review the first set of generalizations of the consonant *c*. Next, present the generalizations for identifying the second sound of *c*. Again, provide practice with real materials. Once you judge the learner capable of using the two sounds separately, provide opportunities to apply the two sounds together in a single lesson. This sequence may take the learner three, four, five, or more days. Focus on the learning that is taking place and not on the time spent. When a learner exhibits any confusion about skills or information, go back to a point where the student can successfully complete a task.

Another reason for taking small steps is that exceptional learners often have short attention spans. The presentation of too much new material at any one time tends to frustrate and confuse them. When a learner's attention appears to be directed to places other than the task at hand, stop the lesson and pursue a different activity in which the learner can take an active part.

Not all exceptional students learn best when provided small instructional steps. Some learn better holistically. Breaking the reading process into component skills, such as identifying and pronouncing the two sounds of c, may subject these exceptional students to more, not less, difficulty. You must teach these youngsters reading in terms of the development of language usage. Always consider the exceptional student's optimum learning style and adapt to it. In general, though, we have found that most students progress best when the reading skills are presented, practiced, and applied in small steps.

*The ability to identify a small enough step in the instructional process does not come easily to a novice teacher—it takes practice. Don't be discouraged if at first you select and present too much material. Learn to correct your errors and take smaller steps when necessary.*

***Expect small increments of change.*** Your expectations for success must match the learner's ability. At times exceptional students do assimilate and apply information readily. At other times no matter how hard the student and teacher try the student appears to achieve little. Don't despair! Change in an exceptional student's ability to acquire and apply skills occurs slowly. Don't set goals beyond a student's capability or you will probably ensure failure. Set goals based on the student's ability, not on the amount of material to be covered.

***Identify specific goals.*** Before beginning to teach any class you must assess the reading needs of the students and develop instructional procedures based on the assessment data. Working with exceptional learners is no different. You cannot provide appropriate instruction, or more specifically, focused instruction (Otto & Chester, 1976), without first identifying and then basing goals on the students' reading strengths and weaknesses. Broad goals, such as "improving word recognition skills," are too vague and often require so much time to attain that both you and the student lose sight of them. Goals should be specific and attainable, such as "identifying main ideas in paragraphs containing topic sentences." Both the teacher and the student can record progress made toward such a goal.

***Be flexible.*** A teacher who is rigid when planning and implementing reading instruction usually creates a classroom atmosphere of apprehension, which can be particularly stressful for exceptional students. Instead, you must adjust plans and teaching methods to the special characteristics and circumstances of these students, establishing attainable goals, adapting materials and tasks to ability levels, assigning activities of appropriate length, and giving clear and simplified directions. You will have to allow exceptional students more time to complete assignments. You may have to adapt or rewrite the reading materials to accommodate their skill levels.

You may find yourself spending a lot of time explaining directions and getting an exceptional student started on a task. This is not unusual; learn to adjust the pace of instruction for exceptional students. Learning to be flexible does not occur automatically—you must work at it. Flexibility may be difficult to attain because of pressures exerted by the principal, superintendent, school board, or parents. They may wonder why progress is so slow or why the same approach is not used for all students. Nevertheless, recognizing that students are different and approaching each student with the differences clearly in mind will be of the most benefit to your students.

***Use modeling, prompting, and shaping.***     Exceptional students respond well to *modeling,* your demonstrating a skill in such a way that they can observe and then imitate your behavior. Before asking an exceptional student to complete a new task, perform the task as the student watches. The learner thus observes each step taken to initiate an action and complete a task. Exceptional students often learn more from watching and then doing than from being told what to do. Modeling provides you with instantaneous assessment and the learner with immediate feedback.

*Prompting,* which is also particularly helpful with exceptional students, involves providing clues or even partial answers to questions to assist a student to complete an activity. Verbal clues, gestures, or pantomine may trigger a thought that, when elaborated upon, enables a learner to understand a concept or skill. Exceptional students tend to be hesitant to take risks when answering a question or performing a task, even when they know the answer. Your prompting can let the learner know that he or she is on the right track and encourage a guess at the answer.

*Shaping* is also helpful with exceptional students. It is a step-by-step process by which learning is fashioned by your responses to a student's actions. You provide immediate feedback to each action taken by the student. For example, if a student incorrectly identifies the first incident in a story, immediately point out the error so the student can alter the answer to provide a more appropriate response. Respond with praise if the student correctly identifies the second incident. For each student response, indicate the direction in which the student's attention should be focused, thereby leading the learner toward success.

***Provide sufficient guided practice.***     The opportunity to practice what one has learned is very important in the learning process. It is extremely valuable for exceptional students because learning and retaining what is learned is so difficult in the first place. When students practice a concept or skill immediately after it is taught, they remember it better and longer. This is especially true for exceptional students, who tend to forget easily.

Be involved in the practice process. Exceptional students frequently make incorrect responses when left on their own during practice sessions. The incorrect responses then become the learned responses. To prevent this, carefully monitor the student's performance during practice sessions. When you are busy with others, another student can monitor an exceptional student's work.

***Provide review.***     The exceptional student should have frequent opportunities to review material already learned. We suggest that you review at the beginning of each instructional session the work covered the preceding day. Always review previously taught material before presenting related new material. Exceptional students need frequent pauses in the progression of learning to review and bring together ideas and skills previously taught. The more frequent the review, the greater the chances that they will retain what they have learned. Remember that exceptional students tend to forget more readily and rapidly than average learners.

***Provide for generalization and transfer of learning.*** One of your primary objectives as a teacher of reading is to have students use reading subskills as they read in various content areas. Therefore, provide your students with opportunities to apply reading skills in all academic areas. Exceptional students, in particular, need you to show them exactly how skills learned during reading instruction can apply to reading a science text or pleasure book.

First help the exceptional student learn to select materials that he or she can read independently. Provide the student with opportunities to talk about a subject of interest and to go to a library to select materials that address that interest. Don't leave generalization and transfer of reading skills to chance. Make every effort to encourage the student to develop interests and to read about those interests. Helpful activities include students' sharing verbal descriptions of the books they have read, your reading books out loud on a regular schedule, displaying students' art work related to a reading experience, and using higher levels of questioning skills and thinking skills during discussions.

*We encourage you to use these general practices as you teach exceptional students who have been mainstreamed into your classroom. Don't be afraid to expand or adapt our suggestions to meet your teaching needs and the learning needs of the exceptional students in your classroom.*

In the following sections of this chapter, we label and define several categories of exceptional learners. We describe some characteristics representative of each category, but only those characteristics important to the acquisition and application of reading skills—such as intelligence, behavioral problems, and variables associated with language development. We also identify and describe effective strategies for teaching reading to exceptional learners in a regular classroom setting.

# Educable Mentally Handicapped (EMH)

The American Association on Mental Deficiency identifies the EMH student as possessing "subaverage intellectual functioning" and "deficits in adaptive behavior" manifested during the developmental period (Grossman, 1973). In terms of teaching and learning, this definition depicts the EMH student as low in intellectual ability, immature, slow to learn, deficient in receptive, associative, and expressive language skills, and low in reading ability. Consequently, an EMH student usually functions academically at a low level of development across subject areas and skills. Dunn (1973) characterizes the EMH student as not reading up to mental age expectancy and being inferior to normal students of the same mental age in locating relevant facts, recognizing main ideas, drawing inferences, drawing conclusions, and using word attack skills. A specialized program of instruction is required to teach the EMH student to read.

## Teaching Strategies

EMH students are usually not capable of participating in a program centered on a basal reader. Generally, they are able to use only a limited amount of language, the size of their sight word vocabularies is extremely small, and they are behind the average reader in general reading ability. Therefore, you and the EMH specialist must jointly develop an individualized program of instruction. Such a program should focus on developing a student's language skills, conceptual competence, and sight vocabulary.

The development of an EMH student's basic sight vocabulary is one of the most important areas for the classroom teacher to consider. Because EMH students usually possess limited vocabularies, they are almost certain to experience receptive, expressive, and associative language difficulties. The EMH student does not develop vocabulary knowledge merely from exposure to words. You must also see that the student uses and understands the words in speaking, listening, reading, and writing.

Teach words that enhance the EMH student's well-being and survival. For example, teach proper names associated with the student's everyday life (names of stores, foods, people, and places), names of concrete objects (table, door, house, window, street, etc.), and basic survival words (stop, hot, cold, yes, no, etc.). An EMH student can learn, retain, and use the names of concrete objects, but usually not words identifying abstract ideas. Even an average reader may have difficulty learning abstract words and ideas; but once the abstract words and ideas are learned the average reader applies them readily. This is not the case with EMH students. For example, the word *table* and the properties associated with a table are easier and more relevant for an EMH student to learn and understand than the ideas associated with the concept *democracy*. You should teach EMH students vocabulary and ideas that they can grasp and that are relevant to them. Your long-term goal is to help the EMH student acquire sufficient language and knowledge to be able to function independently in society.

Develop new words as concepts to enhance EMH students' conceptual competence. Do not expect them to memorize word lists, because they have poor memories. Rather, identify the characteristics of each word, its physical attributes, and the relationship of its characteristics to other words. Rely on actual experiences to build vocabulary competence.

Another strategy for teaching vocabulary to EMH students is to rely on as many of the five senses as possible to identify and illustrate a new word. To teach the word *sugar* you can use at least three of the senses. Sugar has a distinctive taste; it can be identified by sight in crystal, liquid, and powder forms; and it has a granular, smooth, or slippery texture. You can develop the concept of sweetness by presenting a variety of foods containing sugar in one form or another. Whenever possible, ask EMH students to use more than one sense to identify a word. Provide them with oppor-

Rely on *all* the senses. (Photo by Strix Pix)

tunities to relate a new word to other words already within their grasp. Using the senses to acquire information by means of active participation or demonstration has a lasting effect on EMH students.

Provide as many reading experiences as possible. These must not always be those in which the student is an active participant. We suggest that you also develop experiences through in-depth explanation and description. Teaching a word or concept may entail demonstrating properties or attributes of the concept as well as reading a description of the idea you want the student to grasp. Reading to an EMH student is important to the development of the student's reading ability.

The language experience approach (LEA) is effective with EMH students. Language experience stories are ideas about a topic dictated by a student and transcribed by the teacher (see Chapter 7). LEA encourages EMH students to use language, to increase their identification of sight words, and to work on developing competence in the use of syntax.

Use concrete objects as topics or "story starters" with EMH students. Teach word identification in the context of the story and not in isolation or through the use of phonics rules. Words taught in isolation are not easily remembered. EMH students also have difficulty learning and applying phonic generalizations, so teaching phonics "rules" is not likely to be productive.

*We like to use concrete objects for initiating a student's thinking before stories are written. Use as story starters foods of all types and concrete objects that can be manipulated, such as simple woodworking tools or household utensils. We have placed candy (marshmallows) in a plain brown paper bag with no writing on it. We then asked students to "discover" the contents of the bag without looking inside. They develop a language experience story based on their discovery. An instamatic camera that produces a picture immediately is a unique story starter. Making ice cream with a hand-powered ice cream machine and eating the ice cream in the classroom has lead to some interesting and enjoyable story lines by EMH students. Whenever possible allow students an opportunity to use or work with items before beginning a language experience story.*

To enhance an EMH student's use of expressive language, we urge teachers to read stories out loud and to discuss the content of the stories with students. Discussions should focus on questions that ask the student to provide information from what was read. Require students to use their oral language. Establish expectations for students that prohibit them from answering a question with one word. Such brief answers do not reveal the student's knowledge or understanding of story content.

The ability to recall or recognize facts from a written text is important for all students. The ultimate goal is to get them to think and understand beyond the literal level. The goal is no different for EMH students, but getting there is very difficult. Using literal information to learn to make higher level decisions does not come easily for these students. To begin to think at higher levels, they must be guided by questions that help them make an inference, draw a conclusion, identify a relationship, or make an evaluation based on the materials. Ask them to make choices and to support their choices based on story content. Do not ask only literal questions that require the student to parrot back answers from the text. Encourage your EMH students to verbalize and describe their thoughts.

Teaching EMH students the skill of paraphrasing is an important first step toward developing their ability to think at higher levels. A student who is able to paraphrase an author's statement demonstrates real understanding of the author's idea. Begin to teach paraphrasing simply, using short concrete phrases until the students can use their own words to express a single thought unit. Move to paraphrasing whole sentences and finally to paragraphs.

The next set of tasks is to help students develop the ability to draw an inference, make an evaluation, understand a relationship or association, and express an appreciation or a personal point of view.

Helping EMH students learn to think at higher levels is not easy. The process takes much time and energy, but the goal is worthwhile. These students are usually capable of developing thinking and reasoning skills when given the opportunity—an opportunity you can provide in your classroom as you teach reading.

# Learning Disabled (LD)

The National Advisory Committee on Handicapped Children (1968) defines learning disability as a disorder in one or more of the basic psychological processes involved in understanding or using spoken or written language. The learning problems of LD students, then, are not due to environmental disadvantage, mental retardation, or emotional disturbance. Rather, the problems are caused by perceptual handicaps, neurological dysfunction, brain impairment, memory and cognitive difficulties, receptive and expressive language problems, attentional deficits, and like disorders.

Learning disability (LD) is a relatively new addition to the categories included in special education. Coined by Kirk in 1962, the term LD has been adopted by the Association for Children with Learning Disabilities (ACLD) and the United States Office of Education (Kirk & Bateman, 1962). Since Kirk coined the term, specialists have had difficulty determining whether certain children's learning disabilities should be attributed to cultural disadvantage or to disorders in psychological processes (Kappelman, Kaplan, & Ganter, 1976). Specialists have also had trouble diagnosing a disorder in basic psychological processes. There is little agreement among the various disciplines (medicine, psychology, education) regarding the criteria to be used in identifying LD students. According to some criteria, up to 30 percent of the school population exhibits learning disabilities. Furthermore, there is a tendency in many school districts to assign almost any student having difficulty in school to special LD classes so that the district may receive additional funding (Wepman, Cruickshank, Deutsch, Morency, & Strother, 1975).

Hyperactivity, distractibility, and short attention span have historically been associated with LD students. Learning disability specialists seem to agree that many of the conduct disorders and maladaptive behaviors that LD children exhibit in the classroom are related to deficiencies in attention. Obviously a student who is running around the classroom cannot be attending to reading instruction. The student may, however, be running around the room in frustration because of the inability to selectively attend to the relevant discriminating aspects of the reading assignment. In a study of the characteristics of students identified as educable mentally handicapped, learning disabled, or emotionally handicapped, Gajar (1980) found that the students from all three groups ranked highest on a pattern of behaviors labeled immaturity-inadequacy. This pattern includes short attention span, distractibility, inattentiveness to what others say, restlessness, an inability to sit still, excessive daydreaming, irresponsibility, undependability, and laziness in school and in the performance of other tasks (Quay, 1972).

LD students are of average or above-average intelligence (Wallace & McLoughlin, 1979). Nevertheless, they tend to be underachievers in academic subject areas, especially reading. Kirk and Elkins (1975) found, in a survey of the characteristics of 3,000 children enrolled in Child Service Demonstration Centers for learning disabled students in 21 states, that approximately two-thirds of the students were reported to have reading problems. The median reading retardation level was one grade below mental age reading expectancy, and the level in reading and spelling was one-half grade lower than that in arithmetic.

The visual discrimination and auditory discrimination skills of learning disabled students often indicate difficulties with language reception, association, and expression. Wallace and Kauffman (1978) state that students with visual discrimination deficiencies are those "who have normal visual acuity" but who have trouble "differentiating, interpreting, or remembering different shapes, letters, or words" (p. 175). Behaviors of students with visual discrimination deficiencies include: (a) the confusion of letters that are close in shape and form—for instance, b/d, p/q, m/n, z/w; (b) problems with sequencing, such as confusing *stop* with *spot* or *there* with *three;* and (c) problems with reversals, such as reading the word *was* for *saw, on* for *no, part* for *trap.*

LD students may also have problems discriminating individual sounds and words that they hear. Wallace and Kauffman (1978) state that children with auditory discrimination deficiencies ". . . may have normal hearing acuity. However, they have difficulties in differentiating, synthesizing, and remembering the sounds of different letters and words" (p. 184). Behaviors of children with auditory discrimination problems include: (a) requesting that the teacher repeat verbal instructions, (b) incorrectly repeating sounds and words, and (c) incorrectly associating a sound with a symbol or word.

Learning disabled students may have trouble expressing themselves. Their difficulties with spoken language may include trouble with phonology, the production of the sounds of speech; morphology, the formation of correct words and sentences; semantics, the ability to express ideas or problems; or syntax, the ability to construct sentences using the correct word order. Written expression problems include: spelling errors; the omission of letters from words, and words from sentences; difficulty holding a writing utensil; and errors in manuscript or cursive writing.

LD handicaps are complex. Behaviors in a particular classroom may range from the general chaos exhibited (and created) by a hyperactive child to the silence of a withdrawn learner, who quietly goes about doing nothing constructive. Individualized instructional programs and a variety of strategies are needed to teach these children to read. Yet, the LD student must be allowed to participate with the rest of the class in the development of socialization skills.

## Teaching Strategies

Avoid overdrilling on words out of context when teaching vocabulary to LD students. Information out of context has little meaning for learners who have difficulty forming and identifying associations, as do LD readers. Because they also have trouble categorizing information, they may be unable to identify the relationship of an isolated word to other information. They may only learn disjointed bits of information because they cannot combine the new information with ideas and concepts they already know. Teaching words in a specific context provides LD students with ready-made relationships and categories, increasing their chances of learning the new information.

Explain to LD students *why* you are teaching a skill and *how* that skill is related to what they already know. When they understand why they are learning a specific skill and how it fits into the larger scheme of learning to read, they are better able to fit the skill into their stores of previous knowledge. When teaching the skill of "identifying a sequence of events in a story," for instance, relate the skill to counting. Teach your LD students that in telling a story an author identifies certain information and then has a story character react to that information. The author then presents a second bit of information and has the character react again, following this process for all the information necessary to tell the story. As you describe this process, relate the events of the story to the process of counting, something the students know how to do. You thus establish a relationship between a known process and a new skill, thereby increasing LD students' retention of the new information. Because LD readers usually have poor short-term memories, you must identify what knowledge they already possess so new information can be related to that existing knowledge.

Devise listening and read-along activities. LD students often need to develop listening abilities to compensate for their inability to read printed materials. For many LD students, learning occurs mainly through listening. Set a purpose for each listening activity to focus it toward attentive listening, not just hearing sounds. Read-along activities can give LD students an opportunity to follow a story as another individual reads. By directing students' attention to print, read-along activities help LD students not only develop listening skills but also acquire a sight vocabulary. Listening ability does not develop on its own. You must provide instruction to develop the skill. Activities that direct attention and develop effective listening skills are important because they establish a groundwork for learning to read.

## Special Reading Practices for LD Students

Some specialized reading programs for LD students utilize sensory modality training as an aspect of reading instruction. We find two techniques, the VAKT approach and the Neurological Impress Method, particularly useful to classroom teachers of reading.

***VAKT approach.*** The VAKT approach, developed by Grace Fernald (1943), utilizes visual, auditory, kinesthetic, and tactile senses to reinforce learning. Fernald stresses the need for a student to experience words through various sense modalities. Because of the painstaking nature of the approach and the slow progress made by students with whom it is used, we recommend it as a total approach only with highly motivated, seriously learning disabled readers. The Fernald procedure guards against breaking the reading process into component parts; it stresses reading as a meaning-getting process.

The VAKT approach consists of four stages that blend, one stage into the other, as students improve their ability to learn words and to read them in context.

*Stage one.* The student selects a word to be learned, which you write or print on a strip of paper in crayon, large enough for the student to trace. The student traces the word with a finger while saying the word in syllables, repeating the procedure until grasping that word. After the word is removed from sight, the student reproduces it as a unit of memory. Then the student, having learned a few words in this manner, composes a little story incorporating the words. Type the story and have the student read it to you. Write each new word that the student has learned on a separate card and place the cards alphabetically in a word file box. The box is a source for providing an LD reader with the repetition needed to learn the alphabet letters and basic dictionary skills and to master a sight vocabulary.

*Stage two.*    Tracing is no longer necessary at this stage; otherwise, the basic approach remains the same. A student looks at words from a dictated story and vocalizes them to establish a connection between the sound of the words and their form. The student never focuses on individual letter sounds but rather produces words as whole units.

*Stage three.*    At this stage, the student begins to read from books and is taught to identify unknown words by using contextual clues. Tracing or copying is no longer necessary. If a student is unable to identify a word through context, tell the student the word.

*Stage four.*    The student generalizes sufficiently to recognize new words by their similarities to words already known. Encourage him or her to survey reading material before reading and to learn unfamiliar words so the author's message is not interrupted.

### Neurological impress method.

Heckelman (1969) has described a method of reading in unison with a good oral reader to expose a poor reader to accurate, fluid reading patterns rather than to the student's own mistaken-ridden, halting reading. Ask the reader to read in unison with you as you slide a finger along the line of words being spoken so that your finger is always at the location of the word being spoken.

Select materials at the student's independent reading level. Give no attention to the meaning or understanding of the materials. Tell the student to do as well as he or she can in just saying the words along with you. Focus entirely on the flow of the oral reading.

Sit next to and slightly behind the student and read into the student's ear. In the beginning, you should read louder and faster than the student. As the student becomes more capable of assuming the lead in oral reading, lower your voice and lag slightly behind the student's reading. If the student falters, take over the lead again by raising your voice. During the reading, accompany the reading with a smooth, continuous motion of the index finger under the words being read. Eventually the student takes over the finger gliding. The finger movement must be synchronized to tie in the visual and oral senses with the tactile sensation.

Once the procedure is well-established and the student has developed some fluency, begin to ask the student to retell the story. This activity conveys to the student the idea that reading is not just fluent word calling.

With this approach you can help certain learning disabled readers who appear to lack a proper concept of reading, who sound out every word, or who have serious phrasing problems. Of course, the neurological impress method is only one part of a total reading program; it is not a complete approach in itself. For some students, however, it may, at least for a while, constitute a major part of a total reading program.

*Notice that the neurological impress method is similar in some respects to the technique of repeated readings described in Chapter 8. The neurological impress method differs mainly in that it puts more stress on the echoic nature of the reading experience and that it stresses "keeping place" with the finger. We wonder whether "neurological impress" is truly an important aspect of the method's impact; but we do believe that it can be useful with certain severely disabled readers.*

# Emotionally Handicapped (EH)

A widely accepted definition of the emotionally handicapped student does not exist. A variety of personality and social adjustment disorders are associated with EH students. They manifest behaviors that usually exceed the tolerence and understanding of people with whom they are in contact by responding to their environment in socially unacceptable or personally unsatisfying ways. But these students can be taught more socially acceptable and personally gratifying behavior. Three basic forms of behavior are exhibited by an EH student: aggression, withdrawal, and anxiety. Any or all of these forms of behavior may be exhibited at one time. An individual exhibiting aggressive behavior may also express anxiety. Be constantly aware of changes in the classroom atmosphere that may affect the behavior of an emotionally handicapped student. You must also be aware of inappropriate behavior as it is being exhibited.

Kauffman (1981) and Gajar (1980) found that EH students exhibit below-average intelligence. In an earlier survey, however, Morse, Cutler, and Fink (1964) found more EH students at the higher levels of intelligence than would be expected in a normal distribution. A possible explanation for those conflicting reports may be that the behaviors exhibited by EH students interfere with the measurement of intelligence. Disruptive students often have difficulty performing up to their capabilities in testing situations.

EH students' language characteristics (both oral and written) are often quite similar to those of LD students. EH students often exhibit difficulties with visual and/or auditory discrimination skills; as a result, they have problems with language reception, association, and expression. The language problems of EH students, however, are due more to the student's disruptive and inattentive behaviors than to the student's perceptual difficulties.

It is not uncommon for an EH student who has a tenuous hold on his or her emotions to be mainstreamed into a regular classroom. The techniques for teaching reading to an EH student are essentially the same as for teaching normal students, but you must develop ways to manage an emotionally handicapped student's behavior on a personal level differently from the ways you deal with other students.

## Teaching Strategies

An emotionally handicapped student functions best within an established routine. Such a student typically has great difficulty coping with disruption or abrupt changes in classroom routine. Something as simple as changing the reading period from the first activity in the morning to a later time in the day can be traumatic. Changing an EH student's seat location in the classroom may cause the student to "act out" as a result of not understanding the change; or the student may totally withdraw from participating in class activities. Whenever possible, avoid abrupt changes in classroom routine.

EH students need your support and approval; their self-confidence is often very low. Learn to build on their successes both in improved behavior and in learning. Give verbal praise and physical gestures of approval, such as a reassuring touch or pat on the shoulder, when an EH student completes an assignment successfully. Because an emotionally handicapped student usually has a short attention span, presenting too much information at one time is likely to cause frustration followed by unacceptable behavior. Introduce only an amount of material that the student can readily learn and assimilate. Breaking the reading process into individual subskill elements and then providing for the application of all the elements together is a good instructional approach to take with an EH student who is often inattentive.

Take pains to encourage the student to participate in class activities. Isolating an EH student increases the level of anxiety, which may be followed by disruptive classroom behavior. Whenever possible assign these students to classroom groups and encourage them to participate in and contribute to the group. Providing an EH student with opportunities to interact and to work with other students who have similar interests may go a long way toward developing self-confidence and acceptance by other students in the classroom.

Rules of conduct and the enforcement of rules for the EH student should be fair and consistent. The student must understand the rules as well as know the consequences for breaking them. For instance, punishment imposed for a specific behavior at one time must be the same when the behavior occurs at a later time. Ignoring an inappropriate behavior today and punishing the same behavior tomorrow will only confuse the EH student as to what is and what is not acceptable behavior in the classroom.

You cannot expect an EH student to obey a rule that you do not expect other students in the class to obey. Take great care to explain thoroughly the classroom rules and to make an emotionally handicapped student aware of why a particular behavior is unacceptable. To punish a student without an explanation will not alter the student's behavior and may simply cause the behavior to be repeated. Be positive: tell the EH student what to do rather than what not to do.

One additional suggestion is in order: Allow the student to walk around the classroom, or even to walk out into the hall when he or she feels an urgent need to get away from the group. At times a student's anxiety may be so great that the student has to get away from the situation causing the anxiety. Forcing the student to remain in the situation would only result in a breakdown of behavior and a disruption of the learning environment. Of course, you should not let EH students leave at every sign of discomfort; it is important for them to face certain problems and develop adequate coping behaviors. Work out a system of signals by which an EH student warns you of an impending problem. This requires your constant awareness of the EH student and his or her needs.

# Visually Handicapped (VH)

Students who are blind or have visual acuity problems such as partial sight, errors of refraction, and deficits in the muscular control of the eye are identified as *visually handicapped* (VH). For purposes of schooling, a student is blind when vision is so severely impaired that the student must be taught to read Braille or taught with alternative aural methods (audiotapes and records). Students suffering other visual impairments may be able to learn to read by using magnifying devices or books with large print (Hallahan & Kauffman, 1982).

From extensive studies of blind students, Hayes (1950) concluded that blindness did not need to result in depressed intellectual functioning, because most intellectual tasks are primarily verbal in nature. Visually handicapped students may, however, perform at a lower level than their peers on tasks that require abstract thinking.

VH students usually tend to be verbally very proficient, but their language skills associated with writing may not be well-developed. Spache (1976) concluded from a literature review that VH students could progress normally if their handicap was accommodated with large print materials.

Visually handicapped students mainstreamed into regular classrooms present special problems. Reading is an obviously visual process, so VH students are likely to experience difficulties learning to read. You must be prepared to adapt general instructional procedures to accommodate the handicap.

## Teaching Strategies

Mobility and orientation are two special needs of the VH student. We believe that the classroom teacher must take responsibility for developing competence in both areas before reading instruction begins.

*Orientation* refers to an individual's sense of spatial placement in relation to other objects within an environment. *Mobility,* on the other hand, refers to the ability of an individual to move about in an environment. Before the student becomes a member of a classroom group, take time to acquaint the VH student with the layout, not only of the classroom but also of the entire school. Give the VH student time to become familiar and comfortable with the surroundings before expecting him or her to encounter a classroom and school full of students and teachers. The orientation may take place before school is in session or at some time when only the teacher and student can be in the classroom together.

Likewise, before the VH student enters a full classroom train the other students to assist the visually handicapped student. You are the key to preparing the other students to accept and help the VH student. They can guide the VH student around the confines of the classroom as well as around the school. When the VH student signals for help, the other students in the classroom must be ready to respond.

VH students must be taught to read by a multisensory approach that incorporates touch, smell, taste, and hearing. VH students rely heavily upon both auditory and tactile input to process information; therefore, base most instruction for them in both of these senses. Although instruction in phonics is an auditory approach to teaching reading, phonics is seldom taught to a blind student. The reason is that Braille, the main tool for reading for the blind, uses many abbreviations for common words. Because phonics and Braille do not complement each other, phonics is not an appropriate technique for teaching a VH student to read. Instead spoken descriptions and explanations and the handling of objects are essential.

Remember to explain vocabulary words and concepts in nonvisual terms. Provide several sensory experiences when possible. For example, instead of explaining that an apple has a red or green outer skin, is hard, and is usually sweet or tart, give the student several types of apples to handle, smell, and taste. Then describe the appearance of the apple for the student. In this way the concept of apple is fully developed even though the student is unable to see the apple. Concrete objects serve to allow a VH student to "see," but they should be accompanied by explanations. Sound effects are helpful when explaining concepts to VH students.

When teaching vocabulary sight words to a student with limited vision, use large clear pictures to explain ideas and to create language experience stories. Write messages on a blackboard and on labels used to identify objects around the classroom clearly and with very large, well-spaced letters. When presenting print and pictures to a student with limited vision, eliminate as many distractions as possible and provide clear, well-defined writings and objects. The use of contrasting colors such as white on black or yellow and black or dark blue allows the student to better identify the shapes and elements of a word.

The development of listening skills is essential for the VH student, so make the tape recorder your ally. All types of activities can be developed for use with the tape recorder. For example, the student can listen to stories or passages that you have recorded. The student can use the tape recorder to record the answers to taped questions about the passage. You and the student can play back the questions and answers to check for errors. Comprehension skills, such as getting the main idea and developing sequence, and higher level thinking skills can be developed with this activity. A VH student can also use the tape recorder to identify and to respond to various sounds in the environment, telling who or what made the sounds and how the sounds were made. This activity provides the student the opportunity to use and develop oral language fluency based on experiences in the environment. Such experiences help an individual appreciate that there is more to objects than their appearance.

Books with cassette recordings can develop a VH student's ability to understand and can encourage participation in group discussions. By listening to a taped story, a VH student encounters the same descriptions and explanations that a student with normal vision reads. The students have a common experience, which serves as a basis for discussion. You can tape questions to check the comprehension of a VH student after the student has listened to the taped book.

# Hearing Impaired

Students who are either deaf or hard-of-hearing are classified as hearing impaired. Inadequate auditory feedback and the inability to hear an adult model use language significantly detracts from these students' ability to acquire language, to produce speech, and to develop reading skill.

Most hearing impaired students mainstreamed into regular classrooms are capable of verbalizing and developing oral language skills. Many also know and use sign language to receive and to express ideas.

Before describing some strategies for teaching reading to a hearing impaired student, we present some general information to consider when developing an appropriate plan of reading instruction. Many hearing impaired students use some form of amplification, such as a hearing aid, to assist in the reception of spoken language. You should be aware of the student who is using amplification and develop knowledge of the workings of the instrument so that you can make minor adjustments to the instrument, such as changing the battery.

Before making plans for reading instruction, find out how old the student was at the time the hearing loss occurred. The older the student at the onset of a hearing loss, the greater the chance the student has acquired language normally. A student who has been hearing impaired since birth obviously will have a harder time developing and using a language system than a student who suffered a hearing loss at age seven or eight.

Consider also the student's level of intelligence. McConnell (1973), conducting studies of hearing impaired students, used intelligence tests that incorporate nonverbal variables. The students' hearing impairments did not result in depressed intellectual functioning. A hearing impaired student with a high IQ is more adept at developing strategies to compensate for the impairment, however, than a student who has less intellectual ability. Consequently, you have more freedom to vary instruction when teaching a capable student to use language.

Hearing impaired students do exhibit problems with all aspects of language—listening, speaking, reading, and writing—so consider the amount and quality of a student's language development when developing reading plans. A hearing impaired student who does not have a good language model and is not encouraged to use language at home and in daily life must work to develop the ability to use language before learning to read. A student who uses language well is more likely to acquire reading skill.

The hearing impaired student should sit where he or she can see you and other class members during class. This enables the student to employ both amplification and speech reading while attending to instruction. A hearing impaired student often learns best when seated near the front of a classroom; but before assigning a seat allow the student to experiment by sitting in different locations within the classroom. Then decide on a location that best suits the needs of both you and the student.

## Teaching Strategies

There are several strategies you should use when teaching a hearing impaired student as a member of a whole class or group. When teaching at the blackboard, first write on the board and then face the student to explain the idea or give directions. This gives the student an opportunity to see the words and to see you speak the words. In front of a group, avoid moving around, distorting speech, yelling, or placing your hands or any other object near your mouth. Each action detracts from the message and limits the student's ability to understand. Repeat ideas and instructions frequently, always rephrasing what has been said. The repetition of ideas enables a hearing impaired student to focus on ideas missed the first time. We suggest that teachers vary their statements because repeating statements verbatim is not so likely to help the student who failed to understand what was said the first time. Getting and maintaining the student's attention is crucial. Don't assume that because a hearing impaired student is looking in your direction that the student is following what you are saying; the student may be looking beyond you. Check often to see that the student understands directions, assignments, or discussions. Allow hearing impaired students to ask questions, and ask them to give feedback on just how well they understand.

Of course, you should avoid any system based on auditory discrimination. Phonics or sound-symbol relationships are not appropriate. A visual method in which new words and concepts are written down, spoken by you, and repeated by the student in a mimicking fashion works best. If a student has trouble reproducing the sound of a word, place the hand of the student on the speaker's larynx as the speaker says the word. Next, ask the student to place a hand on his or her own larynx while attempting to reproduce the sound of the word. Repeat this procedure as often as necessary until the student is able to produce the sound correctly. Words depicting concrete objects are easier for a hearing impaired student to learn than abstract terms because the student is able to develop an association between an object and the written letters that represent the object.

We suggest teaching sight words that have inherent value to the student and that can help the student to cope and to survive in the home, school, and community. Word cards identifying specific objects around the classroom can be helpful. When introducing new words, use the words in many different sentences and write the sentences down so the student can see the words. This improves the student's use of language skills.

Concrete objects, photographs, and illustrations provide excellent stimuli for developing vocabulary and comprehension skills. Encourage a student to make a picture dictionary, a scrapbook, or picture word cards. Use any of these materials for generating experiences and discussions. Employ the picture word cards, for example, to develop the skills of alphabetizing and categorization. The scrapbook can generate written stories, increasing the student's abilities to use language, to organize thoughts, and to write.

Previewing material to be covered in class is another strategy effective with a hearing impaired student. Previewing allows the student to prepare for a topic before the topic is discussed by the entire class, enabling the student to follow the class discussion with greater attention and ease.

Whatever strategies you select to use, focus on the student's language development by presenting reading in a visual mode.

## Gifted

Gifted readers are another category of exceptional learners found in the regular classroom during reading instruction. The characteristics of a gifted reader are significantly different from the characteristics of an EMH student, a hearing impaired learner, and the other types of exceptional learners.

Federal law (PL 95-561) describes gifted students as possessing demonstrated or potential abilities that give evidence of high performance capabilities in such areas as intellectual functioning, creativity, specific academic ability, leadership ability, and the performing or visual arts. In education, three characteristics are used to identify gifted students: high degree of ability, including high intelligence; high creativity, which includes the ability to formulate new ideas and apply the ideas to solve problems; and a high degree of commitment and motivation to see projects through to completion.

Gifted readers, when working up to their ability levels, are likely to read two or more grade levels above their grade placement. That is, a gifted fourth-grade reader may decode and comprehend material at a sixth or eighth or tenth grade level.

In the not too distant past, gifted readers were intellectually and instructionally neglected. Teachers, in general, have failed to challenge them to develop their reading ability to the fullest. Likewise, teachers have failed to make use of the abilities of gifted readers in classrooms. Creative, sensitive teachers can help gifted readers to be assets in the classroom by setting them as models of reading for less adept readers.

For too long gifted readers have been required to trudge through basal readers and accompanying workbooks just as the average readers have had to do even though the reading ability of a gifted reader may far exceed the level of the basal reader. Even the story content of the basal reader may offer little interest and challenge to gifted readers. They may complete their work but never feel challenged to excel in areas in which they show great potential.

## Teaching Strategies

How can you challenge a gifted reader? First, we recommend a variety of approaches beyond the basal reader. While basal readers may provide a core for skill development, you should also guide the student in developing a reading program based on library and trade books. Once you have determined general reading ability, take time to converse with the reader about general interests and, in particular, reading interests. Identify the types of stories the student likes to read, discover the student's favorite authors, and discuss other interests relevant to reading before compiling a list of books to be read based on those interests and the student's reading level. (See Appendix C for some suggestions.) Allow the student to suggest materials for the list. The school librarian may also be able to make some suggestions.

*We encourage you to involve other classroom teachers by asking them to make book suggestions based on any special talents or interests they may be willing to share with the gifted reader.*

Next describe some activities and goals the gifted reader can work toward while you teach the other class members in reading groups. Make the goals and expectations very explicit, stating exactly when the student is to meet with you, the amount of reading the student is expected to accomplish, and what is to happen during each meeting. Gifted readers do not need to meet with you for reading instruction each day. We recommend that you meet once every two days with students in grades one to

Challenge your gifted students. (Photo by Strix Pix)

three and once per week with gifted readers in grades four and beyond. Make sure the students understand each assignment and when each task is to be completed. Once the preliminaries are taken care of, let the students read.

Unless a gifted reader demonstrates a specific reading problem, do not provide subskill instruction in decoding and comprehension. The reader is developing and applying subskill abilities by reading. If a student does exhibit some skill need, teach and practice the specific subskill in conjunction with the book the student is currently reading. Instruction of this type provides for direct application of the skill.

In addition to reading many books, the gifted reader should have opportunities to demonstrate understanding of the material being read. Caution! Be selective in evaluating a student's progress and avoid the use of tests. We have found that oral discussions that require the reader to relate what has been read to real-life circumstances yield an enormous amount of information about the student's ability to apply higher levels of thinking (evaluating, synthesizing, abstracting, and assimilating). The discussions enable the student and teacher to share ideas and experiences, and to build a relationship.

Activities that incorporate writing skills help develop gifted readers' ability. Encourage them to rewrite an ending to a story, write a description of the personality of a main character, or even write a sequel to a story. Suggest that they create various forms of artwork depicting books or parts of books. Teach gifted readers to acquire more information about a topic through research techniques. Have them draw on a number of sources to write about a topic. Writing tasks can allow gifted readers to expand their thinking abilities beyond the cover of a book.

In addition to encouraging the gifted reader's direct involvement in specific reading activities, you may wish to invite the gifted reader to help tutor students with less reading ability. We have observed fifth-grade gifted readers working with kindergarten students to develop their skills of letter identification and letter-sound matching, fourth-grade gifted children reading to second graders experiencing reading difficulties, and sixth-grade gifted readers helping fellow sixth graders develop vocabulary knowledge. Of course, some of the student exchanges must be planned in conjuction with other classroom teachers. Take care to match students who work well with each other. Once working relationships are established the gifted reader can be an added resource in the classroom reading program.

# Summary

Since the passage and implementation of Public Law 94-142, students with exceptional learning needs (educable mentally handicapped, learning disabled, emotionally handicapped, visually handicapped, hearing impaired, and gifted) have been mainstreamed into regular classrooms. Classroom teachers must be able to plan and deliver reading instruction that meets the various special needs of these exceptional learners.

No "bag of tricks" for teaching learners with exceptional needs exists. Rather, teaching them requires patience, planning, knowledge of the characteristics of the various categories of exceptional learners, knowledge of the reading process, and hard work.

Classroom teachers should work together with learning specialists assigned to their school building or school district to develop plans for teaching exceptional learners to read. Some general teaching practices for working with exceptional learners are a) plan small steps of instruction; b) expect small increments of change; c) identify specific goals; d) maintain a flexible approach, e) use modeling, prompting, and shaping strategies; f) provide for review of previously learned skills; and g) provide for generalization and transfer of learning. We also present specific suggestions for teaching reading to particular categories of exceptional students.

Special characteristics such as intelligence, behavior, and language development of each exceptional student must be considered before instruction begins. The strategies presented in this chapter are designed to help the classroom teacher generate ideas for implementing instructional plans appropriate to the reading needs of a variety of exceptional students.

# References

Bond, G. R., & Tinker, M. A. (1973). *Reading difficulties, their diagnosis and correction* (3rd ed.). Englewood Cliffs, NJ: Prentice-Hall.

Borko, H., Shavelson, R. J., & Stern, P. (1981). Teacher's decisions in the planning of reading instruction. *Reading Research Quarterly, 16* (3), 449–466.

Chall, J. (1967). *Learning to read: The great debate.* New York: McGraw-Hill.

Duffy, G. G. (1983). From turn taking to sense making: broadening the concept of reading teacher effectiveness. *Journal of Educational Research, 76,* 134–139.

Dunn, L. M. (1973). Children with moderate and severe general learning disabilities. In L. S. Dunn (Ed.), *Exceptional children in the schools* (2nd ed.). New York: Holt, Rinehart & Winston, 127–190.

Fernald, G. M. (1943). *Remedial techniques in basic school projects.* New York: McGraw-Hill.

Gajar, A. H. (1980). Characteristics across exceptional categories: EMR, LD, ED. *Journal of Special Education, 14,* 165–173.

Grossman, H. J. (1973). *Manual on terminology and classification in mental retardation.* Baltimore: Garamond-Pridemark.

Hallahan, D. P., & Kauffman, J. M. (1982). *Exceptional children: Introduction to special education* (2nd ed.). Englewood Cliffs, NJ: Prentice-Hall.

Hayes, S. P. (1950). Measuring the intelligence of the blind. In P. A. Zahl (Ed.), *Blindness.* Princeton, NJ: Princeton University Press.

Heckelman, R. G. (1969). A neurological impress method of reading instruction. *Academic Theory, 4* (4), 277–282.

Kappelman, M. K., Kaplan, E., & Ganter, R. L. (1976). A study of learning disorders among disadvantaged children. *Journal of Learning Disabilities, 10,* 411–419.

Kauffman, J. M. (1981). *Characteristics of children's behavior disorders* (2nd ed.). Columbus, OH: Charles E. Merrill.

Kirk, S. A. (1962). *Educating exceptional children.* Boston: Houghton Mifflin.

Kirk, S. A., & Bateman, B. (1962). Diagnosis and remediation of learning disabilities. *Exceptional Children, 29* (2), 73–78.

Kirk, S. A., & Elkins, J. (1975). Characteristics of children enrolled in the child service demonstration centers. *Journal of Learning Disabilities, 8* (10), 31–38.

Kirk, S. A., Kliebhan, S. J. M., & Learner, J. W. (1978). *Teaching reading to slow and disabled learners.* Boston: Houghton Mifflin.

McConnell, F. (1973). Children with hearing disabilities. In L. M. Dunn (Ed.), *Exceptional children in the schools: Special education in transition* (2nd ed.). New York: Holt, Rinehart & Winston.

McDermott, R. P. (1976). Achieving school failure: An anthropological approach to illiteracy and social stratification. In H. Singer and R. Ruddell (Eds.), *Theoretical models and processes of reading.* Newark, DE: International Reading Association.

McGinnis, D. J., & Smith, D. E. (1982). *Analyzing and treating reading problems.* New York: Macmillan.

Morse, W. C., Cutler, R. L., & Fink, A. H. (1964). *Public school classes for the emotionally handicapped: A research analysis.* Washington, DC: Council for Exceptional Children.

National Advisory Committee on Handicapped Children. (1968). *Special education for handicapped children: First annual report.* Washington, DC: U.S. Department of Health, Education, and Welfare.

Otto, W. R., & Chester, R. D. (1976). *Objective-based reading.* Reading, MA: Addison-Wesley.

Otto, W. R., & Smith, R. J. (1980). *Corrective and remedial reading* (3rd ed.). Boston: Houghton Mifflin.

*Public Law 94-142, Education for All Handicapped Children Act of 1975.* Washington, DC: U.S. Office of Education.

Quay, H. S. (1972). Patterns of aggression, withdrawal and immaturity. In H. C. Quay & J. S. Werry (Eds.), *Psychopathological disorders of childhood.* New York: Wiley.

Richek, M. A., List, L. K., & Lerner, J. W. (1983). *Reading problems diagnosis and remediation.* Englewood Cliffs, NJ: Prentice-Hall.

Spache, George D. (1976). *Diagnosing and correcting reading disabilities.* Boston: Allyn & Bacon.

Wallace, G., & Kauffman, J. M. (1978). *Teaching children with learning problems* (2nd ed.). Columbus, OH: Charles E. Merrill.

Wallace, G., & McLoughlin, J. A. (1979). *Learning disabilities: Concepts and characteristics* (2nd ed.). Columbus, OH: Charles E. Merrill.

Wepman, J. M., Cruickshank, W. M., Deutsch, C. P., Morency, A., & Strother, C. R. (1975). Learning disabilities. In N. Hobbs (Ed.), *Issues in the classification of children* (Vol. 1). San Francisco: Jossey-Bass.

# Check Your Reading Comprehension

1. What are some of the guidelines to keep in mind when attempting to obtain information about exceptional students? What other types of information might be helpful?

2. Consider the skill of identifying sequence in a passage of reading material. Respond to items a–h with a particular exceptional child in mind.
   a. Identify two small steps of instruction that you should include in teaching sequencing. (Note: Identify subskills, not activities.)
   b. What might be a realistic expectation of change over a series of three days of lessons?
   c. Identify two specific goals for the learner. (Note: These could be related to your answer to a).
   d. Describe three approaches or methods for instruction that relate to one of your objectives in c.
   e. Identify a strategy (modeling, prompting, or shaping) appropriate for this series of lessons.
   f. Prepare an activity for one of your objectives that would allow for guided practice.
   g. Identify two previously learned skills that should be reviewed as part of this series of lessons.
   h. How might you provide for transfer of this skill to other areas of the curriculum?

**3.** Matching exercise:

_____ **1.** Modeling

_____ **2.** Prompting

_____ **3.** Shaping

_____ **4.** VAKT

_____ **5.** Neurological impress

_____ **6.** Orientation

_____ **7.** Mobility

_____ **8.** Multisensory approach

**a.** An individual's spatial placement in relation to other objects within an environment.

**b.** Fernald method; incorporates language experience and kinesthetic techniques in learning word forms.

**c.** An instructional strategy that involves providing clues and/or partial answers for the learner

**d.** An instructional approach that incorporates the senses of sight, touch, smell, taste, and hearing.

**e.** The ability of an individual to move about in an environment.

**f.** Method in which poor reader reads material in unison with good reader; described by Heckelman.

**g.** An instructional strategy by which the teacher demonstrates a skill for the learner.

**h.** A step-by-step process in which learning is fashioned by the teacher's responses to actions taken by the student.

Answers:

| | |
|---|---|
| 8. d | 4. b |
| 7. e | 3. h |
| 6. a | 2. c |
| 5. f | 1. g |

**4.** There is often an overlap of exceptionalities. Suppose you have a child in your classroom who is visually handicapped and emotionally handicapped. What provisions might you make in teaching this child?

**5.** Consider the following statements from this chapter:

> Gifted readers are another category of exceptional learners found in the regular classroom during reading instruction.

> In the not too distant past, gifted readers were intellectually and instructionally neglected.

Argue both the *pro* and *con* side of each issue.

# 16

# Bilingual Children

In Chapter 1 we met Maria. Unlike Joe, who was mainstreamed from an EMR class, Maria appears to have at least average potential for learning. She was considered a "special needs" student in Chapter 1 because English is not her native language. Many of the good practices in reading instruction that have already been described in the preceding chapters are appropriate for Maria. In this chapter we provide some background information that may be helpful in understanding children like Maria.

**Written by Drs. Joseph O. Prewitt Diaz, Assistant Professor of Education, and Eunice N. Askov, Professor of Education, The Pennsylvania State University.**

Approximately 3.6 million school age children (between the ages of 4 and 18) in the United States are like Maria: they have only limited speaking, reading, and writing skills in English (Bell, 1982; Rorberg, 1982). Bell (1982) reports that only 6 percent of the Limited English Proficiency (LEP) children are receiving instruction that includes assessment of English proficiency, provision of instruction in all instructional areas, and at least five hours weekly of English instruction.

Bilingual education programs have been created to accommodate children like Maria but ordinarily can be operated only in communities that have a large enough non-English speaking population to warrant them. Maria's family is among several Spanish-speaking families, but they do not constitute a large enough group for the school district to offer a bilingual education program. Bell (1982) also indicates that LEP students in the upper grades are less likely to be served by bilingual programs.

Current estimates of the language minority population in the United States (Bell, 1982; O'Malley, 1981) indicate the following:

- An estimated 28 million people in the United States in 1976 had language backgrounds other than English.
- Language minority people in the United States are mostly native born.
- The largest language minority group is Spanish.
- The population of LEP children is concentrated in three states: California, New York, and Texas.
- The number of LEP children in the United States is projected to increase by about 35 percent by the year 2000.
- Ninety-two percent, or 2.7 million, of the projected increase in the LEP children will have Spanish-language background.

These figures do not include immigration from the Caribbean, but they do allow for immigration that may result from political or economic upheavals in the future (Bell, 1982).

The Bilingual Education Act was enacted by Congress in 1968 and amended in 1978 (Public Law 95-561). This act is commonly known as Title VII of the Elementary and Secondary Education Act. The intent of the law is to establish equal opportunity for all children. It encourages the establishment and operation of educational programs using bilingual educational practices, techniques, and methods; and it provides financial assistance to local and state educational agencies.

According to Public Law 95-561, bilingual education programs are defined as follows:

> Instruction given in, and study of, English and, to the extent necessary to allow a child to achieve competence in the English language, the native language of the LEP children, and such instruction is given with appreciation for the cultural heritage of such children and of other children in American society . . . (92 Stat. 2270, 20 USC 3223).

The literature on bilingual education identifies at least four different types of approaches used in the United States. In the first approach instruction is offered in two languages, with the content areas being taught in the student's native language. This is to enable students to function in another language in addition to their native language, with or without equal proficiency (Ogletree, 1976). Usually an English-as-a-Second-Language (ESL) teacher and a reading specialist work with the nonnative speakers. Because they are given remedial reading instruction, they are often grouped with native (English) speakers who have reading difficulties.

A second approach is a bilingual/bicultural approach (Condon, 1974). This calls for instruction in, and reinforcement of, the native language and culture as well as the new, or second, language and culture. The greater emphasis on the native culture sometimes leads to less emphasis on the content areas.

A third approach, described by Fishman and Keller (1982), is the transitional bilingual approach. Students learn English with little or no reinforcement of the native language, except as a starting point to help them make the transition from their native language to English as soon as possible. This approach is based on the "melting pot" concept that all people who come to the United States should give up their native language and culture to be assimilated into the mainstream of the American society and the English language.

In contrast, a fourth approach is to maintain bilingual education (Cohen, 1979). This approach advocates a self-sustaining, continuous program for developing the native language while teaching English to an equal level of proficiency. An example of this approach is found in Dade County, Florida, where one language group (Cuban) has achieved the social status necessary to make Spanish acceptable as an alternative language. This approach is based on cultural pluralism, which recognizes the legitimate right of other languages and cultures in the classroom. This approach is usually possible only when political equality has been achieved by the non–English-speaking group.

*The type of community you teach in is likely to determine the approach to bilingual education. If there are enough non–English-speaking children to warrant a bilingual education program, the approach selected will be influenced by political and economic factors in the community. Considering the growing numbers of non–English-speaking people in the United States, you will probably have some of these children in your classroom. In most states school districts are obligated to provide some type of special assistance to them, but it may be only English-as-a-Second-Language (ESL) instruction rather than an extensive bilingual education program. As the classroom teacher you are responsible for helping these children adjust to a new language and culture.*

# Bilingualism

A range of definitions exists in the literature for bilingualism. These definitions extend from knowledge of the mother tongue with only a slight knowledge of a second language to a command of both languages.

Two types of bilingualism have been studied closely: compound and coordinate (Weinreich, 1953). *Compound* bilinguals have a single underlying semantic, or meaning, network with two distinct modes of expression. In other words, a person has a single set of meaningful associations for a concept, such as freedom of speech, but two different sets of terminology (perhaps one in English and one in Spanish) associated with the concept. Usually compound bilingual children have developed two languages in their early home life.

On the other hand, *coordinate* bilinguals have separate semantic systems. In this group are persons who have learned the second language in school. Such is the case of most of the children, like Maria, you will meet in your classroom. A concept, such as freedom of speech, with associated vocabulary terms, must be developed separately in each language.

The question of whether students are compound or coordinate bilingual is confounded by the age at which they acquired the second language (Rivers, 1983b; Snow and Hoefnagel-Höhle, 1982). A person acquiring two languages in infancy is likely to do so in a different environmental context than individuals acquiring a second language at a later time.

While some tests do exist to determine the type of bilingualism of a given person, the classroom teacher would not be concerned with this type of assessment. Our intent is simply to let you know that different types of bilingualism exist and that you will have children in your classroom with varying degrees of English language competence. The bilingual students in your classroom may be of either type. Furthermore, they might range from having limited reading skills in the native and second languages to being proficient readers in the native language.

# The Bilingual Child

Not all bilingual children are alike. There are three basic types of bilingual children in the United States: the American bilingual child, the immigrant child, and the Limited English Proficiency (LEP) child.

## The American Bilingual Child

The American bilingual child is usually the child of parents who are American citizens but whose native language is other than English. For example, a Puerto Rican family may have lived in mainland United States for less than ten years; they have preserved their native language (Spanish) in the home, church, and neighborhood. The children in this family may have been in the mainland schools all of their school lives. Such children are generally able to shift from their native language to English and vice versa with ease (Simoes, 1979).

Many Puerto Rican children, however, may need to maintain both English and Spanish because they frequently travel back and forth between Puerto Rico and the mainland. In fact, bilingual students range from recent arrivals who do not speak English to students who have spent all their school lives on the mainland and still have poor skills in both Spanish and English (Prewitt Diaz, 1979). Discrepancies between the home and school expectations of the Spanish language skills for these children may result in the children developing resistance to learning English. The students, to bridge the home-school discrepancy, may speak English with a heavy accent to emphasize their Hispanicity (Prewitt Diaz, 1981).

## The Immigrant Child

Immigrant children are children of people who have migrated to the United States and who are contemplating permanent settlement (Gonzalez, 1979; Fishman & Keller, 1982). This group is mainly composed of Asians in the west, Haitians and Cubans in the southeast, Portuguese and Dominicans in the northeast, and Mexicans in the south-southwest. The parents of immigrant children have usually come to the United States because of political and economic problems in their homelands. They want to integrate themselves into the majority community and become American citizens (Gonzalez, 1979). Therefore, they emphasize the learning of English as soon as possible.

Immigrant children from an Asiatic background may have problems both learning a new alphabet and language system, and adapting from an agricultural environment to a highly technical society (Chu-Chang, 1979). Many of these children, however, began the process of learning to speak English in refugee camps. In fact, some of these children might have developed relatively proficient speaking, reading, and writing skills in their native language (Izzo, 1981). It is important to recognize these skills and use them in developing English-language skills.

## The Limited English Proficiency (LEP) Child

LEP children may have been in U.S. schools for a year or more or for all their school lives. They have usually participated in an ESL program and are now in the regular program. While they are able to speak English well enough to get along in everyday life, they have not developed the skills that would allow them to read and understand content materials written in English (Cohen, 1979). The emphasis of instruction should be upon concept acquisition, concept formation, and concept development in English (Bratt-Paulston, 1980). LEP students, however, typically have difficulty incorporating the vocabulary and concepts of the content areas into their current English vocabulary (Izzo, 1981). As a result, they may act shy and embarrassed in the content area classroom about their level of comprehension of the English language.

While all these bilingual children need opportunities for both acquiring and learning about English, all language learning should be kept in context, since this is the way humans develop their native language (Feeley, 1983; Gonzales, 1981; Wheat, Galen, & Norwood, 1979).

# Teaching Bilingual Students to Read

There are basically two approaches to reading instruction in a second language, in this case English. Kupinsky (1983) suggests that one approach is to foster oral mastery for one or two years, and then to provide reading instruction. The second approach consists of teaching oral language skills using controlled materials, at each step teaching the students to read the language just mastered (Cohen, 1979; Gonzales, 1981; Krashen, 1981). While some research (Downing, 1984; Elley and Mangubhai, 1983) suggests that the former approach may be more productive in teaching beginning reading, the philosophy of the school district in which you are teaching will probably determine the approach you use.

Bilingual students, like their native– English-speaking classmates, differ in their individual ways of learning. They need opportunities to try different approaches, ask questions, share ideas, react to situations, and test their ideas and the ideas of other people. The classroom instructional setting should fulfill the student's social and psychological needs. The success or failure of the developmental process of reading depends in large part on the sensitivity of the teacher toward the student's environment and culture (Carrasquillo, 1978).

## Language Experience Approach (LEA)

Described in previous chapters, the language experience approach is also particularly useful in teaching nonnative speakers to read in English. (Feeley, 1979). LEA emphasizes the integration of listening, speaking, reading, and writing, which are listed in the usual order of acquisition for native speakers. The traditional ESL approach tends to emphasize the first two communication areas with little attention paid to reading and writing. If the nonnative speakers in a classroom are receiving ESL instruction in addition to the regular curriculum, you must coordinate efforts closely with the ESL teacher. You can incorporate vocabulary and English skills that the ESL teacher is working on into LEA reading lessons.

Many authorities (Feeley, 1983; Izzo, 1981; and Simoes, 1979) recommend that students act out social situations with accompanying appropriate language. Good citizenship can be reinforced through a series of drills on communication skills pertaining to the home, school, and community. The student might, therefore, either in an ESL class or the regular classroom, role play taking a note from home to the office. Afterwards, the student could dictate reflections about the experience or the language used in the experience as you write it on chart paper. This story becomes the reading material from which to teach reading vocabulary and skills.

Target words that should be taught as part of the lesson can be incorporated into the LEA story while still using the children's own language. (Recall that students use the familiar words and syntax of the story as cues to word recongition. If you substantially rearrange what the students say or substitute different words, the context will no longer provide cues to word recognition.) Write the target words—those from the role playing or from any experience that should be learned in reading—on the board. The students should then dictate a story about their role playing or experience, incorporating those words. Not only do the students learn the target words, but they also gain better understanding of their meanings by having to use them appropriately in sentences in the stories.

Any school or classroom event can provide the basis for an LEA story. But most important in teaching nonnative speakers is the oral language that precedes the dictation of the story. While this step occurs in using LEA with native speakers, it is even more crucial for students like Maria. They must first hear and speak the words that they will later use in their dictated stories. Rivers (1983b) and Thonis (1976) stress that listening and speaking must precede any reading task. Role playing, dialogues, and skits enacting social situations are even more helpful than discussion because they are more concrete and more easily understood. They help students adjust to new social situations and customs as well as to a new language (Rivers, 1983a).

It is important to base English LEA stories on school experiences when working with coordinate bilingual children—those who have usually learned English in school and who have separate meaning systems for words in their native language and in English. Coordinate bilingual children lack the English vocabulary to talk about their homes and families because these personal experiences are all coded in their native language. (They may also have difficulty talking about their school learning, which is in English, to their family in their native language.) Since most LEP children have learned English only in school, and hence are coordinate bilinguals, you must be aware of the difficulties that they may have if asked to share home and family experiences in English.

Key words variation of the Language Experience Approach (LEA).
(Photo by Jean Greenwald)

A variation on the LEA has been formulated by Veatch, Sawicki, Elliott, Barnette, and Blakey (1979), based on Sylvia Ashton-Warner's (1963) approach to teaching the Maori children in New Zealand, as described in Chapter 6. The key words approach suggests that the student (or a group of students working together) say one word that is important to him or her, which is recorded on an index card with a sentence. Each day the student uses those key words in reading and writing. As the words become known, they are separated from the new words studied each day. The important point is that the individual student or group of students supplies the words to be learned, which are, therefore, of more interest and importance and are more easily learned.

As students become more proficient in English, their stories can become more sophisticated. We know of one teacher who used LEA to have the students write letters to friends and relatives in their homeland. This became more than a reading lesson as the students wrote of their personal concerns in their new country. It made the teacher more sensitive to their problems as well as gave them the feeling that the teacher cared about them and their difficulties.

## Cloze Technique

The cloze technique has been discussed in previous chapters both as a measure of text readability and as an instructional tool. Although it is used quite frequently in teaching reading to nonnative speakers, it is difficult for those who lack the native, intuitive sense of the English language. Consequently, it is not an accurate test of whether or not an individual can read a given selection of reading material. But it can help build a sense of context. You can use the cloze with the LEA stories, deleting target words for the students to supply (rather than deleting every fifth word as described in Chapter 5). Or you may choose to delete only nouns or verbs or some other part of speech that the students are learning about in ESL or classroom instruction. Delete sparingly at first until the students learn how to use context.

We recommend the instructional use of cloze as described because it places emphasis on the meanings of words. Nonnative speakers may learn to decode fairly easily, especially if they already know how to read in their native language, but understanding the meaning of what they read is often difficult. The student may decode the symbols and produce the words, but the words fail to trigger an image or reference because the concept represented does not exist for the student or exists in only a limited, vague form (Cohen, 1979; Ebel, 1981; Rivers, 1983b). Do not assume that because the students can say the words they can actually understand the message of the author. The cloze technique helps the student focus on the meaning of a reading selection as well as on the meanings of the words.

## Sentence Patterns

ESL teachers often teach English by using common sentence patterns. One pattern may be used in forming a question and answer pertaining to an everyday situation. For example, the basic sentence pattern Noun + Intransitive Verb + Adverb is used in this dialogue:

"Where are you going?"

"I am going to the supermarket."

(The interrogative "where" and the prepositional phrase "to the supermarket" function as adverbs in this pattern.)

Similarly, you can use sentence patterns in teaching reading. (See May, 1982, for instruction in the basic sentence patterns.) McCracken and McCracken (1972) suggest using a basic sentence pattern with a model sentence. For example, you might select the pattern Noun + Transitive Verb + Noun, in which the first noun functions as the subject and the second noun functions as the direct object. You should write the example sentence on the chalkboard: *The dog bit his brother.* Ask students to come to the board and write words that could be substituted for the various parts of speech. You can have the students act out each new sentence to clarify meaning. Point out what are nonsense sentences (such as *The bridge bit his head* ) so as not to lose meaning. For variety you can also write words on index cards, which the students sort into the function in the sentence and use in creating new sentences. The students can also select one of these sentences to be the first sentence in a paragraph that they write.

Another writing activity—dictation (see Chapter 12)—combined with the study of sentence patterns, is particularly helpful in teaching nonnative speakers to read in English. Read aloud a brief paragraph containing mainly examples of the target sentence pattern being taught. The students write what they think you are saying. Knowledge of the sentence pattern assists them in knowing the positions of the nouns and verbs in the sentences. Dictation reinforces this knowledge and provides practice in applying letter-sound knowledge.

## Concept Development

As mentioned earlier in this chapter, nonnative speakers of English need to develop concepts in English. Vocabulary development is related, especially in the words that are concept labels. The word *democracy* is a concept label; its meaning extends beyond a dictionary definition to a set of associations and understandings. Unfortunately, these understandings are so ingrained in our culture and language that we often do not recognize them as trouble spots for nonnative speakers. Carefully analyze a reading selection to determine what underlying concepts might cause difficulty for someone new to the English language and American culture. Robinett (1978) refers to this process as cultural reading readiness, which is essential if students are to comprehend the meaning of a selection.

Dale's Cone of Experience (1969) is presented in Figure 16.1 as a guide in developing concepts. All elementary school-age children develop concepts better when the learning experience is closer to the bottom of the cone. Nonnative speakers especially need as many concrete experiences as possible in developing concepts.

Take the example of the concepts associated with the words *centrifugal force.* If you simply assign a reading selection from a textbook that explains centrifugal force, the students would be learning about the concept through verbal symbols, the least effective approach to concept development. On the other hand, if you or the students

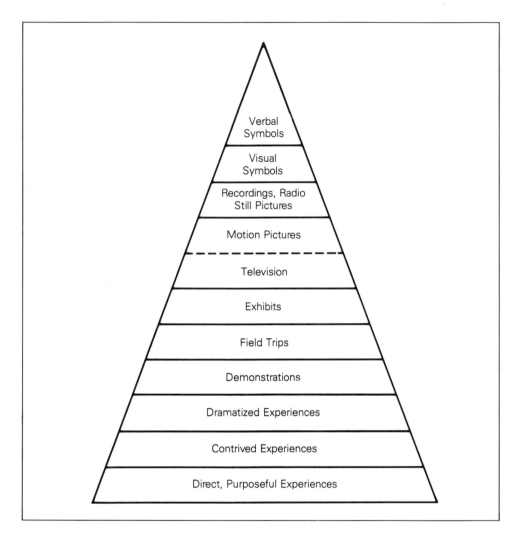

**Figure 16.1** Dale's Cone of Experience. From AUDIOVISUAL METHODS IN TEACH-ING, 3rd ed., by Edgar Dale. Copyright © 1969 by Holt, Rinehart and Winston. Reprinted by permission of Holt, Rinehart and Winston, CBS College Publishing.

swing partially filled buckets of water in circles overhead, the students directly experience centrifugal force (and perhaps also wet clothes!). They would come to a better understanding of this science concept through direct, purposeful experiences.

We know of a teacher who was particularly sensitive to the need to develop background concepts among the nonnative speakers in her classroom. She wanted the students in one of her instructional reading groups to read a story in a basal reader that pertained to a handicapped girl who was confined to a wheelchair. The teacher was unsure what level of understanding any of her students had with regard to the concept of being handicapped. She began the development of the concept with direct, purposeful experiences by arranging to borrow several wheelchairs from the local hospital. The students faced the problems of being confined to wheelchairs as they tried to get through a normal school day with a partner assigned to help. Next, the teacher planned a guest speaker who was handicapped to provide demonstrations of the difficulties of a person confined to a wheelchair. The teacher had also clipped pictures of handicapped children doing normal activities for a bulletin board, thus using visual symbols. After that concept development she felt the students were ready to read the basal story meaningfully because they would better understand how it feels to be handicapped.

Concept development should be part of the directed reading-thinking activity described in Chapter 9. Because it is closely related to vocabulary development, the two processes should be thought of together. Concept development, however, involves a whole host of related understandings that go beyond the mere dictionary definition of a word.

The use of media, while listed only at mid-level on the cone in Figure 16.1, can be very useful in developing concepts for non–English-speaking children. Films that portray historical events, for example, can make concepts associated with a period of history understandable. Sometimes direct, purposeful experiences are not possible or practical, given the demands of the school day. Then films, filmstrips, videotapes, audiotapes, pictures, and other media presentations can serve as good substitutes in concept development.

A variety of reading experiences is also important in developing concepts. Read to the students materials that they cannot read on their own. Discussion, as well as enhancing social and emotional communication, lets you know whether they have understood what you have read. Stimulating recreational reading helps fluency in reading and positive attitudes toward reading. Listening centers containing tapes of good children's literature; filmstrips related to children's literature; a library containing high interest, easy-to-read books in English and the students' first language; storytelling, by both teacher and students; and projects, such as dioramas and puppet shows, all help nonnative speakers develop concepts while learning to read.

Feeley (1983) suggests that when dealing with children whose first language is not English, teachers in English-speaking classrooms must help the nonnative speakers build up a store of knowledge about English vocabulary. You are responsible for providing direction to the children in their process of becoming proficient in English. As Krashen (1981) has suggested, while the children acquire English from their peers and neighbors, they still need formal language learning experiences, especially those related to reading, provided by teachers.

In teaching children who do not speak English as a native language, you must move gradually from the known to the unknown. It is important to build on the experiences that they have had, remembering that some of them may have had to endure hardships that we would never dream of. Refugees, for example, are the survivors who have had to leave family and friends behind in their homelands. We need to respect these children for what they have endured and give them the chance that they deserve in their new country. Never view them as liabilities in the classroom, but as students with special needs who have much to contribute.

# Summary

The number of non–English-speaking students is increasing; the regular classroom teacher is a key person in helping them not only learn to read in English but to function in our culture. The Bilingual Education Act guarantees that these students will be appropriately educated. Bilingual children may be categorized into the American bilingual child, the immigrant child, and the Limited English Proficiency (LEP) child. You should stress oral language as an important prerequisite to reading. Coordination with the student's English-as-a-Second Language (ESL) teacher is essential. Instruction using the language experience approach (LEA), cloze technique, sentence patterns combined with writing, and concept development is appropriate when teaching these nonnative speakers.

# References

Ashton-Warner, S. (1963). *Teacher*. New York: Simon and Schuster.

Barnitz, J. G. (1982). Orthographics, bilingualism and learning to read English as a second language. *The Reading Teacher, 35* (2), 154 – 163.

Bell, T. H. (1982). *The condition of bilingual education in the nation: 1982*. Rosslyn, VA: Inter America Research Associates.

Bratt-Paulston, C. (1980). *Bilingual education: theories and issues*. Rowley, MA: Newbury House Publishers.

Carrasquillo, A. (1978). Integrated reading approaches for bilingual learners. In H. La Fontaine, B. Persky, and L. H. Golubchick (Eds.), *Bilingual Education*. Wayne, NJ: Avery Publishing Group.

Chu-Chang, M. (1979). Procedures in curriculum education. In M. Montero (Ed.), *Bilingual Education Teacher Handbook*. Cambridge, MA: National Assessment and Dissemination Center.

Cohen, B. (1979). *Models and methods for bilingual education*. New York: Teaching Resources Corporation.

Condon, E. C. (1974). Bilingual/bicultural education. *New Jersey Education Association Review, 10,* 9 – 10.

Dale, E. (1969). *Audiovisual methods in teaching* (3rd ed.). New York: Holt, Rinehart & Winston.

Downing, J. (1984). A source of cognitive confusion for beginning readers: learning in a second language. *The Reading Teacher 37* (4), 366 – 370.

Ebel, C. W. (1981). An update: teaching reading to students of English as a second language. *The Reading Teacher, 33* (4), 403 – 407.

Elley, W. B., & Mangubhai, F. (1983). The impact of reading and second language learning. *Reading Research Quarterly, 19* (1), 53 – 67.

Feeley, J. T. (1979). A workshop tried and true: language experience for bilinguals. *The Reading Teacher, 33* (1), 25 – 27.

Feeley, J. T. (1983). Help for the reading teacher: dealing with the limited English proficient (LEP) child in the elementary classroom. *The Reading Teacher, 36* (7), 650 – 655.

Fishman, J. A., & Keller, G. D. (1982). *Bilingual education for Hispanic students in the United States.* New York: Teacher College Press.

Gonzalez, J. (1979). Coming of age in bilingual/bicultural education: a historical perspective. In H. T. Trueba and C. Barnett-Mizran (Eds.), *Bilingual Multicultural Education and the Professional.* Rowley, MA: Newbury House Publishers.

Gonzales, P. C. (1981). Beginning English reading for ESL students. *The Reading Teacher, 35* (2), 154–163.

Izzo, S. (1981). *Second language learning: a review of related studies.* Rosslyn, VA: National Clearinghouse for Bilingual Education.

Krashen, S. D. (1981). *Second language acquisition and second language learning.* Oxford, England: Pergamon Press.

Kupinsky, B. Z. (1983). Bilingual reading instruction in kindergarten. *The Reading Teacher, 37* (2), 132–137.

May, F. B. (1982). *Reading as communication.* Columbus, OH: Charles E. Merrill.

McCracken, R. A., & McCracken, M. J. (1972). *Reading is only the tiger's tail: a language arts program.* San Rafael, CA: Leswing Press.

Ogletree, E. J. (1976). Chicago teachers accept integration, but reject the plans. *Illinois School Journal, 56,* 56–60.

O'Malley, J. M. (1981). *Children's English and services study: language minority children with limited English proficiency in the United States.* Washington, DC: National Clearinghouse for Bilingual Education.

Prewitt Diaz, J. O. (1979). A report of the perceptions of newly arrived Puerto Rican students concerning home-school behavior discrepancies. *Revista Cayey, 13* (3), 32–38.

Prewitt Diaz, J. O. (1981). Considerations for the development of a reading program for Puerto Rican bilingual students. *Reading Improvement, 18* (4), 302–307.

Rivers, W. E. (1983a). *Communicating naturally in a second language.* New York: Cambridge University Press.

Rivers, W. E. (1983b). *Speaking in many tongues* (3rd ed.). New York: Cambridge University Press.

Robinett, B. W. (1978). *Teaching English to speakers of other languages.* Minneapolis, MN: University of Minnesota Press.

Rorberg, I. C. (1982). Federal policy in bilingual education. *Harvard Educational Review, 52* (2), 30–39.

Simoes, A., Jr. (1979). The system-context approach to curriculum theory in bilingual education. In M. Montero (Ed.), *Bilingual Education Teacher Handbook.* Cambridge, MA: National Assessment and Dissemination Center.

Snow, C. E., & Hoefnagel-Höhle, M. (1982). The critical period for language acquisition: evidence from second language acquisition. In S. D. Krashen (Ed.), *Child-Adult Difference in Second Language Acquisition.* Rowley, MA: Newbury House Publishers.

Thonis, E. W. (1976). *Literacy for America's Spanish speaking children.* Newark, DE: International Reading Association.

Veatch, J., Sawicki, F., Elliott, G., Barnette, E., & Blakey, J. (1979). *Key words to reading: the language experience approach begins* (2nd ed.). Columbus, OH: Charles E. Merrill.

Weinreich, U. (1953). *Language in contact.* The Hague: Mouton.

Wheat, T. E., Galen, N. D., & Norwood, M. (1979). Initial reading experiences for linguistically diverse learners. *The Reading Teacher, 33* (1), 28–30.

# Check Your Reading Comprehension

**1.** Matching exercise:

_____ **1.** PL 95-561

_____ **2.** American bilingual children

_____ **3.** Immigrant children

_____ **4.** Limited English Profiency (LEP) children

_____ **5.** Compound bilinguals

_____ **6.** Coordinate bilinguals

_____ **7.** Bilingual education

_____ **8.** Bilingual/bicultural education

_____ **9.** Transitional bilingual approach

_____ **10.** Maintenance bilingual education

**a.** Bilinguals who have separate semantic systems.

**b.** An approach that proposes the learning of English with little or no reinforcement of the native language, except as a starting point.

**c.** An approach to instruction in two languages, enabling the children to function in another language in addition to their native language.

**d.** Children of persons who have migrated to the United States and who are contemplating permanent settlement.

**e.** An approach advocating a self-sustaining continuous program of developing the native language, while learning English.

**f.** Children who exhibit language proficiency in their native language commensurate with their age and have learned English in the oral form.

**g.** Bilingual Education Act; encourages establishment and operation of bilingual programs and provides financial assistance for such programs.

**h.** Bilinguals who have two distinct models of expression for a single underlying semantic network.

**i.** Children (such as Puerto Ricans) who are American citizens and whose parents' native language is other than English.

**j.** An approach that suggests instruction in and reinforcement of the native language and culture as well as the new, or second, language and culture.

Answers:

| | |
|---|---|
| 5. h | 10. e |
| 4. f | 9. b |
| 3. d | 8. j |
| 2. i | 7. c |
| 1. g | 6. a |

**2.** Suppose you have a bilingual child in your classroom. (a) What modifications might you make to better meet this child's needs in reading? Consider materials to be used, modalities of instruction, grouping patterns, and nonreading activities. (b) Would these modifications be appropriate for all bilingual children? Consider the American bilingual child, the immigrant child, and the Limited English Proficiency child.

**3.** In Chapter 7 a variety of approaches to the teaching of reading are discussed. After you have read that chapter, you should answer this question: What advantages and disadvantages do you see in each of these approaches for the bilingual child?

**4.** Imagine you are teaching a fifth-grade class in social studies. You are beginning a chapter on the American Civil War. What concepts do you feel your students need before reading the chapter? How might you help to develop those concepts for the nonnative speakers of English in your class? (Refer to Dale's Cone of Experience in Figure 16.1)

# 17

# Organizing and Managing the Classroom

We consider in this chapter the ingredients of effective schools and effective teachers. Much of the "art" of teaching lies in "getting it all together." Demands are being made on classroom teachers that have never been made before, especially with mainstreaming of special education students. One veteran teacher attributed her success in classroom management to the fact that she had begun her teaching career in a one-room schoolhouse! There she had learned to manage the needs of children of vastly different ages as well as abilities.

Today the classroom teacher faces a class all the same age; however, the range of abilities within the classroom has expanded and the types of special problems have increased. Many of the problems such as learning disabilities existed before, but we did not recognize them. Today we also have the benefit of specialists and special resources to help us.

If you have not yet taught, or are just beginning your career as a teacher, do not be overwhelmed by the tasks of classroom management. Through experience you will learn techniques that work for you that perhaps we have not even thought of. If they work, use them!

Unfortunately, we often teach as we have been taught. New teachers, in spite of methods courses in college, often revert to methods used when they were in school, whether they are pedagogically sound or not. We hope that this chapter will give you some fresh ideas to use in instructional planning and classroom management.

# Effective Schools

Research on effective schools has been primarily limited to urban settings. Despite this limitation, the research has encouraged the view that schools, not students, fail, and it has fostered interest in program development to increase achievement. As Edmonds (1981) stated in his testimony before a House of Representatives subcommittee, "Our thesis is that all children are eminently educable, and the behavior of the school is critical in determining the quality of that education (p. 6)."

Earlier studies (Coleman, et al., 1966) had not been so optimistic, linking school achievement primarily to family background. It had appeared that minority children of a low socioeconomic status (SES) whose families were not oriented toward school would not reach competence in reading. In fact, schools appeared to have little influence on achievement as measured by performance on standardized achievement tests.

This early research had left educators with a sense of helplessness; urban schools drawing from low SES neighborhoods seemed to be doomed to low achievement by the nature of the student body. Perhaps what created the interest in effective schools research was the fact that effective inner-city schools did exist (Weber, 1971). What made these schools produce achievement gains among their low SES students?

Reviewing the results of some research on effective schools, D'Amico (n.d., p. 19) identifies "four operative generalizations":

1. Effective schools have a strong principal who is an instructional leader, a model for the staff, and a firm and fair disciplinarian.
2. Effective schools are staffed by individuals who have high expectations for their students' basic skills achievement and who operate under the assumption that all their students can meet these expectations.
3. Effective schools have clearly stated goals and objectives stressing basic skill acquisition, which receive high priority by staff, act as a basis for instruction, and constitute the reference points for student and staff accountability.
4. Effective schools have a school climate that is not disruptive, disorganized, nor distractive; rather it is orderly and generally reflects the school's role as a place for instructional activity.

Similarly, Edmonds (1981), drawing upon his research in the New York City schools, has identified five characteristics of effective schools: leadership, climate, expectations, instructional emphasis, and assessment.

Effective schools, first of all, are characterized by supportive *leadership*. At the elementary level this leadership usually comes from the building principal. We have observed a variety of principals, ranging from glorified school secretaries to dynamic instructional leaders. The principal who frequently observes teachers' classrooms, who emphasizes achievement, who coordinates instructional programs, and who supports teachers is usually an effective instructional leader (Sweeney, 1982). Teachers are quick to note a principal's expectations and respond accordingly. Sometimes leadership comes from another source, such as from a reading consultant, when the principal does not exert leadership. A new teacher needs to be alert to the source of leadership in a school.

Related to leadership is school *climate*—a strong leader does not permit chaos in a school. We believe that "open" schools, or those without walls between classrooms, are not necessarily "disruptive, disorganized, nor distractive." While a parent may have difficulty adjusting to the noise from other classrooms at a back-to-school night, children usually adjust well if the classrooms are well-managed.

*Expectations* set for all students have proved to be important in determining how much they will learn. Expectations should be high but realistic, particularly for underachievers. The teacher who says in the lounge, "I had his father, and he couldn't learn to read either," is not likely to give the second generation a chance. For a long time we have known that students perform the way we expect them to perform (Rosenthal & Jacobson, 1968). If we expect them to be achievers, they will rise to our expectations. But if we expect little from them, why should they even attempt to work?

*Instructional emphasis* on the basic skills is related to a school's effectiveness. Today's schools must perform a wide variety of roles. Recent research has indicated that those schools that have maintained basic skills instruction as the top priority have been the effective schools, those producing the highest achievement gains. Edmonds (1978) reports that all school staff share a sense of this common mission in the effective schools.

Related to an emphasis on basic skills is the *assessment* of progress in acquiring those basic skills. Regular monitoring of achievement by both the classroom teacher and the school district seems to increase achievement in the basic skills. Effective schools responded to changes in achievement by making instructional program changes. For example, as discussed in Chapter 5, a teacher may use criterion-referenced tests to be sure that students have actually mastered the reading skills that have been taught. A teacher should also occasionally administer informal reading inventories to check application of the skills mastered on criterion-referenced skills tests. Most school districts administer norm-referenced tests regularly to monitor the progress of the school population and to compare local achievement levels with national norms; changes in the instructional program are made on the basis of test results.

These characteristics of effective schools are correlational, not causal, factors. In other words, while we cannot yet say that one or more of the factors will cause an increase in achievement, we can say that these factors have been associated with effective schools.

# Effective Teachers

Parallel to the research on effective schools is a growing body of research on what constitutes effective teaching. Again, this research is limited by the fact that much of it has been conducted in urban sites.

One attempt to study teacher effectiveness was the Beginning Teacher Evaluation Study (Fisher, et al., 1980) conducted in California. The study defined effective teachers as those producing above average gains from the beginning to the end of the school year, using as criteria the achievement gain on standardized achievement tests in reading and mathematics. The study concentrated only on second and fifth graders who did not deviate extremely from expected grade-level performance.

Effective teachers *allocated* more instructional time to reading and math. But even more important, they created more *engaged* time—time when students were actively responding to learning tasks or actively learning—as opposed to off-task behavior—daydreaming, chatting with friends, or doing classroom housekeeping details. In other words, effective teachers used more of the allocated time for active instruction, thereby increasing the amount of engaged time.

The researchers found that effective teachers provided for more engaged time with a *high success rate,* which they called Academic Learning Time (ALT). ALT was in turn positively associated with achievement gains. Conversely, a low success rate was negatively associated with learning. Students did not appear to make as great achievement gains when given difficult tasks as when given tasks with a high success rate. Particularly the younger children seemed to respond better to tasks at which they could easily succeed. It appears that young children especially need successful practice or consolidation of skills before tackling new learning.

Effective teachers permitted less off-task behavior among students. This, however, did not seem to cause more negative student attitudes toward school. Other factors found to be related to effective teaching were accuracy of diagnosis and prescription, and emphasis on academic goals. Students of effective teachers were more responsible for academic work and worked more cooperatively with classmates. Effective teachers more frequently monitored seatwork, had more substantive interaction with students, and gave more academic feedback. Their lessons were more structured, and their directions were more complete and specific.

Engaged time was about 15 percent higher when students were working with the teacher in group work than when in independent seatwork. The researchers did note, however, that students spent approximately two-thirds of the allocated time in independent seatwork. One might conclude that if the teacher worked with the class as a whole most of the time the engagement time would increase. While this might be true, children working below and above the average class performance would undoubtedly have difficulties (Rosenshine, 1980).

Good (1979) concluded from this research that structured learning with a high success rate is particularly important for younger and less capable students. Those with low achievement pretest scores need direct instruction, with a gradual movement toward more independent learning as students grow older and increase in academic competence. He suggests that high-aptitude students may not respond as well to such structured, direct teaching. Peterson (1979) concurs with this suggestion.

A teacher is likely to increase engagement time during seatwork by increasing the amount of substantive interaction during group work, such as by posing problem-solving situations (Rosenshine, 1980). Students need direct, structured instruction in group work with meaningful tasks assigned for independent seatwork. Close monitoring of seatwork and holding students accountable for successfully completing this work should also increase engagement time.

Duffy (1983) has pointed out problems that teachers have traditionally had with substantive interaction during group work. He suggests that the procedure of "turn taking" within a group is based on the fallacious assumption that *all* students can learn by being exposed to reading materials and then being questioned by the teacher. But this process is in fact difficult for poor readers and focuses on obtaining the correct answers rather than on the learning processes. The teacher plays a passive role, according to Duffy—assigning, questioning, and providing feedback rather than teaching. Turn-taking need not be eliminated, but it needs to be modified so that the teacher provides explanation when students do not arrive at the correct answers on their own.

Turn-taking in a reading group. (Photo by Jean Greenwald)

Duffy identifies five characteristics of effective explanation:

1. Explicit information about what is being taught and why it is important.
2. Clarity, "so that the usually invisible cognitive processes are made visible."
3. More "teacher talk" during explanation than during turn-taking.
4. Use of examples and specifics in clarifying students' misunderstandings.
5. Cohesion across the various lessons in a day.

Other summaries of research (for example, Anderson, Evertson, & Emmer, 1979; Brophy, 1979) have reached similar conclusions about what constitutes effective teaching. Anderson et al. (1979) point to three clusters of teacher behaviors:

1. Conveying the purpose and meaning of academic activities (telling students *why* on-task behaviors are important).
2. Instructing students in the skills of good behavior (telling them *how* to behave).
3. Exhibiting a sense of students' level of understanding and need for information and selecting activities that reflect this. (pp. 8–9)

Effective teachers, then, diagnose the amount of independence that each student can handle and plan plenty of direct instruction, with more supervision for those students who lack the ability to function independently. Effective teachers also tell students why they're doing particular classroom activities, because students' engagement levels are greater if they perceive an activity to be meaningful and purposeful.

# Teaching Underachievers to Read

The heterogeneity of most classrooms makes it difficult for teachers to carry out appropriate reading instruction for all students. Observational studies (for example, Allington, 1980) have shown that often poor classroom management causes poor readers to receive less actual instructional time in reading. Much time spent correcting poor readers' behavior that could be spent teaching reading.

Reading, as top priority in most school districts, should be the focus in all the day's activities. You should teach content area studies not only to build concepts and knowledge but to develop expository reading skills. Carefully monitor the work of the underachieving readers to be sure that they apply the reading skills that they do know in the content areas. Help them transfer these reading skills by pointing out opportunities for application. For example, in presenting new science vocabulary words, remind students of their knowledge of roots and affixes to assist in word recognition and meaning.

Some sort of grouping by reading instructional levels becomes necessary, as discussed later in this chapter (Rosenshine, 1980). Because grouping necessarily entails independent seatwork while you are working with other groups, assign seatwork tasks that are not difficult—that are likely to have a high success rate. Block (1980), discussing the Beginning Teacher Evaluation Study, says that success should be continual, not simply at a marking period, especially for younger and less able students.

Instruction for underachievers needs to be structured and direct, following the procedures discussed in Chapter 3. You can build structure into any approach to reading instruction. The important point is that you actively teach new learning before assigning follow-up practice exercises. Some observational studies (for example, Durkin, 1978–1979) have revealed that instead of offering direct instruction in reading skills, teachers are only mentioning skills, doling out worksheets and expecting students to infer what is to be learned. We have often heard parents complain that they must teach their children basic concepts because the teacher has apparently assigned a worksheet without first giving adequate instruction.

You can also increase engagement time for poor readers by spending more direct instructional time with this group, giving them less independent seatwork. Monitor their independent seatwork closely by walking around the classroom and checking quickly over their shoulders to see how they are doing. This only takes a few minutes, perhaps while groups are changing. Check (but don't grade) seatwork daily so that students know that they are held accountable for their work. Positive comments, smiley faces, stickers, and so forth provide positive feedback that stimulates the student to try harder.

We know of one school unit (grades 4, 5, and 6) that attempted to group students for instruction according to the amount of structure they needed, rather than their reading achievement levels. Students who appeared to need direct teacher instruction tended to be in the lower achievement range; they were taught in reading groups using a very structured approach. The goal, however, was to move these students to the semistructured group, which also received much direct group instruction but with more independent seatwork and learning centers. Those deemed capable of independent learning, who tended to be in the higher achievement range, were given an individualized reading program operating on a contract system. The goal was to move as many students as possible into the independent instructional mode.

You can see, then, that poor readers need more structure and direct instruction. They seem to need more group work than others. Learning centers and other independent learning situations are appropriate if you structure their use very carefully. Clarify directions for their use and closely monitor work done independently.

Underachievers also need more successful experiences, especially when working independently. They have too often experienced frustration and failure. You must introduce new learning in small doses in group instruction. Do not assign independent practice materials following instruction unless you are sure the students can successfully complete them. More capable readers, especially older students, can tolerate some ambiguity and can apply their problem-solving skills independently. Poorer readers cannot; and their resulting frustration often leads to disruption in the classroom.

As we have said, all students need to know *how* and *why* they are learning. Students usually cannot infer the reasons behind their assignments, nor should they be expected to. Particularly underachievers in reading need to see the rationale behind their assignments to make them purposeful and meaningful.

# Classroom Management

How does a teacher effectively manage the various needs of some 25 children in developing an effective reading program? The schema presented in Figure 17.1 illustrates the many decision points in managing a classroom reading program.

## Tentative Placement in Instructional Materials

Emmer, Evertson, and Anderson (1980) find that effective classroom managers spend more time initially describing the rules and procedures than teachers rated as ineffective managers. Better managers plan ahead to have all needed materials on hand, thus preventing confusion early in the school year. They give more rewards for appropriate behavior and stop disruptive behavior more quickly. Effective managers expect compliance with the classroom rules and are quick to respond to deviations from the rules. They also closely monitor students' work and hold students accountable for their assignments. Emmer, et al. (1980) state:

> In summary, the more effective managers clearly established themselves as the classroom leaders. They worked on rules and procedures until the children learned them. The teaching of content was important for these teachers, but they stressed, initially, socialization into the classroom system. By the end of the first three weeks, these classes were ready for the rest of the year. (p. 225)

We can reasonably assume that one component of effective classroom management is placement of students in appropriate instructional materials. Because the emphasis during the first several weeks is upon classroom management, rather than content, it is probably best to give students material that is interesting and fairly easy to read. Some teachers do not attempt to group students by reading ability initially; instead, they instruct the class as a whole or group on other bases. Others form tentative groupings based on information from the previous teachers, such as the instructional reading level at the end of the previous school year.

This initial "try-on" of materials is important, particularly with poor readers, to see how well each student is able to function. If the material is much too difficult, they may "turn off" to reading immediately in the new classroom. If it is easy, so much the

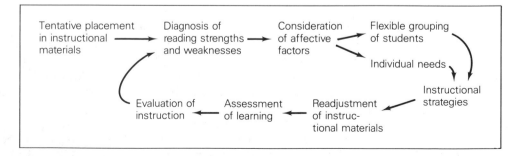

**Figure 17.1**  Managing a Classroom Reading Program

better to build their confidence. Initially using easy, high-interest materials builds confidence, positive attitudes, and understanding of the classroom management procedures.

## Diagnosis of Reading Strengths and Weaknesses

Diagnosis is an ongoing task throughout the school year. Data gathered at the beginning of the school year establish a baseline for later growth and lay the groundwork for effective reading instruction. Unfortunately, many classroom teachers feel ill-equipped to apply diagnostic information obtained from an informal reading inventory to plan instruction. *We hope that you feel more confident for having read this book!*

As described in Chapter 5, the IRI is one of the most commonly used diagnostic tools for the classroom teacher. We recommend testing poor readers first to get their regular instructional program underway as soon as possible. Work closely with the reading specialist to get additional diagnostic information about poor readers.

## Consideration of Affective Factors

As described in Chapter 13, consideration of affective factors—self-concept, attitude, motivation, and interest—can be crucial, especially in working with poor readers. Unless poor readers are interested in the materials they are reading, it is unlikely that they will be motivated to engage in the practice so necessary in building reading fluency. Many poor readers have poor self-concepts because of frustrating school experiences. A negative self-concept, in turn, leads to more failure and frustration. The resourceful teacher must break this cycle if children are to succeed in reading.

## Flexible Grouping of Students

The key considerations in grouping students for reading instruction are flexibility and variety. While reading instructional level is the most common basis for forming groups in elementary schools, it should not be the only basis. If it is, morale problems will surely exist among the lowest group and a stigma be attached to membership in that group. (Parents further complicate the issue by wanting to know what group their child is in and how their child can move into the top group.)

Why group by reading level at all if these problems exist? Obviously, grouping by reading level reduces the range of individual differences within the classroom. In the fifth-grade classroom presented in Chapter 1 the reading levels ranged from 2.4 to 10.0 on a standardized reading test. If the teacher selected materials for the whole class on a fifth-grade reading level, only those students reading on grade level or approximately a year on either side of it would find the material appropriate. Poor readers would be unable to keep up; gifted readers would be bored.

Groups should, however, remain flexible. Some children show sudden growth spurts that enable them to move ahead into the group for the next higher reading level. We know of one boy, a disabled reader, who spent a two-week school holiday in full-time reading simply because he had been grounded to his room for misbehavior. Needless to say, the teacher was at first mystified by his rapid progress but was pleased to readjust the reading groups to accommodate his growth.

Frequent use of other types of groupings also overcomes the stigma associated with the lowest reading group. You might mix students of various reading levels in project work, such as in a unit of study. (See Chapter 11 for a description of units.) Good and poor readers alike can contribute by reading appropriate, but different, materials related to the same project.

You might group by interests, especially in recreational reading. Students may choose to read various books related to sports, for example, and share their findings with other group members. Help guide students in selecting books at appropriate levels that are related to these interests. The group might also prepare a sharing activity, such as a diorama, to present to the rest of the class.

Temporary grouping by skill needs can be effective. Following criterion-referenced testing, you may be able to identify various students in different reading groups with the same skill need. These children can work together for one or two weeks on the deficient skill—for example, learning prefixes, or studying latitude and longitude on a map. Since students from different groups are mixed together, poor readers are not singled out.

Sometimes a better reader can be paired with a less able reader. As long as the partnership is productive, this arrangement can be beneficial to both. The good reader reinforces his or her own skills by teaching them to the poor reader. Monitor peer tutoring carefully to be sure that it does remain constructive. Occasionally assign the poor readers to tutor others in nonreading tasks, such as constructing tables and graphs or creating an art project. If the partners can help each other with various tasks, the relationship is healthier and more productive.

Occasionally students may choose their own groups by signing up to work with a particular leader. These social groupings may or may not involve reading tasks. Social groupings are particularly useful with older students who have developed social interests.

The poor reader does not need to feel stigmatized by group membership as long as different groups are formed for different purposes. If all group members can contribute, then no one feels embarrassed by poor reading skills.

## Individual Needs

Plan instruction around individual needs. A hearing impaired student who probably cannot learn phonics skills successfully might benefit from instruction through the visual and tactile modalities. A partially sighted child may learn to read by phonics combined with the tactile modality.

Special education students who have been mainstreamed into the regular classroom need particular consideration. A slow learner may need much drill, practice, and repetition while learning a reading skill. Carefully plan instruction for an emotionally disturbed child to avoid excessive frustration. Do not confront a learning disabled child with tasks in which sequences are presented in jumbled order, such as scrambled words.

Sometimes consideration of individual needs overrides placement in an instructional group. Some students cannot learn in a group setting; those special students require individual instruction. Be sure to coordinate these efforts with the appropriate special education resource teacher. You may become the coordinator as well as the implementer of instructional efforts for children with multiple special needs.

## Instructional Strategies

The approaches to reading instruction discussed in Chapter 7 range from those with a meaning-getting emphasis to those that emphasize decoding. The basal reader, the most frequently used approach, combines the elements of decoding and meaning-getting and thus was placed at mid-point in the continuum shown in Figure 7.3.

In spite of the many advantages of the basal reader, we do not consider it to be the best approach for underachieving readers. When students fall behind their grade-level peers, the basal reader assigned for their chronological age is no longer appropriate. Basal readers that are appropriate in terms of reading level—those intended for younger children—are inappropriate in terms of the students' interests and are thus unlikely to encourage positive attitudes toward reading.

If a student has not sufficiently mastered word recognition skills—Stage 1 of Chall's stages of reading development (1983) discussed in Chapter 8—use an instructional approach that emphasizes decoding. Phonics may help the student become "glued to print." If, however, the student does not appear to learn to attack words by phonics, then an auditory processing problem may exist. We then recommend a visual approach, such as the linguistic approach. Development of a large sight vocabulary, perhaps through the kinesthetic modality, is another way to glue a student to print until decoding generalizations can be taught.

After the students have mastered the decoding process and are into Stage 2, in which fluency becomes the major objective, then apply meaning-getting approaches. Individualized reading—self-selected, self-paced, silent reading with teacher conferences—encourages the development of fluency through wide reading. In Stage 3, learning from content area materials, the strategies discussed in Chapter 11 become particularly important.

Instructional strategies, therefore, should be adjusted to the stage of reading development of the underachieving readers. Don't forget, however, that a sixth grader, who by chronological age and grade placement ought to be in Stage 3, may actually be only in Stage 1. Draw upon resource personnel, such as the reading specialist and special education teacher, for help in planning instructional strategies for these students.

## Readjustment of Instructional Materials

The process of forming instructional groups and deciding on instructional strategies will probably take at least until October of the school year. As we have said, adjustments throughout the school year are necessary, but you need an instructional plan for each group and for the individuals within the groups.

Following the initial "try-on" of materials and diagnoses of strengths and weaknesses, you may need to readjust instructional materials. You must make decisions not only about reading level but also about instructional strategies, students' prior background experiences, and interests. The decision about instructional materials should follow, not precede, these other decisions. In other words, we do not believe in using the same "canned" materials for all poor readers, regardless of reading problems. These children and their problems can be as different as those portrayed in Chapter 1, and they require different materials.

## Assessment of Learning

Periodic assessments are important in monitoring progress, especially of poor readers. Daily informal monitoring by observation is necessary.

Note students' behaviors during instructional time and assigned seatwork periods. Also check (not necessarily grade) students' independent work. Try to catch problems early and offer immediate correction, preventing problems from escalating. You can usually give corrective instruction in groups when you notice that several children are experiencing a particular problem.

We recommend criterion-referenced assessments to determine whether or not students have mastered given skills. These may be informal teacher-made assessments or more formal tests available commercially or created by a school district.

If a group of assessments are given at the beginning of the school year, use the results for forming groups for specific skill instruction. Children are thus not taught skills they have already mastered or, especially in the case of poor readers, skills they are not ready for. It seems pointless, for example, to teach diphthongs or r-controlled vowels to children who have not yet mastered short and long vowel sounds.

Assessments of mastery after instruction are especially important. Rude, Otto, and Klumb (1976), studying retention of skills over the summer months, found that students required to demonstrate mastery of the skills on criterion-referenced tests at the end of the school year had better retention over the summer than those evaluated only by teacher judgment.

Equally as important is the use of informal reading inventories to check application of skills while reading in context. Some poor readers demonstrate mastery of isolated skills but are unable to apply these skills in attacking words. They need help in building fluency in reading while also being reminded of skill application.

## Evaluation of Instruction

Evaluation is closely related to assessment of students' learning because student progress lets you know how effective your teaching is. Satisfactory progress on the part of every student is unlikely, especially among poor readers. When a student does not progress, you must return to the original diagnosis of strengths and weaknesses and perhaps make modifications. You may have overestimated the student's reading level or failed to notice certain skill weaknesses. Perhaps the problem does not lie in the instructional program at all but in emotionally upsetting events occurring at home or with peers.

Try to discover the source of problems for individual learners as much as possible. However, when a student's problem persists, with no apparent progress toward its solution, refer the child to a specialist, such as the reading specialist or school psychologist. Most learning problems can be more readily helped if detected early, especially in the primary grades, so be alert to problems. Hiding or ignoring a problem, perhaps for fear of being considered an inadequate teacher, is not in any child's best interest.

On the other hand, progress on the part of students who have had reading difficulty can be very rewarding. You can and should feel good about this progress. Besides giving yourself a pat on the back, try to analyze the situation to discover the ingredients of success. You may be able to apply them with another student in the future.

# Scheduling Reading Instruction

Plans for scheduling reading instruction vary enormously depending on school district policies. Some districts allocate the morning to a reading, language arts, and social studies block. Other districts prescribe a certain number of minutes to each curriculum area.

You may or may not have much choice in setting up the schedule for reading instruction. Often special subjects, such as art, music, and physical education, must be scheduled first. Children may be going to and from the classroom to resource rooms or specialists at various times during the day. (One second-grade teacher confided that she finally had to make herself a daily schedule to coordinate the comings and goings of all her mainstreamed children!)

Most school districts require a minimum of one and a half hours of reading instruction in the primary grades, often reduced to an hour in the upper elementary grades. Reading skills in the content areas become much more important in the upper grades, however, so ideally reading in some form should be taught almost all day. You can also provide time for Sustained Silent Reading (SSR), perhaps before or after lunch or recess. Many teachers, even in the upper grades, also use these transition periods as opportunities to read aloud to children.

Our discussion of scheduling options is organized by types of plans; we present a few basic ones in the hope of increasing your understanding of the various possibilities for scheduling reading instruction.

## Self-Contained Classroom

This scheduling option represents traditional reading instruction, which we might have experienced as children. The teacher schedules a heterogeneous class of children in various types of groupings. Usually the class is divided into three or four groups according to reading levels for reading instruction. Of course, within each group a range of reading abilities still exists, but not as great as within the whole class.

One fourth-grade teacher (Elsie Parks, of Jersey Shore, Pennsylvania, Public Schools) has shared her schedule. Four reading groups are placed at different levels within a given basal reader series. The district allocates the morning for reading instruction, but special subjects are also scheduled during that time. On Monday the children have 40 minutes of physical education and 30 minutes of music. On Tuesday, they go to the library for a half hour. On Wednesday they have 30 minutes of art. The teacher sets aside an hour and a half on Fridays to work with the whole class on newspaper reading with accompanying activities. These activities often focus on study skills, such as map reading or research skills.

This teacher rotates her four reading groups in the time spent in direct teacher instruction. She begins with the lowest group first (8:30 – 9:00) because at 9:00 every day they leave for an additional reading class taught by the reading specialist. The other groups work independently on seatwork. Approximately one basal story per week is covered, with a day set aside for each step in the directed reading-thinking activity (DRTA), as described in Chapter 9:

- Preparation for reading
- Directed reading
- Skills instruction
- Enrichment

The teacher spends her daily time with each group on one of these steps (approximately 30 minutes per group). While the students are not working directly with the teacher, they may be working on a variety of assigned tasks:

- Follow-up to teacher instruction related to the DRTA (for example, a vocabulary practice exercise that follows the introduction to new vocabulary)
- Workbook or teacher-made skills practice exercise
- Directed reading of a portion of the story
- Learning centers and games to reinforce previously taught skills
- Listening center using an individualized phonics program on tape
- Reading individualized kit material

Tuesday's schedule appears in Table 17.1. Since Group 4 includes the poorest readers, let's take a closer look at their schedule. On Tuesday the teacher worked with them on the directed reading with comprehension questions and oral rereading of portions of the story. (They did not do "round-robin" reading where everyone reads a paragraph, but instead they read portions aloud to answer comprehension questions and verify information.) They had previously been introduced to new vocabulary and background concepts for the reading. The seatwork for comprehension activities from 9:30 – 10:00 is to follow up on the directed reading, discussion, and questions on the story. For example, they might practice identifying a sequence of events if sequencing had been emphasized in the basal story. The listening center from 10:30 – 11:00 involves activities in following taped directions because the teacher has observed that all but her top reading group has difficulty following directions. Further word recognition skill instruction is planned for Wednesday, using words in the basal story. The teacher assigns the students to begin work on enrichment activities—for example,

**Table 17.1**  Tuesday's Schedule

| Time Period | Group 1* | Group 2 | Group 3 | Group 4 |
|---|---|---|---|---|
| 8:30–9:00 | Learning centers | Listening center | Seatwork: Silent reading | Teacher: Discussion and questions on story. Some oral rereading. Assign enrichment activities. |
| 9:00–9:30 | Independent research project (contract) | Individualized reading kit | Teacher: Discussion conclusion of story. Review vocabulary. Instruct in skills. Assign skills practice | Out for Chapter 1 |
| 9:30–10:00 | Seatwork: Enrichment activities | Teacher: Introduce story, vocabulary, concepts. Set purposes. Assign reading of story. | Listening center | Seatwork: Comprehension activities |
| 10:00–10:30 | Library | Library | Library | Library |
| 10:30–11:00 | Teacher: Students share enrichment activities | Seatwork: Silent reading | Learning centers | Listening center |

*Groups are numbered by reading ability: Group 1 includes the best readers while Group 4 consists of the poorest readers.

reading a related story or writing a paragraph or poem—which extend the students' understanding of the story and motivate them to do further reading. The enrichment activities are to be completed by Friday.

Occasionally the teacher chooses to increase the amount of time spent with one of the lower groups and omit meeting with the top group. Because children in the top group tend to be more self-directed and capable of independent work than those in the lower groups, they need less direct teacher instruction. Because the teacher has the same children all day, she can pull them together for a brief period later in the day if the need arises.

## Joplin Plan

The Joplin Plan is a procedure whereby at a given time all students at a grade level leave their homerooms for reading instruction with a homogeneous group of students. In other words, they are assigned to a teacher specifically for reading instruction according to their reading instructional level. While homogeneous grouping decreases the range of reading abilities within the classroom, it still does not eliminate the need to group children to narrow the range still further. Most teachers form two or three groups, following procedures similar to the teacher in the self-contained room during the time set aside for reading instruction.

Some schools group homogeneously for reading and mathematics instruction, with the rest of the day being spent in heterogeneous groups. This plan works only if specified times can be set aside for all students to pass from room to room.

## Skill Grouping

A modification of the Joplin Plan is to exchange students among teachers only for skill group instruction. The rest of the portions of the DRTA are carried out in regular reading instructional groups. Using a reading management system, whereby the strengths and weaknesses of each student have been determined by pretesting and recorded, teachers can group students temporarily (usually two to three weeks) by skill needs. For example, if four teachers are working together, they might designate a half hour daily for skill group instruction. One teacher might teach all the children who need work in short vowel sounds; another teacher, base words and endings; a third teacher, diphthongs; and a fourth teacher, sight vocabulary development. Depending on the size of the groups, a teacher might have two groups studying different skills. Children who have mastered all of the skills being taught in a particular cycle can work independently on other skills, supervised by one of the teachers.

If teachers from two grade levels work cooperatively for skill instruction, the range of skills being taught can be expanded. For example, if second and third graders are combined, then the best second-grade readers can work primarily in third-grade groups; the weakest third graders can be placed primarily with second graders in skill groups.

Skill groupings can be used in conjuction with either of the preceding two plans if (a) a common time for skill groupings can be found three to five times per week; (b) teachers are willing to cooperate in skill instruction and (c) a reading management plan exists so that strengths and weaknesses in reading skills are identified.

## Implications for Poor Readers

All of the preceding plans can accommodate underachieving readers. The self-contained classroom permits the classroom teacher to know each student well. Because the teacher has the same students for all subjects, he or she can more easily stress application and transfer of reading skills to content area subjects.

On the other hand, the self-contained classroom teacher has an enormous range of reading abilities to deal with. Homogeneous grouping, as in the Joplin Plan, decreases this range. But because a teacher may have different students for reading instruction than for other content areas, that teacher may not know the students' reading strengths and weaknesses as well, making application and transfer of skills during content area instruction difficult.

Skill groupings offer efficiency, since each teacher prepares only one or two skills for instruction during a two- or three-week period. Students receive appropriate instruction according to their skill needs, not according to the lesson that comes next in the basal reader. Readers of all levels may be combined in a skill group if they have the same specific need. But transfer of skill learning to reading in any subject area, including reading instruction using the DRTA, may prove troublesome.

Obviously, no one plan is without flaws. All also offer advantages. With regard to poor readers, remember these two important points:

1. Regardless of the instructional plan, poor readers especially need help with the transfer and application of reading skills. They will not apply skills learned in one setting to another setting without teacher assistance.
2. Grouping should enhance, not erode, poor readers' concepts of themselves as readers. We do not recommend that poor readers be grouped together all day for instruction in all subjects. It is better to plan homogeneous groups for reading and mathematics only, with heterogeneous groupings for all other subjects, thus combining the advantages of ability grouping with the need to group students of all ability levels together.

The plan chosen will be influenced by the local school district's philosophy of reading instruction and by the administrative leadership. While poor readers cannot be the only concern, their needs should certainly be considered i organizing classrooms for reading instruction.

# Computer Technology

Recent research (Kulik, 1983; Mason, Blanchard, & Daniel, 1983; White, 1983), while yielding mixed results at the time of this writing, suggests that computers may be effective tools if used properly.

Cynics, however, recall the high hopes that educators once had for teaching machines and other devices that presumably would solve all learning problems. We have learned from those experiences. This section represents our views on the appropriate uses for computers with underachieving readers.

## Computers for Instruction

The computer can be a tool for instruction, just as the slate was for pioneer children learning to read and the chalkboard is today. Because it is just a tool, the computer is only as effective as the instructional programs written for it. The lesson we learned from teaching machines in the 1960s is that students learn best from machines in small doses. The teacher controls the use of the tool. If the teacher uses a computer effectively, it can become a very significant technological aid in the classroom.

Software companies continue to spring up in basements and garages (many of which belong to college professors!). These new companies are peddling software that is quick and relatively easy to create because elaborate, long-term curriculum development requires extensive funding and expertise. As when buying a car, the teacher who wants to purchase software for the classroom should shop around to find the best bargains. Although car dealers allow you to test drive a car before buying it, many computer companies do not send software to potential customers on approval.

The best alternative for the teacher, as an individual or as a member of a school district seeking good educational software, is to join a consortium that purchases and/or reviews commercial software. In some states the Department of Education has organized this service, which lets the teacher know what is "under the hood" of the software package. (Shiny chrome on the outside may convey a false promise of effectiveness and usefulness!) Finding out what others have used effectively is one solution to the problem. Reading educational computer journals is another. (See the list of journals that review software for classroom use at the end of this section.) Seeing the software demonstrated at professional meetings and workshops is probably the best way to know what a particular software package will do.

But what should you look for in software to teach reading to students who need corrective instruction? Whether you are looking for educational games and practice materials or computer courseware (more or less a complete curriculum), you need to keep some special considerations in mind.

## Software for Underachieving Readers

The process of learning to read has somehow gone wrong for the underachieving reader; the computer offers a new route to learning that is not yet fraught with failure. It is important, therefore, that the software be effective. If the student fails again, this time using the computer as an instructional tool, he or she will inevitably reject reading and possibly all school learning.

For the student to achieve success, good diagnostic tests, administered on the computer or by the teacher, must be part of the software curriculum. Unless the student is placed appropriately according to reading level and skill needs, learning on the computer will not be effective. Likewise, mastery tests must be built in so that both the teacher and the student can see that progress is being made.

Good software should be designed to guarantee success. If a student answers incorrectly, the program should contain "branches" to route the student through instruction on prerequisite skills. New material should be introduced at a pace governed by the student's rate of mastering prior material.

Some software programs do not permit a student to enter a wrong answer; the computer simply does not respond until the correct answer is entered. While this may be appropriate with very young children or with severely retarded individuals, it seems to encourage random guessing. On the other hand, programs ought not say to the student, "You're wrong!" We prefer those programs that provide branching yet give the user the sense of having control rather than being controlled. The student should be able to choose activities within a given lesson or decide which activities to do first.

Directions to the student should be simple and easy to follow. In programs for nonreaders, however, printed directions can be a real problem. Even if a program offers good examples of what the students are to do, nonreaders may not know how to respond. Some software packages have used voice synthesizers to get around this problem. Voice synthesizers can also be very useful in teaching reading to nonnative speakers, who especially need auditory as well as visual input in learning to read English.

Another concern in selecting software is whether the programs are to be used by individuals or groups. Software intended for group use offers both wider usage of the computer and socialization. For children from non–English-speaking backgrounds, like Maria in Chapter 1, the language interaction of group members can have important benefits in helping them learn English. Discussing tasks on the computer can also help shy and withdrawn children.

Remember, though, that underachieving readers are behind others in the acquisition of reading skills. They can benefit from group use of the computer best if they are grouped with others of a similar skill level. In a group of mixed abilities the better readers may set the pace in the learning process, leaving underachieving readers behind. If that happens the underachievers cannot feel any better about themselves while using the computer than in the regular classroom situation. The decision about group versus individual use will have to be made locally, considering the students for whom the software is intended.

Good software should allow you to modify it to "fit" a particular child or a local situation. For example, some software programs allow you to enter vocabulary words that are being studied in reading class or in one of the content areas. Those words become the focus of instruction. It is also possible to personalize the software by using the student's name and incorporating words that pertain to a subject of the student's personal interest. (Human interest and interaction are indeed important to the successful use of computers. John's teacher in Chapter 1 should praise him for the progress he is making in using computer courseware. A pat on the back would still go a long way in making John feel good about himself and his learning.)

A final consideration in selecting computer software is whether you want computer management of instruction (CMI) in addition to computer assisted instruction (CAI). (We have been speaking thus far about CAI.) CMI offers the benefits of record-keeping so that students can begin a lesson where they left off on the previous day. CMI also keeps track of the results of diagnostic and mastery tests for each student and provides class records. As microcomputers become more powerful, they will be able to utilize more sophisticated record-keeping systems and manage more data. You need to be aware of the capabilities of the computers in your school when selecting software, to know whether they will take a particular CMI software package.

You, as a concerned teacher of reading, need to stay informed about developments in computer technology. Progress is being made every day in increasing

Teacher involvement is important in using a computer. (Photo by Paul Conklin)

capabilities while bringing down costs. It is exciting to know that you will have opportunities for using technology in ways that we have not even contemplated.

## Summary

Effective schools focus on the basic skills. Effective teachers, likewise, take basic skills instruction seriously. They manage their time to provide more time and greater involvement in learning for all children.

We outline a step-by-step procedure for organizing the reading instructional program, suggesting various types of groupings, as well as flexibility in group composition, to overcome the stigma that may be attached to membership in the lowest reading group.

There are advantages and disadvantages to various scheduling plans. The self-contained classroom enables the teacher to know students better, facilitating transfer of skills to all content areas. The Joplin Plan reduces the great range of reading abilities within a classroom. Skill groupings provide children with appropriate skill instruction and offer efficiency in instructional effort.

Computers can be effective tools in the classroom. We suggest various features to look for when selecting software, particularly for use with poor readers.

# Journals With Reviews of Software

*Computer Learning Classroom*
Subscription Department
5615 West Cermak Road
Cicero, IL 60650

*Computers, Reading, and Language Arts*
Department M2
P.O. Box 13247
Oakland, CA 94661 – 0247

*The Computing Teacher*
International Council for Computers in Education
Department of Computer and Information Science
University of Oregon
Eugene, OR 97403

*Creative Computing: Magazine of Personal Computer*
   *Applications and Software*
P.O. Box 5214
Boulder, CO 80321

*Educational Computer*
3199 De La Cruz Boulevard
Santa Clara, CA 95050

*Educational Computer Magazine*
P.O. Box 535
Cupertino, CA 95015

*Electronics Learning*
Scholastic, Inc.
50 West 44th Street
New York, NY 10036

*MECC Users Newsletter*
MECC Publications
2520 Broadway Drive
St. Paul, MN 55113

*Personal Software*
P.O. Box 2919
Boulder, CO 80321

# References

Allington, R. (1980). Teacher interruption behaviors during primary grade oral reading. *Journal of Educational Psychology, 72* (3), 371–377.

Anderson, L. M., Evertson, C. M., & Emmer, E. T. (1979, April 8–12). *Dimensions in classroom management derived from recent research.* Paper presented at the annual meeting of the American Educational Research Association, San Francisco.

Block, J. H. (1980). Success rate. In C. Denham & A. Lieberman (Eds.), *Time to Learn.* Washington, DC: National Institute of Education.

Brophy, J. E. (1979). Teacher behavior and its effects. *Journal of Educational Psychology, 71* (6), 733–750.

Carnine, D., & Silbert, J. (1979). *Direct instruction reading.* Columbus, OH: Charles E. Merrill.

Chall, J. (1983). *Stages of reading development.* New York: McGraw-Hill.

Coleman, J. S., Campbell, E. Q., Hobson, C. J., McPartland, J., Mood, S. M., Weinfeld, F. D., & York, R. L. (1966). *Equality of educational opportunity.* Washington, DC: United States Office of Education.

D'Amico, J. J. (n.d.). *The effective schools movement: Studies, issues, and approaches.* Philadelphia, PA: Research for Better Schools.

Duffy, G. G. (1983). From turn taking to sense making: broadening the concept of reading teacher effectiveness. *Journal of Educational Research, 76* (3), 134–139.

Durkin, D. (1978–1979). What classroom observations reveal about reading comprehension instruction. *Reading Research Quarterly, 14,* 481–533.

Edmonds, R. (1978, July). *A discussion of the literature and issues related to effective schooling.* Paper presented at the National Conference on Urban Education, St. Louis.

Edmonds, R. (1981, October 27). *Characteristics of effective schools: research and implementation.* Testimony before the House of Representatives Subcommittee on Elementary, Secondary, and Vocational Education, Washington, DC.

Emmer, E. T., Evertson, C. M., & Anderson, L. M. (1980). Effective classroom management at the beginning of the school year. *Elementary School Journal, 80,* 219–231.

Fisher, C. W., Berliner, D. C., Filby, N. N., Marliave, R., Cahen, L. S., & Dishaw, M. M. (1980). Teaching behaviors, academic learning time, and student achievement: an overview. In C. Denham & A. Lieberman (Eds.), *Time to Learn.* Washington, DC: National Institute of Education.

Good, T. L. (1979). Teacher effectiveness in the elementary school. *Journal of Teacher Education, 30* (2), 52–64.

Kulik, J. A. (1983). Synthesis of research on computer-based instruction. *Educational Leadership, 41* (1), 19–21.

Mason, G. E., Blanchard, J. S., & Daniel, D. B. (1983). *Computer applications in reading.* Newark, DE: International Reading Association.

Peterson, P. L. (1979). Direct instruction: Effective for what and for whom? *Educational Leadership, 37* (1), 46–48.

Rosenshine, B. V. (1980). How time is spent in elementary classrooms. In C. Denham & A. Lieberman (Eds.), *Time to Learn.* Washington, DC: National Institute of Education.

Rosenthal, R., & Jacobson, L. (1968). *Pygmalion in the classroom.* New York: Holt, Rinehart & Winston.

Rude, R. T., Otto, W., & Klumb, R. W. (1976). Retention of specific reading skills by primary grade pupils under varied teacher incentive conditions. *Journal of Educational Research, 69* (9), 323–330.

Sweeney, J. (1982). Research synthesis on effective school leadership. *Educational Leadership, 39* (5), 346–352.

Weber, G. (1971). *Inner-city children can be taught to read: four successful schools.* Washington, DC: Council for Basic Education.

White, M. A. (1983). Synthesis of research on electronic learning. *Educational Leadership, 40* (8), 13–15.

# Check Your Reading Comprehension

1.  Several views of the effective school were presented in this chapter. What are the characteristics commonly associated with such schools?

2.  A growing body of research concerning effective teaching is also available. According to the research cited in this chapter, what are the characteristics associated with effective teachers?

3.  Three types of scheduling plans for reading were presented in this chapter. Identify them:

    _____ In this plan students have a scheduled reading period. During this time slot, they leave their homerooms and meet in homogeneous groups (according to their reading level) for instruction.

    _____ In this plan, part of the DRTA is carried out in regular reading groups. Students move to other teachers for homogeneously grouped skill development.

    _____ This plan is the traditional reading organizational plan. A heterogeneous class is subdivided and stays with the same teacher for all reading instruction.

4.  After considering the advantages and disadvantages of each scheduling plan, which would you choose to use for your classroom? Why?

5.  As pointed out in this chapter, grouping of students does not have to be done by reading levels. What are other types of groups that could be established? Using the children in Table 1.1 (Chapter 1), form groups based on reading levels and on another criterion.

6.  Plan a grouping scheme for your class based on a criterion other than reading level.

7.  In Chapter 11 you began to develop a unit for your class. Units may include large group activities, small group activities, and individual activities. Attempt to build activities of each type into your unit. Try different grouping strategies within your unit.

# A

## Annotated List of Standardized Tests with Publishers' Addresses

*California Achievement Tests: Reading* (1970), by E. W. Tiegs and W. W. Clark, is a group-administered survey test for grades 1.5 to 12. It includes vocabulary and comprehension subtests and is available in five levels. Levels 1 and 2 cost $10.15 per 35 tests. Levels 3–5 cost $12.25 per 35 tests. Order from California Achievement Test Bureau, McGraw-Hill, Del Monte Research Park, Monterey, CA 93940.

*Doren Diagnostic Test of Word Recognition Skills* (1973), by M. Doren, is a group-administered diagnostic test for grades 1 to 4. It includes subtests for letter recognition, beginning sounds, whole word recognition, words within words, speech consonants, ending sounds, blending, rhyming, vowels, discriminate-guessing, spelling, and sight words. It costs $6.80 per 25 tests (plus $2.35 for a manual). Order from American Guidance Service, Inc., Publishers Building, Circle Pine, MN 55014.

*Durrell Analysis of Reading Difficulty,* rev. ed. (1980), by D. D. Durrell, is an individually administered diagnostic test for grades 1 to 6. It includes oral reading and silent reading subtests. It costs $3.75 per 35 record booklets. Order from Psychology Corporation, 757 Third Avenue, New York, NY 10017.

*Gates-MacGinitie Reading Tests* (1978), by W. H. MacGinitie, is a group-administered survey battery for grades 1 to 9. It includes vocabulary and comprehension subtests (and a speed and accuracy subtest in the upper levels). It is available in seven levels. It costs $3.60 per 35 tests. Order from Riverside Publishing Co., 8420 Bryn Mawr, Chicago, IL 60631.

*Gates-McKillop Reading Diagnostic Tests,* rev. ed. (1981), A. I. Gates and A. S. McKillop, is an individually administered diagnostic battery for grades 2 to 6. It includes subtests for oral reading, word perception, flashed word presentation, untimed word presentation, phrase perception, syllabication, letter names and sounds, visual and auditory blending, and spelling. It costs $6.50 per 25 record booklets (plus $.50 for a manual). Order from Teachers College Press, 1234 Amsterdam Avenue, New York, NY 10027.

*Iowa Tests of Basic Skills* (1975), by E. F. Linquist, A. N. Hieronymus, and others, is a group-administered survey battery for grades 1 to 9. It includes vocabulary, comprehension, and reference materials subtests as well as other nonreading subtests. The reading subtests cannot be purchased separately. The total battery costs $14.97 per 25 tests (plus $3.39 for a manual) for the primary level and $12.60 per 35 answer sheets (plus $2.97 per test booklet) for the upper levels. Order from Houghton Mifflin Co., 2 Park Street, Boston, MA 02107.

*Metropolitan Achievement Tests: Reading Tests* (1973), by W. N. Curost and others, is a group-administered survey battery for grades 2.5 to 9.5. It includes word knowledge and reading subtests. It costs $8.50 per 35 tests (plus $7.00 for a manual). Order from Psychology Corporation, 757 Third Avenue, New York, NY 10017.

*Peabody Individual Achievement Test* (1970), by L. M. Dunn and F. C. Markwardt, is an individually administered survey test for grades K–12. It includes reading recognition, reading comprehension, and spelling subtests as well as general information and mathematics subtests. It costs $36.00 per set of materials and 25 record booklets. Order from American Guidance Service, Inc., Publishers Building, Circle Pine, MN 55014.

*Silent Reading Diagnostic Test* (1970), by G. L. Bond, B. Balow, and C. J. Hoyt, is a group-administered diagnostic test for grades 2 to 6. It includes subtests for words in isolation, words in context, visual-structural analysis, syllabication, word synthesis, beginning sounds, ending sounds, and vowel and consonant sounds. It costs $5.00 per 20 tests. Order from Rand McNally and Company, Box 7600, Chicago, IL 60680.

*Spache Diagnostic Reading Scales,* rev. ed. (1981), by G. D. Spache, is an individually administered diagnostic battery for grades 1 to 8. It includes a word recognition test, graded reading passages, and a supplementary phonics test. It costs $5.00 per student book and $35.00 per 35 examiner's record booklets (plus $7.00 for a manual). Order from California Test Bureau, McGraw-Hill, Del Monte Research Park, Monterey, CA 93940.

*Stanford Achievement Tests: Reading Tests* (1973), by R. Madden and others, is a group-administered survey battery for grades 1.5 to 9.5. It includes vocabulary and comprehension subtests as well as additional subtests—such as word study skills—in some levels. It is available in four levels. The Primary I level costs $8.95 per 35 tests; other levels cost $10.25 per 35 tests. Order from Psychology Corporation, 757 Third Avenue, New York, NY 10017.

*Stanford Diagnostic Reading Test* (1976), by B. Karlsen, R. Madden, and E. F. Gardner, is a group-administered diagnostic test for grades 1.5 to 13. It includes various subtests depending upon level, such as word reading, vocabulary, comprehension, literal comprehension, inferential comprehension, phonetic analysis, and structural analysis. It is available in four levels. Levels A– C cost $12.50 per 35 tests; Level D costs $14.50 per 35 tests. Order from Psychology Corporation, 757 Third Avenue, New York, NY 10017.

*Wide Range Achievement Test* (1978), by J. F. Jastak, S. R. Jastak, and S. W. Bijou, is an individually administered survey test for kindergarten to adulthood. It includes reading, spelling, and arithmetic subtests. It costs $5.70 per 50 tests (plus $8.00 for a manual). Order from Jastak Associates, Inc., 1526 Gilpin Avenue, Wilmington, DE 19806.

*Woodcock Reading Mastery Tests* (1973), by R. W. Woodcock, is an individually administered survey test for grades K to 12. It includes subtests for letter identification, word identification, word attack, word comprehension, and passage comprehension. It costs $22.00 per kit with 25 response forms, and $3.85 per additional 25 response forms. Order from American Guidance Service, Inc., Publishers Building, Circle Pine, MN 55014.

*Woodcock-Johnson Psychoeducational Battery* (1977), by R. W. Woodcock and M. B. Johnson, is an individually administered survey battery for preschool to adulthood. It includes subtests for cognitive ability, achievement, and interest. It costs $118.00 for a complete battery, $9.00 per 25 additional cognitive ability record forms, and $9.00 per 25 additional achievement and interest (combined) record forms. Order from Teaching Resources Corporation, 50 Pond Park Road, Hingham, MA 02043.

# B

## Selected Textbooks and Journals of Interest to Teachers of Reading

## Textbooks

The following textbooks focus on the diagnosis and remediation of reading difficulties. (Prices are, of course, subject to change by the publishers.)

Aulls, Mark W. *Developmental and Remedial Reading in the Middle Grades.* Abridged edition. Paper, 1978. This text includes chapters describing instructional programs for students in grades 4–8 with varying degrees of disability and chapters suggesting methods of organizing classroom instruction.
It is available from Allyn and Bacon, Inc., Rockleigh, NJ 07647, for $11.95.

Bader, Lois A. *Reading Diagnosis and Remediation in Classroom and Clinic.* Paper, 1980. This text includes many practical procedures for both diagnosis and remediation of reading difficulties, especially in the area of comprehension.
It is available from Macmillan Inc., 866 Third Avenue, New York, NY 10022, for $13.95.

Bond, Guy L., Tinker, Miles A. and Wasson, Barbara, B. *Reading Difficulties: Their Diagnosis and Correction.* Fourth edition, 1979. This is a comprehensive text. Although it includes a chapter about meeting individual differences through diagnostic teaching in the classroom, most of its planning suggestions are for individual remediation by a reading specialist.
It is available from Prentice-Hall, Inc., Englewood Cliffs, NJ 07632, for $23.95.

Brown, Don A. *Reading Diagnosis and Remediation.* 1982. This text includes a chapter describing organizational procedures for groups of students in remedial and corrective programs.

It is available from Prentice-Hall, Inc., Englewood Cliffs, NJ 07623, for $22.95.

Cheek, Martha Collins, and Cheek, Earl H., Jr. *Diagnostic-Prescriptive Reading Instruction: A Guide for Classroom Teachers.* 1980. This is a basic text that emphasizes classroom-oriented corrective reading instruction. It includes a chapter on organizing, analyzing, and interpreting the data obtained from diagnosis to put it to best use in prescriptive instruction.

It is available from William C. Brown Co., 2460 Kerper Blvd., Dubuque, IA 52001, for $18.00.

Ekwall, Eldon E., & Shanker, James L. *Diagnosis and Remediation of the Disabled Reader.* Second edition, 1983. This is a basic text. Its discussions of skills groups and problems contributing to reading disability include separate sections about diagnosis and about remediation.

It is available from Allyn and Bacon, Inc., Rockleigh, NJ 07647, for $20.95.

Ekwall, Eldon E. *Locating and Correcting Reading Difficulties.* Fourth edition. Paper, 1985. This is a "cookbook" for the corrective reading teacher. It is organized by "difficulties" (e.g., "Repetitions," "Unable to Use Context Clues") for each of which there are sections titled "Recognized By," "Discussion," and "Recommendations."

It is available from Charles E. Merrill Publishing Co., 1300 Alum Creek Drive, Columbus, OH 43216.

Kennedy, Eddie. *Classroom Approaches to Remedial Reading.* Second edition, 1977. This is a basic remedial text. Attention is given to the role of the classroom teacher in remediation, but the emphasis is on instruction, materials, and organization for teaching students needing remediation outside of the regular classroom.

It is available from Peacock Publishers, 115 North Prospect Avenue, Itasca, IL 60143, for $17.50.

Otto, Wayne, and Smith, Richard J. *Corrective and Remedial Teaching.* Third edition, 1980. This text is written for teachers working with underachievers in the regular classroom. By including chapters devoted to other basic skills, it puts reading disability in the context of the larger school curriculum.

It is available from Houghton Mifflin Co., 1 Beacon Street, Boston, MA 02107, for $20.75.

Roswell, Florence G., and Natchez, Glady. *Reading Disabilities: Diagnosis and Treatment.* Third edition. Paper, 1980. This basic text includes a chapter on evaluation by the classroom teacher.

It is available from Basic Books, Inc., 10 East 53rd Street, New York, NY 10022, for $7.95.

Rubin, Dorothy. *Diagnosis and Correction in Reading Instruction,* 1982. This text includes practical suggestions and a program description for making diagnosis and correction an integral part of the daily reading program.

It is available from Holt, Rinehart & Winston, 383 Madison Avenue, New York, NY 10017, for $24.95.

Rupley, William H., and Blair, Timothy R. *Reading Diagnosis and Remediation: Classroom and Clinic.* Second edition, 1983. This comprehensive text includes chapters describing methods for classroom implementation of a diagnostic model for reading instruction.

It is available from Houghton Mifflin, Co., 1 Beacon Street, Boston, MA 02107, for $22.50.

**Zintz, Miles V.** *Corrective Reading.* Fourth edition, 1981. This text is for classroom teachers. It includes chapters about appraising reading problems in the classroom, scheduling time and planning instruction for corrective reading, and working cooperatively with parents.

It is available from William C. Brown Co., 2460 Kerper Blvd., Dubuque, IA 52001, for $17.95.

# Journals

The following educational journals carry articles, research reports, and commentary of interest to reading teachers.

*Harvard Education Review* includes learned articles pertaining to many aspects of education and very informative book reviews. The latter call attention to many books that reading teachers will find interesting but may not see reviewed elsewhere (e.g., *Biting the Apple: Accounts of First Year Teachers; GNYS at Work: A Child Learns to Write and Read; runnin' down some lines: the language and culture of black teenagers* ).

*HER* is available from the Business Office, Longfellow Hall, 13 Appian Way, Cambridge, MA 02138, for $23.00 per year (four issues).

*Journal of Educational Research* includes reports of experimental research across many areas in education. Besides reports directly concerned with the teaching of reading, research about classroom practices, school organization, and student and teacher attitudes are of interest to reading teachers.

*JER* is available from Heldref Publications, 4000 Albemarle Street, NW, Washington, DC 20016, for $22.00 per year (six issues).

*Journal of Learning Disabilities* includes articles offering practical suggestions and discussions of issues, research reports, and brief book reviews related to learning disabilities. As a multidisciplinary publication, it includes many entries per issue that are of interest to reading teachers.

*JLD* is available from The Professional Press, Inc., 101 E. Ontario Street, Chicago, IL 60611, for $27.00 per year (10 issues).

*Journal of Reading* includes articles offering practical teaching suggestions and discussions of issues for teachers of reading at the secondary school, college, and adult levels. It also includes reviews of trade books, instructional materials, and professional books.

*JR* is available from the International Reading Association, 800 Barksdale Road, P.O. Box 8139, Newark, DE 19711, for $25.00 per year (eight issues), or for $35.00 per year with one of the following, $45.00 per year with two of the following, or $55.00 per year with three of the following: *Reading Teacher, Reading Research Quarterly, Lectura y Vida.* The subscription fee includes membership in the International Reading Association.

*Journal of Reading Behavior* includes reports of experimental research and book reviews specifically concerned with reading. The latter are concise reviews of reading and language arts methods texts, theoretical books, and collections of research.

*JRB* is available from the National Reading Conference, Inc., 1970 Sibly Tower, Rochester, NY 14604, for $25.00 per year (four issues); or *JRB* and a National Reading Conference yearbook may be obtained along with membership in the National Reading Conference, which costs $35.00.

*Reading Horizons* includes articles offering practical teaching suggestions and discussions of issues for reading teachers at all levels. A small portion of its space is given to research reports and reviews that emphasize implications for practitioners.
*RH* is available from the College of Education, Western Michigan University, Kalamazoo, MI 49008, for $10.00 per year (four issues).

*Reading Improvement* includes reports of experimental research, articles offering practical teaching suggestions and discussions of issues, and theoretical papers related to the teaching of reading at all levels. One-paragraph reviews of books—most of which are interesting though not all are directly concerned with reading—are page fillers.
*RI* is available from Project Innovation, Box 566, Chula Vista, CA 92010, for $8.00 per year (four issues).

*Reading Psychology* includes reports of experimental research, theoretical articles, essays about issues, and book reviews, all specifically concerned with reading. One section of each issue is titled "For the Practitioner"; the book reviews include a wide variety of books of interest to reading teachers; and interesting quotations about books and reading from expected and not-so-expected sources (e.g., Harper Lee, Carl Sagan, Paul "Bear" Bryant, and Ronald Reagan among others, in one issue) are page fillers.
*RP* is available from Hemisphere Publishing Corp., 1025 Vermont Avenue, NW, Washington, DC 20005, for $19.75 per year (four issues).

*Reading Research Quarterly* includes scholarly reports of experimental research directly concerned with reading. *RRQ,* which describes itself as a forum for exchange of information and opinion, prints reactions to previous articles in a section titled, "Commentary."
*RRQ* is available from the International Reading Association, 800 Barksdale Road, P.O. Box 8130, Newark, DE 19711, for $25.00 per year (four issues) or with the same discounts for subscriptions to more than one International Reading Association journal that are described for *Journal of Reading.* The subscription fee includes membership in the International Reading Association.

*Reading Teacher* includes articles offering practical teaching suggestions and discussions of issues for teachers at the elementary level. *RT* also includes reviews of children's books, instructional materials, and professional books.
*RT* is available from the International Reading Association, 800 Barksdale Road, P.O. Box 8139, Newark, DE 19711, for $25.00 per year (eight issues) or with the same discounts for subscriptions to more than one International Reading Association journal that are described for *Journal of Reading.* The subscription fee includes membership in the International Reading Association.

*Review of Educational Research* includes thoroughly documented reviews of the literature pertaining to a wide variety of subjects in education. Though only a few reviews per volume specifically address the subject of reading (e.g., articles about adjunct questions in texts or integrating information from texts), many are concerned with subjects of at least indirect interest to reading teachers (e.g., pre- and post-testing, criterion referenced testing, clinical teaching, teacher praise).
*RER* is available from the American Education Research Association, 1230 17th Street, NW, Washington, DC 20036, for $16.00 per year (four issues) or *RER* and two other American Educational Research Association journals may be obtained with membership in the American Educational Research Association, which costs $35.00 (for students, $15.00).

# C

## Children's Literature Selected by the CCBC

The purpose of this appendix is to offer a list of good trade books for children that may have a potential motivational function for corrective students. Compiling such a list presented us with a formidable selection task. Happily, two university colleagues, Susan C. Griffith and Ginny Moore Kruse, had developed a list similar to what we hoped to present here. They had already selected trade books they considered excellent for various reasons for an annual publication of the Cooperative Children's Book Center (CCBC), a children's literature research library and examination center at the University of W sconsin—Madison, 4290 Helen C. White Hall, 600 N. Park Street, Madison, WI 53706. We reprint their selection list, "CCBC Choices: 1981" here as an example of the wide variety just one year's publications offer in high quality reading to supplement teachers' standard favorites and past award-winning books.

### CCBC Choices: 1981

Several perspectives on the books published in 1981 for children through 14 years of age are available to those associated with the CCBC. Monthly CCBC book discussions, content evaluations by Wisconsin specialists, and our own participation on national and state book evaluation committees provide the basis for this selective listing developed in February, 1982. The books are organized into eleven sections. Suggested interest levels are provided.

## History, People, and Places

Alihi. *Digging Up Dinosaurs.* Crowell. 33 p. (A Let's-Read-and-Find-Out Science Book)
An engaging and informative brief description of how scientists uncover, preserve, and study fossilized dinosaur bones provides background for youngsters who see such skeletons reconstructed in museums. (4–11 years)

Barton, Byron. *Building a House.* Greenwillow. 32 p.
A step-by-step outline of the process of building a house is illustrated with rudimentary drawings painted in solid, deep, bright colors. (3–7 years)

Bober, Natalie S. *A Restless Spirit; The Story of Robert Frost.* Atheneum. 197 p.
An objective biography of Robert Frost reveals the importance of his farming experiences and his relationship with his wife Elinor in writing his poetry. The responsible notes include a Source Guide for Quoted Material, bibliography, two poetry indexes, and a standard index. (11 years and older)

Coerr, Eleanor. *The Big Balloon Race.* Pictures by Carolyn Croll. Harper & Row. 62 p. (An I Can Read Book)
Three easy-to-read chapters tell a story based on an actual family of balloonists: the Myers Family of whom Carlotta was the most expert and popular aeronaut in the 1880s. In this book, young Ariel first almost causes her mother to lose a balloon race and then is instrumental in gaining the victory. (4–9 years)

Curtis, Patricia. *Cindy a Hearing Ear Dog.* Photographs by David Cupp. Dutton. 55 p.
The training of young dogs for use by people with hearing impairments is detailed in text and photographs in this account of such a training center. (7–14 years)

Fritz, Jean. *Traitor, the Case of Benedict Arnold.* Putnam. 192 p.
Benedict Arnold's life is deftly and sensibly recounted in light of his personality and the temper of the times. The account of Major Andre's foray into enemy territory includes researched material found in no other biography of Arnold. A bibliography, notes, and index supplement a fine example of biography writing in which the material in quotation marks is taken from primary sources only. (11 years and older)

Biglin, James Cross. *The Skyscraper Book.* Illustrations by Anthony Kramer. Photographs by David Anderson. Crowell. 86 p.
A compact volume in a clear, easily understood format relates the history of skyscrapers and the technical principles upon which their construction is based. The precise text integrates human interest details and anecdotes with information. Includes a list of "Fabulous Facts about Famous Skyscrapers." (9 years and older)

Hirsch, Karen. *Becky.* Pictures by Jo Esco. Carolrhoda Books. 36 p.
A youngster learns to live with her part-time sister, a child whose hearing impairment and resulting educational needs requires her to live in a foster home during school weeks. The author lives in Eau Claire, WI. (4–9 years)

Howe, James. *The Hospital Book.* Photographs by Mal Warshaw. Crown. 94 p.
An up-to-date look at hospital experiences includes black-and-white photographs of modern hospital scenes and equipment as well as information about feelings that might be a part of a hospital experience. Photographs make it possible to use with younger children; the text makes it useful for older readers as well. (4–13 years)

Ingalls, Robert P. *Point of Order; a Profile of Senator Joe McCarthy.* Putnam. 159 p.
A chronological account of the factors, incidents, and influences instrumental in Joseph McCarthy's rise to power and eventual political downfall in the 1950s. Facts are presented within the context of opinion and of the time period. (11 years and older)

**Leoper, John J.** *By Hook and Ladder: the Story of Fire Fighting in America.* Atheneum. 74 p.
An interesting and readable perspective on firefighting includes information about equipment, techniques, personnel, and famous fires in U.S. history. (9 – 13 years)

**Sadler, Catherine Edwards.** *Two Chinese Families.* Photographs by Alan Sadler. Atheneum. 70 p.
The lives of two contemporary Chinese families are compared and contrasted in a short text and many photographs, which capture the rhythm of life in China today. (7 – 11 years)

**Sandin, Joan.** *The Long Way to a New Land.* Harper & Row. 63 p. (An I Can Read History Book)
Four chapters chronicle a family journey from Sweden to the U.S. during the famine of 1868. Illustrations in three colors by the author provide visual information and interest on every page-spread. An author's note at the end gives historical background in this unusually fine, easy-to-read historical fiction. (7 – 11 years)

**Sarnoff, Jane, and Riffins, Reynolds.** *Words: A Book about the Origins of Everyday Words and Phrases.* Scribner. 64 p.
A compendium of information about the origin of specific words is organized into categories such as family, ships at sea, mystery, and names. Interestingly illustrated with black silhouetted figures and indexed by key word. (7 – 13 years)

**Siegal, Aranka.** *Upon the Head of the Goat; A Childhood in Hungary 1939 – 1944.* Farrar, Straus & Giroux. 214 p.
An autobiographical account of rural and urban circumstances relating to Hitler's take-over of Hungary and one family's subsequent fate in a concentration camp. Restraint and integrity mark this unique personal narrative told through young Piri's point of view. A 1982 Newbery Honor Book. (11 years and older)

**Sobol, Harriet Langsam.** *The Interns.* Photographs by Patricia Agre. Coward. 61 p.
An in-depth narrative with black and white photographs follows two interns through the intense responsibility of their first year of postgraduate medical education at the Babies Hospital or the Columbia Presbyterian Medical Center. (11 years and older)

**Tang, Yungmei.** *China, Here We Come! Visiting the People's Republic of China.* Putnam. 64 p.
A photographic essay records a trip to China through the eyes of a group of thirteen-year-old New York City children. The impressions and actions of these children provide the connection and interest for young readers in the United States. (9 – 13 years)

**Tax, Meredith.** *Families.* Illustrated by Marylin Hafner. Little, Brown. An Atlantic Monthly Press Book. 32 p.
Black and white drawings portray many kinds of family structures. Regardless of where or with whom you live, "families are who you live with and who you love." (4 – 9 years)

**Thomas, Art.** *Merry-go-rounds.* Pictures by George Overlie. Carolrhoda Books. 48 p. (A Carolrhoda On My Own Book)
An easy-to-read history and description of merry-go-rounds presents material already of entertainment interest to youngsters in a format they can approach and enjoy. (7 – 9 years)

**Yates, Elizabeth.** *My Diary — My World.* Westminster. 186 p.
Elizabeth's determination to become the woman she wants to be strikes the universal chord of experience in her diary, a journal of her life as a daughter and aspiring writer in a wealthy upstate New York family in the 1900s. The author is the author of the Newbery Award-winning *Amos Fortune, Free Man.* (11 years and older)

Zerman, Melvyn Bernard. *Beyond a Reasonable Doubt; Inside the American Jury System.* Crowell. 217 p.

Zerman discusses issues surrounding the jury system and tells how the system works. The clearly organized text uses understandable terminology and attention-getting (and appropriate) examples. (11 years and older)

Ziefein, Melvin B. *Flight, a Panorama of Aviation.* Illustrated by Tobert Andrew Parker. Pantheon. 119 p. (available in hardcover and paperback)

Watercolor paintings illustrate every page of this history of human flight, which begins with early theories and concludes with the SST. The author is Deputy Director of the National Air and Space Museum at the Smithsonian Institute. (all ages)

## Issues in Today's World

Bernstein, Joanne E. *Dmitry: A Young Soviet Immigrant.* Photographs by Michael J. Bernstein. Clarion/Houghton. 80 p.

A warmly told account of the immigration of a Soviet family to the United States is a balanced and fair look at the awesomeness of adjustment to a new culture in contemporary times. Information about daily life in the Soviet Union and about the situation of Jews in the Soviet Union is carefully and clearly presented from the family's perspective. (9–13 years)

Booher, Dianna Daniels. *Rape: What Would You Do If . . .?* Messner. 159 p.

Practical, helpful information about prevention and protection. (12 years and older, and parents)

Jacobs, Francine. *Bermuda Petrel; The Bird That Would Not Die.* Illustrated by Ted Lewin. Morrow. 38 p.

When Christopher Columbus sailed in 1492, there were probably more than a million cahows, or Bermuda petrels. By 1620 the bird was believed to be extinct, and not until 1906 was seen again. Then the work of Bermudian David Wingate on behalf of the cahows began, and with this individual effort, the dramatic comeback of an endangered species. Unusually interesting drawings complement every page-spread. (7–13 years)

*The Kids Book of Divorce: By, For and About Kids.* By the Unit at the Fayerweather Street School. Lewis/distributed by Stephen Greene Press. 123 p.

Children aged 11–14 discuss personal and legal impacts of divorcing (ed) parents. (10 years and older, and parents)

Kiefer, Irene. *Poisoned Land; The Problem of Hazardous Waste.* Atheneum. 90 p.

A subject specialist describes EPA guidelines and new waste disposal systems for land and sea that can deal with chemical wastes. A glossary and index are included. (11 years and older)

LeShan, Eda. *The Roots of Crime; What You Need to Know about Crime and What You Can Do About It.* Four Winds. 166 p.

LeShan examines the criminal justice system, showing how people with few opportunities and little hope become victims of antiquated laws. A sobering look at the roots of crime—poverty, racial prejudice, slum neighborhoods, the climate of corruption in society, and strong feelings of anger and self-hatred born of unhappy families and inadequate schools—in a hopeful, commonsense manner. She integrates interviews with people who have committed crimes. (11 years and older)

Poynter, Margaret. *Too Few Happy Endings: The Dilemma of the Humane Societies.* Atheneum. 130 p.

An account of the daily life of Humane Society workers identifies and discusses issues caused by overcrowded shelters and overworked staffs. (9 years and older)

Pringle, Laurence. *What Shall We Do with the Land? Land Choices for America.* Illustrated with photographs. Crowell. 120 p.

Choices about land use presently facing the United States are all thoroughly explained and placed in ecological and political contexts. Division of chapters is by type and aids in the use of the book as a reference tool; farmland, rangeland, forests, wild places, and coasts. An excellent list of further reading is appended. Carefully captioned occasional photographs add interest and value to this eloquent statement regarding responsibility and stewardship for land across time. (11 years and older)

## Seasons and Celebrations

Ancona, George. *Dancing Is.* Dutton. 48 p.

Dancing has different meanings depending on circumstances or culture. "Dancing is a skip and a hop and a kick and a stomp and just feeling good." One does not always need to take lessons to enjoy movement. Abundant black and white photographs expand the concept of dance and picture celebrations and entertainments in many parts of the world. (4–11 years)

Cohen, Barbara. *Yussel's Prayer; a Yom Kippur Story.* Retold by Barbara Cohen. Illustrated by Michael J. Deraney. Lothrop. 28 p.

A poor child's heartfelt, simple gift means more than the traditional gifts of the older, wiser, and wealthier. Illustrated in soft pencil drawings in sepia tones. (4–9 years)

Cosman, Madeleine Pelner. *Medieval Holidays and Festivals; a Calendar of Celebrations.* Scribner. 136 p.

Medieval celebrations organized by month include material not easily located in other books for children: Twelfth Night customs, Lammas Day, Michaelmas, and Catherning, along with unusual information about Valentine's Day and Halloween. Decorations, costumes, and food are detailed. Further reading is listed, and source notes document archival photographs. The author is Director of the Institute for Medieval and Renaissance Studies at City College of the City University of New York. (9 years and older)

Drucker, Malka. *Passover: A Season of Freedom.* Drawings by Brom Hoban. Holiday House. 95 p. (A Jewish Holidays Book)

The Exodus story, the meaning of the Seder meal, and Passover preparations are clearly explained and illustrated with photographs from many museums and archives. (9 years and older)

Greenfield, Howard. *Bar Mitzvah.* Illustrated by Helen Grove. Holt. 28 p.

The origin and importance of this significant Jewish ceremony are described in detail in a handsomely designed book. (9 years and older)

## The Natural World

Bonners, Susan. *A Penguin Year.* Written and illustrated by Susan Bonners. Delacorte. 44 p.

Blue and black watercolor paintings enliven 48 pages of fascinating material about the life cycle of the Adelie penguin of Antarctica. (7–11 years)

Cole, Joanna. *A Horse's Body.* Photographs by Jerome Wexler. Morrow. 45 p.

The parts of a horse's body and their functions are described in a brief text printed in large type. Black and white photographs and simple diagrams precisely illustrate the information.

**Cole, Joanna.** *A Snake's Body.* Photographs by Jerome Wexler. Morrow. 48 p.
Remarkable close-up black and white photographs illustrate a study of the functions and features of a snake's body.

**Goldner, Kathryn Allen, and Vogel, Carole Garbuny.** *Why Mount St. Helens Blew Its Top.*
Illustrations by Robert Aggarwal. Dillon. 88 p.
An unusually large variety of photographs, charts, and other graphics—many in two colors or full color, illustrate and expand the information about one volcano as well as that about general characteristics of volcanoes, how eruptions can be predicted, and some famous eruptions. The author is a science teacher who grew up near Verona and Mount Horeb, WI. (9 years and older)

**Goor, Ron and Nancy.** *Shadows: Here, There, and Everywhere.* Crowell. 47 p.
How shadows are formed, why they change, and their importance in the world are demonstrated in a series of black and white photographs with accompanying text. People interested in art and design as well as science topics will find this book to be of unusual interest. (7–11 years)

**Isenbart, Hans-Heinrich.** *A Duckling Is Born.* Illustrated by Othmar Baumli. Translated from the German by Catherine Edwards. Putnam. 38 p.
Full-color photographs trace the life cycle of mallard ducks. A stunning sequence of photographs shows the development of a duckling inside an unhatched egg. (4–11 years)

**Lauber, Patricia.** *Seeds, Pop, Stick, Glide.* Photographs by Jerome Wexler. Crown. 57 p.
A remarkable combination of photographs and text describe the ways seeds travel with animals and people, the wind and water. Seeds that scatter themselves are also described and pictured. (7 years and older)

**McLoughlin, John C.** *The Tree of Animal Life; A Tale of Changing Forms and Fortunes.*
Dodd, Mead. 160 p.
The evolution of the major animals' phyla from the first primitive cells is pictured in drawings and explained in text in a hefty, oversized book that also discusses transformations of animal life through natural selection processes acting on genetic material. A compelling conclusion reminds readers that evolution continues and that human decisions can affect the process drastically. An extensive glossary and many charts add to the value of this unusual book developed by a zoologist and scientific illustrator whose works for adults are widely respected. (for good readers 11 years and older)

**Pringle, Laurence.** *Frost Hollows and Other Microclimates.* Morrow. 62 p.
Small climates affect plants and animals; architects as well as farmers often use this knowledge of microclimates to advantage. "Whether you want to save energy, fly a kite, grow plants, or keep cool on a hot summer day, knowledge of the little climates that surround you will be helpful." The book is a good introduction to an aspect of the natural world to which increased attention is being given as people seek to live harmoniously with nature. Pringle's reputation as a careful researcher and fine writer is upheld. The book contains excellent photographs and charts on almost every page-spread; each has an interesting caption. A glossary, further reading, and an index complete this excellent example of science writing and bookmaking. (7–13 years)

**Sattler, Helen Roney.** *Dinosaurs of North America.* Illustrated by Anthony Rao. Lothrop.
151 p.
Dinosaur history is told against a background of vast geological changes. More than 80 kinds of dinosaurs are described in accurate detail and shown in lifelike drawings. North American dinosaur discoveries are indexed by geographic region, state, prov-

ince, etc. A topical and illustration index are included as is a list of further reading. (all ages)

Simon, Hilda. *The Magic of Color.* Lothrop. 55 p.

A concise, understandable explanation of color and color perception includes information about the difference between light color and paint color. The color separation process used in printing books is also outlined. (9 – 13 ages)

Simon, Seymour. *Einstein Anderson Tells a Comet's Tale.* Illustrated by Fred Winkowski. Viking. 73 p.

A sequence of ten fictionalized science mysteries gives readers a chance to solve each puzzle before the story is concluded. Some prior information about each science topic is usually necessary. In this fourth book of a series, Adam "Einstein" Anderson solves puzzles related to astronomy, optics, rocketry, zoology, change of state, inventions, and motion. The author is a noted science writer who once taught science. An ideal "read-aloud" book for science classes; excellent for use with or by gifted/ talented children. (7 – 11 years)

## The Arts

Anno, Mitsumasa, and Anno, Masaichiro. *Anno's Magical ABC; An Anamorphic Alphabet.* Philomel. 62 p.

A double treatment of upper and lower case letters introduces the negative perspective of reflected painting and drawing used by early Greek painters and sculptors. Younger children can make an entertainment of seeing the ABC's in a new perspective using foil around a small cyclindrical object. Art educators and teachers in gifted and talented programs will appreciate the graphs and instructions that guide older children in experimentation with reverse drawing. (4 – 13 years)

Crane, Walter. *An Alphabet of Old Friends; and, The Absurd ABC.* Metropolitan Museum of Art and Thames and Hudson. 28 p.

Two of Crane's original, comical alphabets are handsomely and faithfully reproduced in an elegant and interesting single volume picture book first published in 1874. (up to 6 years)

Haddad, Helen R. *Potato Printing.* Crowell. 64 p.

Attractive potato prints accompanied by careful explanations of process and step-by-step instructions in words and drawings are arranged by increasing difficulty. Useful as a craft primer or as a design challenge to the knowledgeable craftsperson or adult leader or teacher. (7 – 13 years)

Lasky, Kathryn. *The Weaver's Gift.* Photographs by Christopher G. Knight. Warne. 64 p.

Carolyne Frye's respect for her medium and her technical skills are a basis for this personal and comprehensive photo essay about the weaving process, taken from the birth of a lamb to the weaving of a blanket for a child. (7 – 11 years)

## Poetry

Adoff, Arnold. *OUTside INside Poems.* Illustrated by John Steptoe. Lothrop. 32 p.

An original collection of free-form poetry, which can be read as a collection of individual poems or as a loose narrative, explores the inner and outer life of a boy who aspires to be a baseball star. "OUTside my pants are torn and there is a scrape on my knee /INside an eagle takes off from its nest and flies free." The illustrations convey the internal and external realities by emphasizing perspective. (7 – 13 years)

**Baylor, Byrd, and Parnall, Peter.** *Desert Voices.* Scribner. 32 p.
>    Nine desert creatures (Pack Rat, Tortoise, Coyote, etc.) speak for themselves in poems that convey their natural behavior. Drawings and paintings expand the ideas with the colors reminiscent of U.S. Southwest desert areas. A final poem features a desert person. (4–13 years)

*Dusk to Dawn; Poems of Night.* Selected by Helen Hill, Agnes Perkins, and Althea Helbig. Illustrated by Anne Burgess. Crowell. 49 p.
>    Both the enchantment and the threat of night are balanced in this fine collection of 35 British and American poems illustrated with somewhat humorous black and white drawings. Indexed by poet, first line, and title. (9 years and older)

**Hearn, Michael Patrick** (Ed.). *Breakfast, Books, & Dreams: A Day in Verse.* With etchings by Barbara Garrison. Warne. 34 p.
>    Stylized browntone etchings illustrate a well-balanced, cohesive selection of poems that take a child through a school day: breakfast, inside a lab, at the lunchroom, during recess, in the library, with the family, etc. An entertaining variety of poems in an unusual and beautiful book gives a new view of dailiness. (4–11 years)

**Hughes, Ted.** *Under the North Star.* Illustrated by Leonard Baskin. Viking. 47 p.
>    A sophisticated sequence of poems accompanied by full-color drawings captures the barren and isolated environment in which 24 creatures survive: loon, wolverine, muskellunge, heron, brook trout, skunk, and others are presented by an internationally known poet and artist. (11 years and older)

**Morrison, Lillian.** *Overheard in a Bubble Chamber and Other Science Poems.* Paintings by Eyre de Lanux. Lothrop. 64 p.
>    Human emotions are expressed with modern scientific terminology in this collection of original poetry, appropriately illustrated with abstract paintings in black and white. (14 years and older)

**Thomas, Joyce Carol.** *Black Child.* Illustrated by Tom Feelings. Zamani Productions (31 West 31st Street, New York, NY 10001) paperback. 34 p.
>    A compassionate, haunting collection of poetry celebrates "the beauty and promise of the children." The poems and black-and-white portraits of children in the United States, Ghana, Guyana, and Senegal express innocence and angst in the face of an uncertain, perhaps hostile, future. (9 years and older)

**Willard, Nancy.** *A Visit to William Blake's Inn; Poems for Innocent and Experienced Travelers.* Illustrated by Alice and Martin Provensen. Harcourt. 45 p.
>    Stylized illustrations in an array of textures and warm harmonious brown/golds/grays/blues complement and extend the logical nonsense in a collection of whimsical, original poetry. The poems were inspired by Willard's childhood experience with the poetry of William Blake. 1982 Newbery Medal Winner. 1982 Caldecott Honor Book. Winner: CCBC Straw Caldecott Vote. (4–11 years)

## Folklore

**Aardema, Verna.** *Bringing the Rain to Kaptiti Plain; A Nandi Tale.* Pictures by Beatriz Vidal. Dial. 32 p.
>    A tale discovered in Kenya, Africa, has been retold with a cumulative refrain bringing the rhythm of "The House that Jack Built," the English nursery rhyme to which the similarity of this variant was noticed more than seventy years ago. The artist, originally from Argentina, used brilliant colors, stylized forms, and space to illustrate the story. (4–9 years)

**Bang, Molly Garrett.** *Tye May and the Magic Brush.* Adapted from the Chinese by Molly Garrett Bang. Greenwillow. 55 p. (A Greenwillow Read-Alone Book)
A six-chapter retelling of a Chinese tale about a child with no parents who dreams she has a brush that brings to life everything she paints. Careful use of red highlights details of the black and white drawings throughout the text. Short sentences and simple words relate the story of a girl whose name means "Iron Plum Flower." (4–9 years)

**Billout, Guy.** *Thunderbolt & Rainbow; A Look at Greek Mythology.* Prentice-Hall. 32 p.
Very brief retellings of 13 myths explaining the stars, moon, sun, dawn, wind, seasons, etc., are interpreted for today by bright and spare poster-like full-page illustrations. Readers' eyes will first see each unusual visual presentation and only after "seeing" the familiar urban or technological panorama will the earlier myth seem related. A remarkable and often humorous introduction to mythology. (7 years and older)

**Diop, Birago.** *Mother Crocodile/Maman-Caiman.* Translated and adapted by Rosa Guy. Illustrated by John Steptoe. Delacorte. 32 p.
When Mother Crocodile warns her children to swim away, they close their ears. Only later, in fact almost too late, do they realize the truth in her words. A cautionary Ovolof tale from Senegal, West Africa, illustrated with abstract drawings in a spectrum of underwater color can also be seen as a symbolic history. Honor Book: CCBC Caldecott Straw Vote. (7–11 years)

**Jaquith, Priscilla.** *Bo Rabbit Smart for True; Folktales from the Gullah.* Retold by Priscilla Jaquith. Drawings by Ed Young. Philomel. 55 p.
Humorous, action-filled cartoon-like frames vertically border each page of four trickster tales from the tradition of the coastal islands off Georgia and South Carolina. Gullah is the dialect mixing African usage with Elizabethan English and other linguistic elements. Source notes, a brief explanation of Gullah culture, and a bibliography add to the value of this unusual and highly entertaining book printed in two colors and designed in an original manner. (4–9 years)

**Otsuka, Yuzo.** *Suho and the White Horse.* Retold by Yuzo Otsuka. Adapted from the translation by Ann Herring. Illustrated by Suekichi Akaba. Viking. 48 p.
When a young Mongolian shepherd enters his beautiful white horse in a race and wins, a nobleman claims the horse for his own. An oversize format, spacious design and sensitive use of color capture the grandeur of the Mongolian landscape and the power of a treasured tale. (4–9 years)

**Schwartz, Alvin.** *Scary Stories to Tell in the Dark.* Drawings by Stephen Gammell. Lippincott. 111 p.
Gross, scary, frightening, silly, gory, creepy, and well-told fully documented tales are illustrated with black-and-white drawings of vague eerie tones, which accentuate the gruesome detail. All stories were responsibly collected from contemporary American folklore. An extensive, thought-provoking bibliography is included. Solid scariness usually told by memory on overnights, camping trips, and at Halloween from generation to generation has a validity that the trendy horror or macabre of other recent books cannot match. (9 years and older)

**Shannon, George.** *The Piney Woods Peddler.* Pictures by Nancy Tafuri. Greenwillow. 32 p.
An amiable peddler will swap or trade almost anything to get a shiny silver dollar for his dear darling daughter. A lilting refrain links episodes pictured in bright, boldly shaped paintings and drawings in this version by Eau Claire, WI, storyteller George Shannon of a tale some know as "The Twice-Bitten Stick." Detailed border designs give contrast as well as another way to see what's happening. (4–9 years)

**Yagawa, Sumiko.** *The Crane Wife.* Retold by Sumiko Yagawa. Translation from the Japanese by Katherine Paterson. Illustrated by Suekichi Akaba. Morrow. 32 p.
>In one of the most beautiful books of the year, a heartbreaking Japanese tale unfolds in understated and evocative illustrations that reflect Japanese art and culture in line and form. The sadness resulting from the inevitability of events is conveyed without sentimentality in this translation, which employs several Japanese onomatopoeic words. A note to readers says that *The Crane Wife* is perhaps Japan's most loved folktale and has been made into plays, movies, and even an opera. Every year thousands of Japanese will experience some version of the story. (7 years and older)

## Books for the Youngest

**Ahlberg, Janet and Allan,** *Funnybones.* Greenwillow. 32 p.
>A big skeleton, a little skeleton, and a dog skeleton spend a night on the town swinging and singing and scaring each other. White cartoon skeletons on dark backgrounds and white print on black backgrounds emphasize the nocturnal nature of this light-hearted adventure. (4–6 years)

**Ahlberg, Janet and Allan.** *Peek-a-boo!* Viking. 32 p.
>Perfectly placed cut-out circles highlight the details of a baby's perspective on family happenings. Borders frame each full-color picture of one family's comfortably cluttered life. (up to 4 years)

**Crews, Donald.** *Light.* 32 p.
>A presentation of daylight and nightlight(s) employs deep colors and broad shapes and invites comparisons that are most impressive from a distance or with a group. (up to 6 years)

**Henkes, Kevin.** *All Alone.* Greenwillow. 32 p.
>"No one looks just like me or thinks just like I do." A young child reflects upon the importance of time to imagine, think, and enjoy being by himself. A beautifully designed jacket and endpapers introduce and conclude this carefully made book illustrated with drawings and paintings in blue, green, brown, and rose hues. The author/artist grew up in Racine, WI, and developed this book when he was a freshman at University of Wisconsin—Madison. (up to 9 years)

**Hill, Eric.** *Spot's First Walk.* 20 p.
>A pop-up story features a frisky puppy's foray into a garden, a puddle, and other nearby places. Bright color, a large typeface, and study page stock distinguish a "first" book. (up to 3 years)

**Knotts, Howard.** *The Summer Cat.* Story and pictures by Howard Knotts. Harper. 32 p.
>Ben becomes attached to a mysterious cat that appears in his yard regularly on summer evenings. When he discovered that the cat is owned by a woman who lives on the other side of the woods during the summer only, he tries to make the cat "love me more than that summer lady," Black and white drawings give detail and reinforce the story with delicacy. (4–9 years)

**Le Tord, Bijou.** *Arf, Boo, Click; An Alphabet of Sounds.* Four Winds. 52 p.
>An ingenious concept book uses "sound words" such as "arf, boo, and click" to delineate the alphabet. Red, yellow, green, and black line drawings and type of many sizes add variety to an unusual alphabet book. (up to 6 years)

**Lewin, Betsy.** *Cat Count.* Dodd, Mead. 32 p.
>Cartoon cats with mischievous grins participate in lively, silly activity accompanied by simple rhythmic lyrics. A continuing equation in the upper right hand corner of

each page-spread extends the use of the book beyond those children just learning to count. The surprise at the end is in keeping with the "up" beat of the book. (up to 9 years)

**Lobel, Arnold.** *Uncle Elephant.* Harper. 64 p. (An I Can Read Book)
Nine chapters tell the story of an uncle's relationship to his nephew during an urgent time in the family. Readers will find a wonderful relationship revealed story by story. (4–9 years)

**Marshall, Edward.** *Three by the Sea.* Pictures by James Marshall. Dial. 48 p.
Three children make up stories to entertain each other while spending a day at the beach. The three types of stories within one story are a welcome technique in an unusually fine beginning reader.

**Rabe, Berniece.** *The Balancing Girl.* Pictures by Lillian Hoban. Dutton. 32 p.
Margaret can balance a book on her head and blocks in a tower. A determined and competitive child finds yet another way to be successful at the school carnival; the wheelchair and leg braces she uses are incidental to her full involvement in classroom and peer activities. The subdued colors of the drawings and paintings picture a contemporary classroom. (4–9 years)

**Sendak, Maurice.** *Outside Over There.* Harper. 36 p.
Ida ventures into "outside over there" to rescue her baby sister from the boglins. A pastiche of images and artistic styles embodies the dreamlike nature of this fantasy. A 1982 Caldecott Honor Book. (all ages)

**Shannon, George.** *The Gang and Mrs. Higgins.* Pictures by Andrew Vines. Greenwillow. 47 p. (A Greenwillow Read-Alone Book)
A tale he heard as a child in Kansas gave the author the idea for this story for beginning readers. Quick action and robust characters earmark an adventure for beginning readers to enjoy. (4–9 years)

**Shannon, George.** *Lizard's Song.* Illustrated by Jose Aruego and Ariane Dewey. Greenwillow. 32 p.
Bear discovers that singing his own song is much better than trying to copy that of a friend. A bright, flat, poster-like use of images and spaces suits this story by an Eau Claire, WI, writer. (up to 9 years)

**Van Allsburg, Chris.** *Jumanji.* Written and illustrated by Chris Van Allsburg. Houghton. 32 p.
Striking black-and-white pencil drawings from shifting and unusual perspectives juxtapose daily detail with fantastic absurdity as two bored and restless children play Jumanji, "a jungle adventure game, fun for some but not for all." 1982 Caldecott Medal Winner. (4–9 years)

**Waterton, Betty.** *Pettranella.* With illustrations by Ann Blades. Vanguard. 28 p.
A Canadian prize-winning book presents brightly colored paintings illustrating the brief story of a pioneer family's oxcart journey during which a child loses the bag of her grandmother's seeds she promised to plant at ther new Wisconsin home. (4–9 years)

**Williams, Vera.** *Three Days on a River in a Red Canoe.* Greenwillow. 32 p.
Childlike text and colored drawings report and record a canoe trip down a river. Details of preparation and practicalities of camping are interwoven with the adventure and fun of the trip. (4–9 years)

## Fiction for Younger Readers

**Byars, Betsy.** *The Cybil War.* Illustrated by Gail Owens. Viking. 126 p.
Simon and Tony vie for the attention of the same classmate: Cybil Ackerman. A light-

hearted look at a classroom romance and at the nature of friendship and loyalty. (9–11 years)

**Cameron, Ann.** *The Stories Julian Tells.* Illustrated by Ann Struggnell. Pantheon. 71 p. Large typeface and frequent illustrations will invite new readers to try a chapter book of six family stories beginning with a pudding episode that is easy to enjoy and hard to forget! An especially sympathetic father is one of the memorable aspects of the series of episodic stories. The author grew up in Rice Lake, WI. (4–9 years)

**Hautzig, Esther.** *A Gift for Mama.* Illustrated by Donna Diamond. Viking. 56 p. Ten-year-old Sara is determined to buy rather than make a gift for her mother. Her aunt helps her find a way to earn the money in a story with a universal theme of giving and receiving set in a particular time in Vilna, Poland. Black-and-white monoprints illustrate a story for which extraordinary care has been taken to make a beautifully bound and designed book. (7–9 years)

**Lewis, Naomi.** *The Silent Playmate: A Collection of Doll Stories.* Edited and with an introduction by Naomi Lewis. Illustrated by Harold Jones. Macmillan. 223 p. A fine collection of stories about all kinds of dolls includes excerpts from longer works of fiction, folktales, short stories, and poetry from several cultures. Lewis's excellent introduction broadly interprets dolls to include tin soldiers, wind-up toys, and stuffed animals. A list of more doll stories is appended. Authors represented include Charles Kingsley, Laura Ingalls Wilder, Robert Louis Stevenson, E. Nesbit, Katherine Mansfield, Laurence Housman, and Kenneth Grahame. (4–11 years)

**Pellowski, Anne.** *Stairstep Farm: Anna Rose's Story.* Pictures by Wendy Watson. Philomel. 176 p. Episodic stories of rural Wisconsin living in the 1930s tell of cookie baking, ghostly games, dress up, thistle chopping, a tornado and holiday customs in a large, happy, Catholic, Polish-American family. The author grew up in Trempealeau County where this and other books in a generation-by-generation sequence are set. She gathered information for them from archival records in Wisconsin and even in Poland as well as from people living there at the time. The first book to be published, *Willow Wind Farm,* is set in the 1960s. The other books will be published next year and are set early in the 20th century and late in the 19th century. (7–11 years)

## Fiction for Middle Readers

**Alexander, Lloyd.** *Westmark.* Dutton. 184 p. Theo, a fugitive from the law, becomes embroiled in adventures with a roguish doctor and in incendiary plots of revolutionaries in Westmark, a land ruled by villainous Chief Minister Cabbarus. Episodic chapters with cliff hanging endings and plenty of action make this exciting as a read-aloud. (9–13 years)

**Ames, Mildred.** *Anna to the Infinite Power.* Scribner. 198 p. A twelve-year-old math whiz who almost seems to be a human computer accidentally finds out that she is a clone and that she is part of an experiment with somewhat ominous overtones. The time is the 1990s. (9–13 years)

**Baker, Olaf.** *Where the Buffaloes Begin.* Drawings by Stephen Gammell. Warne. 46 p. A legend-like story features 10-year-old Little Wolf who could run the fastest, catch and ride with wildest pony, and know no fear. As he goes to "where the buffaloes begin" he is catapulted into riding to save his people. Black-and-white drawings perfectly complement the story, which was first published in the magazine *St. Nicholas* in February, 1915. Excellent and accurate drawings of objects from Little Wolf's life and culture divide sections of the story. A 1982 Caldecott Honor Book. (7–11 years)

**Bond, Nancy.** *The Voyage Begun.* Atheneum/A Margaret K. McElderry Book. 319 p.
Set in a not-too-distant future on an almost deserted Cape Cod, a long novel unfolds the impact of energy resource depletion. Eleven-year-old Mickey is defiant and independent as she learns to work for an old boat builder. An older brother is in a gang "The Salvages," which burns the boat and gives trouble to 16-year-old Paul, a thoughtful newcomer to the area. Parents and other adult characters are as powerfully drawn as children and teenagers. Threads of subplots and lives intersect in a remarkably well-written, original work that thrusts readers into considering what might happen next in the book as well as in real life. Gifted readers will enjoy the depth and scope of the story. Winner: CCBC Straw Newbery Vote. (9 years and older)

**Donnelly, Elfie.** *So Long, Grandpa.* Translated by Anthea Bell. Crown. 90 p.
Childhood perceptions of life and death are interwoven with the practical, daily routine of living with a terminally ill person. A touching first-person narrative notable for the warmth and humor of ten-year-old Michael's relationship with his grandpa, a character who is extremely well-developed. Winner: 1979 German Children's Book Prize. (9–13 years)

**Heide, Florence Parry.** *Treehorn's Treasure.* Drawings by Edward Gorey. Holiday House. 64 p.
The unforgettable boy of *The Shrinking of Treehorn* returns in a similarly designed book. One day Treehorn notices the leaves on a tree changing into dollar bills. Since this occurs shortly after Treehorn's father announces that money doesn't grow on trees, and they must save for a rainy day, Treehorn tries but fails to get the attention of adults to what he is saying. Puns, irony, and droll social observations mark the witty text by a Kenosha, WI, writer, and "Goreyesque" illustrations enhance each page-spread. (9 years and older).

**Keller, Beverly.** *The Sea Watch.* Four Winds. 134 p.
A funny, punny mystery filled with outlandish events, dastardly deeds, and unlikely heroes. (9–13 years)

**Lively, Penelope.** *The Revenge of Samuel Stokes.* Dutton. 122 p.
A washing machine smells of roast venison. Tobacco smoke comes from the television. A greenhouse turns into a Greek temple. The ghost of Samuel Stokes asserts itself when Charstock Park, a housing estate, is built on the site of an 18th-century garden he'd designed. (9–13 years)

**McGraw, Eloise Jarvis.** *The Money Room.* Atheneum/A Margaret K. McElderry Book. 182 p.
Shortly after moving onto the Oregon property their great-grandfather left their mother, Scott and Lindy determine to find his near-legendary Money Room. A series of unusual and baffling incidents soon has them wondering just who else is looking for the Money Room. (9–13 years)

**Rodowsky, Colby.** *The Gathering Room.* Farrar. 186 p.
The self-imposed isolation of nine-year-old Mudge and his parents as caretakers of Edgemount Cemetery begins to change when Aunt Ernestus comes for a visit. (9–13 years)

**Sargent, Sarah.** *Secret Lies.* Crown. 118 p.
Thirteen-year-old Elvira Judson travels to stay with relatives she barely knows in Virginia and finds the distinction between her romantic fantasies and the realities of her life and theirs. The author lives in Oshkosh, WI. (9–13 years)

**Uchida, Yoshiko.** *A Jar of Dreams.* Atheneum/A Margaret K. McElderry Book. 131 p.
Eleven-year-old Rinko lives in California during the Depression. She discovers the nature of racism and the prejudice against people born in Japan, as were her parents and aunt. (9–13 years)

Wiseman, David. *Jeremy Visick*. Houghton. 170 p.
> Twelve-year-old Matthew begins a school assignment by observing epitaphs in a local cemetery and is drawn to find out more about and even to assist a boy lost in a mining disaster a century earlier in Cornwall where they both live(d). (9–13 years)

Caring, Jane. *The Return of the Dragon*. Illustrated by Polly Broman. Houghton. 146 p.
> The dragon Carador must prove he is no longer the terror of Wales by doing twelve good deeds. Unlikely facts in the Carador stories are historically true, but the adventures are more firmly rooted in geography than history. (9–13 years)

## Fiction for Older Readers

Childress, Alice. *Rainbow Jordan*. Coward. 123 p.
> Women of four generations are portrayed as 14-year-old Rainbow attempts to find hope and promise in her life. Rainbow's mother was a child herself when she became a parent. Rainbow's involvement with other women of differing social and economic classes helps her to figure out who she is with respect to demands on her from a foster parent, a social worker, a boyfriend, and others. The syntax of black English is used skillfully and the characterizations are splendid. Honor Book: CCBC Straw Newbery Vote. (14 years and older)

Hamilton, Virginia. *The Gathering*. Greenwillow. 179 p.
> In the third and final book of The Justice Cycle, four modern day children return to Dustland, the world of the distant future, bringing with them The Watcher, a genetic gift necessary to the survival of all future life forms. The author has created an extraordinary fantasy world within the framework of modern evolutionary theory in which she explores the concepts of time, change, power, and responsibility. (14 years and older)

Hunter, Mollie. *You Never Knew Her As I Did*. Harper. 216 p.
> Young Will Douglas is devoted to the imprisoned Mary, Queen of Scots. His role in plotting and carrying out her escape is fascinating adventure. A genealogical chart at the end of the book assists in unraveling the web of royal and political interrelationships, which are essential to the story. (14 years and older)

Kerr, M. E. *Little Little*. Harper. 183 p.
> Narratives from the alternating viewpoints of 18-year-old Little Little LaBelle and Sydney Cinnamon provide the vehicle for an outrageous satire on contemporary middle-class U.S. mores and customs—conventions, personalized cars, and television evangelists—to name a few targets of the author. The perspective, astonishingly, does not ridicule the American Diminutives and other dwarfs who are central to the novel. (14 years and older)

Kullman, Harry. *The Battle Horse*. Translated from the Swedish by George Blecher and Lone Thygesen-Blecher. Bradbury. 183 p.
> A poor public school kid in Sweden during the Depression is thrilled to become involved in the popular jousting tournaments in which upper class teenagers are the knights riding on the shoulders of the lower class participants who become horses. A sombre, compelling, important novel examines conflicts between classes and sexes. Literary allusions from *Call of the Wild, Gulliver's Travels* and *Ivanhoe* develop themes of survival, justice, and romance. The author was runner-up for the 1980 Hans Christian Andersen Medal, which honors a total body of writing; Kullman has written 19 novels for young readers in Sweden. 1982 Batchelder Award Winner. (14 years and older)

McHargue, Georgess. *The Horseman's Word*. Delacorte. 259 p.

Champion rider Leigh Powers leaves Boston for the summer to manage her ailing uncle's pony-trekking business in Scotland. Her growing friendship with neighboring Rob Tinto ultimately leads to her participation in the secret, for males only, ceremony, the Horseman's Word. (14 years and older)

Nostingler, Christine. *Luke and Angela*. Translated by Anthea Bell. Harcourt. 144 p.

As two lifelong friends and neighbors approach adolescence, changes inevitably occur in their relationship. Their school life and apartment house community in Vienna are pictured well as are the dilemmas of being caught between childhood and adulthood. Humor marks a story that, in its hardcover edition, looks much "younger" in appeal than its content actually is. (14 years and older)

Schlee, Ann. *The Vandal*. Crown. 188 p.

Paul's violent outbursts and continual questions disrupt a repressive society dependent on its members retaining memory for no longer than three days. A psychologically suspenseful novel of the future. Winner: 1980 Guardian Award in England. (14 years and older)

Skurzynski, Gloria. *Manwolf*. Houghton/Clarion. 175 p.

As he reaches adolescence, Adam realizes that people think he is a werewolf. The details of life in medieval Poland are well-developed, as is a plot based on knowledge of an actual inherited disease so rare that only seventy cases are recorded. Victims of this incurable disease have an excess of porphyrins or red dyes in their blood, causing their bones, teeth, and urine to become red. (14 years and older)

Slepian, Jan. *Lester's Turn*. Macmillan. 139 p.

Lester, a teenager with cerebral palsy, struggles to bring warmth and friendship to his institutionalized friend Alfred. The narrative, a story set in the 1940s, is marked with the cynicism and hope typical of adolescents approaching adulthood. (14 years and older)

Taylor, Mildred. *Let the Circle Be Unbroken*. Dial. 394 p.

The Logans find strength and support in their family and their community as they and other blacks encounter the racism and the impact of government policy in rural Mississippi during the Depression of the 1930s. Honor Book: CCBC Straw Newbery Vote. (14 years and older)

Tolan, Stephanie S. *No Safe Harbors*. Scribner. 184 p.

Sixteen-year-old Amanda Sterling's safe, middle class world is challenged when her father, the mayor of an Ohio River city, is indicted for accepting a bribe. Her unexpected friendship with Jo Schmidt, a mechanic working to finance the college education for which his father refuses to pay, helps her look beneath the surface and begin to accept differences and weaknesses in others. The author grew up in Kenosha, WI. (14 years and older)

Westall, Robert. *The Scarecrows*. Greenwillow. 185 p.

Thirteen-year-old Simon's perceptions of reality are drastically altered by his rage and jealousy at his mother's remarriage to a sloppy, good-hearted artist, so unlike his soldier father. A powerful and frightening account of one boy's struggle to accept the circumstances around him. (14 years and older)

Noteworthy new editions of classic novels:

Twain, Mark. *The Annotated HUCKLEBERRY FINN: Adventures of Huckleberry Finn*. By Mark Twain (Samuel L. Clemens), with an introduction, notes, and bibliography by Michael Patrick Hearn. Clarkson N. Potter, Inc./distributed by Crown. 378 p.

Stevenson, Robert Louis. *Treasure Island*. Illustrated by N. C. Wyeth. Reissued by Charles Scribner's Sons to commemorate the 10th anniversary of the story's original publication. First published in this edition in 1911. 273 p.

# D

## Word Attack Objectives: Wisconsin Design for Reading Skill Development

### Level A

1. Listens for rhyming elements
   a. Words ①
      Objective: Given familiar words pronounced by the teacher, the child

      - indicates which of three words rhymes with a stimulus word; or
      - tells whether two words do or do not rhyme.

   b. Phrases and verses ②
      Objective: In real or nonsense verses read by the teacher, the child

      - supplies the missing word in a verse (e.g., "The big tall man/ Fried eggs in a _____"); or
      - identifies the rhyming words.

2. Notices likenesses and differences

   a. Pictures (shapes) ③
      Objective: The child identifies shapes that are the same or different in form and orientation.
   b. Letters and numbers ④
      Objective: The child selects the letter (upper or lower case) or number in a series that is identical to a key number or letter.

**Distributed by Learning Multi-Systems, Inc.,**
**340 Coyier Lane, Madison, WI 53713.**

[The child points to the letter that is the same as the first letter or number in a row—e.g.,

$$
\begin{array}{lcccc}
\text{P:} & \text{B} & \text{T} & \text{P} & \text{K} \\
\text{s:} & \text{s} & \text{z} & \text{e} & \text{c} \\
\text{9:} & \text{6} & \text{0} & \text{9} & \text{8]}
\end{array}
$$

  **c.**  Words and phrases  ⑤

Objective: The child selects the word or phrase in a series that is identical to a stimulus word or phrase (e.g., down: want, down, bone, find; back and forth: bank and find, back and forth, found it).

**3.**  Distinguishes colors  ⑥ᶦ *

Objective: The child identifies the colors blue, green, black, yellow, red, orange, white, brown, purple, when named by the teacher.

**4.**  Listens for initial consonant sounds  ⑦

Objective: Given a familiar word pronounced by the teacher, the child indicates which of three other words begin with the same consonant sound.

# Level B

**1.**  Has a sight word vocabulary  ①ᶦ

Objective: Given a maximum one-second exposure per word, the child recognizes preprimer and primer level words from the adapted Dolch sight vocabulary list.

Note: The specific preprimer and primer words are given in the list that appears on page 441. The child should be able to recognize additional sight words in instructional materials to which he has been exposed.

**2.**  Follows left-to-right sequence  ②ᶦ

Objective: The child reacts to number or letter stimuli in a left-to-right sequence. [The child names the letters or numbers presented in rows—e.g.,

$$
\begin{array}{cccc}
\text{N} & \text{C} & \text{H} & \text{P} \\
\text{c} & \text{o} & \text{e} & \text{g} \\
\text{4} & \text{7} & \text{1} & \text{2}
\end{array}
$$

— in a left-to-right sequence.]

---

*An *i* after the small numeral designates a skill that is assessed individually.

**3.** Has phonic analysis skills

    **a.** Consonant sounds

        **1)** Beginning consonant sounds ③

        Objective: Given real or nonsense words pronounced by the teacher, the child

- identifies the letter that stands for the initial sound and
- tells whether two words do or do not begin alike; or
- supplies another word that begins with the same sound.

        **2)** Ending consonant sounds ④

        Objective: Given real or nonsense words pronounced by the teacher, the child

- identifies the letter that stands for the ending sound and
- tells whether two words do or do not end alike; or
- supplies another word that ends with the same sound.

    **b.** Consonant blends ⑤
    Objective: Given real or nonsense words that begin with the consonant blends bl, cl, fl, gl, pl, sl, br, cr, dr, fr, gr, pr, tr, the child

- identifies the two letters that stand for the initial blend in words pronounced by the teacher; or
- identifies words that begin with the same blend as a stimulus word pronounced by the teacher and
- pronounces words that begin with the blends listed above.

    **c.** Rhyming elements ⑥
    Objective: Given a word, the child

- selects a rhyming word based on structure (e.g., man, pan, and fan are from the same word family); or
- supplies a real or nonsense rhyming word based on structure.

    **d.** Short vowels ⑦
    Objective: Given a one-syllable word with a single short vowel sound pronounced by the teacher (e.g., man, duck, doll, hop), the child

- identifies the letter that stands for the vowel sound; or
- reproduces the vowel sound.

    **e.** Simple consonant digraphs ⑧
    Objective: Given real or nonsense words pronounced by the teacher, the child identifies the letters in the simple two-consonant combinations sh, ch, th, that results in a single new sound.

**4.** Has structural analysis skills

  **a.** Compound words  ⑨
     Objective: The child

- identifies compound words; or
- specifies the elements of a compound word.

  **b.** Contractions  ⑩
     Objective: The child

- identifies simple contractions (e.g., I'm, it's, can't)
- uses contractions correctly in sentences.

  **c.** Base words and endings  ⑪
     Objective: The child identifies the root word in familiar inflected words (e.g., jumping, catches, runs).

  **d.** Plurals  ⑫
     Objective: The child tells whether familiar words (noun plus s or es) are singular or plural.

  **e.** Possessive forms  ⑬
     Objective: the child identifies the possessive forms of nouns used in context.

## Level C

**1.** Has a sight word vocabulary  ①

Objective: Given a maximum one-second exposure per word, the child recognizes first-grade words from the adapted Dolch sight vocabulary list. Note: See the list on page 441 for specific words. The child should be able to recognize additional sight words in the instructional materials to which he has been exposed.

**2.** Has phonic analysis skills

  **a.** Consonants and their variant sounds  ②
     Objective: Given words containing variant sounds of c, s, and g (e.g., cake/city, sit/trees, go/giant), the child indicates whether the underlined letters in given pairs of words have the same or different sounds. Note: Although the consonants c, g, s, q, d, x, t, and z have more than one sound, variant sounds of c, s, and g are most common at this level.

  **b.** Consonant blends  ③
     Objective: Given real or nonsense words beginning with the consonant blends st, sk, sm, sp, sw, sn, the child

- identifies the two letters that stand for the initial blend in words pronounced by the teacher; or

- identifies words that begin with the same blend as a stimulus word pronounced by the teacher and
- pronounces words that begin with the blends listed above.

**c.** Vowel sounds

**1)** Long vowel sounds ④

Objective: the child

- identifies the letter that stands for a single vowel sound in real or nonsense words pronounced by the teacher (e.g., nose, brile, cheese, seat, labe, run, mab) and indicates whether the sound is long or short; or
- pronounces real or nonsense words with a single vowel sound.

**2)** Vowel plus r ⑤

Objective: The child

- identifies the vowel that is with r in real or nonsense words pronounced by the teacher (e.g., darl, der, mur, form, girt) or
- pronounces words with r-controlled vowels (e.g., part, fur, hurt, bird)

Note: Because er, ir, and ur have the same sound, e, i, or u is the appropriate response in er, ir, and ur words.

**3)** a plus l ⑤

Objective: The child

- identifies the letters that stand for the al sound in real or nonsense words pronounced by the teacher; or
- pronounces words in which there is an al combination (e.g., salt, ball, zall).

**4)** a plus w ⑤

Objective: The child

- identifies the letters that stand for the aw sound in real or nonsense words pronounced by the teacher; or
- pronounces words in which there is aw combination (e.g., draw, saw, blaw).

**5)** Diphthongs ew, oi, oy, ou, ow ⑥

Objective: Given words containing ew, oi, oy, ou, ow, the child

- identifies the diphthong in real or nonsense words pronounced by the teacher; or
- pronounces words containing diphthongs.

**6)** Long and short oo ⑦

Objective: The child

- indicates whether the oo in words has the long oo (e.g., choose) or the short oo (e.g., book) sound; or
- pronounces words in which there is an oo combination.

**d.** Vowel generalizations ⑧
   **1)** Short vowel generalization

Objective: Given real or nonsense words in which there is a single vowel and a final consonant (e.g., bag, his, cat, gum), the child

- tells whether the words are pronounced according to the generalization; or
- pronounces the words giving the vowel its short sound.

Note: Children should learn that some familiar sight words are exceptions to this generalization (e.g., bold, find, sight, wild).

**2)** Silent e generalization ⑨

Objective: Given real or nonsense words that have two vowels, one of which is a final e separated from the first vowel by a consonant (e.g., cake, cube, mape, jome), the child

- tells whether the words are pronounced according to the generalization; or
- first attempts pronunciation by making the first vowel long and the final e silent.

Note: Children should learn that some familiar sight words are exceptions to this generalization (e.g., come, have, prove).

**3)** Two vowels together generalization ⑩

Objective: Given real or nonsense words that have two consecutive vowels (e.g., boat, meet, bait, deech), the child

- tells whether the words are pronounced according to the generalization; or
- first attempts pronunciation by making the first vowel long and the second vowel silent.

Note: Children should learn that some familiar sight words (e.g., bread, August) and words containing diphthongs are exceptions to this generalization.

**4)** Final vowel generalization ⑪

Objective: Given real or nonsense words in which the only vowel is at the end (e.g., go, she, thi), the child

- tells whether the words are pronounced according to the generalization; or
- pronounces the words giving the vowel its long sound.

Note: Children should learn that some familiar sight words are exceptions to this generalization (e.g., do, who).

**e.** Common consonant digraphs ⑫

Objective: Given real or nonsense words pronounced by the teacher, the child identifies the letters in the two-consonant combinations ch, nk, sh, ng, th, wh, that result in a single new sound.

**3.** Has structural analysis skills

**a.** Base words with prefixes and suffixes ⑬
Objective: The child selects base words with or without affixes that are appropriate to the context.

**b.** More difficult plural forms ⑭
Objective: The child tells whether more difficult plural forms (e.g., mice, ladies, children) are singular or plural.

**4.** Distinguishes among homonyms, synonyms, and antonyms

**a.** Homonyms ⑮
Objective: Given a sentence context, the child chooses between homonyms (e.g., Mother brought some meet/meat for dinner).

**b.** Synonyms and antonyms ⑯
Objective: The child tells whether words in a pair have the same, opposite, or simply different meanings.

**5.** Has independent and varied word attack skills ⑰

Objective: In both self-directed and teacher-directed reading, the child uses a variety of skills (e.g., picture, clues, context clues, structural analysis, sound/symbol analysis, comparison of new to known words) in attacking unknown words.

Note: The objective can be assessed through an individually administered informal reading inventory or by teacher observation.

**6.** Chooses appropriate meaning of multiple meaning words ⑱

Objective: Given a multiple-meaning word in varied contexts, the child chooses the meaning appropriate to a particular context.

## Level D

**1.** Has a sight word vocabulary ⑪

Objective: Given a maximum one-second exposure per word, the child recognizes second- and third-grade words from the adapted Dolch sight vocabulary list.
Note: See the list given on page 442 for specific words. The child should be able to recognize additional sight words in instructional materials to which he has been exposed.

**2.** Has phonic analysis skills
   **a.** Three-letter consonant blends ②
   Objective: The child identifies the letters in the three-letter blends scr, shr, spl, spr, str, thr, in real or nonsense words pronounced by the teacher.
   **b.** Simple principles of silent letters ③
   Objective: Given words containing silent letters (e.g., knife, gnat, write, dumb, doubt, high, flight, eat, four, believed), the child

   - identifies the silent letters; or
   - pronounces words containing silent letters

   Note: silent consonants commonly occur in the following combinations: (k)n, (g)n, (w)r, m(b), (b)t, i(gh), (t)ch.

**3.** Has structural analysis skills

   **a.** Syllabication ④
   Objective: The child divides words into single-vowel sound units by applying syllabication generalizations.

   **b.** Accent ⑤
   Objective: The child indicates the accented part (syllable) in familiar words, primarily two-syllable ones.

   **c.** Unaccented schwa ⑥
   Note: *If the unaccented schwa is included in the developmental reading program, this skill can be taught; if the schwa is not included, this skill can be omitted. Although the ability to identify the schwa sound has little inherent value, the child who is aware of the existence of the schwa sound may be more successful in sounding vowels than the child who is not.*
   Objective: Given words that he knows, the child specifies the unaccented syllable containing a schwa.
   Note: Although the short sound of u in, say, puppy has the same sound as that of the schwa, it is not a schwa because it is in the accented syllable.

    **d.**  Possessive forms ⑦

        Objective: The child identifies possessive nouns and pronouns used in context.

# Breakdown of the Adapted Dolch Basic Word List by Levels

## Level B: Preprimer

| | | | | |
|---|---|---|---|---|
| a | find | is | not | three |
| and | for | it | one | to |
| away | funny | jump | play | two |
| big | go | little | red | up |
| blue | help | look | run | we |
| can | here | make | said | where |
| come | I | me | see | yellow |
| down | in | my | the | you |

## Level B: Primer

| | | | | |
|---|---|---|---|---|
| all | do | no | say | want |
| am | eat | now | she | was |
| are | four | on | so | well |
| at | get | our | soon | went |
| ate | good | out | that | what |
| be | have | please | there | white |
| black | he | pretty | they | who |
| brown | into | ran | this | will |
| but | like | ride | too | with |
| came | must | saw | under | yes |
| did | new | | | |

## Level C: First Grade

| | | | | |
|---|---|---|---|---|
| after | fly | his | old | take |
| again | from | how | once | thank |
| an | give | just | open | them |
| any | going | know | over | then |
| as | had | let | put | think |
| ask | has | live | round | walk |
| by | her | may | some | were |
| could | him | of | stop | when |
| every | | | | |

## Level D: Second Grade

| | | | | |
|---|---|---|---|---|
| always | does | its | sit | very |
| around | don't | made | sleep | wash |
| because | fast | many | tell | which |
| been | first | off | their | why |
| before | five | or | these | wish |
| best | found | pull | those | work |
| both | gave | read | upon | would |
| buy | goes | right | us | write |
| call | green | sing | use | your |
| cold | | | | |

## Level E: Third Grade

| | | | | |
|---|---|---|---|---|
| about | eight | hurt | myself | six |
| better | fall | if | never | small |
| bring | far | keep | only | start |
| carry | full | kind | own | ten |
| clean | got | laugh | pick | today |
| cut | grow | light | seven | together |
| done | hold | long | shall | try |
| draw | hot | much | show | warm |
| drink | | | | |

# E

# Primary Pupil Reading Attitude Inventory: Samples

## Directions for Administration

In the inventory there are 30 pages, or 30 choices between two pictured activities. Of the 30 choices, 18 involve a reading activity. The rest are distractors—choices that don't involve reading.

The pictures represent the following situations in each version:

Girl's Version

Boy's Version

Reading Activities

Reading a book indoors
Reading a book outside

Reading a book indoors
Reading a book outside

Recreational Activities

Swimming
Climbing on monkey bars
Play with dolls
Swinging on a swing
Riding a bike
Jumping rope
Drawing a picture
Making a puppet
Watching TV

Swimming
Climbing on monkey bars
Playing with toy trucks
Swinging on a rope
Riding a bike
Climbing a tree
Drawing a picture
Building a model airplane
Watching TV

Each of the two reading pictures is paired with each of the nine other pictures, making a total of 18 opportunities to choose reading as a favorite activity. Included in this appendix are a sample page from the girl's version and a sample page from the boy's version. Both complete versions are in the Instructor's Manual.

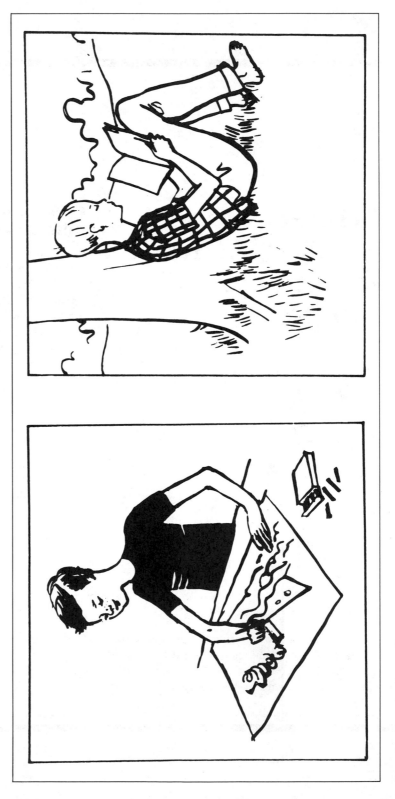

Sample page: boy's version.

444

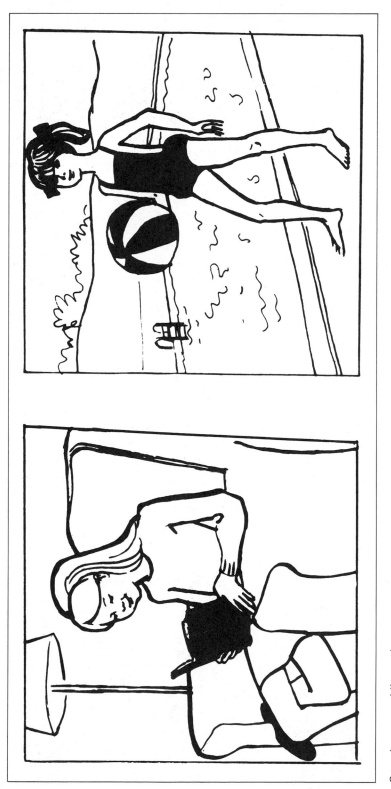

Sample page: girl's version.

## Instructions to Children

*Does every girl have a booklet with pictures of girls and does every boy have one with pictures of boys? Now get out a pencil and one crayon. In pencil, print your first and last name, grade, teacher, and date.* (Put this information on the board.).

*First look up here while I go through the pictures so you understand what each one is showing.* (Explain what activity is portrayed in each picture both for the girl's and boy's versions. It is helpful to have cut out a picture of each activity to explain to the pupils what each picture represents.)

*Now let's look at the first page of your booklet. With your crayon put a big X through the picture of the activity you like best. If you like to climb on the monkey bars better than you like to go swimming, put an X through the picture of the child on the monkey bars with your crayon. If you like to go swimming better than climbing on the monkey bars, put an X through the picture of the child going swimming.*

*Do the same thing on the rest of the pages. Choose which of the two activities you like to do better on each page and put an X through that picture with your crayon. Be sure you choose only one activity on a page, and be sure you mark one on every page. Don't look back to see what you have chosen earlier—just choose between the two pictures on each page. All of the pictures will appear in your booklet several times so don't worry if some of the pages seem alike.*

## Scoring

Count the total number of times that reading was chosen over other activities. The highest possible score a child can receive is 18. In previous studies (Askov, 1972) mean scores have tended to range from 8 to 13 with girls usually scoring higher than boys. Grade placement (Grade 1 as opposed to Grade 3) has not been found to have a significant relation to attitude toward recreational reading.

# Reference

Askov, Eunice N. (1972). *Assessment of attitudes toward reading in primary pupils.* Wisconsin Research and Development Center for Cognitive Learning (Technical Report No. 206).

# Index

# About the Authors

**Eunice N. Askov**

**Wayne Otto**

Eunice N. Askov teaches reading education courses at The Pennsylvania State University and serves on the board of directors of the American Reading Forum. Her teaching experience covers remedial reading, high school English and reading, and adult basic education. In addition to publishing and lecturing widely on reading instruction and study skills, Dr. Askov has devised inservice materials for the Wisconsin Research and Development Center for Individualized Schooling. At the University of Western Australia, where she received a Fulbright Senior Scholar's Award, she developed computer-based adult literacy courseware. She is on the research committee of the International Reading Association and co-directs a state program of inservice training to integrate reading skills into content subjects.

Wayne Otto teaches reading courses in the Department of Curriculum and Instruction at the University of Wisconsin (Madison), where he is currently chairman. His background includes experiences as a Marine, an English teacher and school librarian, and a university professor. He has been a principal investigator and co-director of the Wisconsin Research and Development Center for Individualized Schooling. In recent years he has been a Lansdowne Visitor and visiting professor to British Columbia's University of Victoria. He has served on the board of directors of the American Reading Forum and the National Reading Conference, and on the research committee of the International Reading Association. He is an executive editor of the Journal of Educational Research and an advisory editor to two reading journals. His favorite areas of study and publication are how children learn and common-sense ways to teach them.